INDIAN BUDDHIST THEORIES OF PERSONS

Vasubandhu's "Refutation of the Theory of a Self"

James Duerlinger

RoutledgeCurzon
Taylor & Francis Group
LONDON AND NEW YORK

First published 2003
by RoutledgeCurzon
11 New Fetter Lane, London EC4P 4EE

Simultaneously published in the USA and Canada
by RoutledgeCurzon
29 West 35th Street, New York, NY 10001

RoutledgeCurzon is an imprint of the Taylor & Francis Group

Typeset in Sabon by
Florence Production Ltd, Stoodleigh, Devon
Printed and bound in Great Britain by
Antony Rowe Ltd, Chippenham, Wiltshire

British Library Cataloguing in Publication Data
A catalogue record for this book is available
from the British Library

Library of Congress Cataloging in Publication Data
Duerlinger, James.
Indian Buddhist theories of persons/James Duerlinger.
p. cm. – (RoutledgeCurzon critical studies in Buddhism)
Includes bibliographical references and index.
1. Vasubandhu. Abhidharmakośabhāṣya. atmavadapratioeda.
2. Anatman. 3. Man (Buddhism) I. Title. II. Series
BQ2682.E5D84 2003
126–dc21 2002037127

ISBN 0–415–31835–1

INDIAN BUDDHIST THEORIES OF PERSONS

In this book, Vasubandhu's classic work "Refutation of the Theory of a Self" is translated and provided with an introduction and commentary. The translation, the first into a modern Western language from the Sanskrit text, is intended for use by those who wish to begin a careful philosophical study of Indian Buddhist theories of persons. Special features of the introduction and commentary are their extensive explanations of the arguments for the theories of persons of Vasubandhu and the Pudgalavādins, the Buddhist philosophers whose theory is the central target of Vasubandhu's refutation of the theory of a self.

James Duerlinger has taught in the Philosophy Department at the University of Iowa since 1971. He has published on topics in Greek philosophy, philosophy of religion, and Buddhist philosophy, which are also his current teaching and research interests.

RoutledgeCurzon Critical Studies in Buddhism
General Editors:
Charles S. Prebish and Damien Keown

RoutledgeCurzon Critical Studies in Buddhism is a comprehensive study of the Buddhist tradition. The series explores this complex and extensive tradition from a variety of perspectives, using a range of different methodologies.

The Series is diverse in its focus, including historical studies, textual translations and commentaries, sociological investigations, bibliographic studies, and considerations of religious practice as an expression of Buddhism's integral religiosity. It also presents materials on modern intellectual historical studies, including the role of Buddhist thought and scholarship in a contemporary, critical context and in the light of current social issues. The series is expansive and imaginative in scope, spanning more than two and a half millennia of Buddhist history. It is receptive to all research works that inform and advance our knowledge and understanding of the Buddhist tradition.

THE REFLEXIVE NATURE OF AWARENESS
Paul Williams

BUDDHISM AND HUMAN RIGHTS
Edited by Damien Keown, Charles Prebish and Wayne Husted

ALTRUISM AND REALITY
Paul Williams

WOMEN IN THE FOOTSTEPS OF THE BUDDHA
Kathryn R. Blackstone

THE RESONANCE OF EMPTINESS
Gay Watson

IMAGING WISDOM
Jacob N. Kinnard

AMERICAN BUDDHISM
Edited by Duncan Ryuken Williams and Christopher Queen

PAIN AND ITS ENDING
Carol S. Anderson

THE SOUND OF LIBERATING TRUTH
Edited by Sallie B. King and Paul O. Ingram

BUDDHIST THEOLOGY
Edited by Roger R. Jackson and John J. Makransky

EMPTINESS APPRAISED
David F. Burton

THE GLORIOUS DEEDS OF PURNA
Joel Tatelman

CONTEMPORARY BUDDHIST ETHICS
Edited by Damien Keown

INNOVATIVE BUDDHIST WOMEN
Edited by Karma Lekshe Tsomo

TEACHING BUDDHISM IN THE WEST
Edited by V. S. Hori, R. P. Hayes and J. M. Shields

EMPTY VISION
David L. McMahan

SELF, REALITY AND REASON IN TIBETAN PHILOSOPHY
Thupten Jinpa

BUDDHIST PHENOMENOLOGY
Dan Lusthaus

ZEN WAR STORIES
Brian Victoria

IN DEFENSE OF DHARMA
Tessa J. Bartholomeusz

RELIGIOUS MOTIVATION AND THE ORIGINS OF BUDDHISM
Torkel Brekke

DEVELOPMENTS IN AUSTRALIAN BUDDHISM
Michelle Spuler

THE BUDDHIST UNCONSCIOUS
William S. Waldron

ACTION DHARMA
Edited by Christopher Queen, Charles Prebish and Damien Keown

INDIAN BUDDHIST THEORIES OF PERSONS
James Duerlinger

CONTENTS

PREFACE

The "Refutation of the Theory of a Self" is an Indian treatise (fourth or fifth century CE) on the selflessness of persons that was composed by a Buddhist philosopher known as Vasubandhu. The "Refutation," as I will call it, is basically an attempt to refute the view that persons are selves. In this book I offer a Translation of the "Refutation," along with an Introduction and Commentary, for the use of readers who wish to begin detailed research on Indian Buddhist theories of persons by making a careful philosophical study of this classic of Indian Buddhist philosophy. The Translation is the first into a modern Western language to be made from the Sanskrit text and avoids errors I believe to be contained in earlier translations, which were based on a Sanskrit commentary (sixth century CE) by Yaśomitra, and either the Tibetan translation by Jinamitra and dPal brtsegs (twelfth century CE) or the Chinese translations by Paramārtha (sixth century), and by Xúanzàng (seventh century CE).

In the Introduction I provide readers with information and explanations that will introduce them to the main three kinds of Indian Buddhist theories of persons and enable them to do a careful philosophical study of the "Refutation." In the Translation an attempt is made both to translate terms in a way that will promote a better understanding of the theses and arguments it contains and to help readers through its more difficult passages by indicating in brackets key unexpressed parts of the theses and arguments it contains. The notes to the Translation explain the translation and call attention to problems I believe to exist with previous modern translations. In the Commentary, the theses and arguments contained in the "Refutation" are explained and assessed.

In the "Refutation" Vasubandhu first argues that we are not selves, which are persons who can be identified without reference to the collections of aggregates that comprise their bodies and minds, and that, nonetheless, we do ultimately exist, since we are the same in existence as the collections of these aggregates. Then he presents a series of objections to the theory of the Pudgalavādins, who belong to the Indian Buddhist schools in which it is claimed that, even though we are not independently identifiable, we ultimately exist without being the same in existence as collections of such aggregates. Then Vasubandhu replies to their objections to his own theory of persons. Finally, he replies to objections raised by the Nyāya-Vaiśeṣikas, non-Buddhist Indian philosophers who claim that we are selves in the sense that we are substances that exist independently of our bodies and momentary mental states.

Vasubandhu not only discusses and rejects the theories of persons put forward by the Pudgalavādins and Nyāya-Vaiśeṣikas, but also dismisses, in a single sentence, the thesis of Nāgārjuna, the founder of the Mādhyamika school of Indian Buddhism, that no phenomena ultimately exist, as an adequate basis for a theory of persons. In Nāgārjuna's extant works (second century CE) a Buddhist theory of persons is not presented in any great detail. But in the seventh century CE Candrakīrti worked out the implications of Nāgārjuna's thesis for the interpretation of the Buddha's theory of persons. This interpretation became the basis of the only Buddhist critique, other than that of the Pudgalavādins, of interpretations of the sort presented by Vasubandhu. The three basic kinds of Indian Buddhist theories of persons are those presented by Vasubandhu, the Pudgalavādins, and Candrakīrti. Since one of my objectives in the Introduction and Commentary of this book is to provide readers of the "Refutation" with an introduction to the three different kinds of Indian Buddhist theories of persons, I have intermittently included brief discussions of Candrakīrti's interpretation of the Buddha's theory and his opposition to the interpretations of Vasubandhu and the Pudgalavādins. At some point I hope to provide readers with a translation of Candrakīrti's discussion of the selflessness of persons, along with an introduction and commentary of the sort presented here. What I have to say in this book about Candrakīrti's objections to the sorts of theories of persons held by Vasubandhu and the Pudgalavādins, therefore, may have to be revised in the light of my further research on his discussion. But my portrayal of his own theory, I believe, is on the mark, and will serve the purpose of a presentation of the three main Indian Buddhist theories of persons.

Elaborate explanations of the other parts of the philosophies of the Pudgalavādins, the Nyāya-Vaiśeṣikas, and Candrakīrti are not presented in this book because they would have unnecessarily lengthened and complicated my discussion and because they are not needed for the sort of examination of the theses and arguments in the "Refutation" undertaken here. The exact nature of the Pudgalavādins' theory of persons, I believe, has not yet been explained by scholars. Although I think that I have here correctly explained the nature of their theory, much more needs to be done to ground this explanation in more detailed examinations of the Buddhist sources than could be included in a book primarily devoted to an account of Vasubandhu's "Refutation." The theories of persons of the Nyāya-Vaiśeṣikas and Candrakīrti are generally better understood, and my accounts of them owe a great deal to the work of Indian, Tibetan, and Western scholars.

For the sake of readers unfamiliar with the Sanskrit language I have attempted to keep the use of anglicized Sanskrit words and names to a minimum. However, since readers who are new to this subject and wish to continue their study of Indian Buddhist theories of persons need to become familiar with at least some of the most common and/or important Sanskrit words and names used in our source materials, I have retained Sanskrit names of Indian philosophers, philosophical schools, and many texts, as well as a few well-known Buddhist Sanskrit technical terms (such as nirvāṇa, saṃsāra, sūtra, etc.). I have also added, in parentheses, after the first occurrence of my translations of the most important technical terms, the Sanskrit terms being translated. Since there do not exist standardized translations of Buddhist Sanskrit terms into English, readers without a familiarity with these Sanskrit terms need to learn them in order to negotiate the secondary literature and English translations of Sanskrit philosophical texts. Readers who need help in the task of mastering the recognition and pronunciation of Sanskrit terms are encouraged to read the Introduction to Monier Williams' *A Sanskrit–English Dictionary* (Delhi: Motilal Banarsidass, 1899, esp. xxxvi). For readers who also require a general introduction to Indian Buddhist thought I recommend *The Foundations of Buddhism*, by Rupert Gethin (Oxford: Oxford University Press, 1998).

ACKNOWLEDGMENTS

I wish to acknowledge the help I received from the University of Iowa, which provided me with semester sabbaticals in 1988 and 1993, and from the Fulbright-Hays Foundation, which in 1993 provided me with a Fulbright Senior Scholar Research Grant in India, so that I could find the time and resources needed to work on this book. I also wish to thank the publishers of *The Journal of Indian Philosophy* for permission to draw freely from my articles on the "Refutation" published there, which include "Vasubandhu's 'Refutation of the Theory of Selfhood,'" vol. 17, 1989, pp. 129–35, "A Translation of Vasubandhu's 'Refutation of the Theory of Selfhood': A Resolution of Questions about Persons," vol. 17, 1989, pp. 137–87, "Reductionist and Nonreductionist Theories of Persons in Indian Buddhist Philosophy," vol. 21, 1993, pp. 79–101 (reprinted in *Essays in Indian Philosophy*, ed. Roy Perrett, Duckworth), "Vasubandhu's Philosophical Critique of the Vātsīputrīyas' Theory of Persons (I)," vol. 25, 1997, pp. 307–35, "Vasubandhu's Philosophical Critique of the Vātsīputrīyas' Theory of Persons (II)," vol. 26, 1998, pp. 573–605, and "Vasubandhu's Philosophical Critique of the Vātsīputrīyas' Theory of Persons (III)," vol. 28, 2000, pp. 1–46. Much of what I wrote in these articles, however, has been superseded in the present book.

I also wish to thank Professors Panyot Butchvarov, Richard Fumerton, Paul Hackett, Michael Myers, Jonardon Ganeri, James Powell, and David Stern for their comments on earlier drafts of the Introduction. Professor N. H. Samtani met with me regularly in Sarnath, India, in February and March 1993 to check my translation of the "Refutation." His attention to detail and concern that my English renderings of Sanskrit words be faithful to their Abhidharma definitions provided me with the opportunity to rethink many of my attempts to render Vasubandhu's technical terminology into a suitable philosophical idiom. His kindness in this matter is a good example of his Buddhist practice. I wish to thank Mr Michael Olson, who worked with me as a research assistant for two years, during which time he made detailed criticisms of the first draft of my translation of the "Refutation" and translated for me numerous passages from the Chinese translations of the "Refutation" and their Chinese commentaries. I am grateful to Mr Yoshi Iwai, who provided valuable bibliographical and editorial assistance, to Dr Aydeet Mueller, who assisted me in consulting secondary source materials in German, and to my wife, Evelyn, who graciously tolerated my absences during the times I worked on this project. I take full responsibility for whatever errors remain in this work, since I have not always heeded the advice of the scholars who were kind enough to comment on it.

Finally, I wish to express my appreciation to all of the Tibetan Buddhist scholar-monks and their Western students with whom I have had the opportunity to study Buddhism over the years. It is to them that I dedicate this volume.

1

INTRODUCTION TO THE TRANSLATION

Vasubandhu's "Refutation" and the central philosophical questions about which Indian Buddhist theories of persons are concerned

The text translated in this book is a Buddhist treatise on "the selflessness of persons" (*pudgalanairātmya*) composed by Vasubandhu, who is generally regarded as one of the most important philosophers of the scholastic period of Buddhist thought in India.[1] The treatise, which I will call the "Refutation," after its full title, "Refutation of the Theory of a Self," deals with philosophical questions about persons that are different from, but closely related to, a number of important philosophical questions about persons discussed in the West. For this reason it should be of considerable interest not only to Buddhists and scholars of Buddhism, but also to those who are familiar with the relevant discussions in Western philosophy. Although not all of the philosophical questions discussed by the Indian Buddhists are explicitly raised in the "Refutation," I believe that a careful study of this treatise is the best way to gain initial access to them. To facilitate this access this Introduction begins with a sketch of these questions and how they are related to the study of Vasubandhu's treatise.

According to the Indian Buddhists, when we conceive ourselves from the first-person singular perspective and ascribe attributes to ourselves in dependence upon our bodies and minds,[2] we create a false appearance of ourselves as selves, the acceptance of which appearance is the root cause of our suffering. Vasubandhu agrees with the Pudgalavādins, his Buddhist opponents in the "Refutation," that the selves we falsely appear to be are persons who can be identified independently of our bodies and minds. His chief non-Buddhist opponents, the Nyāya-Vaiśeṣikas, believe that we are selves of this sort, since they claim that we are substances that exist apart from our bodies and minds. The most basic philosophical issue Vasubandhu addresses, therefore, is whether or not we are selves. Whether or not the acceptance of a false appearance of ourselves as selves is the root cause of our suffering is a further issue, of course, but it is not an issue Vasubandhu discusses. Nor does he discuss whether or not we actually create such an appearance when we conceive ourselves from the first-person singular perceptive and ascribe attributes to ourselves. An issue he does raise, however, concerns in what form we ultimately exist if we do not exist as entities that can be independently identified. In the "Refutation," discussion of this issue takes the form of a debate with the Pudgalavādins. According to Vasubandhu, our ultimate existence – the existence we possess apart from being conceived – is the existence of the bodies and minds in dependence upon which we are conceived. According to the Pudgalavādins, we ultimately exist without being the same in existence as our bodies and minds and without being separate substances.

There are, in addition, Indian Buddhists who believe that we do not ultimately exist. The most articulate of these Buddhists, Candrakīrti, thinks that we suffer because we give assent to our false appearance of existing by ourselves, apart from being conceived. So another issue that is discussed by the Indian Buddhists is whether or not we ultimately exist. This issue is only alluded to in the "Refutation," but it is important to a proper assessment of the central issue it does concern, which is whether or not, if we cannot be identified independently of our bodies and minds, we can still exist independently of our bodies and minds.

Because Candrakīrti believes that nothing ultimately exists, he thinks that first-person singular reference to ourselves does not depend upon a reference to something that ultimately exists. This does not mean that he thinks that "I" is not a referring expression. Rather, it means that it refers to a mentally constructed "I" and to nothing else. Vasubandhu and the Pudgalavādins believe that first-person singular reference to us is possible because it is also a reference to something that ultimately exists. So another issue that arises from a consideration of Indian Buddhist theories of persons is whether or not first-person singular reference to ourselves is possible if we are not the same in existence as something that exists apart from being conceived.

These disagreements about whether or not we ultimately exist, and if we do, in what form we ultimately exist, and if we do not, whether reference to ourselves is possible, cannot be settled without an answer to the more general question of what it means to exist. Although most Indian Buddhist philosophers agree that what exists can enter into causal relationships with other things, they do not all define existence in this way. Different conceptions of existence play a crucial role in Buddhist debates about the existence of persons. One view is that to exist is to be a substance or an attribute of a substance, and another is that it is to be either a substance or a collection of substances conceived for practical purposes as a distinct entity of some sort. A third view is that it is to exist apart from being conceived, and a fourth is that it is to exist in dependence upon being conceived.

There is also a set of issues that arise from the arguments used by those who propound the different theories of persons presented in the

"Refutation." Among these are questions about how exactly appeals to our conventional ascriptions of attributes to ourselves are to count for or against theories concerning our mode of existence and/or identity. Vasubandhu's opponents seem to believe that his theory, that we are the same in existence as our bodies and minds, should be rejected because it fails to account for our intuitions concerning the subjects of the attributes we ascribe to ourselves. Such attributes include our being the same at different times (and in different lives), being single entities rather than many, remembering objects experienced in the past, having perceptions, feelings and other mental states, being agents of actions who experience the results of our actions, etc. At issue here is whether or not the form in which we ultimately exist undermines these ascriptions of attributes. Vasubandhu argues that the Nyāya-Vaiśeṣikas' theory, that we are separate substances, cannot be used to explain ascriptions of these attributes to ourselves, and that the Pudgalavādins' theory, that we ultimately exist without being either separate substances or the same in existence as our bodies and minds, is both logically incoherent and contrary to the teachings of the Buddha. He believes that the intuitions upon which the objections to his theory are based are expressions of our mistaken view of ourselves.

An issue raised by Candrakīrti concerns whether or not, if we ultimately exist, our ascriptions of these attributes to ourselves can be explained. He believes, following the lead of Nāgārjuna, the founder of the Mādhyamika school of Buddhist philosophers, that if we ultimately exist, we possess natures of our own by virtue of which we exist, and so, cannot enter into causal relationships with other phenomena, for which reason we could not come to be, cease to be, change, or perform any of the functions we, as persons, are believed to perform. This issue, although not discussed in the "Refutation," is relevant to an assessment of the debate between Vasubandhu and his opponents concerning the form in which we ultimately exist.

Finally, there are different views concerning knowledge of our existence. The Nyāya-Vaiśeṣikas think that we are known to exist as separate substances by means of inference. In the "Refutation," Vasubandhu attempts to show that a number of these inferences are incorrect. Vasubandhu believes that knowledge of our existence apart from being conceived is knowledge of the existence of our bodies and minds. The Pudgalavādins think that by means of perception we are known to exist apart from being conceived without being separate substances or being the same in existence as our bodies and minds. In the "Refutation," Vasubandhu challenges their account of how we are known to exist if we exist in this way. Candrakīrti thinks that we are known to exist only as part of the conceptual scheme that creates us. However, both Vasubandhu and the Pudgalavādins can ask how, if we do not ultimately exist, knowledge of our existence is even possible, and if so, how.

This is a very brief statement of the central philosophical questions to which a study of the "Refutation" gives rise. In this Introduction and in the Commentary I will explain how they arise when the treatise is carefully read and its theses and arguments are carefully assessed.

The Sanskrit text and its translation

Vasubandhu probably composed the "Refutation" as a separate work, and then added it, as a ninth chapter or appendix, either to his *Treasury of Knowledge* (*Abhidharmakośa*), which I will call the *Treasury*, or to his *Commentary on the Treasury of Knowledge* (*Abhidharmakośabhāṣya*), which I will simply call the *Commentary*.[3] Although many scholars have assigned to this treatise the title, "An Examination of the Person" (*Pudgalaviniścāyaḥ*), which was used by Yaśomitra, one of the Indian Buddhist commentators of the *Treasury*, the title that Vasubandhu himself uses is "Refutation of the Theory of a Self" (*ātmavādapratiṣedha*).[4] The *Treasury*, its *Commentary*, and the "Refutation" were composed in India during the fourth or fifth century CE. In the *Treasury* the theses (*siddhānta*-s) that typify those held in the Vaibhāṣika (Exposition follower) schools of Indian Buddhism are explained. In the *Commentary* these theses are evaluated from the point of view of the teachings of the Buddha in his sūtras (discourses) and on the basis of independent reasoning. The Vaibhāṣika schools are the schools named after a work called the *Mahāvibhāṣā* (*Great Exposition*), a second century CE compendium of Indian Buddhist philosophy.[5] The school of Indian Buddhist philosophy from whose point of view Vasubandhu composed most of the *Commentary* and the "Refutation" is called the "Sautrāntika" (Sūtra follower) school.

Sanskrit copies of the *Treasury* and its *Commentary*, which included the "Refutation," were discovered in Tibet in 1936 by Rahula Samkrtyayana.[6] Before that time modern scholars were in possession only of a Sanskrit copy of Yaśomitra's commentary (sixth century CE) on the *Treasury*, called *Gloss of Full Meaning on the Treasury of Knowledge* (*Sphuṭārthābhidharmakośavyakhyā*), which I will hereafter call the *Gloss*.[7] The manuscripts found by Samkrtyayana were first edited in 1967 by Prahlad Pradhan,[8] and then in 1970–3 by Dwarikadas Shastri.[9] For my translation of the "Refutation" I consulted the editions of both Pradhan and Shastri, as well as the corrected reprint of Pradhan's edition made by Aruna Haldar in 1975,[10] Yaśomitra's *Gloss*, and the careful work done by Akira Hirakawa, *et al.*[11] and Yasunori Ejima[12] on the Sanskrit text of Pradhan's edition. My Translation is an extensive revision of a translation I did that was first published in 1988.[13]

The "Refutation" was translated once into Tibetan[14] and twice into Chinese.[15] Yaśomitra's *Gloss* is the only commentary that seems to have survived in Sanskrit. There are three Chinese commentaries on the Chinese translations, composed by Pû-guâng, Fâ-bâu, and Yuán-huî,[16] that still exist. There were commentaries on the *Treasury* and/or *Commentary* written in Sanskrit by Saṃghabhadra, Sthirāmati, Pūrṇavardhana, Śamathadeva, Dignāga, and Vinītadeva. Although the original Sanskrit texts have been lost, they exist in Tibetan translation. Among these commentaries, those composed by Saṃghabhadra, Sthirāmati, and Vinītadeva do not deal with the "Refutation." Since the commentary of Śamathadeva deals primarily with the identification of the sūtras quoted in the "Refutation," and Dignāga's commentary on the "Refutation" is brief and merely quotes some of its arguments, they do not provide useful information pertinent to the present study, which concerns its philosophical import. The commentary on the "Refutation" composed by Pūrṇavardhana has not been consulted, since I first learned of it after my own work on the treatise had been completed.

In reliance upon Yaśomitra's *Gloss* and the Tibetan translation, Theodore Stcherbatsky composed an interpretative English translation, entitled "The Soul Theory of the Buddhists."[17] A French translation, by Louis de La Vallée Poussin[18] is based on Yaśomitra's *Gloss*, the Chinese translations by Paramārtha and by Xúanzàng, and the commentaries by Pû-guâng, Fâ-bâu, and Yuán-huî. (The commentary of Pūrṇavardhana, which in the Tibetan translation is included as the last portion of the commentary on the eighth chapter of the *Treasury*, is not mentioned by Stcherbatsky or by La Vallée Poussin. It may have been overlooked by them, as it was by me, because it is included as part of his commentary on the eighth chapter of the *Treasury*.) There is also a complete English translation of La Vallée Poussin's translation made by Leo Pruden.[19] However, these earlier translations, which were not based on the Sanskrit text, do not in my opinion always accurately convey the meaning of important theses and arguments in the Sanskrit original. Although I disagree on many substantive points with these translations, I have not taken readers through all of the tedious details about where, how, and why I disagree, except for crucial passages. My major disagreements with these translations are for the most part included in my notes to the Translation, although some are also discussed in the Commentary on the Translation. The pioneering work of Stcherbatsky and La Vallée Poussin was a great achievement, but our understanding of Indian Buddhist philosophy has now advanced to the point at which its errors need to be corrected. Nonetheless, I gratefully acknowledge that without the help of their work I might easily have gone astray in my reading of the text in numerous passages. Relatively little has appeared in print more recently to advance our understanding of the "Refutation" as a Buddhist treatise on the selflessness of persons.[20]

Vasubandhu's abbreviated style of composition in the "Refutation" is suitable for study by scholarly monks steeped in Buddhist doctrine and privy to oral traditions of commentary, but it creates difficulties of translation for a Western readership. These difficulties, along with the apparent absence in modern times of an oral commentarial tradition on the text, are surely two of the reasons this very important work of Indian Buddhist philosophy has not received the detailed philosophical attention it deserves. In my Translation I have often in brackets included words, phrases, and sentences that I believe will help readers to grasp unexpressed parts of the theses and arguments presented in the text. The additions most often are made in reliance upon information supplied by Yaśomitra's *Gloss*, though I also rely on the commentaries of Pû-guâng, Fâ-bâu, and Yuán-huî when their views seem reasonable and helpful, but at times I simply supply what the context of argument seems to demand or our current knowledge of Indian Buddhist philosophy seems to require. Readers may read the text without my bracketed additions because I have translated the text so that it can stand alone and be read without them. To make grammatical sense of the unembellished Translation readers need to reinterpret punctuation and capitalization required for the readability of the expanded translation.

Because the argument of Vasubandhu's treatise is often presented in an abbreviated debate style, Stcherbatsky and La Vallée Poussin chose to translate it as a philosophical dialog between proponents of different schools of Indian philosophy. But translating the "Refutation" as a dialog of this sort creates the impression, which I believe to be false, that Vasubandhu meant to compose a dialog instead of a treatise in which brief statements of opposing theses and arguments are alternatively presented. My Translation does not reproduce every question and answer that occurs in the text, since many add nothing to the course of the argument. But I have retained the question and answer format when the question raises a significant point. When direct discourse is used to have the opponents put forth an objection, reply or question, we may assume that the words used are being attributed to the opponents. When indirect discourse is used to have the opponents put forth an objection, reply or question, the words may be Vasubandhu's paraphrase. Although my unembellished translation slightly alters the literary style of the text, I believe that it accurately captures its philosophical nuances and shows its character as an Indian Buddhist polemical treatise on the selflessness of persons.

Throughout I have tried to avoid distortions engendered by the use of special Western philosophical terms and theories that have often been used to translate Indian Buddhist philosophical terms and to explain Indian Buddhist philosophical views. The use of this terminology and explanations of this sort, in my opinion, have in the past seriously compromised our attempts to understand clearly the indigenous philosophical concerns of the Indian philosophers. This purging of special Western philosophical terminology and theory I assume to be necessary in a genuine effort to understand the "Refutation" in the way it was understood by the Indian

Buddhist philosophers themselves. I have not, however, restricted myself to the use of traditional Indian Buddhist classifications and explanations. I believe that the terminology I introduce is easy to understand and not based on a special Western philosophical prototype, and that the classifications and explanations I employ, which are grounded in careful analyses of the theses and arguments presented in the "Refutation," are needed for a better analytical understanding of the philosophical issues it raises. So readers will not find in the Introduction and the Commentary a mere summary of the theses and arguments employed in the "Refutation." It has been my intention to give readers of Vasubandhu's treatise an opportunity to consider some of the actual issues with which it is concerned from an Indian Buddhist point of view. Although I have surely not dealt with all of these issues and perhaps only scratched the surface of those with which I do deal, I hope to have provided a platform from which further work on them can be done.

The use of unfamiliar English and Sanskritized English expressions to translate technical philosophical Sanskrit terms is also avoided. Such translations, which are seldom carefully explained in terms Western readers can easily understand, I believe to have unnecessarily obscured the meanings of their Sanskrit originals and to have overly complicated the attempt of those without a knowledge of Sanskrit to do a careful study of Indian Buddhist philosophical texts. In addition, section headings are supplied, numbered according to related issues raised in the "Refutation," as an aid to reference and to comprehension of the twists and turns of Vasubandhu's argumentation. For the purposes of spoken reference to sections the numbers may be orally cited without mention of the periods. So Section 2.1.1, for instance, would be cited as two one one, and so on. The sequence of numbers used to mark the subsections of each major section usually indicates, in order, the introduction of a new objection or reply, different arguments devoted primarily to the same objection or reply, and disagreements about these arguments. The numbering depends upon my own interpretation of the significance and place of an argument within the course of the argumentation of which it is a part. To obtain an overview of the argumentation of the "Refutation" readers need only to read the section headings in the order presented.

Readers who seek information about the scriptural sources of quotations in the text and about philological matters may consult the extensive notes La Vallée Poussin added to his French translation, which were translated by Pruden. I do not attempt to reproduce the work he has done on these matters. The notes of Stcherbatsky that deal with questions of meaning are sometimes helpful, but they are brief and of little help for close philosophical analysis. The notes to my Translation include explanations of translations and additions, sources consulted for the additions, or clarifications of the meanings of theses and arguments.

The Buddha formulated his theory of persons as a part of his theory about what causes suffering and how to destroy this cause. His theory is that the root cause of suffering is that persons give assent to a naturally occurring false appearance of themselves as selves and that they can eliminate this assent by meditating on the selflessness of persons. Section 1 of the Translation contains a brief statement of Vasubandhu's interpretation of the Buddha's theory of persons. According to his interpretation, persons are not "selves" in the sense that they are not persons who can be identified independently of the phenomena that comprise their bodies and minds. He argues that, nonetheless, persons ultimately exist, since they are the same in existence as these phenomena, which do really exist.[21] Section 2 contains Vasubandhu's objections to the interpretation of the Buddha's theory of persons put forward by the Pudgalavādins. The Pudgalavādins, I believe, may be characterized as the Indian Buddhist philosophers who, while agreeing that persons are not selves in the above sense, deny that persons are the same in existence as the phenomena that comprise their bodies and minds, since they can exist by themselves without possessing any character or identity at all.[22] According to Xúanzàng, a Chinese monk who traveled to India in the seventh century CE, about a quarter of the monks in India belonged to the Sāṃmitīya school, which is one of the Pudgalavādin schools. Vasubandhu, following tradition, calls the Pudgalavādins the "Vātsīputrīyas" (followers of Vātsīputra).[23] Section 3 is primarily concerned with Vasubandhu's replies to the Pudgalavādins' objections to his own interpretation of the Buddha's theory. In Section 4 Vasubandhu replies to the objections of the non-Buddhist Indian philosophers he calls the "Tīrthikas" (Forders).[24] These philosophers claim that persons are selves in the sense of being substances that exist apart from their bodies and minds. In Section 4, Vasubandhu also presents objections of his own to their arguments for the existence of selves of this sort, which we may call "separate substances." The only non-Buddhist Indian philosophers whose views Vasubandhu considers in Section 4, I believe, are those of the Nyāya-Vaiśeṣikas.

The theories of persons of the Pudgalavādins and the Nyāya-Vaiśeṣikas

It seems clear that Vasubandhu composed the "Refutation" primarily for the purpose of purging Buddhism of what he took to be the Pudgalavādins' heretical interpretation of the Buddha's theory that persons are not selves. For this purpose, in the greater part of the "Refutation" he presents objections to their interpretation and replies to their objections to the sort of interpretation he himself accepts. He then devotes the last part of the work to replies to the Nyāya-Vaiśeṣikas' objections to his theory. Although his purpose in the "Refutation" is to purge Buddhism of the Pudgalavādins' heresy, he includes replies to the objections presented by the Nyāya-Vaiśeṣikas, I suspect, because he believes that it may have been their objections that led the Pudgalavādins to reject the sort of interpretation of the Buddha's theory of persons presented by Vasubandhu and to substitute a theory that, as we shall see, closely resembles the one held by the Nyāya-Vaiśeṣikas. The ways in which the theory of the Pudgalavādins resembles that of the Nyāya-Vaiśeṣikas are explained later in this Introduction and in the Commentary.

Our knowledge of the theories of persons presented by the Pudgalavādins and the Nyāya-Vaiśeṣikas is not exhausted by what Vasubandhu reports in the "Refutation," and a consideration of our other sources of information would be helpful in understanding Vasubandhu's critique of their theories.

One text that scholars believe to be composed from the viewpoint of a Pudgalavādin school and to contain information about its theory of persons is the *Sāṃmitīyanikāya Śāstra*, a pre-sixth century CE treatise preserved only in Chinese translation.[25] Since Yaśomitra identifies the Pudgalavādin school with which Vasubandhu contends in the "Refutation" as the Āryasāṃmitīyas, Vasubandhu's opponent in the "Refutation" could be the school from whose point of view the *Sāṃmitīyanikāya Śāstra* was composed.[26]

The *Sāṃmitīyanikāya Śāstra* is basically a discussion of two questions, one concerning Buddhist views about the existence of persons and the other concerning Buddhist views about the possibility of a transitional state of persons between rebirths. In its discussion of the first question, seven opinions are considered and rejected concerning the existence of persons. The persons concerning whose existence different opinions are considered are "persons conceived from a basis" (*āśrayaprajñaptapudgala*), which seems to be equivalent to the idea that they are persons who are "conventional realities" (*saṃvṛtisatya*-s).[27] That the Sāṃmitīyas assume that persons are conventional realities does not mean, however, that they assume them to be conventional realities in the sense in which they are defined in the *Treasury* and *Commentary*. Indeed, in Section 2.1.1 of the "Refutation" the Pudgalavādins are made to deny that persons are conventional realities in that sense. Later in this Introduction I shall take up the question of the sense in which the Sāṃmitīyas, and indeed, all Pudgalavādins, believe that persons are conventional realities. The seven rejected opinions about the existence of conventionally real persons are (1) that although the aggregates exist, persons do not, (2) that persons neither do nor do not exist, (3) that persons really exist (i.e. exist as substances), (4) that persons and their aggregates are the same, (5) that persons and their aggregates are other than one another, (6) that persons are permanent phenomena, and (7) that persons are impermanent phenomena.

After rejecting the above-mentioned seven opinions about the existence of persons conceived from a basis, the Sāṃmitīyas distinguish persons of this sort from persons conceived from transition and from persons conceived from cessation. Since the basis upon which persons are conceived are the "aggregates" (*skandha*-s), the fact that these aggregates, which are impermanent, form a causal continuum over time enables persons to be conceived as the same persons at different times. Since, as well, the causal continuum of the aggregates that are the basis upon which persons are conceived ceases to exist when "final release from saṃsāra" (*parinirvāṇa*) is reached, persons are conceived, even after the continuum of their aggregates has ceased, by reference to the cessation of that continuum. In the "Refutation," the Pudgalavādins are represented as holding the view that persons are conceived in reliance upon aggregates that belong to them, are acquired by them, and exist in the present. How exactly this view is related to the view, expressed in the *Sāṃmitīyanikāya Śāstra*, that there are these three kinds of persons, will be explained below.

Another work that contains information relevant to an understanding of Indian Buddhist theories of persons has been attributed to the Pudgalavādins by Thích Thiên Châu.[28] This work, whose Sanskrit name was probably the *Tridharmaka Śāstra*, seems to have survived only in two fourth century CE Chinese translations. It contains a summary of Buddhist views composed by Vasubhadra and a commentary on the summary composed by Sanghasena. The work as a whole is divided into three parts, which are divided into three sections, which are divided into three topics, etc. Of the basic nine sections, three are concerned with positive qualities the acquisition of which facilitates the attainment of "nirvāṇa" (release from saṃsāra), three are concerned with negative qualities the retention of which keeps us in "saṃsāra" (the rebirth cycle), and three are concerned with the basic phenomena the knowledge of which enables us to attain nirvāṇa. Among the negative qualities the retention of which keeps us in saṃsāra the following are mentioned: ignorance of phenomena that are "inexplicable" (*avaktavya*),[29] and doubt concerning the three "realities" (*satya*-s).[30]

Inexplicable phenomena, the ignorance of which keeps us in saṃsāra, are persons who are conceived in dependence upon (1) the fact that they acquire aggregates, (2) the fact that the aggregates they acquire exist in the past, present, and future, or (3) the fact that they have ceased acquiring aggregates.[31] If these persons are inexplicable in the sense that persons are said to be inexplicable in the "Refutation," they are persons who are neither other than nor the same as the collections of aggregates in dependence upon which they are conceived. The aggregates are the substances of which the bodies and minds of persons are composed. The three ways inexplicable persons are said to be conceived are comparable to the three kinds of persons mentioned in the *Sāṃmitīyanikāya Śāstra*.[32] We may also assume, I believe, that the Pudgalavādins think that the persons who are conceived in these three ways are conventional realities.

That persons, just insofar as they are conceived, are thought to be conventional realities is not contradicted by the claim, made in the *Tridharmaka Śāstra*, that doubt concerning the three realities prevents us from escaping saṃsāra. Among the realities mentioned there are conventional reality, which is equated with worldly convention, ultimate reality, which is equated with the causally unconditioned phenomenon called nirvāṇa, and the reality that includes all of the causally conditioned phenomena that comprise suffering, the origin of suffering and the path to nirvāṇa. This third reality, which seems to have been called "the reality of phenomena that possess defining characteristics" (*lakṣaṇasatya*), and ultimate reality, so conceived, include all of the substances (*dravya*-s) that are called ultimate realities by those who belonged to the closely allied Vaibhāṣika schools.[33] It seems that in order to retain the motif of dividing topics into three divisions, the doctrine that there are two realities, ultimate and conventional, is redescribed in the *Tridharmaka Śāstra* as three. According to this threefold division of realities, persons will be conventional realities, which are unlike other conventional realities insofar as they are inexplicable.[34]

In addition to the *Sāṃmitīyanikāya Śāstra* and the *Tridharmaka Śāstra*, there are a number of works composed by the Buddhists in which the theory of persons of the Pudgalavādins is presented and criticized. The works included, in addition to the "Refutation" of Vasubandhu, are Moggaliputta-tissa's *Kathāvatthu* (second century CE),[35] Devaśarman's *Vijñānakāya* (second century CE),[36] Harivarman's *Satyasiddhi Śāstra* (third century CE),[37] Asaṅga's *Mahāyānasūtralaṃkāra* (fifth century CE),[38] Bhāvaviveka's *Madhyamakahṛdayavṛtti*, along with its commentary, the *Tarkajvālā* (sixth century CE),[39] Candrakīrti's *Madhyamakāvatāra* and *Madhyamakāvatārabhāṣya* (seventh century CE),[40] Śāntideva's *Bodhicaryāvatāra* (eighth century CE),[41] and Śāntarakṣita's *Tattvasaṃgraha*, along with Kamalaśīla's *Pañjika* commentary on Śāntarakṣita's work (eighth century CE).[42] Among these sources, the *Kathāvatthu*, the *Vijñānakāya* and the *Satyasiddhi Śāstra* were composed before Vasubandhu's "Refutation" was composed. So it should be to them that we look for antecedents of Vasubandhu's critique of the Pudgalavādins' theory of persons.

In the first chapter of the *Kathāvatthu*, an extensive and very stylized debate between the proponents of the Pudgalavādins' theory of persons and the Theravādin theory is presented. Since it was not composed in Sanskrit, it is not a likely source upon which Vasubandhu draws in the "Refutation," but it does seem to represent the Pudgalavādins' theory of persons more or less in the form in which Vasubandhu represents it.[43] In the first chapter of the *Kathāvatthu* many of the same arguments used by Vasubandhu in the "Refutation" appear, albeit in a peculiar form, devised to facilitate memorization.[44] The major thrust of the *Kathāvatthu* critique of the Pudgalavādins' theory of persons is that conventionally real persons do not, as they claim, ultimately exist, since they do not exist in the way ultimate things exist, and are not known to exist in the way other ultimate things are known to exist. To exist in the way ultimate things exist, the Theravādins seem to assume, is to exist in the way a substance exists. The Pudgalavādins, of course, do not think that persons exist as substances, but *in the way* substances exist, which is apart from being conceived. To exist ultimately is to exist apart from being conceived. The Theravādins, apparently, do not think that anything possesses ultimate existence other than substances.

The Theravādins themselves surely also believe that in some sense conventional realities ultimately exist. But the ultimate existence of conventional realities, they think, is the existence of the collections of substances in dependence upon which they are conceived as single entities. From this point of view, their main criticisms of the Pudgalavādins' theory of persons are that if conventionally real persons are neither other than nor the same in existence as collections of substances, they do not possess ultimate existence, since they are neither substances nor collections of substances, and are not known to exist since they are not known to exist in the way substances are known to exist. So understood, their main objections to the Pudgalavādins' theory of persons are basically the same as those put forward by Vasubandhu in the "Refutation." Their objections, however, are more difficult to understand because of the convoluted form in which they are presented.

The other major issue taken up in the *Kathāvatthu* concerns how, if inexplicable persons ultimately exist, they can be, as the Pudgalavādins claim, neither the same nor different in different lives. Vasubandhu does not discuss the Pudgalavādins' claim, that persons are neither the same nor different in different lives, but he does criticize their claim that the only way to explain the convention that persons are reborn is to suppose that they are inexplicable phenomena.

In the second chapter of the *Vijñānakāya* a debate between the Pudgalavādins and their opponents is represented. The arguments of this chapter are similar to, but simpler than, the arguments of the first chapter of the *Kathâvatthu*. If Vasubandhu studied the *Vijñānakāya*, however, his study did not have much influence on his argumentation in the "Refutation," which is much more extensive and more carefully articulated. In the *Vijñānakāya* the arguments primarily turn on questions about whether or not the Pudgalavādins' theory of persons is consistent with the Buddha's different classifications of persons, about whether or not it can explain the relationship between persons in one of their rebirths and these same persons in another rebirth, and about whether or not it is consistent with the Buddha's classifications of phenomena. In the "Refutation" Vasubandhu totally ignores arguments of the first kind, but does include arguments of the second and third kinds. He first concentrates upon questions of the internal consistency of the Pudgalavādins' theory, and then upon scriptural refutations, after which he takes up their objections to his own theory.

The arguments in Sections 34 and 35 of the first chapter of the *Satyasiddhi Śāstra* are much more like those in the "Refutation" in a number of important respects. The English translation and paraphrase by N. Aiyaswami Shastri contains some of the same basic arguments used by Vasubandhu and the Pudgalavādins in the "Refutation," although they are formulated slightly differently and occur in a slightly different context and order. In fact, some of the same quotations from the Buddha's sūtras are employed. In Section 34 a series of scriptural objections is advanced against the Pudgalavādin theory that a person is inexplicable, some of which Vasubandhu employs in the "Refutation." Then in Section 35 a number of Pudgalavādin arguments for the existence of an inexplicable person are presented and objections to these arguments are posed.[45] But the arguments in these sections are not so rigorously formulated as they are in the "Refutation." Nonetheless, the strong similarities between some of the arguments in these sections and arguments in the "Refutation" suggest either that Vasubandhu was familiar with the *Satyasiddhi Śāstra*, that the author of the *Satyasiddhi Śāstra* was familiar with Vasubandhu's examination in the "Refutation," or that both examinations were based on an earlier examination that has been lost.

The later polemical treatments of the Pudgalavādins' theory of persons, for the most part, seem to draw upon Vasubandhu's "Refutation" or upon these other earlier treatments. Indeed, La Vallée Poussin often calls attention in the notes to his translation of the "Refutation" to similarities between its arguments and the arguments in these later works. Except for the arguments in Candrakīrti's *Madhyamakāvatāra*, which are directed against theories of persons of the sort held by Vasubandhu and the Pudgalavādins, and for the arguments in Śāntarakṣita's *Tattvasaṃgraha*, along with Kamalaśīla's commentary on them, which call attention to the most basic issue involved in the dispute between the Pudgalavādins and their Buddhist critics concerning the existence of inexplicable persons, I will not be concerned here with these later developments, which is a topic that cries out for special study.

Among more recent secondary sources, relatively brief discussions of the Pudgalavādins' theory of persons are presented by Edward Conze, Nalinaksha Dutt, S. N. Dube, and L. S. Cousins.[46] More extensive treatments of the Pudgalavādins' theory of persons are to be found in Thích Thiên Châu's *The Early Literature of the Personalists* and Leonard Priestley's *Pudgalavāda Buddhism*. Although I have consulted all of these secondary sources in my attempts to clarify the debate between Vasubandhu and the Pudgalavādins, and I have found all helpful in different ways, I failed to find in them what I consider to be clear philosophical accounts of the theories of persons of the Pudgalavādins and their Buddhist critics, and hence, a clear philosophical understanding of what exactly the debate is about.

The key to understanding their different theories of persons and the philosophical issues involved in the dispute between them, I believe, is that Vasubandhu and the Pudgalavādins actually agree that persons are conventional realities that ultimately exist, but disagree about the form in which persons ultimately exist, and so, about what can and cannot be a conventional reality. That they agree that persons are conventional realities I concluded from my study of the surviving works of the Pudgalavādins themselves and their early Buddhist critics. I found Priestley's *Pudgalavāda Buddhism* to be especially helpful to me in the process of arriving at this conclusion.[47] That Vasubandhu and the Pudgalavādins agree that conventionally real persons ultimately exist was finally called to my attention when I realized that the major criticism of their theories by the philosophers belonging to the Mādhyamika (middle way follower) schools of Indian Buddhist philosophy is that they assume that persons ultimately exist.[48]

The only non-Buddhist theory of persons Vasubandhu seems to discuss explicitly in the "Refutation" is that of the Nyāya-Vaiśeṣika school of philosophy. Although nominally distinct, the Vaiśeṣika and Nyāya schools of philosophy are usually treated as a single school, the Nyāya-Vaiśeṣika school, whose metaphysical views are most often presented by the Vaiśeṣikas and whose epistemological and logical views are usually presented by the Naiyāyikas. The root texts of this school are Kaṇāda's *Vaiśeṣika Sūtras* (sixth century BCE) and Gotama's *Nyāya Sūtras* (sixth century BCE).[49] Vasubandhu is likely to have studied the theory of persons presented in these seminal works, as well as the elucidation of the Vaiśeṣika theory of persons by Praśastapāda in his *Padārthadharmasaṃgraha* (second century CE)[50] and the elucidation of the Nyāya theory of persons by Vātsyāyaṇa in his *Nyāya Bhāṣya* (second century CE).[51] In Gotama's *Nyāya Sūtras* the principal arguments for the existence of a self occur in Book I, Chapter 1 and in Book III, Chapter 1. In Kaṇāda's *Vaiśeṣika Sūtras* the principal arguments occur in Book III, Chapters 1 and 2.[52] Readers will find a study of these texts very helpful for an assessment of Vasubandhu's replies to the Nyāya-Vaiśeṣika school objections to his theory of persons and his own objections to their theory. There are, moreover, a number of later treatises that develop the Nyāya-Vaiśeṣika arguments for the existence of the self that may be consulted for elaborations of the objections of the Nyāya-Vaiśeṣikas to the sort of theory of persons presented by Vasubandhu.[53]

The Nyāya-Vaiśeṣikas claim that, from the point of view of their ultimate reality, persons are "selves" in the sense of being permanent and partless separate substances, and that, through contact with an internal organ (*manas*), these selves become conceivers of objects. By means of becoming conceivers of objects, they acquire characters of a kind only such entities can possess and begin to function as agents of bodily motion. The existence of selves is known by means of a correct inference from the existence of the characters and agency they possess. In Section 4 of the "Refutation" a variety of arguments used by the Nyāya-Vaiśeṣikas to prove the existence of selves are presented, many of which are made the basis of objections to Vasubandhu's theory of persons. Although consciousness of objects is made a proof of the existence of selves, it is not thought that selves are by their own natures conscious of objects. The practical goal of the practice of the Nyāya-Vaiśeṣika philosophy is to free persons from consciousness of objects, since suffering is the inevitable consequence of consciousness of objects. But in India, among those who identify selves with owners or possessors of consciousness and agents of bodily motion, the essentialist viewpoint predominates. The Jains, Pūrva Mīmāṃsās, Viśiṣṭādvaita Vedāntins, and Dvaita Vedāntins all hold versions of the theory that selves by their own natures are conscious of objects and are agents of bodily motion.

Another non-Buddhist theory of persons to which Vasubandhu alludes, according to Yaśomitra, is that of the Sāṃkhyas. The basic text in which the Sāṃkhyas' theory of persons is presented is the *Sāṃkhyakārikas* (fifth century CE), which is attributed to Īśvarakṛṣṇa. In verses 17–20 of this work, proofs of the existence, nature, and number of selves are presented.[54] Although this text may have been composed about the time Vasubandhu composed the *Treasury*, the doctrines it contains are quite ancient. So we may assume that Vasubandhu is familiar with the theory of persons it contains, even if he does not openly criticize it in the "Refutation." The Sāṃkhyas claim that there are just two basic kinds of substances. The first kind is a "self" (*puruṣa* or *ātman*), which they believe to be a permanent and partless consciousness that is a subject that can exist without an object, that can exist without an owner or possessor, and that cannot itself be made an object of consciousness. The second kind of substance is an unmanifest form of "matter" (*prakṛti*) that, for the enjoyment of selves, causes itself, by combining its three causally inseparable fundamental "constituents" or "qualities" (*guṇa*-s) in different ways, to evolve into different kinds of objects for subjects to witness. The first of these evolutes is an agent "intellect" (*buddhi*), which causes itself to evolve into "a mind that conceives an I" (*ahaṃkāra*), which mind, in dependence upon how its own causally inseparable three constituents are combined, causes itself to evolve into many other kinds of objects for selves to witness. The practical goal of the Sāṃkhya philosophy is for persons to become free from the illusion that they are objects of consciousness. The Sāṃkhyas' pluralistic version of selves as permanent and partless instances of pure consciousnesses is later transformed by the Advaita Vedāntins into a theory according to which every self is in the last analysis one universal permanent and partless consciousness that is identical to "absolute reality" (*brahman*).

The Indian Buddhist philosophical schools and the two realities

The traditional Buddhist classification of the Buddhist philosophical schools is to some extent an artificial creation of later Buddhist scholars. But the classification does serve the purpose of placing the theses and arguments contained in Vasubandhu's "Refutation" into an Indian Buddhist philosophical context without getting bogged down in difficult questions concerning the interpretation of the views of particular philosophers. The four major philosophical schools are called the "Vaibhāṣika" (Exposition follower) school, the "Sautrāntika" (Sūtra follower) school, the "Cittamātrika" (Mind Only follower) school,[55] and the "Mādhyamika" (Middle Way follower) school.[56] Each of the four Buddhist philosophical schools is in fact a collection of two or more schools whose most fundamental theses are very similar.

In the Indian Buddhist philosophical schools, it is clearly asserted or implied that all phenomena known to exist are classified as either "conventional realities" (*saṃvṛtisatya*-s) or "ultimate realities" (*paramārthasatya*-s), even though the distinction between these realities may not be stressed in their extant literature. The distinction needs to be incorporated into the theories set out in the different schools because it is made in the Buddha's sūtras. The two realities, in general, may be characterized as two ways in which objects known to exist possess reality. The etymology of *saṃvṛti* in *saṃvṛtisatya* suggests that a conventional reality, or perhaps the mind that apprehends it, conceals or hides an ultimate reality. In a generic sense, I suggest, a conventional reality may be said to be the conventional nature of an object established by conventional means, apart from the use of the sort of analysis that reveals its ultimate nature or reality, which is known by means of such an analysis. This is not a very informative account, but it is about all that can be said about the general meaning of the terms. In all schools it is agreed that we need to rely upon both conventional realities and ultimate realities in order to traverse the path to nirvāṇa. It is important to rely on conventional realities, for instance, for the purpose of explaining what the problem of suffering is and how to solve it. In particular, the Buddha taught his disciples to rely on conventional realities in their practice of morality. Although we are not agents of actions or subjects of experience in the domain of ultimate realities, for instance, we are such agents and subjects in the domain of the conventional realities, which are the foundation of the practice of morality. We are to rely on ultimate realities in the practice of wisdom on the path, he taught, insofar as direct yogic perception of ultimate realities is the means by which we can effectively eliminate the mistaken view of a self, which is the root cause of suffering in saṃsāra. Different interpretations of the exact natures of the two realities are presented in most of the Indian Buddhist philosophical schools. The Pudgalavādins' interpretation, however, will need to be reconstructed on the basis of what is said in the *Tridharmaka Śāstra* about the three realities and the fact that many of their theses are comparable to those held in other Vaibhāṣika schools.

In all Indian Buddhist philosophical schools other than the Pudgalavāda schools, phenomena known to exist are also classified as either "causally conditioned" (*saṃskṛta*) or "causally unconditioned" (*asaṃskṛta*), as "impermanent" (*anitya*) or "permanent" (*nitya*), as one of the twelve "bases of perception" (*āyatana*-s) and as one of the eighteen "elements" (*dhātu*-s).[57] The Pudgalavādins claim that there are, in addition, phenomena that are "inexplicable" (*avaktavya*). According to most Vaibhāṣika schools, and perhaps to the Sautrāntika school from whose perspective Vasubandhu composed the bulk of the *Commentary*, there are four kinds of phenomena that are causally conditioned and impermanent: "bodily forms" (*rūpa*-s), "minds" (*citta*-s), "mental factors" (*caitta*-s), and "causal factors not associated with minds or mental factors" (*viprayuktasaṃskāra*-s). Moreover, there are three kinds of phenomena that are causally unconditioned and permanent: space, cessations not brought about by analysis, and cessations brought about by analysis. Nirvāṇa, which is included as one of the cessations brought about by analysis, is the cessation of all suffering and saṃsāra.

In the Indian Buddhist philosophical schools it is believed that the twelve bases of perception are six kinds of organs of perception, five of which are sense-organs and one of which is a "mental organ" (*manas*), and six kinds of objects of direct perception, each of which consists of different kinds of objects directly apprehended by means of one of the organs of perception. When the minds that directly apprehend these objects by means of these organs are added to the list, one mind answering to each of the six organs, the resultant eighteen phenomena are called "the elements." The same phenomena are contained in both the classification into twelve bases of perception and the classification into eighteen elements, since the six minds included in the latter classification are counted in the former classification as objects directly apprehended by means of the mental organ.

A classification of causally conditioned and impermanent phenomena that is accepted in all schools is employed in the context of an analysis of the phenomena of which bodies and minds are composed. It is the classification of causally conditioned and impermanent phenomena into the following five "aggregates" (*skandha*-s): "bodily forms" (*rūpa*-s), "feeling" (*vedanā*), "discrimination" (*saṃjñā*), "volitional forces" (*saṃskāra*-s), and "consciousness" (*vijñāna*).[58] The aggregate of bodily forms includes all of the most basic bodily phenomena in dependence upon which the Buddha believed we conceive bodies. If these bodies are the bodies of persons, the aggregate of bodily forms includes the sense-organs. The remaining aggregates include all of the most basic mental phenomena in dependence upon which he believed we conceive minds. A more detailed account of

Vasubandhu's explanation of the aggregates will be presented later in this Introduction.

Most Indian Buddhist scholars have distinguished eighteen different Vaibhāṣika schools.[59] For our purposes these may be divided into fourteen orthodox Vaibhāṣika schools and four Pudgalavādin schools.[60] According to the orthodox Vaibhāṣika schools, what we normally call bodies are collections of elements that are "substantially real" (*dravyasat*). There are two sorts of elements of bodies, those that are themselves "substances" (*dravya*-s), which always exist together in differently configured inseparable combinations, and the combinations themselves, of which it is said that they cannot be physically or mentally broken down into their constituent substances. In all bodies other than the sense-organs, the most basic configuration of inseparable elements is that some, the "primary elements" (*mahābhūta*-s), provide an underlying support (*āśraya*) for others, called the "secondary elements" (*bhautika*-s). The sense-organs, by contrast, are differently configured inseparable combinations of subtle forms of the four primary elements known as earth, air or wind, fire, and water. In addition, what we normally call minds are composed of temporally partless mental substances. These mental substances also exist together in inseparable combinations. One of them, called "mind" (*citta*), is the underlying support for the others, called "mental factors" (*caitta*-s).

We need not here explore any further the orthodox Vaibhāṣika account of the elements of which bodies and minds are composed or attempt to pursue the many the questions it raises.[61] Nor do we need to explore Vasubandhu's critique of this account. However, since to my knowledge Vasubandhu does not explain what is meant by "substantially real" (*dravyasat*) and "substance" (*dravya*) and these terms play an important role in the argumentation of the "Refutation," we need to employ an interpretation of their meaning if we are to get a clear understanding of that argumentation. The interpretation that I believe explains their use in the "Refutation" is (1) that substantially real phenomena are phenomena that possess natures of their own by virtue of which they exist and can be identified independently of one another, (2) that substances and inseparable combinations of substances are substantially real phenomena, (3) that substances are the basic kinds of phenomena that exist, and (4) that among substances, those that are causally conditioned exist in inseparable combinations with others, and those that are causally unconditioned do not.[62] Among the substances that the orthodox Vaibhāṣikas believe to exist are seventy-two kinds of causally conditioned phenomena and three kinds of causally unconditioned phenomena. The seventy-two kinds of causally conditioned phenomena are the phenomena that are included in the five aggregates of which bodies and minds are composed. The causally unconditioned phenomena are, as mentioned above, space, cessations occasioned by analysis, and cessations not occasioned by analysis.[63]

Substantially real phenomena, which are also called phenomena that possess substantial reality (*dravyasiddhi*), are to be distinguished from phenomena whose reality is substantially established (*dravyasiddha*). Substantially established realities are entities whose identities are mentally constructed, but exist by reason of being composed of different kinds of substances in dependence upon which their identity is constructed.[64] They are unlike inseparable combinations of substances insofar as they lack separate identities. On the basis of Vasubandhu's account of their views in the *Treasury*, I believe, it may be inferred that the orthodox Vaibhāṣikas think that all and only substantial realities are ultimate realities, while all and only substantially established realities are conventional realities.

In verse 4 of Book VI of the *Treasury*, the orthodox Vaibhāṣika schools' interpretation of the Buddha's doctrine of the two realities is presented. The interpretation, which Vasubandhu endorses in the *Commentary*, consists of a pair of definitions in which we are given the means by which to determine whether an object known to exist is a conventional reality or an ultimate reality. It is said that an object of knowledge is a conventional reality just in case it is no longer conceived to be what it is conceived to be if analyzed or broken into parts. The implication is that a conventional reality is an object of knowledge that does not possess an identity by itself, but instead possesses an identity in dependence upon possessing parts the collection of which is the basis of its being conceived as a single entity of some sort. It is not implied that a conventional reality does not exist apart from being conceived, since what has been shown is only that the mind has superimposed an identity upon a collection of phenomena conceived by that mind as its parts. The standard example of a conventional reality is a pot, since when subjected to analysis or breakage it is no longer conceived as a pot. A person is another example. If the phenomena in a collection of phenomena upon which an identity is superimposed lose their identities when analyzed into parts or broken into parts, they too are conventional realities. This process of analysis or physical breakage of the object continues until the mind arrives at phenomena whose identity is not lost when analyzed or broken into parts.

An ultimate reality, by contrast, is an object of knowledge whose identity is retained if analyzed or broken into parts. Because ultimate realities are substantially real phenomena, they exist and have identities apart from being conceived. Although Vasubandhu himself seems to reject the Vaibhāṣikas' view that the ultimate realities of which bodies are composed are spatially unextended, he does accept the idea that there are, in some sense, minimally sized phenomena of which they are composed and that they are ultimate realities. Since in Section 4.8 of the "Refutation" he implies that the five aggregates in their uncontaminated forms are substances, in Section 2.1 that bodily forms, which are included in the collection of aggregates, are substantially real phenomena, and in Section 2.1.5

that the four primary elements are substances, I assume that he accepts the Vaibhāṣika view that the aggregates and the four elements are substances, and so, are ultimate realities.[65]

The Pudgalavādin schools do not accept the orthodox Vaibhāṣika identification of ultimate realities with substantial realities, or of conventional realities with substantially established realities. In Section 2.1.1 of the "Refutation" the Pudgalavādins are in effect made to deny that persons are either substantial realities or substantially established realities. This denial, however, does not mean that they deny that persons are conventional realities. Rather, the reason for their denial is that they believe that conventional realities may be either substantially established or inexplicable, and that persons are of the second kind.[66] What is inexplicable, therefore, is basically what ultimately exists without being a substantial reality or a substantially established reality. Since substantial realities and substantially established realities exhaust the entities that possess separate identities, it is clear that ultimately existent inexplicable phenomena are entities without separate identities.

In the "Refutation" the idea of inexplicable persons is usually conveyed by the statements that persons neither are nor are not the aggregates, and that persons neither are nor are not other than the aggregates. But "are the aggregates" and "are not other than the aggregates" in these statements mean "are the same in existence as collections of aggregates," and "are not the aggregates" means "are other than collections of aggregates as a separate substance." The assumption is that what exists is either a collection of aggregates (which are substances) or a substance. This "logic" of being and not being the aggregates and of being other and not being other than the aggregates is grounded in the orthodox Vaibhāṣika belief that everything that exists is a substantial reality or a substantially established reality. The Pudgalavādins are basically claiming that this "logic" excludes the existence of entities without separate identities, and so, excludes the existence of persons.

When the Pudgalavādins say in the "Refutation" that persons exist, they are assuming that persons are inexplicable phenomena and that the existence they possess is ultimate existence. This is the existence, I believe, that the Pudgalavādins of the *Kathāvatthu* called "existing in the way an ultimate thing exists." We need to be clear, however, what this means. The meaning is that although inexplicable persons, insofar as they are conceived, exist in dependence upon aggregates, they do exist apart from the aggregates and from being conceived in dependence upon aggregates as entities that lack separate identities. So inexplicable persons are conventional realities insofar as they are conceived in dependence upon collections of aggregates, but ultimately exist insofar as they exist apart from being conceived, as entities without separate identities. We do exist by ourselves, in other words, but insofar as we do, we cannot be conceived. Because we are inexplicable phenomena we cannot be conceived apart from the aggregates we are said to acquire.

We need to realize, as well, that Vasubandhu does not reject the view that persons ultimately exist. For he too believes that conventionally real persons ultimately exist by reason of being the same in existence as collections of aggregates. What he rejects is the Pudgalavādins' thesis that persons, who are conventionally real and ultimately exist, are inexplicable phenomena.

Whether or not the Pudgalavādins believe that there are other conventionally real inexplicable phenomena that ultimately exist is not clear. In the Commentary I will offer suggestions concerning whether or not they believe that fire, to which they compare persons, is a conventionally real inexplicable phenomenon that ultimately exists. In general, the Pudgalavādins' theories, other than their theory of persons, may not be significantly different from those of the orthodox Vaibhāṣika schools, save for their penchant, demonstrated in the *Tridharmaka Śāstra*, to reclassify phenomena into triads and their restriction of the notion of ultimate reality to nirvāṇa. Indeed, as we shall see, if Vasubandhu's philosophical critique of their theory of persons is correct, they do in fact accept a number of orthodox Vaibhāṣika theses that are incompatible with their theory of persons.

Although the form in which the Pudgalavādins formulated the Buddha's doctrine of the two realities is not to be found in any of our ancient sources, it is clear that they do not formulate it in the way Vasubandhu does in the *Treasury*. For our purposes, however, we need not reconstruct their view of both of these realities. We need only provide evidence for the view that they believe that persons are conventional realities that are neither substantial realities or substantially established realities. In the *Kathāvatthu*, the Pudgalavādins are represented as claiming that persons, like the aggregates, exist in an ultimate way, but their ultimate existence is of a different sort and is established in a different way. Although we cannot know, at this point, what the Pudgalavādins of the *Kathāvatthu* meant by the claim that both persons and aggregates ultimately exist, the most reasonable hypothesis, I believe, is that it means that they exist by themselves, apart from being conceived. In this case, the aggregates ultimately exist by virtue of possessing substantial reality and persons ultimately exist by virtue of being entities without separate identities. According to the Theravādins, we may presume, persons ultimately exist in the sense that their existence is the same as the existence of collections of aggregates. Hence, their complaint in the *Kathāvatthu* is only to the view that persons who are inexplicable ultimately exist. Accordingly, the different way in which the Pudgalavādins in this work claimed that persons are known to possess ultimate existence seems to be that which is explained in Section 2.5 of the "Refutation."

The Pudgalavādin schools, like all other Indian Buddhist philosophical schools, surely accept the doctrine of two realities, since it was extensively taught by the Buddha. In the *Tridharmaka Śāstra*, I have suggested above, they recast the original Vaibhāṣika theory of the two realities into three realities, two of which are what the orthodox Vaibhāṣikas call ultimate realities, and include persons among conventional realities, which is the third reality. Although they do not, in their extant works, provide a clear account of what conventional realities are, I think we can easily reconstruct their account. That the persons about whom they make their claims are conventional realities is clear from their discussions of persons in the *Sāṃmitīyanikāya Śāstra* and the *Tridharmaka Śāstra*, and from the claims made on their behalf in the treatises critical of their theory. The simplest and, for this reason, the most plausible reconstruction of their view is that persons are conventional realities insofar as they exist in dependence upon being conceived on the basis of collections of aggregates. In the *Sāṃmitīyanikāya Śāstra* two different ways in which phenomena are conceived in dependence upon a basis are presented. They may be conceived in dependence upon a basis in the way milk is conceived in dependence upon its elements or in the way fire is conceived in dependence upon fuel. In other words, they may be conceived in dependence upon a basis with which they are the same in existence or they may be conceived in dependence upon a basis with which they are not the same in existence. Persons, of course, are conceived on the basis of aggregates in the way fire is conceived on the basis of fuel. This is exactly the view that Vasubandhu attributes to the Pudgalavādins in the "Refutation." When in Section 2.1.2 Vasubandhu claims that if persons are conceived on the basis of their aggregates, they are the same in existence as their aggregates, just as milk is the same in existence as the elements on the basis of which it is conceived, the Pudgalavādins answer, in Section 2.1.3, that persons are not conceived in this way, but in the way that fire is conceived in reliance upon fuel.

There are two Sautrāntika schools. The first, which I call the original Sautrāntika school, is the school upon whose theses Vasubandhu seems most often to rely in his *Commentary*.[67] Many of the theses of the Vaibhāṣika schools are accepted in the original Sautrāntika school. The major differences between the orthodox Vaibhāṣika schools and the original Sautrāntika school are that the Sautrāntikas (1) drastically reduce the number of substances posited by the Vaibhāṣikas to explain the functioning of causally conditioned phenomena, and (2) reject the Vaibhāṣika theses that impermanent bodily phenomena may exist for more than a moment and that there are causes and effects that occur simultaneously.

The theses of the second Sautrāntika school, which I call the revised Sautrāntika school, incorporate many of the logical and epistemological ideas that were first formulated by Dignāga and then developed by Dharmakīrti in a series of logical and epistemological treatises.[68] The treatises of Dignāga and Dharmakīrti deal with the "valid cognitions" (*pramāṇa*-s) by means of which phenomena are known to exist. They had a profound effect on later developments in Indian Buddhist philosophy. The treatises were attempts to counter the Nyāya "theory of valid cognitions" (*pramāṇavāda*) with a distinctive Buddhist theory.[69] We will not be concerned here with the theses of the revised Sautrāntika school, which arose after the time Vasubandhu composed the "Refutation."

The Cittamātrika school was also made up of two major schools. The original fourth century CE Cittamātrika school is based on works composed by Asaṅga and his brother Vasubandhu.[70] According to the Buddhist tradition this Vasubandhu is the same Vasubandhu who composed the *Treasury*. Some scholars doubt that these two Vasubandhus can be the same person, but we need not deal with this issue here,[71] since the Vasubandhu who composed the *Commentary* does not seem to have relied on the theses of the Cittamātrika school in his critique of the theories of persons of the Pudgalavādins and Nyāya-Vaiśeṣikas. The major thesis of this school is that external objects, which are objects that exist apart from minds, do not exist. Later a revised Cittamātrika school was formed in which ideas set out in the works on logic and epistemology composed by Dharmakīrti are employed. Since in the "Refutation" there would seem to be no clear references to the theses of the Cittamātrika school, we need not discuss them here.

The Mādhyamika school was founded by Nāgārjuna during the second century CE. The major thesis of this school is that no phenomenon is "an independent reality" (*svabhāva*). This thesis was interpreted in different ways by Bhāvaviveka in the sixth century CE[72] and by Candrakīrti in the seventh century CE.[73] They agree, however, that what lacks independent reality lacks ultimate existence in the sense that it does not exist apart from being conceived. According to Bhāvaviveka, however, even though phenomena do not exist apart from being conceived, they also exist from their own side in dependence upon being conceived. According to Candrakīrti, phenomena cannot exist from their own side in dependence upon being conceived if they exist in dependence upon being conceived.[74] These different interpretations gave birth to a classification of different Mādhyamika schools. Bhāvaviveka is said to be the founder of the "Svātantrika" (Autonomy follower) branch of the Mādhyamika school, while Candrakīrti is usually said to be the founder of the "Prāsaṅgika" (Consequence follower) branch.[75] The Svātantrika-Mādhyamika school itself is believed to have divided into two branches, the Sautrāntika (Sūtra follower) branch, which continued Bhāvaviveka's interpretation of Nāgārjuna's Mādhyamika philosophy, and the Cittamātrika (Mind Only follower) branch, which revised it. Śāntarakṣita and Kamalaśīla (eighth century CE) are usually said to be the founders of the Cittamātrika-Svātantrika school. Candrakīrti, Bhāvaviveka, Śāntarakṣita, and Kamalaśīla all included in their work objections to the Pudgalavādins' theory of persons. Vasubandhu implies in Section 3.10 that Nāgārjuna is committed to a nihilism interpretation of the Buddha's teaching. The implication of his remark, which is that they deny the existence of everything, is that they deny the ultimate existence of persons, since they deny the existence of the collection of aggregates. In what follows I shall follow the practice of stating that the main thesis of the Mādhyamika school is that no phenomena possess ultimate existence, since this is the form in which it can most easily be seen to contradict the claims of Vasubandhu and the Pudgalavādins that we possess ultimate existence.

Candrakīrti also claims that persons are conventional realities. He seems to think that conventional realities are objects of knowledge that appear to minds in dependence upon the causally efficacious conventional framework of conceptions used by them during their beginningless journey through saṃsāra. Ultimate realities, by contrast, are objects of knowledge that appear to minds in dependence upon an analysis that dissolves this conventional framework of conceptions.[76] An ultimate reality, in this scheme, is an object's emptiness of ultimate existence. Every object of knowledge, including this emptiness, is empty of ultimate existence. For this reason, in his system of thought, conventional realities may be defined as all existent phenomena other than emptinesses.

Many different analyses are used by Candrakīrti to show that conventionally real persons are empty of ultimate existence. Among them is the argument that persons do not possess ultimate existence because they are neither other than nor the same in existence as the collections of aggregates in dependence upon which they conceive themselves. This argument seems to be the same argument used by the Pudgalavādins in Section 2.1.1 to deny that persons must be either substantial realities or substantially established realities. Unlike Candrakīrti, the Pudgalavādins believe that persons who are neither other than nor the same in existence as the collections of aggregates in dependence upon which they are conceived can possess ultimate existence. They believe that persons must ultimately exist, since they cause perceptions of themselves when their aggregates are present and the causes of such effects must ultimately exist if they are to cause their effects. Vasubandhu himself believes that if persons are neither other than nor the same in existence as collections of aggregates, they do not ultimately exist. He thinks that if persons are neither other than nor the same in existence as collections of aggregates, they cannot possess either substantial reality or substantially established reality, which are the only forms of existence he recognizes.

The selflessness of persons thesis and Indian Buddhist theories of persons

In all Indian Buddhist philosophical schools four theses are accepted. The first, which we may call the impermanence thesis, is that all causally conditioned phenomena are impermanent. Causally conditioned phenomena are phenomena that come to be by means of causes and conditions. They are opposed to causally unconditioned phenomena, which are phenomena that do not come to be by means of causes and conditions, since they do not come to be at all. Impermanence is conceived as the condition of a phenomenon being able to pass away. Its opposite, permanence, which is conceived as the condition of a phenomenon not being able to pass away, belongs to all causally unconditioned phenomena. Bodies in space, for instance, are cited as examples of causally conditioned impermanent phenomena, since they come to be by means of causes and conditions and then pass away. The space in which bodies come to be and pass away is cited as an example of a causally unconditioned permanent phenomenon, since it does not come to be or pass away.

In all Buddhist philosophical schools other than the orthodox Vaibhāṣika schools a momentariness interpretation of the impermanence thesis is accepted. According to this interpretation, all impermanent phenomena are momentary in existence, i.e. immediately pass away after having come to be for a moment. Bodies are believed to appear to remain the same for more than a moment because the minds that perceive them by means of the sense-organs cannot perceive the comings to be and passings away of the temporal parts of the causal series of phenomena of which they are composed. The momentariness of bodies is called their "subtle" impermanence, while the mere fact that they pass away after having come to be even in their gross appearance is called their "coarse" impermanence. What in the West we call "minds" are believed to be uninterrupted causal series of momentarily existent mental phenomena whose subtle comings to be and passings away cannot be detected by those who have not been trained to detect them.

The second thesis accepted in all Indian Buddhist philosophical schools is that all contaminated phenomena constitute suffering. Contaminated phenomena are mental afflictions or phenomena contaminated by mental afflictions.[77] The root mental affliction is "the mistaken view arising from a perishable collection of aggregates" (*satkāyadṛṣṭi*), which is our assent to a naturally occurring false appearance of ourselves as selves and of our aggregates as possessions of a self. This mental affliction contaminates all other phenomena in the collection of phenomena in dependence upon which we are conceived. The elimination of all contaminated phenomena is the goal of Buddhist practice, since it will result in the cessation of suffering. Uncontaminated phenomena are phenomena that are neither mental afflictions nor contaminated by them. This second thesis we may call the contamination thesis. The third thesis, which may be called "the cessation thesis," is that nirvāṇa is the peace that is the cessation of all suffering and rebirth. The differences between the Buddhist philosophical schools' interpretations of the contamination and cessation theses need not concern us here, since they have no bearing on the theories of persons we will discuss.

The fourth thesis accepted by all Indian Buddhist philosophical schools is the selflessness thesis. This is the thesis that all phenomena are "selfless" (*anātman*). The selflessness thesis is generally considered to be the one that distinguishes the teachings of the Buddha from the teachings of the Indian sages who base their teachings on the claim that a "self" (*ātman*) exists. In the "Refutation," those who explicitly teach that there is a self Vasubandhu calls the Tīrthikas.[78] In the different Indian Buddhist philosophical schools, different interpretations of the selflessness thesis are given. In the Cittamātrika and Mādhyamika schools the selflessness thesis is divided into two parts, one of which pertains only to persons and the other to all other phenomena, and different interpretations of each are given. In the Vaibhāṣika and Sautrāntika schools it is the thesis that no phenomenon is a self or a possession of a self, where a "self" is conceived as a person that can be independently identified.[79] As the Vaibhāṣikas and Sautrāntikas understand it, I will call it the selflessness of persons thesis.

The conception of a person is the conception of an object (1) to which we refer when we use the first-person singular pronoun to refer, and (2) of which we say, by convention, that it possesses as parts a body and mind that enable us to perceive objects, think about them, have feelings when they are perceived or thought about, perform actions for the sake of acquiring or avoiding them, etc. We may call (1) the referential component of the conception of a person, and (2) the descriptive component. In the Indian Buddhist philosophical schools it is generally agreed that the conception has both a referential and descriptive component. Vasubandhu asserts that the referent of the conception of a person is the same in existence as a collection of aggregates. The Pudgalavādins and Candrakīrti deny this is so. Vasubandhu and the Pudgalavādins believe that the referent of the conception ultimately exists, but Vasubandhu thinks this to be true because that referent is the same in existence as a collection of aggregates, while the Pudgalavādins think it to be true in spite of not being the same in existence as the collection. Candrakīrti not only denies that persons ultimately exist in either of these two ways, but also that reference to them is simultaneously a reference to the phenomena in dependence upon which they are conceived.

I will often call the conception of a person the conception of ourselves, and when I use "we" in what follows I mean "persons" in the sense that persons are the objects to which we refer when we use the first-person singular pronoun to refer and of which we say, by convention, that they possess bodies and minds, etc. When Vasubandhu says that a person is conceived, we may assume that he usually means that we conceive ourselves as persons. The view, that we conceive ourselves as persons, may be rendered simply as "we conceive ourselves." I mean that we conceive ourselves as persons. To conceive ourselves, however, is not to conceive ourselves as selves, since persons are not selves.

Vasubandhu, the Pudgalavādins, and Candrakīrti agree that the conception of ourselves is formed in dependence upon collections of aggregates and that insofar as we are conceived on this basis we are conventional realities.[80] Accordingly, collections of aggregates may be called "the causal basis" of the conception of ourselves. Included in the causal basis of the conception of ourselves, depending upon the context in which we refer to ourselves, are (1) all of the aggregates present at the moment we are referring to ourselves, (2) these same aggregates, along with previous aggregates in the causal continuum of aggregates of which the present aggregates are a part, and (3) these same aggregates, along with future aggregates in the causal continuum of aggregates of which the present aggregates are a part. So the causal basis of the conception of myself when I say, "I am writing this sentence," includes all of my present aggregates, the causal basis when I say, "I wrote this sentence yesterday," includes both all of my present aggregates plus the aggregates in dependence upon which I referred to myself yesterday, and the causal basis when I say, "I will write another sentence tomorrow," includes both all of my present aggregates plus the aggregates in dependence upon which I will refer to myself tomorrow. When I speak of "collections of aggregates" I will usually mean "collections of aggregates in dependence upon which we conceive ourselves," and when I speak of "our aggregates" I will mean "the aggregates in the collections in dependence upon which we conceive ourselves."[81] Finally, when I use "he" and "him" to refer to a person I do so without prejudice. The various devices commonly used to avoid "gender bias" in our language (e.g. using "she," "she/he," or even "it") seem to me either not to solve the problem or to be too awkward.

In what follows I will not discuss the Cittamātrika and Mādhyamika interpretations of the selflessness thesis as a thesis about phenomena other than persons and their possessions, since to do so would involve complications not pertinent to an understanding of the issues raised in the "Refutation." I will discuss only their interpretations of the selflessness of persons thesis, since they are the proper analogs of the selflessness thesis as it is interpreted by Vasubandhu and the Pudgalavādins.

There are two interpretations of the selflessness of persons thesis accepted in all of the Indian Buddhist philosophical schools. According to the first, it is the thesis that we are not other than collections of aggregates. To be other than collections of aggregates is to be a separate substance. So let us call this interpretation of the selflessness of persons "the separate substance" interpretation. The Tīrthikas, who claim that we are separate substances, add that we are also causally unconditioned, permanent and partless.[82]

The second interpretation of the selflessness of persons thesis accepted by Vasubandhu, the Pudgalavādins, and Candrakīrti is that we do not possess any attributes apart from being conceived in dependence upon collections of aggregates. They also agree that when we conceive ourselves, we naturally appear to ourselves to possess attributes apart from being conceived in dependence upon collections of aggregates. In other words, they believe that when we conceive ourselves, we naturally appear to be independently identifiable. Vasubandhu and the Pudgalavādins believe that we suffer in saṃsāra primarily because we assent to this appearance. Candrakīrti does not agree. None, however, believes that we naturally appear to ourselves to be separate substances when we conceive ourselves. The idea is that when we conceive ourselves from the first-person singular perspective and ascribe attributes to ourselves we never appear to exist apart from our aggregates in the way, for instance, one color appears to exist separately from another or in the way a color appears to exist separately from a sound. For the one can appear to the mind without the other appearing to it. However, we do naturally appear to be identifiable by ourselves, apart from our aggregates, as their owners or possessors, in spite of never appearing to our minds when our aggregates do not appear. When we investigate, therefore, we discover that we cannot be identified except in relation to these phenomena. Let us call the view that we cannot be identified independently "the no independent identifiability" interpretation of the selflessness of persons thesis. As a thesis of a Buddhist theory of persons, it may be called "the no independent identifiability thesis." According to Vasubandhu and the Pudgalavādins, the realization of our selflessness in the no independent identifiability sense is the chief means by which we become free from the sufferings of saṃsāra.

Vasubandhu assumes that if we cannot be identified except in relation to collections of aggregates, we cannot exist apart from collections of aggregates. For this reason in Section 1.2 of the "Refutation" he assumes that the argument he uses to show that we cannot be identified independently also shows that the Tīrthika thesis, that we are separate substances, is false.[83] In the Pudgalavādin schools,[84] I believe, it is also assumed that if we cannot be identified without reference to our aggregates, we are not separate substances. But in these schools the assumption is made because it is believed that our lack of an independent identifiability implies that we are not substances that exist apart from our aggregates, not because it is believed that our lack of an independent identifiability implies that we do not exist apart from our aggregates. For the Pudgalavādins believe that we can ultimately exist without being independently identifiable or being separate substances, since ultimate existence does not require independent identifiability. This is thought to be possible, as I explained above (p. 20), because persons are entities without separate identities.

Candrakīrti accepts the claims that the Buddha taught the selflessness of persons thesis according to its no separate substance interpretation to oppose the Tīrthikas' theory of persons and taught the no independent identifiability interpretation to oppose a naturally occurring false appearance of ourselves when we conceive ourselves. But he believes that the thesis requires another interpretation, since our assent to the naturally occurring appearance of ourselves as being independently identifiable is not the root cause of suffering in saṃsāra. He thinks that the Buddha gave an interpretation according to which the thesis is meant to oppose a subtle false appearance of ourselves, the assent to which is the actual root cause of suffering in saṃsāra. This subtle appearance is our false appearance of possessing ultimate existence in the sense of appearing to exist from our own side, apart from being conceived. Let us call his interpretation of the selflessness of persons thesis "the no ultimate existence interpretation." As a thesis of a Buddhist theory of persons, it may be called "the no ultimate existence thesis."

Candrakīrti believes that to be a self is to possess ultimate existence. So he thinks that we are selfless in the sense that we lack ultimate existence.[85] Even if we are not separate substances and are not independently identifiable, we can still possess ultimate existence. Such, in fact, is the claim of the Pudgalavādins. Hence, Candrakīrti believes that even if we realize that we are selfless in the no separate substance sense and in the no independent identifiability sense, we have not realized yet that we are selfless in the no ultimate existence sense. Since he believes that we suffer because we assent to a naturally occurring false appearance of ourselves possessing ultimate existence, he claims that the realization of our selflessness in its other two senses will not free us from suffering.

Vasubandhu believes that we ultimately exist in spite of not existing apart from our aggregates. But if he denies that we exist apart from our aggregates, how can he believe that we possess ultimate existence? To explain how this is possible we need to introduce a special thesis he has concerning the ontology of persons. The key to formulating this thesis is a proper understanding of what Vasubandhu means when he claims that we are collections of aggregates and what he means when he says that we are "real by way of a conception" (*prajñaptisat*).[86] In the "Refutation," he assumes that the aggregates are the substances of which our bodies and minds are composed and that we are conceived in dependence upon collections of such aggregates.[87] Nonetheless, he asserts in Section 2.1 that we are real by way of a conception. But how it is possible for us, if we are real by way of a conception, to be the collections of aggregates of which our bodies and minds are composed and in dependence upon which we are conceived?

We can answer this question, I believe, if we assume that Vasubandhu, like the Vaibhāṣikas, holds the view that all phenomena either are "substantially real" (*dravyasat*) or possess a reality that is "substantially established" (*dravyasiddha*). In this case, persons will be phenomena that possess substantially established reality rather than substantial reality. Substantially established realities are entities that possess mentally constructed identities and yet possess ultimate existence by reason of possessing as extrinsic parts different kinds of substances in dependence upon which their identity is constructed. If so, Vasubandhu's thesis, that we are collections of aggregates, implies that we possess substantially established reality, i.e. that we exist as entities to which we can refer because we are the same in existence as the collections of substances in dependence upon which we are conceived. So what it means to say that we are collections of aggregates is that we are the same in existence as collections of aggregates, not that we are, in all respects, the same as the collections. Collections of aggregates, moreover, possesses ultimate existence, since they exist from their own side, independently of being conceived. Hence, when Vasubandhu says that we are our aggregates, he means to imply that we ultimately exist, in spite of the fact that our identity is mentally constructed and we exist in dependence upon our aggregates.

But how can Vasubandhu's claim, that we are real by way of a conception, be made consistent with the view that we possess ultimate existence? It should be clear that to be real by way of a conception cannot mean to be real only as a conception if what is real by way of a conception possesses ultimate existence. It is for this very reason that I have translated his use of *prajñaptitas asti* in Section 2.1 as "is real by way of a conception" instead of "is real as a conception," which implies lack of ultimate existence.[88] What he means by making a person *prajñaptitas asti*, I submit, is that a person exists as a person in dependence upon a collection of aggregates being conceived as a person. It does not mean that the existence of a person is the existence of the conception formed in dependence upon that collection. If this is correct, his view is that we are real by way of a conception in the sense that we are persons in dependence upon being conceived as persons on the basis of collections of aggregates. However, apart from being conceived as persons, we do exist, he thinks, since the collections of aggregates of which we are composed and in dependence upon which we are conceived exist by themselves, apart from being conceived. Hence, his view is that even though we are not independently identifiable and we exist in dependence upon our aggregates, we exist apart from being conceived as persons, since we are the same in existence as our aggregates.

In order to make room for Vasubandhu's claims that we are collections of aggregates and that we are real by way of a conception, let us say that he asserts the thesis that we are entities that possess mentally constructed identities and ultimately exist insofar as we possess, as extrinsic parts, the different kinds of substances in dependence upon which our identities are constructed. Let us call this "the substantially established reality thesis." The opposed thesis is simply that we do not possess substantially established reality.

What exactly is it that possesses substantially established reality? According to Vasubandhu, we are, as objects of the conception of ourselves, conventional realities rather than mere collections of substantially real phenomena. In other words, the things to which we refer, when we use "I" to refer in everyday life, are conventional realities. So the reality that is substantially established in this case is our conventional reality. When Vasubandhu says that a person is his aggregates, he means that a conventionally real person is the same in existence as a collection of aggregates. The implication is that when reference is made to ourselves, as conventional realities, the ontological ground of the reference is a collection of substances that ultimately exists. He is not denying that we refer to ourselves as conventional realities. In fact, he must be referring to us as conventional realities in order to claim that we are the same in existence as collections of aggregates. But because he thinks that the reference to ourselves as conventional realities is based on our creating for ourselves a mentally constructed identity, he says that we are real by way of a conception, and because this same reference is simultaneously a reference to collections of aggregates, which are substances, he says that our reality is substantially established. He is assuming that our existence can be distinguished from our identity, and that what enables us to refer to ourselves, as conventional realities, is the fact that we can refer to collections of aggregates that comprise our extrinsic parts. Vasubandhu says that we are our aggregates in order to explain how reference to ourselves as conventional realities is possible.

So Vasubandhu marks off two domains of entities to which we can refer, conventionally real entities and ultimately real entities. The existence of the entities in the first domain is the same as that of collections of entities in the second, but their identities, which also determine reference to them, are determined by convention rather than by an analysis that reveals the way in which they ultimately exist. If this is correct, a reference to persons, although simultaneously a reference to collections of aggregates, is distinct from a reference to collections of aggregates, which are not by themselves persons. In ultimate reality, so to speak, there are no persons, since in it only collections of aggregates can be found, but in conventional reality there are persons, since in it persons are entities to which we can refer. Moreover, in conventional reality there are no collections of aggregates of the sort in dependence upon which persons are conceived, since the aggregates, from the point of view of conventional reality, are by definition the intrinsic parts of persons, but from the ultimate point of view, are extrinsic parts, since they are substances in their own right. Persons are entities to which we can refer, in the peculiar sense that they are entities reference to which depends upon the convention that they exist when the aggregates in dependence upon which they are conceived are present.

The conception of a person and its causal basis

Vasubandhu seems to assume that we are, from a conventional point of view, wholes of parts. Although the parts of these wholes are in fact identifiable independently of the wholes, the wholes themselves are not identifiable independently of their parts. Our parts he believes to be the aggregates in the collections of aggregates that are the causal basis of the conception of ourselves. The aggregates in these collections, he assumes, exist in a beginningless causal continuum perpetuated by the mistaken view of a self. When we conceive ourselves, who are wholes of parts, he believes, we falsely appear to ourselves to be wholes that are identifiable independently of our parts and our parts falsely appear to be identifiable in dependence upon the wholes of which they are parts. As a result of assenting to the first false appearance we acquire the false idea of "I," and as a result of assenting to the second false appearance, we acquire the false idea of "mine." The false ideas of "I" and "mine" are what, together, are called "the mistaken view arising from a perishable collection of aggregates" (*satkāyadṛṣṭi*). Were we wholes that are identifiable independently of our parts, we should be found, along with our aggregates, among the collection of phenomena in dependence upon which we conceive ourselves. However, nothing but the aggregates are found among this collection of phenomena. Hence, he concludes, we are not selves. Nonetheless, he believes, what is defined when a person is defined is a whole that cannot be identified independently of reference to its parts and whose parts can be identified independently of the whole of which they are the parts.[89]

The conventional definition of a person Vasubandhu seems to have accepted is the one I presented earlier. It is, I believe, a definition based on what the Buddha said about how the aggregates are related to persons. The Buddha often referred to the aggregates in the collections in dependence upon which we are conceived as the *upādānaskandha*-s. The term, I believe, is best understood in English to mean "aggregates that have been acquired." Acquired by what or whom? Vasubandhu, I conjecture, assumed that the Buddha meant that the aggregates are, according to convention, said to be acquired by persons. Hence, a person, as a conventional reality, is the acquirer (*upādātṛ*) of these aggregates. But in what sense does a person acquire aggregates? Surely, the sense, according to Vasubandhu, is that in which a table, for instance, is a whole that acquires different parts when its legs are replaced. Of course, if we can be said to acquire aggregates, we can also be said to possess them, just as a table is said to possess the parts it has acquired. In the sense in which the surface of a table is a part of a table, moreover, we also attribute the color of this part of the table to the table itself. Likewise, the attributes of the aggregates are also ascribed to the person. In general, when we take into account the functions performed by the aggregates of a person, the implication is that the descriptive content of the conception of a person is that of being an owner or possessor of aggregates who acquires different aggregates moment by moment, and by reason of possessing them is said, e.g., to perceive objects, since consciousness does so, and to walk, since the legs of the person do so, etc.

The Pudgalavādins are also likely to have believed that the object of the conception of a person, from a conventional point of view, is a whole of parts. But in their case, the whole includes not only the aggregates as extrinsic parts, but also an entity without a separate identity. They clearly agree with Vasubandhu that we are conceived in dependence upon collections of aggregates. But they do not agree that we are said to acquire and possess aggregates in the way in which a table acquires and possesses parts, since the table is the same in existence as the collection of its parts. In Section 3.4.2 of the "Refutation" they argue that we acquire aggregates in the way, for instance, that we acquire knowledge when we become grammarians. The implication is that persons are the same in existence as the underlying supports (*āśraya*-s) for the parts they acquire, not the collections of the parts acquired. This idea seems to have been borrowed from the Nyāya-Vaiśeṣikas, who believe that persons, as separate substances, are underlying supports for mental states. The Pudgalavādins, however, construe persons as inexplicable phenomena rather than as substances. Moreover, they do not believe, as the Nyāya-Vaiśeṣikas do, that by their own natures persons are, apart from being conceived as persons, underlying supports for mental states, for in that case they would possess separate identities.

Although Candrakīrti shares the view of Vasubandhu and the Pudgalavādins, that we are conceived in dependence upon collections of aggregates, he rejects their view that the aggregates are substances. Moreover, he believes not only that we are conceived in dependence upon collections of aggregates, but also that these collections of aggregates are conceived in dependence upon us. All wholes, he believes, are conceived in dependence upon their parts and all parts are conceived in dependence upon the wholes of which they are parts. The idea of extrinsic parts, therefore, is incoherent. For instance, the aggregate of consciousness, in his opinion, cannot exist apart from a person any more than a person can exist apart from the aggregate of consciousness. So he shares the Pudgalavādins' view that our existence is not the same as that of collections of aggregates.

Vasubandhu, the Pudgalavādins, and Candrakīrti seem to agree that we are able to ascribe to ourselves the functions our aggregates perform because we are not other than our aggregates. For instance, because consciousnesses present within the collections of aggregates in dependence upon which we conceive ourselves perceive objects and we are not other than these consciousnesses, by convention we can say that we perceive objects and that we are perceivers of objects. Similarly, because bodily forms are present within these collections of aggregates and we are not other than these bodily forms, by convention we can say that we possess bodies and ascribe the attributes of our bodies to ourselves. When we conceive ourselves as performing the functions of different aggregates, however, we appear to possess an identity not possessed by any of our aggregates.

By assenting to this false appearance, we acquire a mistaken view of the object of the conception of ourselves.

The fact that the aggregates in the collections in dependence upon which we conceive ourselves exist in a single uninterrupted causal continuum, Vasubandhu and Candrakīrti assume, explains the success of the convention that we are the same persons at different times. The Pudgalavādins, presumably, believe that a better explanation of the success of the convention is that we are the inexplicable underlying supports of all of the aggregates in the causal continuum of the collection of aggregates in dependence upon which we are conceived. It is precisely because they believe that we are the inexplicable underlying supports of all such aggregates, we may assume, that they claim, as reported in our Chinese sources, that we are neither the same persons over time nor different persons over time. The meaning of this view, of course, is that we are neither the same persons over time in the way substantially real underlying supports of aggregates would be nor different persons over time in the way we could be if we were the same in existence as collections of momentary aggregates.

The fact that the aggregates in the causal continuum of aggregates in dependence upon which we are conceived are not the same as one another from moment to moment, Vasubandhu, Candrakīrti, and even the Pudgalavādins seem to assume, explains why we can, by convention, be conceived as different over time. When we conceive ourselves as different over time, however, our difference over time is not conceived as our being different persons over time (except perhaps in a special sense of "persons"), but as our possessing different parts over time. In this way, they are able to explain the convention that we change over time without ceasing to be persons.

When we conceive ourselves as single individuals simultaneously performing the functions of different aggregates, Vasubandhu seems to believe, we appear not only to be independently identifiable, but also to be independently one, i.e. to be wholes whose existence is not the same as the existence of their extrinsic parts. The Pudgalavādins may believe that the conception of ourselves as irreducibly one has a different explanation. They are in a position to claim that the basis upon which the simultaneous performance of the functions of different aggregates can be attributed to us is that, ultimately, we are single entities without separate identities. So perhaps they would say that we possess what might be called an "inexplicable unity," which is our being one without being either a separate substance or a collection of substances being conceived as a single entity. Vasubandhu, Candrakīrti, and perhaps even the Pudgalavādins would seem to believe that aggregates, although not functioning independently of one another, are not the same as one another, which explains why we can, by convention, be conceived as possessing different parts.

Even though Vasubandhu, the Pudgalavādins, and Candrakīrti agree that the conception of a person does not have an object that can be identified independently, they never conclude that the conception has no object, since the view that it has no object is considered to be a nihilism view rejected by the Buddha. To what then does the conception refer? On this question there is disagreement among the philosophers whose theories of persons we are discussing. Although Vasubandhu, the Pudgalavādins, and Candrakīrti agree that the object of the conception of ourselves is a conventional reality, they disagree about what it means to be a conventional reality and about whether or not the conception is used to refer to us in dependence upon its reference to something else, and if it is, to what else. According to Vasubandhu, the conception is used to refer to us as conventional realities because it also refers to our aggregates as a collection. This reference to us, of course, also depends upon the convention that we are present when the aggregates in the collection of aggregates of which we are composed are present. According to the Pudgalavādins, I believe, it is used to refer to us as conventional realities because it also refers to an entity that cannot be independently identified. This entity, they claim, is perceived when the aggregates in the collection in dependence upon which we are conceived are present. According to Candrakīrti, the conception is used to refer to us in dependence upon collections of aggregates, but it itself does not also refer to the collection of our aggregates or to an entity without a separate identity, since we are not the same in existence as either of them. All reference, he believes, relies on phenomena that are not the same in existence as the phenomena to which reference is made, and for this reason, there is no independent reference to anything else on the basis of which a dependent reference to ourselves is made. So the only object of reference to ourselves, in his view, is ourselves. No Indian Buddhist philosopher, of course, believes that the conception of ourselves refers to us because it also refers to a separate substance. Vasubandhu and the Pudgalavādins, of course, would object that reference to what does not ultimately exist is not possible.

A classification of Indian theories of persons may be formed on the basis of the different theses assumed to be true by Indian philosophers concerning our modes of existence and/or identity and how we are related to the collections of aggregates in dependence upon which we are conceived. The two basic kinds of theories are the no ultimate existence theory, which is held by Candrakīrti, and the ultimate existence theory, which is held not only by Vasubandhu and the Pudgalavādins, but also by the Tīrthikas. Vasubandhu's theory we may call the substantially established reality version of the ultimate existence theory of persons, since in it the thesis is asserted that we are the same in existence as collections of aggregates. The Pudgalavādins' theory we may call the entity without a separate identity version of the ultimate existence theory of persons, since in it the thesis is asserted that we are the same in existence as an entity without a separate identity. These two theories, therefore, may be contrasted to the Tīrthikas' separate substance version of the ultimate existence theory of persons, according to which we are separate substances.

Candrakīrti argues that we do not possess ultimate existence precisely because we are neither other than nor the same in existence as the collections of aggregates in dependence upon which we conceive ourselves. Nonetheless, he claims, we do exist, since by convention we exist and possess identity in dependence upon being conceived when our aggre-gates are present. Vasubandhu, the Pudgalavādins, and the Tīrthikas are committed to the view that the no ultimate existence theory of persons implies that we do not exist at all, since what does not ultimately exist could not perform the causal functions we by definition perform. Since what exists performs a causal function, they believe, the thesis that we do not possess ultimate existence fails to preserve our existence. Candrakīrti, however, believes that if we were to possess ultimate existence, we could not perform the causal functions persons by definition perform. His view is that since what possesses ultimate existence must exist by itself, what exists by itself is causally unconditioned, and since what is causally unconditioned cannot perform a causal function, what possesses ultimate existence cannot perform a causal function. He agrees with Vasubandhu that an entity without a separate identity does not ultimately exist. In fact, both deny that such an entity exists even by convention.

The five aggregates in dependence upon which persons are conceived

Although in the Buddhist tradition the order in which the aggregates are usually listed is bodily forms, feelings, discriminations, volitional forces, and consciousnesses, it will be convenient for our purposes first to explain bodily forms, and then, in turn, consciousnesses, discriminations, volitional forces, and feelings. In what follows I will explain the aggregates according to the view of Vasubandhu in the *Commentary*, as opposed to the view of Asaṅga, which is presented in his *Compendium of Knowledge* (*Abhidharma-samuccaya*), since it is Vasubandhu's interpretation that is followed in the "Refutation."

The account of bodily forms in the *Treasury* and its *Commentary* is far from complete and is believed by most scholars to be problematic. But since Vasubandhu seems to rely on parts of this account in important arguments in the "Refutation," I will comment on the parts most relevant to an appraisal of these arguments. Included among bodily forms are the five sense-organs, the five kinds of secondary elements that are the objects perceived by means of these sense-organs, and the four primary elements of which the sense-organs are composed and are said to provide underlying supports for the secondary elements perceived by means of the sense-organs.[90] The four primary elements, which are earth, water, fire, and air or wind, are not earth, water, fire, and air or wind as they are usually conventionally conceived, but substances whose existence is inferred in order to explain the facts that tactile objects can repel one another (earth), can attract one another (water), can become hot (fire), and can move (air or wind).[91] The different configurations of the primary elements in the inseparable combinations of elements of which the sense-organs are composed is assumed to explain the functional differences between the sense-organs. In Vasubandhu's argument with the Pudgalavādins in Section 2 of the "Refutation" he relies on the Vaibhāṣika view that the fire-element is a substance that always exists in conjunction with the other primary elements of which inseparable combinations of substances are composed.

The five kinds of secondary elements directly perceived by means of the five sense-organs are visible forms, sounds, odors, flavors, and tactile phenomena. Each of these five is distinguished into different kinds.[92] In the desire realm,[93] the four primary elements and visible forms, odors, flavors, and tangible objects are present in all combined material particles. For obvious reasons, sound need not be present.[94] Bodily forms are said to be included among the collection of aggregates in dependence upon which we are conceived, presumably, because we are in part defined as owners or possessors of bodies we use to perceive the secondary elements, to feel bodily pleasure and pain when we perceive them, to have physical desires and aversions towards them, and to perform bodily actions to acquire or avoid them, etc.

Consciousness as we normally think of it is revealed in meditation to be a causal continuum of momentary consciousnesses, each of which is a mental substance. The primary cause of each momentary consciousness is its immediate predecessor in a beginningless causal continuum. Its secondary causes are an organ of perception and an object of perception, both of which exist in the preceding moment and are in contact.[95] According to the Vaibhāṣikas, and, we may assume, according to Vasubandhu, a consciousness of the sort to which reference is made in the list of the five aggregates is the substance that performs the function of apprehending the existence of an object, as opposed to apprehending a character it possesses.

A consciousness, so defined, is often called a "mind" (*citta*), and when it is, it is being contrasted to "mental factors" (*caitta*-s). The general function of a consciousness, insofar as it includes both a mind and its mental factors, is the perception of an object. According to the Vaibhāṣikas, mental factors are distinct substances that combine with a mind to comprise a perception of an object. Vasubandhu seems to agree with the Vaibhāṣikas that every mind is attended by ten mental factors, among which are a feeling, a discrimination of a character the object possesses, and a number of other mental factors included among the volitional forces that comprise the fourth aggregate. Although in the *Commentary* Vasubandhu seems to reject the orthodox Vaibhāṣika school view that minds and their mental factors are separate substances, in the "Refutation" he does not, since in Section 4.8 he refers to the five aggregates as substances in their uncontaminated forms.

Consciousnesses are of six different kinds when classified according to the six different kinds of organs of perception by means of which they are produced. The first five kinds of consciousnesses are those that arise in dependence upon the five sense-organs and the different objects within their separate domains. They are the eye-consciousness, ear-consciousness, tongue-consciousness, nose-consciousness, and body-consciousness. The sense-objects in their domains, respectively, are the secondary elements, which are visible form, sound, flavor, odor, and tactile phenomena. The sixth kind of consciousness is called a "mental consciousness" (*manovijñāna*), which is a consciousness that arises in dependence upon a "mental organ" (*manas*) and one of the mental objects within its special domain. A mental consciousness can directly perceive an object in its own special domain, conceive an object in the domain of one of the sense-organs, be a thought about one of these objects, and be the conclusion of a correct inference that establishes the existence of one of these objects.

A mental organ is a consciousness that produces, in the next moment of a continuum of consciousnesses of which it is a part, a direct perception of itself and/or of one or more of its mental factors. The consciousness that has this perception is the mental consciousness. An eye-consciousness, for instance, can give rise to a mental consciousness that directly perceives this same eye-consciousness in the next moment. For this reason it is said to be the organ by means of which it itself is directly perceived. In this case, the eye-consciousness is both the object directly perceived by the immediately following mental consciousness and the mental organ by means of which it itself is directly perceived by that consciousness. A perception to which an eye-consciousness, as an organ of perception, gives rise, however, need not be a direct perception of the eye-consciousness and/or its attendant mental factors. It might instead be an indirect perception of the object of the eye-consciousness. In this case, the perception involves a mental image of an object of the eye-consciousness, and the perceiving consciousness is said to conceive the object. The conception of an object is a consciousness that conceives the object.

Consequently, there are six kinds of objects the Vaibhāṣikas and Sautrāntikas believe to be directly perceived by the six consciousnesses, but the sixth consciousness, which is the mental consciousness, can not only directly perceive the immediately preceding mind and/or its attendant mental factors in the same causal continuum, but can also conceive the objects of the six consciousnesses. Both a direct and an indirect perception of an object is called a "cognition" (*buddhi*). A cognition of an object is said to occur in dependence upon contact that occurs between an organ of perception and an object of perception. If a cognition establishes the existence of an object, it is called a "valid cognition" (*pramāṇa*) and if it does not it is called an "invalid cognition" (*apramāṇa*). The two kinds of valid cognition acknowledged in Section 2.1 of the "Refutation" are "direct perception" (*pratyakṣa*) and "correct inference" (*anumāṇa*).

Since the object of a direct perception is one of the causes of its direct perception and the causal efficacy of a phenomenon is one of the criteria of its existence, Vasubandhu believes that the direct perception of an object establishes its existence. If the object is a substantial reality, the existence established, he believes, is that of a substantial reality. If the object is a substantially established reality, the existence established is that of a substantially established reality. The Pudgalavādins, by contrast, believe that some objects known to exist are inexplicable in the sense of being neither substantial realities nor substantially established realities. Since there are inexplicable phenomena that cause themselves to be directly perceived, they believe, they must exist. They assume that an entity need not possess substantial reality or substantially established reality in order to be causally efficacious. In Section 2.5 they claim that an inexplicable person is known to exist by perception.

The orthodox Vaibhāṣikas hold the view that a consciousness can directly perceive an external object without reproducing in itself a character the object possesses. In fact, it may be the acceptance of this very view that made it possible for the Pudgalavādins, who in effect deny that persons have separate identities, to claim that persons are directly perceived. In Section 4.6 of the "Refutation," Vasubandhu presents the Sautrāntika theory of direct perception according to which a character an object possesses is reproduced in a consciousness that perceives the object. The impression created in the perceiving consciousness, however, is not a mental image of the sort present in a conceiving consciousness, since only a conception of an object is a mental image of it. But what exactly this reproduced character is is not explained. Vasubandhu relies on the Sautrāntika view of the nature and functions of minds and their mental factors throughout the "Refutation."

In the *Treasury* and its *Commentary* Vasubandhu says very little about discrimination. In other Buddhist texts, however, the function of discrimination is said to be to distinguish an object apprehended from other objects that can be apprehended, and it is said to do this by discriminating a character it possesses. A character of an object not only marks off the object from objects of a different kind but also from other objects of the same kind. We may assume that Vasubandhu also holds these views. At least some of his other views about discrimination we might be able to infer from views he holds about closely related matters. On this basis, for instance, we may assume that he believes that a consciousness whose perception establishes the existence of an object always discriminates a character it possesses, since he assumes that an object whose existence is established by a valid cognition possesses a character by means of which it is conceived. Since he holds the view that objects of conceptions known to exist are either substantial realities or substantially established realities, he is also committed to the view that both substantial realities and substantially established realities possess characters discriminated when their existence is established.[96]

If the causal basis of the conception of an object is a substantial reality, Vasubandhu surely believes, it is a substantially real phenomenon whose character has been discriminated. But substantially established realities, in his view, are collections of different kinds of substances that are conceived as single entities of a certain sort, and so do not, from their own side, possess the character on the basis of which they are conceived. Only the collections of different sorts of substances on the basis of which single entities of some sort are conceived are the causal basis of the conception of the collections as single entities. When the causal basis of a conception of an object is a collection of different kinds of substances, the existence of the object is, by convention, established by a valid cognition of any of the substances present in its causal basis. It is for this reason that in Section 2.5.1 of the "Refutation" Vasubandhu assumes that milk is known to exist if any of the substances in the collection of different kinds of substances in dependence upon which milk is conceived is known to exist. Since a substantially established reality like milk can be known to exist by a valid cognition, it must possess a character by means of whose discrimination one of its parts is conceived. Hence, milk, for instance, is not identifiable as the single entity of the sort it is conceived to be apart from the substances in the collection of substances of different sorts of which it is composed. But since milk, insofar as it is conceived as milk, has a mentally constructed component, it is not identifiable apart from the convention that the collection of substances that are its ultimate parts is the causal basis of its conception as milk.

According to Vasubandhu, what has been said here of milk is also true of persons. We may assume, first of all, that he believes that a person, who is the object of the conception of ourselves, is known to exist just in case there is a valid cognition of at least one of the aggregates in the collection of aggregates that is the causal basis of the conception. But a valid cognition of this sort does not establish the identity of the person as a person. For instance, the existence of a person who performs an action can be established by a valid cognition of an action that is present in the collection of aggregates in dependence upon which that person is conceived, but it does not establish the identity of the person as an agent of the action. What is needed to establish the identity of the person as an agent of the action are the conventions that the collection of aggregates in which the action occurs is the causal basis of the conception of a person and that the causal functions performed by the aggregates in this collection are ascribed to the person conceived in dependence upon the collection of aggregates. For this reason, I believe, he thinks that the identity of a person must be established both by valid cognitions of the aggregates that are his constituents and by convention.

Central to Vasubandhu's philosophical critique of the Pudgalavādins' theory of persons is the principle that the object of a conception must be the same in existence as its causal basis. According to this principle, which I shall call the causal reference principle, the object of the conception of ourselves must be the same in existence as the collections of aggregates in dependence upon which we are conceived. It is this principle that the Pudgalavādins attempt to refute when, in Section 2.1.3, they argue that we are conceived in reliance upon our aggregates in the way fire is conceived in reliance upon fuel. The conception of ourselves, they believe, is not formed on the basis of perceptions of ourselves, but only on the basis of the aggregates that are present when we are perceived. Because, from an ultimate point of view, we are entities without separate identities, moreover, we are known to exist by means of perceptions of ourselves that do not include a discrimination of a character we possess by ourselves. Nevertheless, the Pudgalavādins claim in Section 2.5 that we are known to exist by the six consciousnesses that perceive the objects in the domains of their associated organs of perception. However, they do not abandon the general principle that every consciousness is attended by the mental factor of discrimination. For we will discover, on the basis of a close examination of Sections 2.5–2.5.2.2 of the "Refutation," that they believe that a consciousness that perceives an object within the domain of its associated organ of perception also perceives us and that this consciousness is attended by a discrimination of the character of the object within the domain of its associated organ of perception. The idea that there is an awareness of ourselves as entities without separate identities when our consciousnesses are aware of objects in their own domains is a key element in the Pudgalavādins' establishment of their own theory of persons. Whether or not Vasubandhu succeeds in undermining this idea and their attempt to refute the causal reference principle will be discussed at length in my Commentary on Sections 2.1–2.5.2.2.

Since by convention a name (a significant spoken sound) is associated with the conception of an object, this name is also applied to the object of the conception. Vasubandhu calls both this conception and its associated name *prajñapti*. In the Translation and Commentary I translate this term as a "conception" in order to convey the idea that at its root it is a conception of an object and to show its etymological connection to *prajñapyate*, which I translate as "is conceived." When readers see "conceived" and "conception" in the Translation, therefore, they should understand them, respectively, to mean "conceived or named" and "conception or name."

Vasubandhu distinguishes between true and false discriminations, but he does not provide us with an account of the distinction. He says only that false discriminations are one of two causes of rebirth, the other being attachment to feelings.[97] False discriminations cause rebirth because they give rise to false views. A false discrimination, I conjecture, he would define as what seems to be, but is not, a discrimination of a character possessed by an object. Among discriminations that are true are discriminations of the characters of aggregates, which are substantially real phenomena. But also included are discriminations of the characters of persons, since discriminations of their characters are assumed to be nothing but discriminations of the characters of the aggregates in the collections of aggregates in dependence upon which persons are conceived. Since by convention a perception of one of the aggregates of a person is a perception of the person, it can be said that there is a true discrimination of a character possessed by a person, even though the person is real by way of a conception. In general, we may say, a true discrimination is an actual discrimination of a character an object possesses. Although Vasubandhu does not give an example of a false discrimination, we can be sure that he thinks that our assent to our false appearance of being independently identifiable involves a false discrimination.

Although I have chosen to translate the name of the aggregate, *saṃskāra*-s, as "volitional forces," a more literal meaning of the name is "things that causally condition," and what they causally condition are called *saṃskṛta*-s, whose literal meaning is "things causally conditioned." There are many mental phenomena included in the aggregate of volitional forces. Included are all mental factors other than discrimination and feeling. These mental factors are positive, negative, or neutral in dependence upon the positive, negative, or neutral result they bring about when they motivate actions. At the head of the list is the mental factor called "volition" or "intention" (*cetanā*), which is the mental action that gives rise to actions of body and speech. Also included are the mental afflictions that contaminate mental actions, and thereby cause us to suffer. The mental affliction that contaminates all of our mental actions is the mistaken view arising from a perishable collection of aggregates. That volitional forces are singled out as one division of the aggregates implies that it is believed that an important descriptive component of the conception of ourselves is the idea that we are agents of actions.

The view that we are agents of actions surfaces several times in the "Refutation." The Pudgalavādins would seem to believe that their theory of persons provides a better metaphysical explanation of the convention that we are agents of action than Vasubandhu's theory does. The analogy they make in Section 2.2.1 of the "Refutation" between a person and his aggregates and fire and its fuel strongly suggests that they believe that just as fire can unite with fuel and provide a metaphysical explanation for the convention that fire is what burns fuel, so a person can unite with the aggregates and provide a metaphysical explanation for the convention that a person acquires aggregates. The idea that the convention, that a person is an agent of action, requires, as a metaphysical explanation, the substantial reality of an agent of action, underlies the Nyāya-Vaiśeṣika arguments for the existence of a self in Sections 4.2, 4.4, 4.5, and 4.12. Vasubandhu not only denies that his opponents' explanations of this convention are better than his, but also vigorously attacks them. The most notable instance of this is in Section 4.7.1, where Vasubandhu launches an extended critique of the Nyāya-Vaiśeṣika explanation of the role played by a self in the production of the different kinds of minds that arise in persons. Nonetheless, since volitional forces are included among the collection of aggregates that is the causal basis of the conception of ourselves, Vasubandhu believes, as all Buddhists do, that the convention that we are agents of actions is a central part of the descriptive component of the conception, and so requires an explanation in terms of the causal basis of the conception.

When it is said that suffering results from our contaminated actions, the reference is usually to feeling. A feeling, Vasubandhu believes, is one of three kinds: pleasure, pain, and a feeling that is neither pleasure nor pain. A feeling, which is part of every perception, arises in dependence upon contact between an organ of perception and an object of perception. Which of the three kinds of feeling occurs when an object is perceived is determined, in accord with the law of actions and their results, by the character of the prior action that caused it. All feelings that arise because of contaminated actions are forms of suffering. Even pleasure and indifferent feeling are forms of suffering, since suffering includes not only obvious suffering such as pain, but also the suffering latent in temporary pleasure and in perception that arises direct or indirectly in dependence upon the organs of perception. Feeling is said to be included in the aggregates precisely because attachment to it is a cause of rebirth.[98] Attachment to feeling is a cause of rebirth because it leads us to perform contaminated actions.

The centrality given to feeling in our conventional idea of ourselves is indicated not only by the fact that it is the paradigmatic case of the suffering that results from contaminated actions, but also by the fact that its occurrence is argued by the Nyāya-Vaiśeṣika in Section 4.11 to be a proof of the existence of a self. Since volitional forces are coupled with feeling as two of the five aggregates, it becomes clear that the Buddha assumed that the descriptive component of the conception of ourselves includes the idea of our being agents of actions and subjects that suffer the results of these actions. Of course, since consciousness and discrimination are also included among the aggregates, another part of its descriptive component is the idea that we are rational agents of actions and subjects of such experiences.

The middle way between extreme views

The Buddha warned his followers that they must be careful not to abandon the belief that we exist, since although we are not selves, we do exist. A theory of persons in which selfhood is attributed to us the Buddha called the "eternal transcendence theory" (*śāśvatavāda*) and the contrary theory, that we do not exist at all, he called a "nihilism theory" (*ucchedavāda*). The correct theory, he said, is a middle way between these extremes. In all Indian Buddhist philosophical schools an attempt is made to identify correctly what exactly these extremes are and what exactly the middle way between them is.

In his sūtras the Buddha opposed his theory of persons to that of the Tīrthikas. It is to their "theory of a self" (*ātmavāda*) that the Buddha initially opposed his own "no-self theory" (*anātmavāda*). The separate substance version of the ultimate existence theory of persons propounded by the Tīrthikas is claimed by all Indian Buddhist philosophers to fall to the eternal transcendence extreme. In Section 4 of the "Refutation," however, Vasubandhu seems to discuss only the eternal transcendence theory of persons presented by the Nyāya-Vaiśeṣikas.

Vasubandhu believes not only that the separate substance theory of persons falls to the eternal transcendence extreme, but also the independent identifiability theory, since what can be identified independently of collections of aggregates must be a separate substance. He believes that his theory avoids the nihilism extreme because in it we are said to be the same in existence as collections of aggregates. He thinks that the Tīrthikas hold an explicit form of the eternal transcendence theory, since they assert that we are separate substances, and that the Pudgalavādins hold an implicit form of the theory, since even though they deny that we can be identified independently, they assert that we ultimately exist without being the same in existence as collections of aggregates, and this assertion implies that we are separate substances. It is for this same reason, I suspect, that later Buddhist critics of the Pudgalavādins' theory of persons attribute to them the view that we are substantially real.

In the "Refutation" Vasubandhu also implies, in a single sentence, that Nāgārjuna holds a nihilism position because he claims that no phenomena possess ultimate existence. Vasubandhu does not explain his rejection of Nāgārjuna's view. The reason he does not, surely, is that he thinks that it patently contradicts the Buddha's rejection of nihilism. Since he accepts the view that to exist is to exist apart from being conceived, he believes that Nāgārjuna's denial of the ultimate existence of all phenomena commits him to nihilism. Unfortunately, he does not attempt to answer any of Nāgārjuna's objections to the view that phenomena possess ultimate existence.

In the "Refutation," Vasubandhu rejects the eternal transcendence thesis concerning our existence by arguing that neither by means of direct perception nor by means of correct inference can selves be found among the collections of phenomena in dependence upon which we are conceived. He rejects the nihilism thesis by implying in this same argument that we ultimately exist because what are found are collections of aggregates, which are known to exist by means of direct perception and correct inference.

According to the Pudgalavādins' theory, that we are entities without separate identities, the eternal transcendence extreme is also avoided by the standard Buddhist arguments against the view that we are selves, but these arguments are not believed to imply that we do not exist apart from collections of aggregates. The nihilism extreme is avoided by our perceptions of ourselves when the aggregates in the collections in dependence upon which we conceive ourselves are present. The Pudgalavādins also imply that Vasubandhu's view, that we are the same in existence as collections of aggregates, falls to the nihilism extreme. To claim that our existence is the same as that of collections of aggregates, they think, is to deny that we can exist apart from them, and this is a nihilism view.

Candrakīrti claims to avoid the eternal transcendence extreme because, according to his theory, we do not possess ultimate existence. If we were to possess ultimate existence, he reasons, we would exist by our own nature, and so be causally unconditioned separate substances. He claims that his theory avoids the nihilism extreme because it posits our existence in dependence upon being conceived on a basis that is valid by convention. The nihilism extreme, he believes, is not to exist at all, not even in dependence upon being conceived on such a basis.

The problematic character of Vasubandhu's exchange with the Pudgalavādins

Vasubandhu's objections to the Pudgalavādins' theory of persons and replies to their objections may be divided into those that are attempts to show, on the basis of independent reasoning, its logical incoherence, and those that are attempts to show that they contradict the teachings of the Buddha. Most of the objections based on independent reasoning, the Commentary will make clear, are based on premises the Pudgalavādins are not likely to have accepted as true. The Pudgalavādins, for instance, clearly reject (1) the all-inclusiveness of the sort of distinction Vasubandhu makes between the two realities when he presents his basic objection to their theory of persons, (2) the truth of the causal reference principle that he first uses in his attack on their reply to his basic objection, and (3) the correctness of most of his interpretations of the theses and arguments that follow this initial exchange. Nonetheless, since the replies the Pudgalavādins are represented as making to Vasubandhu's objections do not include explicit denials of the truth of the key premises used in his objections, we may concede that many of his objections at least succeed to the extent that they usually show that their theories are inconsistent with the premises used in the objections. These premises are theses of the orthodox Vaibhāṣika schools. Hence, it would seem that Vasubandhu believes that he has shown that the Pudgalavādins' views are logically incoherent because they are inconsistent with theses of the orthodox Vaibhāṣika schools and they do not explicitly repudiate these theses in the exchange.

That Vasubandhu believes that he has shown in this way that the Pudgalavādins' views are logically incoherent because they are inconsistent with orthodox Vaibhāṣika theses supports the hypothesis that his general purpose in composing the "Refutation" is to purge Buddhism of heretical views concerning persons. In this case he would be assuming that the central theses he has set out in the verses of the *Treasury* are theses of the Vaibhāṣikas the Pudgalavādins do or should accept, and that since he has established that their views are inconsistent with these theses, he has shown them to be heretical. Vasubandhu's belief that his objections show that their views are logically incoherent is at least based on his assumption that the Pudgalavādins must accept the truth of the theses of the orthodox Vaibhāṣikas used in his objections if they are not explicitly repudiated by them in the exchange.

The most plausible explanation of why Vasubandhu did not have the Pudgalavādins challenge the correctness of the specific orthodox Vaibhāṣika theses used in his critique of their theory of persons is that he was not aware that they challenged them. This does not mean that the Pudgalavādins themselves did not challenge these particular theses or were unaware that they needed to reject these theses. Perhaps they were reluctant for some reason to present the arguments needed to reject them or they were unable to do so for some reason. If they were reluctant to reject these theses, it may be because they would have been charged with further heresies. If they were unable to find the arguments to refute these theses, Vasubandhu's objections would much more closely have hit their mark. In either case, their theory would appear to the orthodox Vaibhāṣikas to be heretical. Other explanations, of course, are possible. Whatever the explanation for their failure to challenge these theses, it seems likely that they were aware that their theory of persons committed them to the rejection of these theses.

But Vasubandhu's arguments, when viewed apart from Vasubandhu's assumption that the Pudgalavādins are committed to the acceptance of the orthodox Vaibhāṣika theses he uses, fail to show that the Pudgalavādins' theory of persons and objections to his own theory are logically incoherent. This failure, perhaps, provides us with a partial explanation of why, in spite of his critique, Pudgalavāda Buddhism remained a significant force in India until much later times. One person's heresy, it is said, is another's orthodoxy. Although their theory may in fact be logically incoherent, it cannot be said, if we are to judge Vasubandhu's critique of the theory by contemporary standards, that Vasubandhu has shown this to be so. Moreover, Vasubandhu's scriptural objections to their theory, as I will argue in the Commentary, are equally ineffective, since there seem to be differences among the sūtras accepted by both parties and passages from the sūtras they both accept seem to avail themselves of their different interpretations. So neither Vasubandhu's apparent philosophical critique nor his critique on the basis of scripture can be said to be compelling.

The Pudgalavādins' replies to Vasubandhu's objections, as well as their objections to his theory of persons, almost always fail as replies and objections because they tend to be stated in an ambiguous and incomplete form. But why are they ambiguously and incompletely stated? Although the supposition, that Vasubandhu's intention in his critique of the Pudgalavādins' views is to demonstrate their heretical character, goes a long way toward explaining why his objections do not show them to be logically incoherent, it does not at all explain why their replies to his logical objections are so ambiguously and incompletely stated.

It is true, in general, that the polemical works of Indian Buddhist philosophers are mere summaries of their critiques of their opponents' views and do not always do justice to the views or arguments of their opponents.[99] But this need not mean that they intentionally misrepresent the views and arguments of their opponents. It is, of course, possible that Vasubandhu's summary reflects the circumstance that the Pudgalavādins themselves poorly stated and defended their views, but we do not, I believe, have enough evidence to make such an uncharitable accusation. Nor do I believe that I have misrepresented their views and arguments in my reconstructions of them, since these reconstructions very closely follow the language and logic used in the "Refutation" to state and defend these views and they help us to explain the views they express in the *Sāṃmitīyanikāya Śāstra* and *Tridharmaka Śāstra* and the views attributed to them in their critics' polemical works. The fact that I am able to reconstruct their views and arguments on this basis also leads me to believe that Vasubandhu is usually representing views and arguments they presented.

Even if the Pudgalavādins did express their views in the ambiguous and incomplete ways in which they are presented by Vasubandhu in the "Refutation," why does he not employ more adequate expressions of their views and arguments in his examination? Why does he not put forward the best statements of their views and arguments so that it may become clear what their faults really are? At this point, I believe, we need to recall that a Buddhist polemic is not in fact an impartial investigation of theses and arguments, but an attempt to reject theses and arguments that do not agree with those employed in the school from whose point of view the polemic is written. So perhaps Vasubandhu does not attempt to present the theses and arguments of his opponents in a more adequate form because his main concern is to reveal to the followers of the Sautrāntika school the ways in which the Pudgalavādins' theory of persons are inconsistent with the theses of its own system of thought.

Problems and implications of the Pudgalavādins' theory of persons

Vasubandhu's failure, from a third party perspective, to show that the Pudgalavādins' theory of persons is logically incoherent and does not accord with scripture does not imply that it is without problems. There are at least three problems raised by the Pudgalavādins' theory for which solutions are needed if it is to be taken seriously as a Buddhist no-self theory.

The first problem, which is actually a set of problems, concerns the implications of their claim that persons are conceived in reliance upon aggregates in the way fire is conceived in reliance upon fuel. It might be objected that the analogy fails because the fire said to be conceived in reliance upon fuel exists in dependence upon its fuel, while a person, according to the Pudgalavādins, does not exist in dependence upon his aggregates. Indeed, a number of modern scholars seem to have assumed, on the basis of the Pudgalavādins' use of the analogy and their own belief that fire does not exist apart from fuel, that the Pudgalavādins do not believe that persons exist apart from aggregates.[100] But can we assume that the Pudgalavādins believe that a fire conceived in reliance upon fuel exists in dependence upon fuel? If they do believe this, we have no record of such a belief. Nor do we, consequently, have any record of how they could employ such an idea in the explanation of physical phenomena. Whether or not they reject the orthodox Vaibhāṣika theory that the fire-element is a substance depends in part upon whether or not they believe that they can add the idea of a conventionally real inexplicable fire to the orthodox Vaibhāṣika account of phenomena and still retain the view that the fire-element itself is a substance. The fact that, in Section 2.1.5 Vasubandhu thinks that he is entitled to identify what the Pudgalavādins call fire with a collection of elements conceived as fire, suggests that he himself was not aware of an attempt by them to use the idea of a conventionally real inexplicable fire to explain physical phenomena. So, in the absence of any knowledge concerning the ontological status and function of conventionally real fire within the Pudgalavādins' philosophy, it seems that their use of the analogy to fire and fuel is problematic. In the Commentary, nonetheless, I attempt a brief sketch of how they might have attempted to replace the orthodox Vaibhāṣika idea of a fire-element with the idea of a conventionally real inexplicable fire-element.

But even if we suppose that the Pudgalavādins believe that fire is a conventionally real inexplicable entity that ultimately exists, the question arises concerning how this entity is known to exist. Inexplicable persons, they are made to imply in Section 2.5 of the "Refutation," are known to exist by inexplicable perceptions. Do they believe that we have inexplicable perceptions of inexplicable fire? I argue in the Commentary that they think that an inexplicable perception of ourselves is an incidental perception of ourselves by a consciousness that is perceiving its own proper object. But an incidental perception of this sort is not likely to have fire as its object, since it seems to be the self-awareness many believe to occur when we are aware of objects. So then is a conventionally real inexplicable fire known to exist by correct inference? How exactly such an inference would be explained is not clear. One inference, perhaps, would be needed to establish the inexplicability of fire, and another to establish its ultimate existence. In any case, the Pudgalavādins owe us an account of how a conventionally real inexplicable fire is known to exist.

A second problem with the Pudgalavādins' theory of persons concerns their doctrine, expressed in Section 2.5.2.1, that we are known to exist by means of a perception that is inexplicable. This perception, they believe, is an incidental perception of ourselves that occurs when a consciousness perceives its own proper object. It is inexplicable in the sense that it is neither other than nor the same in existence as the perception of this object. But this perception does not exist apart from the perception of the object, since the consciousness that has both perceptions does not exist unless it perceives the object. Neither does it possess substantial reality or substantially established reality, since it is neither a substance, a defining property of a substance, or a collection of substances conceived as a single entity of some sort. Nor does it exist in the very same way a person exists, which is apart from the phenomena in dependence upon which it is conceived. So how does it exist? If it does not exist, of course, inexplicable persons are not known to exist. Perhaps the Pudgalavādins could claim that inexplicable perceptions of persons possess ultimate existence, even if they do not exist independently of perceptions that are not inexplicable. In this case, they would accept the existence of two different kinds of entities that exist without separate identities: those that exist apart from the phenomena in dependence upon which they are conceived and those that do not. Whether or not they would accept this is not clear. But if they did, we need to know more about how they went about explaining the difference between such phenomena.

A third problem with the Pudgalavādins' theory of persons concerns their assumption that it is possible for anything to possess ultimate existence without possessing a separate identity. The deep issue here is whether or not anything inconceivable or nonidentifiable by itself, apart from being conceived, can exist by itself. This is a problem that Vasubandhu never explicitly raises in the "Refutation." He must, however, realize that it is a problem with their theory, since the assumption is in effect challenged when he argues in Section 2.1 of the "Refutation" that if we exist, we must be either substantial realities or substantially established realities. Vasubandhu merely assumes, but does not argue, that if we ultimately exist, we are independently identifiable or the same in existence as collections of independently identifiable phenomena. The Pudgalavādins, of course, believe that they can avoid this third problem, since inexplicable persons are known to exist by reason of being perceived when aggregates in the collections in reliance upon which they are conceived are present. But is this so-called perception of ourselves a means by which our ultimate existence is known or is it an illusion created by the mind's habit of conceiving itself as a possession of a person? Indeed, the question of the actual nature of this so-called perception of ourselves needs to be pursued much further before the Pudgalavādins' claim, that we know that we exist apart from being conceived, can be properly assessed.

This last problem is one aspect of the most fundamental ontological issue raised by an investigation of Vasubandhu's critique of the Pudgalavādins' theory of persons. He assumes that what exists is either a substantial reality or a substantially established reality and that we are substantially established realities because we are not substantial realities. He does not reject the Pudgalavādins' assumption that we ultimately exist, since he believes that our ultimate existence is guaranteed by the fact that we are the same in existence as our aggregates. He rejects only their claim that we are inexplicable phenomena. He also rejects Candrakīrti's view that we can exist without possessing ultimate existence. The Pudgalavādins believe that, in addition to substantial realities and substantially established realities, there are entities without separate identities. So they would reject both Vasubandhu's view, that we do not exist at all unless we possess substantial reality or substantially established reality, and Candrakīrti's view, that we lack ultimate existence. Since Candrakīrti believes that to exist is to exist in dependence upon being conceived, he must reject Vasubandhu's view, that we ultimately exist because we are substantially established realities, and the Pudgalavādins' view, that we ultimately exist because we are entities without separate identities. The primary ontological issue raised by the dispute between Vasubandhu, the Pudgalavādins and Candrakīrti about persons, therefore, concerns the nature of existence. Although this issue is not explicitly discussed in the "Refutation," later Buddhist philosophers came to realize its importance.

In Śāntarakṣita's *Tattvasaṃgraha*, for instance, objections are raised against the Pudgalavādins' assumption that what ultimately exists can lack a separate identity. Although Candrakīrti had already argued that persons do not ultimately exist because they are neither other than nor the same in existence as their aggregates, he does not seem to have made the attempt to justify the principle upon which this inference relies, which is that there is no entity without a separate identity. What these later Buddhists have to say about the Pudgalavādins' theory of persons may serve as an introduction to this issue.

Candrakīrti's objections to the Pudgalavādins' theory of persons are set out in verses 146–9 of Book VI of his *Madhyamakāvatāra* and in his own commentary on the verses. In verse 146 he attributes to them the views that we are substantially real (*dravyasat*), that we are neither other than nor the same as our aggregates, that we are neither permanent phenomena nor impermanent phenomena, and that we are the objects of the mind that conceives an "I." However, the Pudgalavādins against whom Vasubandhu argues in the "Refutation" explicitly deny that we are substantially real. Hence, when in verse 147 Candrakīrti argues that if we are substantially real we cannot be inexplicable phenomena, his argument is based on the assumption that what ultimately exists possesses a separate identity. But this assumption is unargued.

Candrakīrti's second argument, in verse 148, is that the Pudgalavādins must say that we do not exist by ourselves, since they agree that a pot does not exist as an entity (i.e. as a substance) because it is neither other than nor the same as any of its parts. On the assumption that to be an entity is to be a substance, it is reasonable that the Pudgalavādins would have claimed (though no such claim is made in their extant treatises) that a pot does not exist as an entity because it is neither other than nor the same as its parts. But since the Pudgalavādins do not think that a person is a substance, Candrakīrti's criticism misses the mark. Again, he is assuming that there is no entity without a separate identity. The Pudgalavādins about whom Vasubandhu speaks in the "Refutation" do in fact assume that a pot is a conventional reality because it ultimately exists and is not a substance, but if they hold, as I believe they do, that there are two different kinds of conventional realities, and that a pot is an example of one kind and an inexplicable person is an example of the other, it does not follow that a person does not exist apart from his aggregates if he is not a substance.

Finally, in verse 149, Candrakīrti argues that since functional entities (*bhāva*-s) are not other than themselves and are other than other functional entities, and persons are not other than their aggregates, which are other functional entities, they are not entities. Entities, of course, are things that are substantially real, so the conclusion is that a self is not substantially real, as the Pudgalavādins claim they are. The problem with this objection, of course, is that if the Pudgalavādins should agree that we are functional entities, they would not accept the view that all functional entities are other than other functional entities. If they should believe that we are functional entities, they would believe that we are so only insofar as we are conceived to be so in reliance upon collections of aggregates. Moreover, it is not clear that the Pudgalavādins would agree that only functional entities exist.

Candrakīrti seems to believe that the Pudgalavādins, like Vasubandhu, are afraid that if we do not exist apart from being conceived, we do not exist at all. From his point of view, he believes, their attempt to save the ultimate existence of persons by introducing the idea of a phenomenon that could exist by itself without possessing a separate identity is misguided, since there can be no entity without a separate identity. But here again, he merely assumes that such an entity cannot exist; he does not argue that it cannot.

In verses 336–49 of Chapter VII of the *Tattvasaṃgraha*, Śāntarakṣita takes up the Pudgalavādins' theory of persons. After explaining their theory in verses 336–7, he states in verse 338 that if a person is inexplicable, he cannot really exist (i.e. cannot be an entity), since, as Kamalaśīla explains in his commentary on verse 339, what is inexplicable lacks a character of its own, and in verses 340–2, what lacks a character of its own is not an entity. But in this argument, as in the arguments of Candrakīrti, it is simply assumed that there can be no entity without a separate identity. However, in verses 343–4, Śāntarakṣita argues that if persons are not other than their aggregates, they possess the character of being not other than their aggregates, and that if they are not the same as their aggregates, they possess the character of being other than the aggregates, in which case they do in fact possess characters of their own. Moreover, he says in verse 345 that since the Pudgalavādins say that persons are incapable of being said to be other or not other than any of their aggregates, while the aggregates are capable of being said to be other than one another, they imply that persons do possess a character not possessed by their aggregates. In verse 346 he argues that since they say that the aggregates are capable of being said to be impermanent, while persons are incapable of being said to be impermanent, they imply that persons do possess a character not possessed by the aggregates. The upshot of the objections in verses 343–6 is that if phenomena are inexplicable, then nothing at all can be said about them, since the very statement of what they are implies that they possess characters of their own by virtue of which they are distinguished from phenomena that are not inexplicable. Finally, in verse 347, Śāntarakṣita argues that since causal efficacy is the mark of an entity, and only momentary phenomena possess causal efficacy, persons are not entities if they cannot be said to be momentary. The force of this last objection, however, does not derive from the denial that persons are momentary phenomena. Its force amounts to the claim that if inexplicable phenomena are not by their own natures causally efficacious, they cannot be said to possess ultimate existence.

Among the issues raised by these objections to the idea that there are entities without separate identities is whether or not the Pudgalavādins, when they say that persons are inexplicable, are trying to say anything about entities that are inconceivable. We have seen above that, as a matter of fact, their statement, that persons are inexplicable phenomena, is made about conventional realities, i.e. phenomena insofar as they are conceived on a basis, not about entities that are inconceivable. So the characters persons possess that are not possessed by the aggregates are not characters possessed by inconceivable entities, but by persons insofar as they are conceived in dependence upon collections of aggregates. Another issue raised by these objections is whether or not a causal efficacy that belongs to an entity by its own nature is in fact a criterion the Pudgalavādins would use to determine what exists. If they are to be consistent, of course, they do not use such a criterion. Although they seem to believe that we are known to exist because we are perceived when our aggregates are present, and even that we can be said to be known to exist because we cause the perception of ourselves, these beliefs are not predicated, surely, on the ideas that by our own natures we are causes of the perceptions of ourselves or even that consciousness by its own nature perceives us when it perceives an object. But if natural causal efficacy is not the Pudgalavādins' criterion of existence, we may ask, what criterion do they use? This question and others need to be discussed if we are to arrive at a reasonable assessment of their theory of persons.

The objections to Vasubandhu's theory of persons

The philosophical objections the Pudgalavādins and Nyāya-Vaiśeṣikas most often raise against Vasubandhu's theory of persons take the form of claiming that if it is true, a number of important attributes it is necessary to ascribe to ourselves do not in fact belong to us. They object that it is not true, if we are the same in existence as collections of aggregates and not inexplicable persons or selves, to claim that we bear the aggregates as a burden (Section 3.2), that each of us is one person (Section 3.4), that we wander in saṃsāra (Section 3.7), that we refer to our past lives (Section 3.8), that we remember objects experienced in the past (Section 4.1), that we are what remembers such objects (Section 4.2), that we possess a memory (Section 4.3), that we walk and are conscious of objects (Section 4.5), that we possess mental attributes (Section 4.8), that we have a reason to undertake an action (Section 4.9), that we possess a mind that conceives an "I" (Section 4.10), that we are agents of actions and subjects that experience their results (Section 4.12), or that we accumulate merit and demerit (Section 4.13). But if we do not bear the aggregates as a burden, etc. we are not persons. If we are not persons, there are no persons at all. Hence, Vasubandhu's theory is a form of the nihilism extreme.

It is being assumed, in all such objections, that unless we are, from an ultimate point of view, underlying supports for our aggregates, there is in fact nothing to which these attributes of persons belong, and so, that persons do not possess ultimate existence. The basic disagreement between Vasubandhu, the Pudgalavādins, and the Nyāya-Vaiśeṣikas, we may infer, concerns in what form we need to exist ultimately in order to make it possible for us to possess the attributes of persons. It is agreed that, as we are conventionally conceived, we are wholes of parts. The disagreement concerns whether we ultimately exist as collections of the extrinsic parts of these wholes, as inexplicable entities that are the underlying supports of these collections, or as substances that are the underlying supports of these collections. The basic intuition of the objections to Vasubandhu's theory is that we do not exist at all unless we are the underlying supports of the aggregates that comprise our bodies and minds. On the basis of this intuition it is claimed that we are one rather than many and that we are the same over time in a way that provides a basis for the claim that we receive the results of actions performed in the past.

Vasubandhu's replies to such objections do not, as we might expect, take the form of arguing that his opponents' assumption, that we are the underlying supports of our aggregates, is itself an expression of the mistaken view of a self. Instead, he explains how the attributes we seem to be ascribing to underlying supports of the aggregates are attributes we ascribe to conventionally real persons in dependence upon causal connections he believes to obtain between the aggregates in the collections in dependence upon which such persons are conceived. Since the objections take the form of claiming that he cannot explain our possession of these attributes without calling upon an inexplicable person or a person that is a separate substance, he usually replies simply by supplying such an explanation. He does, however, indirectly attack the idea that we must be underlying supports for our aggregates in Section 3.2, when he explains how we can be bearers of the aggregates as our burden. In Sections 4.7.1 and 4.8, moreover, he explicitly attacks the Nyāya-Vaiśeṣikas' view that we are underlying supports for our bodies and minds. These attacks, however, do little more than show Vasubandhu's disagreement with their view.

Candrakīrti's basic objections to the thesis, that we are the same in existence as our aggregates, are presented in verses 126–41 of Book VI of his *Madhyamakāvatāra* and his commentary on the verses. Some of the objections he raises against this thesis, which he surely believes to have been held by the orthodox Vaibhāṣikas and original Sautrāntikas, are based on the assumption that it undermines the ascription of the attributes of persons to ourselves. For instance, in verse 127, Candrakīrti objects that if we are the same in existence as collections of aggregates and we ultimately exist, we are many persons, since collections of aggregates are just many aggregates. In this case, he assumes that if we are the same in existence as collections of aggregates, we are the same in existence as each of the aggregates in the collections. Moreover, he assumes, as Vasubandhu would not, that if we are the same in existence as each of our aggregates, each of our aggregates is a person. Hence, this objection would not seem to apply to the view in the form it is held by Vasubandhu.

In verse 128, Candrakīrti bases a number of objections to the thesis on the assumption that if we are the same in existence as collections of impermanent aggregates, which are not the same over time, we are not the same persons over time. In verse 134 he argues that we cannot be the same in existence as collections of aggregates, which are assumed to be entities, since we are, as persons, not mere collections of entities. These last two objections, of course, are basically the same as some of those presented by Vasubandhu's opponents in the "Refutation," and so are no more compelling than they are. To the objections in verses 128 and 134 Vasubandhu can reply that, from the ultimate point of view, there are no persons, and so, they are not, from that point of view, the one or the same over time. But from a conventional point of view, which is the basis of our form of life in which we possess bodies and minds, he can say that persons are the same over time and one. These points of view, he believes, do not contradict one another, since they create separate domains of thought and discourse. His claims concern only our non-existence as part of ultimate reality, not our existence, and hence, our identity over time and/or unity, as conventional realities. Vasubandhu does not deny the existence of conventionally real persons or their identity over time or their unity, since he has a two-tiered conception of what is real.

Candrakīrti in effect believes that the orthodox Vaibhāṣikas and original Sautrāntikas mistakenly attributed to the Buddha the view that ultimate realities are substantial realities and that conventional realities are substantially established realities. Hence, he thinks that they assume that when we search for our ultimate reality, what we find are collections of substantial realities. However, Candrakīrti objects, although the purpose of the Buddha's search for ourselves among the phenomena in dependence upon which we conceive ourselves is to reveal our ultimate reality, he did not mean to imply that the phenomena we actually find constitute our ultimate reality. Rather, what he meant to imply is that since we are not found among these phenomena, we do not possess ultimate existence. Our ultimate reality, Candrakīrti contends, is our absence among these phenomena, not the phenomena themselves. From this point of view, Vasubandhu's error, according to Candrakīrti, is to confuse the search for our ultimate reality with the search for the collections of substances in dependence upon which we conceive ourselves.

Vasubandhu thinks that we must be the same in existence as collections of aggregates because he assumes that we must possess ultimate existence if we exist at all. The analysis of ourselves into the collections of aggregates in dependence upon which we conceive ourselves shows, he thinks, that we are not independently identifiable, but it does not show that we do not ultimately exist. He equates our ultimate existence with the existence of the causal basis of the conception of ourselves, which is a collection of aggregates. So if we are not the same in existence as collections of aggregates, he reasons, we do not ultimately exist, and hence, do not exist at all.

But this view, Candrakīrti believes, confuses existence with ultimate existence. It also confuses, as the Pudgalavādins themselves argue it does in the "Refutation," the existence of the causal basis of the conception of ourselves with the existence of the object of the conception. In Candrakīrti's view, since we exist *in dependence upon* collections of aggregates, our existence and the existence of collections of aggregates are not the same, and for this reason the object of the conception of ourselves is not the same in existence as collections of aggregates. In Vasubandhu's opinion, apparently, the Buddha's search for us among the phenomena in dependence upon which we are conceived was meant to have the twofold purpose of showing that we are not selves and that we exist. But the Buddha, Candrakīrti objects, taught that no phenomenon can exist apart from being conceived, apart from having distinguishable parts, aspects or attributes, or apart from its causes and conditions. Hence, Candrakīrti thinks that the reason for asserting that we are the same in existence as collections of aggregates is the failure to understand properly the Buddha's teaching of "dependent-arising" (*pratītya-samutpāda*), which is, he believes, the doctrine that all phenomena exist in dependence upon being conceived in relation to other phenomena. If the very idea of one thing existing in dependence upon a second implies that it is not the same in existence as the second, the fact that persons exist in dependence upon the collections of their aggregates implies that they are not the same in existence as the collections of their aggregates.

An initial reflection on the theories of persons discussed in this study of Vasubandhu's "Refutation"

A study of Vasubandhu's "Refutation," of course, can be only a beginning of a search for the answers to the sorts of questions it raises, and I do not here presume to have done anything other than to have provided a possible starting point for the search. For this reason, in part, I have tried to avoid a final assessment of the theses and arguments contained in the "Refutation." Such an assessment, I believe, needs to wait upon an equally careful study of the theories of persons of Candrakīrti, the Nyāya-Vaiśeṣikas, the Sāṃkhyas, the Jains, and the various schools of Vedānta, along with the critique of Indian theories of persons set out by Śāntarakṣita and Kamalaśīla. In addition, I believe, an assessment of the Indian attempts to answer the questions about persons raised by a study of Vasubandhu's "Refutation" should also be based on a thorough study of the works of the many philosophers in the West who have considered questions about the nature, mode of existence, unity and identity over time of persons. With these considerations in mind, I would like here to offer some first thoughts on the theories of persons discussed in this study, in the hope that they may stimulate further thought by readers rather than settle any issues.

Whether or not we are inclined to accept the various objections Vasubandhu's opponents have raised against his thesis, that we are the same in existence as collections of aggregates, seems to depend upon the "pull" of a number of different intuitions we have about ourselves and the world in which we live. These intuitions seem to rely on the different perspectives from which we and our world are experienced. Some of us, like the Nyāya-Vaiśeṣikas and the Pudgalavādins, cling to the idea that we are not the same in existence as our bodies and minds because for various reasons the first-person singular perspective on the world commands our assent. In spite of not being able to perceive directly a separately identifiable referent for the conception of ourselves in the bodies and minds in dependence upon which we create the descriptive content of the conception, they persist in the belief that there is an ultimately existent referent for the conception, and they renounce the intuition that this referent needs to possess the attributes of the bodies and minds in dependence upon which it is conceived. Whether or not they think that this referent must be a separate substance depends on how much they are influenced by the intuition that no ultimately existent entity can exist without a separate identity. Others, like Candrakīrti, are not inclined to believe that we are not the same in existence as our bodies and minds because of their intuitions that the first-person singular perspective reveals an ineliminable part of ultimate reality. They believe this simply because it entails the abandonment of the convention that we possess different attributes than are possessed by our bodies and minds, and that once this convention is abandoned, thought and discourse about us cease to be able to perform their customary functions. In his case, the first-person singular perspective is thought to command our assent as part of the conventional framework required for our form of life, and the so-called intuition, that we ultimately exist, is deconstructed by the analysis that shows that we are neither other than nor the same in existence as our bodies and minds. Others of us welcome the idea that we are the same in existence as our bodies and minds because for various reasons the third-person singular perspective on the world commands their assent, and enables them to dismiss the first-person singular perspective in dependence upon which we appear to be the underlying supports for the attributes we ascribe to ourselves in dependence upon our bodies and minds. They are likely to argue that by convention the object of the conception of ourselves possesses the attributes we normally ascribe to ourselves, but apart from this convention, our existence must be nothing but that of our bodies and minds as they appear from the third-person perspective.

The fact is that both the first-person singular and third-person singular perspectives from which we view the world exist, and whether or not we deem the first-person singular perspective to create an illusion is not ultimately a function of the arguments used to assert or deny that it does, but a function of one's ultimate orientation toward life, which largely determines which intuitions we ultimately accept. In the case of the dispute between Vasubandhu, the Pudgalavādins, and the Nyāya-Vaiśeṣikas, this orientation is dominated by the intuition that the world exists apart from our representation of it in thought and discourse. Vasubandhu's view will be found most satisfying by those of us who are intellectually committed to the existence of a world that contains only something like substances and collections of different sorts of substances conceived as single entities for practical purposes. If they discover that the basis upon which we conceive ourselves from the first-person singular perspective is a collection of substances (or perhaps, impersonal facts), they can willingly embrace the theory, in spite of its counter-intuitive character, that our existence is nothing but that of collections of such substances (or impersonal facts). Others, who are unable, because of their strong practical approach to life, to abandon the intuitions that we ultimately exist and are not the same in existence as our bodies and minds, will find either the Nyāya-Vaiśeṣikas' theory or the Pudgalavādin theory more acceptable. They cannot shake the sense that they exist in the world independently of being identified by means of their bodies and minds. Those who are inclined to accept Candrakīrti's theory, by contrast, are those who feel the pull of the more "developed" intuitions that things in our world, including ourselves, are identifiable only in dependence upon other things and that separately existent entities, if there were any, could not be without separate identities.

In the end, it seems, rational argument alone will not convince us that we are separate substances, separately existent entities without separate identities, the same in existence as collections of aggregates, or merely mentally constructed phenomena that exist in dependence upon collections of aggregates. Rather, the view we are likely to favor is the one that reflects best our basic orientation towards life, along with its favored intuitions. This orientation is what I believe provides life with what meaning it has for us. For some of us this orientation is a matter of religious belief, for others, a commitment to a secular ideology of some sort. For both, I believe, a study of Indian Buddhist theories of persons should help to clarify their basic orientations. Those who have neither a religious nor a secular basic orientation towards life are either on a path that leads them to one of these two sorts of orientations or they are not. Those on either one of these paths should find a consideration of Indian Buddhist theories of persons helpful in their pursuit of a meaningful life. Those who are not consciously on either path should find in a study of Indian Buddhist theories of persons an incentive to begin a path, since a serious consideration of these theories, I believe, is likely to raise questions about ourselves that are so basic that, once asked, will lead them to set out to find one for themselves.

Notes

1 There is disagreement about the dates of Vasubandhu's life because it is not clear whether or not the author of the text translated here is the same

Vasubandhu who composed a number of works from the point of view of the Cittamātrika school of Indian Buddhist philosophy during the fourth century CE. I shall not take a position on this controversy, the final resolution of which seems to me not to be possible on the basis of the evidence now available. For the view that there are two different Vasubandhus see Erich Frauwallner's *On the Date of the Buddhist Master of the Law, Vasubandhu* (Rome: IsMeo, 1951); against the view see Stefan Anacher's *Seven Works of Vasubandhu*, corrected edition (Delhi: Motilal Banarsidass, 1998). For further references, see Peter Skilling, "Vasubandhu and the Vyākhyāyukti Literature," *Journal of the International Association of Buddhist Studies*, 23 (2000, pp. 297–350), in which a recent bibliography on this topic can be found in the second footnote.

2 Instead of saying that we conceive ourselves from a first-person singular perspective, I could have said that we use the first-person singular pronoun to refer in conjunction with using a predicate term to ascribe an attribute to ourselves, since the Sanskrit equivalents cover the same cases. Also, "minds" in this statement and elsewhere in this book, is used, in accord with the Indian Buddhist usage of its Sanskrit equivalents, to refer to momentary mental states or to a series of causally connected momentary mental states.

3 Vasubandhu himself probably did not compose all or most of the verses in Chs 1–8 in the *Treasury*, but he certainly did compile them and write its *Commentary*. But even if Vasubandhu did not himself compose these verses, it is generally agreed by scholars that he composed the treatise on the selflessness of persons. So the question of whether the treatise is part of the *Treasury* or a part of the *Commentary* is not important for the purposes of my discussion in this book.

4 Yaśomitra uses this title in the *Sphuṭārthābhidharmakośavyakhyā*, where he discusses verse 73ab of Book IV of the *Treasury*. Vasubandhu uses his own title in the part of the *Commentary* in which he discusses verse 27c of Book V of the *Treasury*.

5 For information on *The Great Exposition*, which has survived in Chinese translation, see Karl Potter, ed., *Encyclopedia of Indian Philosophies, vol. VII, Abhidharma Buddhism to AD 150* (Delhi: Motilal Banarsidass, 1996, pp. 110–19 and 511–68).

6 See "Second Search of Sanskrit Palm-leaf Manuscripts in Tibet," *Journal of the Bihar and Orissa Research Society*, XXIII (1937, pp. 1–57, especially pp. 18–19 and 53–4).

7 See *Sphuṭārthābhidharmakośavyakhyā, the Work of Yaśomitra*, ed. Unrai Wogihara (Tokyo: Publishing Association of the Abhidharmakośavyakhyā, 1936, pp. 697–723).

8 Prahlad Pradhan, ed., *The Abhidharmakośabhāṣyam of Vasubandhu*, Tibetan Sanskrit Works Series, vol. VIII (Patna: K.P. Jayaswal Research Institute, 1967).

9 Dwarikadass Shastri, ed., *Abhidharmakośa and Bhāṣya of Ācārya Vasubandhu with Sphuṭārthā Commentary of Ācārya Yaśomitra*. Bauddha Bharati Series, vols 7–8 (Varanasi, 1970–3). Reprinted in 1981 in two volumes with continuous pagination.

10 Aruna Haldar, ed., *Abhidharmakośabhāṣyam of Vasubandhu*, the Tibetan Sanskrit Works Series, vol. VIII, revised second edition with introduction and indices, 1975.

11 Akira Hirakawa, *et al.*, *Index to the Abhidharmakośabhāṣya* (Pradhan edition), vol. 1 (Tokyo: Daizo Shuppan, 1973). It contains an Introduction in English.

12 Yasunori Ejima, "Textcritical Remarks on the Ninth Chapter of the *Abhidharmakośabhāṣya*," *Bukkyo Bunka*, 20 (1987, pp. 1–40).

13 James Duerlinger, "Vasubandhu's Refutation of the Theory of Selfhood," *The Journal of Indian Philosophy*, 17 (1988, pp. 129–87).

14 Translated by Jinamitra and dPal brtsegs, entitled *Chos mṅon paḥi mdsod kyi bśad pa*. This work is preserved in PT, 5591 Ñu 93b7–109a7.

15 See the *Ē-pí-dá-mó-jù-shè-shì-lùn* (563–7 CE), which is the translation by Paramārtha, in TT 1559, vol. 29, 304a17–310c17, and the *Ē-pí-dá-mó-jù-shè-lùn* (651–4 CE), which is the translation by Xúanzàng, in TT 1558, vol. 29, 152b23–59b15.

16 See Pû-guâng's *Jú-shè-lùn-jì* (664 CE) in TT 1821, vol. 41, 438c15–452b4; Fâ-bâu's *Jú-shè-lùn-shû* (703 CE) in TT 1821, vol. 41, 803b14–812c1; and Yuán-huî's *Jú-shè-lùn-sòng-shû* (654 CE) in TT 1823, vol. 41, 978a9–981c14.

17 First published by the *Bulletin de l'Académie des Sciences de Russie*, Vol. XIII, nos. 12–18 (1919, pp. 823–54, 937–58), and then reprinted as "The Soul Theory of the Buddhists" (Delhi: Bharatiya Vidya Prakashan, 1976).

18 La Vallée Poussin's translation of the "Refutation" is in the penultimate volume of his six-volume *L'Abhidharmakośa de Vasubandhu* (Brussels: Institute Belge des Hautes Études Chinoises, 1923–31, reprint edition, 1971, pp. 227–302).

19 Leo Pruden's translation is in the fourth volume of *Abhidharmakośabhāṣyam* (Berkeley: Asian Humanities Press, 1990, pp. 1313–80).

20 Summaries of the "Refutation" have been made by Klaus Oetke in *"Ich" und Das Ich* (Stuttgart: Franz Steiner Verlag Wiesbaden GmbH, 1988), and by Stefan Aneckar in *Encyclopedia of Indian Philosophies, vol. VIII, Abhidharma Buddhism*, ed. Karl Potter (Delhi: Motilal Benarsidass, 1999, pp. 510–16). (Hereafter, I will refer to this volume as *Encyclopedia*, VIII). The summary by Stefan Anacher seems to be based on Stcherbatsky's translation. Oetke also comments on Vasubandhu's theory of persons from the perspective of how it might be construed from a contemporary analytical perspective (pp. 195–241), but in doing so, I believe, he does not advance our understanding of Vasubandhu's theory according to its original intent.

21 What I here call "the same in existence" a Western philosopher would call "the same in extension" (as opposed to "the same in intension"), but the adoption of the extension–intension terminology, I believe, brings with it too much baggage from Western versions of logical theory.

22 When I speak of the identity of an entity I mean its possession of a character or attribute, as opposed to its existence. An entity may possess its identity by its own nature or in dependence upon reference to something else. Likewise, an entity may possess existence by its own nature or in dependence upon reference to something else. A central issue that arises from a consideration of the Pudgalavādins' theory of persons is whether or not an entity that exists by its own nature can lack a separate identity.

23 The dating of the life of Vātsīputra is difficult to determine. He was either a contemporary of the Buddha or flourished about 200 years after the death of the Buddha. For a discussion of problems about the sources of our information about the founder of this school see Leonard Priestley's *Pudgalavāda Buddhism* (Toronto: University of Toronto Centre for South Asian Studies, 1999, pp. 32–6). (Hereafter, I will refer to Priestley's book simply as *Pudgalavāda*.)

24 The Sanskrit dictionaries of Apte and Monier Williams define *tīrthika* as a member of any school other than one's own, and so many translators render it as "non-Buddhists" or "outsiders," which loses any connection the word has with *tīrtha*, which is basically a passage, way, road, ford, etc. I prefer to translate the word as "Forders" in order to incorporate the gracious suggestion of the Indian Buddhists that these outsiders think of themselves as forders over the ocean of "saṃsāra" (the rebirth cycle).

25 The views in the *Sāṃmitīyanikāya Śāstra*, which is also known as the *āśrayaprajñapti Śāstra*, are outlined in Sara Boin's English translation of a dissertation that Thích Thiên Châu composed in French at the Sorbonne. The translation is entitled *The Literature of the Personalists of Early Buddhism* (Delhi: Motilal Banarsidass, 1999, pp. 99–117). (Hereafter, this work will be referred to as *Personalists.*) For a translation into English, see "*Sāṃmitīyanikāyaśāstram*," trans. by K. Venkataramanan in the *Visva-Bharati Annals*, V (1953, pp. 153–242).

26 Unfortunately, we cannot be certain whether the *Sāṃmitīyanikāya Śāstra* predates or postdates the "Refutation," or whether one of the authors of these works was aware of the work of the other.

27 Persons conceived from a basis, in other words, are persons *as conceived*, not as they exist by themselves, apart from being conceived.

28 See *Personalists*, pp. 33–85. A detailed examination of its implications for the Pudgalavādins' theory of persons is included in *Pudgalavāda*, pp. 45–7, 55–63, 104–6.

29 The term, *avaktavya*, has been variously translated into English. Most of its translations are meant to convey the idea of being incapable of being spoken about or described. Nowhere, I believe, do the Pudgalavādins define the term in this way. The meaning of the term is "inexplicable," i.e. incapable of being explained as either other than or the same in existence as the phenomena in dependence upon which it is conceived.

30 See *Personalists*, p. 70.

31 Priestley, in *Pudgalavāda*, p. 60, likens the first way of conceiving a person, which he calls "by appropriation," to the way set out in the "Refutation," which he translates as "the person is conceived by appropriating the present aggregates appropriated as internal." But there is a difference, since what Priestley translates as "by appropriating" (*upādāya*) in the "Refutation" must mean "in reliance upon," as the objection Vasubandhu presents in Section 2.1.1 makes clear. The main difference between the "Refutation" account of how an inexplicable person is conceived and the first account in the *Tridharmaka Śāstra* is that in the "Refutation" a person is said to be conceived in reliance upon aggregates, while in the *Tridharmaka Śāstra* he is said to be conceived in dependence upon the present act of acquiring the aggregates. In the *Tridharmaka Śāstra* the three ways of conceiving an inexplicable person are made possible by the difference between the act of acquiring aggregates, the causal continuity of the acquired aggregates over time, and the cessation of the act of acquiring aggregates. The grammar and sense of the passage in the "Refutation" makes it equally clear that what is being said is that these aggregates are acquired, belong to oneself, and exist at the time they are being acquired. Priestley attempts (Ch. 4) to reconcile the *Sāṃmitīyanikāya Śāstra* account of the three ways inexplicable persons are conceived with the account in the *Tridharmaka Śāstra*, but does not attempt to reconcile the account in the "Refutation" with these two accounts.

32 See *Pudgalavāda*, Ch. 4.

33 An explanation of the Vaibhāṣika schools will be given below. The Pudgalavādins seem to have rejected the Vaibhāṣika claim that there are three kinds of causally unconditioned phenomena.

34 See *Pudgalavāda*, Ch. 4, for a radically different interpretation of the Pudgalavādins' view concerning to which of these three realities persons belong.

35 This work is translated from Pali by S. Z. Aung and C. A. F. Rhys Davids in *Points of Controversy* (London: Pali Text Society, 1915).

36 Chs 1 and 2 of Xúanzàng's Chinese translation of this work are translated into French by Louis de La Vallée Poussin as "La Controverse du Temps et du Pudgala dans le *Vijñānakāya*" in *Études asiatiques oubliées a l'occasion du 25e anniversair de l'École-francaise de l'Extrême Orient*, vol. 1 (1925, pp. 343–76). The second chapter, on the Pudgalavādins' theory of persons, has been translated into English in Fumimaro Watanabe, *Philosophy and its Development in the Nikāyas and Abhidhamma* (Patna: Motilal Banarsidass, 1983, pp. 177–208).

37 This work, which survived only in a Chinese translation made by Kumārajīva, has been reconstructed into Sanskrit and then given a "free English translation," by N. Aiyaswami Shastri under the title *Satyasiddhiśāstra of Harivarman*, 2 vols (Baroda: Oriental Institute, 1978).

38 This work has been translated into English by Surekha Vijay Limaye, *Mahāyānasūtralaṃkāra by Asaṅga* (Delhi: Sri Satguru Publications, 1992). Unfortunately, the portion of the text that deals with the Pudgalavādins' theory of persons seems to have been mistranslated.

39 Ch. III of the *Madhyamakahṛdayavṛtti*, along with its commentary, the *Tarkajvālā*, has been edited and translated by S. Iida in *Reason and Emptiness* (Tokyo: Hokuseido, 1980).

40 These works exist now only in Tibetan. Candrakīrti's *Madhyamakāvatāra* has been translated into English from Tibetan by C. W. Huntington, Jr with Geshe N. Wangchen, as *The Emptiness of Emptiness* (Honolulu: University of Hawaii Press, 1989).

41 There are numerous translations of this work. Its most recent translations from the Sanskrit are by K. Crosby and A. Skilton, *Śāntideva: Bodhicaryāvatāra* (Oxford: Oxford University Press, 1995) and V. A. Wallace and B. Alan Wallace, *A Guide to the Bodhisattva Way of Life* (Ithaca: Snow Lion, 1997).

42 This work has been translated from Sanskrit by G. Jha as *The Tattvasamgraha of Śāntarakṣita with the Commentary by Kamalaśīla*, 2 vols (Baroda: Central Library, 1937).

43 In particular, it should be seen that in the *Kathāvatthu* the Pudgalavādins are not represented as holding the view that persons do not exist apart from the aggregates of their bodies and minds, but only that they are not conceived apart them.

44 In the *Kathāvatthu* it is basically argued that persons do not, as the Pudgalavādins claim they do, possess ultimate existence, since they do not possess it in the way other ultimately existent phenomena do, that persons are not, as the Pudgalavādins claim they are, known to possess such existence, since they are not known to possess it in the way other ultimately existent phenomena are known to possess it, that persons who ultimately exist and transmigrate must, contrary to the belief of the Pudgalavādins, be either different persons or the same persons in different lives, and that persons who possess ultimate existence and perform actions must, contrary to their belief, be either different persons or the same persons who collect the results of their actions. The arguments in the *Kathāvatthu*, of course, are much more complex than this synopsis of their general import indicates. For discussions of its arguments see S. N. Dube's *Cross Currents in Early Buddhism* (New Delhi: Monohar Publications, 1980, pp. 234–45) and Watanabe, op. cit., pp. 154–74.

45 Shastri's paraphrase of the Chinese translation, however, can be misleading. For instance, he has the Pudgalavādins say (p. 70) that "We, however, plead that the five aggregates put together form the soul," which makes it appear as if they hold the view that there is a soul that is the same in existence as a

collection of aggregates! The meaning of the original Sanskrit sentence must surely have been that the five aggregates are the basis upon which a person is conceived, which is a view the Pudgalavādins actually hold. Other infelicitous translations may be noted: "the unspeakable soul" instead of "the inexplicable self" and "indescribable dharma" instead of "inexplicable dharma."

46 See E. Conze, op. cit., pp. 122–34; N. Dutt, *Buddhist Sects in India* (Delhi: Motilal Banarsidass, 1970), Ch. VIII; S. N. Dube, op. cit., Ch. 8; and L. S. Cousins' "Person and Self," in *Proceedings: 'Buddhism into the Year 2000'* (Bangkok and Los Angeles: Dhammakaya Foundation, 1994, pp. 15–31).

47 In particular, by posing the problem of how persons can be "conceptual entities" and yet ultimately exist, Priestley led me to question the idea that the disputants believed that conventional realities are in fact simply conceptual entities. See Chs 7 and 8 of *Pudgalavāda*.

48 Perhaps a few warnings about recent discussions of the Pudgalavādins' theory of persons and the debate it started among the Buddhists may be helpful. Although Conze's discussion (1962) is helpful, he claims, without blinking, that the Pudgalavādins believe that a person does not exist apart from the aggregates and is a kind of structural unity they possess. He makes this claim, perhaps, because he, like many others, over-interprets the fire and fuel analogy the Pudgalavādins use to explain how persons are conceived in reliance upon aggregates. It is clear, however, that the Pudgalavādins believe that in some way persons exist independently of their aggregates. Dutt's discussion (1970) of the *Sāṃmitīyanikāya Śāstra* seems to rely heavily on Venkataramanan's English translation of the Chinese translation of this work and incorporates a number of inconsistencies without calling attention to them. For instance, he seems, in different places, to attribute to the Pudgalavādins the views (1) that we are impermanent and changing and that we are neither permanent nor impermanent, (2) that we are not ultimate realities and that we are substances, (3) that we are and are not agents of action that collect the results of our action, and (4) that we (I) exist in dependence upon collections of aggregates, (II) cease to exist when the continuum of the collection of our aggregates ceases to exist, and (III) are not the same in existence as the collection of our aggregates. In general, Dutt reproduces the different claims he believes that the Pudgalavādins are making without attempting to reconcile them. The most surprising of the claims he makes, derived from his reading of the *Sāṃmitīyanikāya Śāstra*, is that the Pudgalavādins believe that we are relative in existence and exist in dependence upon collections of aggregates, since in this case there would be no reason for the other Buddhist philosophical schools to oppose their theory. Dube (1980) outlines the exchange about the existence of persons between the Theravādins and Pudgalavādins in the *Kathāvatthu* and between Vasubandhu and the Pudgalavādins in the "Refutation," but he does not include a consideration of the Pudgalavādins' theory as it is set out in our Chinese sources. His discussion of the "Refutation" seems to rely on Stcherbatsky's translation and interpretation of the argumentation it contains and reflects their biases. For instance, he includes among the objections the Pudgalavādins raise against Vasubandhu's theory a number of objections that I believe should be attributed to the Nyāya-Vaiśeṣikas, and his evaluations of Vasubandhu's arguments against the Pudgalavādins' theory reflect those of Stcherbatsky. Cousins (1994) presents a brief summary of the critiques of the Pudgalavādins' theory of persons in the *Sāṃmitīyanikāya Śāstra*, the *Vijñānakāya* and the *Kathāvatthu*, and outlines four main areas of debate concerning the theory. But he does not evaluate their theory. Thích Thiên Châu's much fuller account of their theory of persons

(1977), while valuable for the wealth of material it includes, does not come to terms with the problem of how, if a person is a conventional reality, their theory of persons really differs from those of most of its Buddhist critics. Leonard Priestley's book (1999), by contrast, is a concerted attempt to reconstruct the Pudgalavādins' theory of persons in a way that reconciles the apparently conflicting information we have about their theory from Buddhist sources. His reconstruction, however, does not take Vasubandhu's extended discussion of their theory of persons into careful analytical consideration. But such a consideration, I believe, provides the key to untying most of the knots in our understanding of these other texts. Moreover, the view that Priestley tentatively attributes to the Pudgalavādins is a theory of persons that more closely resembles a Vedic theory than any theory of persons held within the other Indian Buddhist schools. This is rather surprising, since he subjects Venkataramanan's Brahminical interpretation of the *Sāṃmitīyanikāya Śāstra* to criticism (see *Pudgalavāda*, pp. 88–94). By contrast, Robert Buswell Jr (1996), in his summary of the *Sāṃmitīyanikāya Śāstra* in *Encyclopedia* VIII, pp. 353–65, claims that the Pudgalavādins are simply espousing the standard view that persons are conventional realities. He fails to notice, however, that the sort of conventional realities they must be are quite different from those accepted in the other schools.

49 See Mrinalkanti Gangopadhyay's English translation of the *Nyāya Sūtras*, in his *The Nyāya-Sūtra with Vātsyāyana's Commentary* (Calcutta: D. Chattopadhyaya, 1982) and Basu, B. D., ed., *The Sacred Books of the Hindus, The Vaiśeṣika Sūtra. The Vaiśeṣika Darśaṇa with the commentaries of Śaṅkārā Miśra and Jayanarayana Tarka Pañchanana* (Allahabad: AMS Press, 1911).

50 See *Padārthadharmasaṃgraha of Praśastapāda, with the Nyāyakandalī of Śrīdhara*, trans. Ganganatha Jha (Allahabad: AMS Press, NY, 1974).

51 An English translation of Vātsyāyana's *Nyāya Bhāṣya* is included in Ganganatha Jha's *The Nyāya Sūtra of Gautama (with commentaries of Vātsyāyana and Uddyotakara)*, 4 vols (Delhi: Motilal Banarsidass, 1986).

52 Useful discussions of these arguments can be found in Arindam Chakrabarti's "The Nyāya Proofs for the Existence of the Soul," *Journal of Indian Philosophy*, vol. 10 (1982); Arindam Chakrabarti's "I Touch What I Saw," *Philosophy and Phenomenological Research*, vol. LII, No. 1 (1992); and especially Kisor Kumar Chakrabarti's *Classical Indian Philosophy of Mind: The Nyāya Dualist Tradition* (Albany: State University of New York Press, 1999).

53 Among the later commentaries the most useful are Uddyotakara's *Nyāyavārttika* (sixth century CE), Vācaspati Miśra's *Nyāyavārttika-Tatparyatīkā* (ninth century CE), Śrīdhara's *Nyāyakandalī* (tenth century CE), Jayanta Bhaṭṭa's *Nyāyamañjarī* (tenth century CE), Udayana's *Kiraṇāvalī, Pariśuddhi, Nyāyakusumāñjali*, and especially his *Ātmatattvaviveka* (eleventh century CE), Śrīvallabha's *Nyāyalīlāvati* (eleventh century CE), Śaṃkaramiśra's *Upaskāra* (fifteenth century CE), Annambhatta's *Tarkasaṃgraha* with *Dīpikā* and *Adhyāpanā* (eighteenth century CE), and Viśvanātha's *Bhāṣāpariccheda* and *Siddhāntamuktāvali* (eighteenth century CE). For summaries of the doctrines these works contain see *The Encyclopedia of Indian Philosophies*, vols II and IV, ed. Karl Potter (Princeton: Princeton University Press, 1977 and 1993).

54 There are numerous translations of this text. For extensive information about this work, its origins in oral traditions, and its many commentaries see Gerald James Larson and Ram Shankar Bhattacharya, *Sāṃkhya: A Dualist Tradition in Indian Philosophy* (Princeton: Princeton University Press, 1987).

55 This school is also called the Yogacāra (Yogic Practitioner) school.

56 A handy summary of the major theses of these philosophical schools can be found in Dkon mchog 'jigs med dbang po's *Precious Garland of Tenets* (*Grub pa'i mtha'i rnam par bzhag pa rin poche'i phreng ba*), translated with commentary by Geshe L. Sopa and J. Hopkins in *Cutting Through Appearances* (Ithaca: Snow Lion Publications, 1989, pp. 139–322).

57 Even the Pudgalavādin schools, which add a classification of phenomena called "inexplicable" (*avaktavya*), seem to accept the view that all other phenomena are either impermanent or permanent, either causally conditioned or causally unconditioned, are among the twelve bases of perception, and are among the eighteen elements. See Section 2.2 and its commentary for their classification of phenomena known to exist. They do not explain, in our extant sources, how the generally accepted classification of all phenomena known to exist into ultimate and conventional realities is affected by the introduction of this other category of phenomena. The view that there are three realities, which is presented in the *Tridharmaka Śāstra*, does not contradict the view that all phenomena known to exist are one of these two realities if the classification into three realities is made from a different perspective. I shall offer an interpretation later in the Introduction concerning how the Pudgalavādins may have accepted the doctrine of two realities.

58 English translations of the Sanskrit names of the aggregates vary widely, reflecting different interpretations of their exact functions and the philosophical predilections of the translators.

59 See André Bareau, *Les Sectes Bouddhiques du Petit Véhicule* (Saigon: École Française D'Extrême-Orient Publications, 1955).

60 The four Pudgalavādin schools are usually identified as the Dharmottarīya, Bhadrāyāṇiya, Saṃmitīya, and Channagirka. These schools are considered to be offshoots of the Vātsīputrīya school, which is the school that originally broke off from the Sthaviras. I have chosen to call them Pudgalavādin schools because they are popularly known as the *Paudgalikas*, a term that means those who ascribe to the existence of a person.

61 The elements of bodies, according to the orthodox Vaibhāṣika schools, are spatially unextended. It is not explained in the *Treasury* or its *Commentary* how spatially unextended inseparable combinations of substances can be composed of spatially unextended substances, or how, in general, some parts of the combined elements provide a support for others. See Guy Newland, *Appearance and Reality* (Ithaca: Snow Lion Press, 1999, p. 22) for a brief introduction to the problems associated with these ideas. Vasubandhu rejects the Vaibhāṣikas' view that the past, present and future of phenomena are substances. See his *Commentary* discussion of verses 24–6 of Book V of the *Treasury*. Stcherbatsky translates the discussion in *The Central Conception of Buddhism* (Delhi: Motilal Banarsidass, 1974, pp. 76–91).

62 According to Tibetan scholars, also included among substantially real phenomena are what might be called the "inseparable defining characteristics" of substances and of inseparable combinations of substances. But even if this is correct, the inseparable defining characteristics of substances and of inseparable combinations of substances would seem to be the same in existence as the phenomena of which they are the defining characteristics. For our purposes, I believe, we may set aside the complications involved in including these defining characteristics among substantially real phenomena. Since in the Western philosophical tradition "substance" has taken on a number of different meanings, we must be careful not to assume that my use of this term to translate *dravya* is meant to have any meaning other than the one I assign to it here.

63 See T. Stcherbatsky's *The Central Conception of Buddhism and the Meaning of the Word Dharma* (London: Royal Asiatic Society Publication Fund 7, 1923).

64 Such mentally constructed entities, we may say, possess extrinsic parts. A part of an entity is an intrinsic part if its conception presupposes the existence of the entity, and it is an extrinsic part if it does not. Substantially established realities, according to Vasubandhu, are conceived in dependence upon their extrinsic parts rather than in dependence upon their intrinsic parts.

65 See the *Commentary* discussion of verse 20 of Book I of the *Treasury*. Vasubandhu need not be interpreted in this passage to be implying that the aggregates are not ultimate realities.

66 There is quite a bit of confusion in the secondary literature about the meaning of *avaktavya*, which I here render as "inexplicable." Because this term has been interpreted to refer to what cannot be conceived or named, it has seemed that a person who is *avaktavya* could not be a conventional reality. However, the term can hardly be used to refer to what cannot be conceived or named, since in that case a person could not, strictly speaking, be said to be *avaktavya*. What it means for something to be *avaktavya*, in fact, is that it cannot be explained as either other than (as a separate substance) or as the same in existence as the phenomena in dependence upon which it is conceived and named.

67 Among Vasubandhu's Sautrāntika school predecessors would seem to be Śrilāta, whose works are lost, and Kumāralāta, whose *Kalpanāmaṇḍitikā* has not yet been translated into English. It has been suggested by some scholars that the school originated from the "Dārṣṭantika" (Exemplarist) school, which is one of the orthodox Vaibhāṣika schools. See, for instance, A. K. Warder, *Indian Buddhism* (Delhi: Motilal Banarsidass, 1980, pp. 345, 421) and the *Encyclopedia*, VIII, pp. 111 and 132.

68 Dignāga's principal treatise is the *Pramāṇasamuccaya* (*Compendium on Primary Cognition*). Dharmakīrti's principal treatise is the *Pramāṇavārttika* (*Exposition of Primary Cognition*), which is his commentary on Dignāga's *Pramāṇasamuccaya*. See A. K. Warder, op. cit., pp. 469–74 for further information.

69 Scholars do not agree about the school to which Dignāga and Dharmakīrti belong, some saying the Sautrāntika school itself, others saying the Cittamātrika school, and yet others saying that they belonged to none of the traditional four. See Roger Jackson, *Is Enlightenment Possible? Dharmakīrti and rGyal tshab rje on Knowledge, Rebirth, No-Self and Liberation* (Ithaca: Snow Lion Publications, 1993), pp. 111–13, A. K. Warder, op. cit., pp. 448ff., and Georges Dreyfus, *Recognizing Reality* (Albany: SUNY Press, 1997, pp. 428–42). Whatever may be the truth of their affiliation, it is clear that their logical and epistemological ideas were turned to use in an attempt to bring greater logical and epistemological sophistication into the Sautrāntika school critique of the theses of the orthodox Vaibhāṣika schools.

70 There is a scholarly dispute concerning exactly what works were composed by Asaṅga, since many modern scholars attribute to him works traditionally ascribed to Maitreya. All agree, however, that he authored the *Abhidharmasamuccaya* (*Compendium of Knowledge*) and the *Mahāyānasaṃgraha* (*Compendium of the Universal Vehicle*). The works always ascribed to his brother, Vasubandhu, are the *Viṃśatikā* (*Twenty Verses*) and the *Triṃśikā* (*Thirty Verses*).

71 See note 1 for references.

72 Bhāvaviveka's chief philosophical work is the *Madhyamakahṛdayavṛtti*, along with its commentary, the *Tarkajvālā*. There is a partial translation of this work in S. Iida, *Reason and Emptiness* (Tokyo: Hokuseido, 1980).

73 Candrakīrti's chief philosophical works are the *Prasannapadā* (*The Clear Worded*), a commentary on Nāgārjuna's *Mūlamadhyamakakārikā*, and *the Madhyamakāvatāra* (*Introduction to the Middle Way*), along with his commentary on it, which is preserved only in Tibetan.

74 An example of just how complicated the understanding of the dispute between Bhāvaviveka and Candrakīrti on this issue can get, see Donald Lopez, Jr, *A Study of Svātantrika* (Ithaca: Snow Lion Publications, 1987).

75 In the "Svātantrika" (Independent Reasoning follower) schools, it was held that a phenomenon's lack of ultimate existence could be demonstrated to others by presenting them with reasoning based on its possession of a character by itself. In the "Prāsaṅgika" (Reasoning to Consequences follower) school, it was held that a phenomenon's lack of ultimate existence could be demonstrated to others only by reasoning in which absurd consequences are drawn from their assumption that the phenomenon possessed a character of its own.

76 The minds of all beings other than Buddhas, according to Candrakīrti, cannot simultaneously apprehend the two realities, since the conventional realities that appear to their minds falsely appear to possess ultimate existence. But the minds of Buddhas simultaneously apprehend both of the two realities, since the false appearance of conventional realities possessing ultimate existence has been eliminated from their minds by the practice of the Bodhisattva path. Because Buddhas are omniscient, their minds can apprehend the same conventional realities that appear to the convention-laden minds of other beings.

77 The three root mental afflictions are ignorance, ignorant desire, and ignorant aversion. When present, they contaminate both the apprehension of an object and the object being apprehended.

78 Because the appearance of the three schools of Vedānta post-date the works and life of Vasubandhu, they are not included among the Tīrthikas at this point of time. Included are the Sāṃkhya and Yoga schools and the Nyāya and Vaiśeṣika schools, and perhaps the Vaiyākaraṇas.

79 A self that cannot be identified independently of the aggregates is, I believe, what the Tibetans say is substantially existent in the sense of being self-sufficient.

80 Not all Indian Buddhist philosophers seem to believe that the conception of ourselves arises in dependence upon collections of aggregates. Some seem to believe that it arises in dependence upon a subtle form of the mental consciousness aggregate, and others that it arises in dependence upon a foundational consciousness (*ālayavijñāna*) that retains the seeds of contaminated actions until they give rise to their fruit. In what follows, I shall be concerned only with the view that the conception arises in dependence upon collections of aggregates, since it is the view accepted by Vasubandhu, the Pudgalavādins, and Candrakīrti.

81 Likewise, when I speak of "the collection of their aggregates" I will mean, in dependence upon context, either "the collection of aggregates of which they are composed" or " the collection of aggregates in dependence upon which they conceive themselves," and when I speak of "their aggregates" I will mean, in dependence upon context, either "the aggregates in the collection of which they are composed" or "the aggregates in the collection in dependence upon which they conceive themselves."

82 The no separate substance interpretation of the selflessness of persons thesis needs to be distinguished from what Tibetan Buddhist scholars call the coarse view of the selflessness of persons, which is the view that we are not permanent and partless separate substances.

83 The arguments against the Tīrthikas' theory of persons can take the form of arguing that we are not separate substances, that we are not permanent phenomena, or that we are not partless phenomena. The argument in Section 1.2 is directed only against the view that we are separate substances.

84 According to Tibetan scholars, the Pudgalavādins interpret the selflessness of persons thesis to be the denial that we are permanent and partless substances that exist apart from collections of aggregates. If these scholars are correct, the Pudgalavādins would seem to be committed to the view that we suffer because we assent to a naturally occurring false appearance of ourselves as permanent and partless substances that exist apart from the collection of our aggregates. But I doubt that the Pudgalavādins would have held the view that we all naturally appear to our minds in this way, since a simple inspection of how we naturally appear to our minds when we conceive ourselves will disconfirm the view. In any case, we need not attribute such a view to them, since if an entity can exist without a separate identity, the view that we cannot be independently identified is consistent with the view that we exist apart from the collections of our aggregates.

85 In general, to be a self, he believes, is to be ultimately existent, so that to deny the existence of a self is to deny the existence of an ultimately existent phenomenon. However, in the case of saying that there is no self in the context of denying that a person is a self, we may also say that a self is person that possesses ultimate existence.

86 Vasubandhu usually expresses the view that we are the same as collections of aggregates as the view that we are the same as aggregates, as the view that we are not other than aggregates, as the view that we are aggregates, and as the view that we are nothing but aggregates. In what has preceded and in what follows I employ the full expression of his view. The rendering of *prajñaptisat* as "is real by way of a conception" instead of "nominally exists," "conceptually exists," or "exists as a name or conception," will be explained below.

87 In his *Commentary* discussion of verse 20ab of Book I of the *Treasury*, Vasubandhu asks whether the aggregates are substantially real, as the Vaibhāṣikas claim, or are real by way of a conception, as the Sautrāntikas claim. (See pp. 79–80 of Pruden's English translation of La Vallée Poussin's translation of the Chinese translation of the *Commentary* discussion of verse 20ab of Book I of the *Treasury*.) La Vallée Poussin seems to think that in this discussion (see note 97, p. 141 of the Pruden translation) Vasubandhu unequivocally commits himself to the view that the aggregates are real by way of a conception. But at the very end of the discussion Vasubandhu calls attention to a passage from the *Mahāvibhāṣā* (*Great Exposition*) in support of the view that reference to the aggregates can be interpreted as a reference either to aggregates being conceived as collections or to the phenomena in these collections. Vasubandhu's intention in quoting this passage, I believe, is to suggest that insofar as the aggregates are conceived as collections they are real by way of a conception, but the phenomena included in these collections are substantially real. From this point of view, the aggregates, apart from being conceived as collections, will not be real by way of a conception.

Hence, in Section 4.8 of the "Refutation," Vasubandhu is able to endorse the view that the five aggregates, in their purified states, are substances, and in Section 2.1 to say that visible forms, which are aggregates, are substantially real. So when Vasubandhu in effect says that we are the same in existence as collections of aggregates, he means to imply that we ultimately exist. Since to be the same in existence as collections of aggregates is not to be conceived as collections of aggregates, he can say that we are the same in existence as collections of aggregates without implying that the collections are real by way of a conception.

88 In general, it seems that scholars have interpreted *prajñaptisat* and *prajñaptitas asti* as mere conceptual or nominal existence. But this is in fact only the meaning that the Prāsaṅgika-Mādhyamikas assign to them. In all other schools, the phenomena to which these terms refer ultimate exist, since they could not otherwise perform a causal function. Some scholars have even gone so far as to conclude, because of this error, that Indian Buddhists deny that conventional realities possess causal efficacy.

89 We must distinguish the Buddhist view about what we are, from a conventional point of view, from the Buddhist view that some people, out of ignorance, identify us with an aggregate, others with what possesses an aggregate, others with that in which an aggregate exists, and yet others with something which is in an aggregate. These are wrong views.

90 There is an eleventh kind of bodily form not included within the sense-organs or their objects or the four primary elements, but we need not discuss this complication of the orthodox Vaibhāṣikas' categorization of bodily forms. Vasubandhu rejects the Vaibhāṣikas' view that this bodily form possesses substantial reality.

91 What exactly Vasubandhu could mean by saying that air or wind is responsible for motion is not clear, since motion is not possible in a world in which all causally conditioned phenomena are momentary. Perhaps the meaning is that it is the presence in a body of the air-element that is responsible for what by convention we call its motion.

92 Visible forms are divided into color and shape, colors into primary and secondary colors, etc. Tactile objects are divided into eleven kinds, four of which are the distinguishing characters of earth, water, fire, and air or wind.

93 The desire realm is the realm of objects of consciousness in which desire is its most salient feature. It is the realm in which we normally reside. Its contrasts are the form realm and formless realms, which can be accessed by means of yogic concentration.

94 See verses 12–13 of Book I of the *Treasury*. For a detailed interpretation of Vasubandhu's theory of the elements, see Verdu, *Early Buddhist Philosophy* (Delhi: Motilal Banarsidass, 1985, pp. 21–34).

95 This is Vasubandhu's view, which is rejected in the Cittamātrika school, according to which a consciousness and the object it perceives must exist at the same moment. Vasubandhu thinks that a consciousness which is immediately produced by an object and organ may be said to perceive it directly. What I am here calling the principal cause of a consciousness of an object is often called "the efficient condition," while the object is called "the objective condition," and the organ "the dominant condition" of the consciousness of the object.

96 There is a problem here if among ultimate realities there are such phenomena as impermanence, which would seem itself to be a defining character of causally conditioned phenomena. For if it too is an ultimate reality, would it not possesses a character by virtue of which it is conceived? But if that character is also to be conceived, would there not have to be a character by virtue of which it is conceived, and so on, ad infinitum? Perhaps impermanence is not an ultimate reality.

97 See Vasubandhu's *Commentary* discussion of verse 21 of Book I of The *Treasury*.

98 Ibid.

99 Indeed, it would seem to be true of the polemical works in all Indian philosophical schools, not just the Buddhist schools, that they do not adequately represent the views and arguments of their opponents.

100 This may be the source of the views put forward by some scholars, that the Pudgalavādins believe that a person is "the structural unity" of the aggregates and that a person is a whole of parts that is not reducible in existence to his parts, since these views seem to rest on the assumption that persons cannot exist apart from the collection of their aggregates.

2

TRANSLATION OF VASUBANDHU'S "REFUTATION OF THE THEORY OF A SELF"

Section 1

Vasubandhu's theory of persons

1.1 Only the practice of the Buddha's teachings can free us from suffering

There is no liberation [from suffering] other than this [liberation, the path to which I have just explained], since [the Tīrthikas, who also teach a path to liberation from suffering, fail to recognize that] there is a mistaken view of a self [that causes all suffering.[1] Those who follow their teachings will not be liberated from suffering,] for they do not understand that the conception of a self[2] refers only to a continuum of aggregates;[3] they believe that a self is a separate substance;[4] but the mental afflictions, [which cause suffering,] arise from self-grasping, [which cannot be eliminated by those who believe that a self is a separate substance].

1.2 How it is known that we are the same in existence as collections of aggregates and are not selves

It is known that the expression, "self," refers to a continuum of aggregates and not to anything else because [direct perception and correct inference establish that the phenomena in dependence upon which a person is conceived are the aggregates, and] there is no direct perception or correct inference [of anything else among these phenomena].[5]

[If anything else exists among these phenomena, its existence would be established by direct perception or correct inference,] for of all phenomena [that exist] there is direct perception [that establishes their existence], as there is of the six objects and the mental organ unless [direct] perception of them is impeded, or there is correct inference [that establishes their existence], as there is of the five [sense] organs.

[For instance,] this is a correct inference [by which a sense-organ is known to exist]: [1] it is common knowledge that an effect does not arise when all but one of its causes are present, but does arise when all are present; [2] for instance, a sprout [does not arise when all of its causes are present except its seed, but does arise when the seed is also present]; [3] we know that there are some who do not perceive an object when both the object and attentiveness are present as causes [of the perception of the object], and that there are others who perceive the object when these causes are present; [4] [for instance,] the blind and the deaf [do not perceive the object when these causes are present] and those with sight and hearing [do]; [5] thus we may conclude that in the first case one of the causes [of perception] is absent, while in the second case it is present. This other cause is a [sense] organ.[6] This is a correct inference [by which a sense-organ is known to exist].

There is no correct inference of this sort to [establish that] a self [exists. Nor is there any direct perception of a self]. Therefore, [we know that] there is no self.

Section 2

Vasubandhu's objections to the Pudgalavādins' theory of persons

2.1 Is the Pudgalavādins' theory of persons consistent with the doctrine of the two realities?

The Pudgalavādins,[7] [who profess to be followers of the Buddha's teachings,] assert that a person exists.[8] [To determine whether or not their assertion conforms to the Buddha's teachings,] we must first consider whether in their view a person is substantially real or is real by way of a conception.[9]

If a person is a distinct entity like visible form and other such things, he is substantially real; but if [by analysis] he is [shown to be] a collection [of substances], like milk and other such things, he is real by way of a conception. Consequently, if a person is substantially real, it must be said that he is other than aggregates in the way each of them is other than the others, since he will possess a different nature [than possessed by any of the aggregates. If he is other than aggregates, he must be either causally conditioned or causally unconditioned. If he is other than aggregates and is causally conditioned,] his causes should be explained.[10] But if he is [other than aggregates and is] causally unconditioned, the false theory [of persons] espoused by the Tīrthikas is held and a person does not function[11] [as a person. So since the Pudgalavādins cannot say that a person is other than aggregates, they cannot say that he is substantially real]. If he is real by way of a conception, [he is his aggregates, and] this is the theory [of persons found in the Buddha's sūtras and is] held by us.

2.1.1 *They answer that we are neither substantially real nor real by way of a conception because we are conceived in reliance upon collections of aggregates*

[But the Pudgalavādins assert that] a person is not substantially real or real by way of a conception, since he is conceived[12] in reliance upon aggregates[13] which pertain to himself,[14] are acquired,[15] and exist in the present.[16]

2.1.2 *But if we are conceived in reliance upon collections of aggregates we must be the same in existence as the collections*

If we are to understand this obscure statement [of why a person is neither substantially real nor real by way of a conception], its meaning must be disclosed. What is meant by [saying that a person is conceived] "in reliance upon [aggregates]"? If it means [that a person is conceived] "on the condition that aggregates have been perceived," then the conception [of a person] refers only to them, [not to an independently existent person,] just as when visible forms and other such things [that comprise milk] have been perceived, the conception of milk refers only to them, [not to an independently existent milk]. If [saying that a person is conceived "in reliance upon aggregates" means that he is conceived] "in dependence upon aggregates," then [once again, the conception of a person refers only to them, not to a person,] because aggregates themselves will cause him to be conceived. [Therefore,] there is the same difficulty [that the Pudgalavādins must say that a person is his aggregates].

2.1.3 *They reply that we are conceived in reliance upon collections of aggregates without being other than or the same in existence as them in the way that fire is conceived in reliance upon fuel without being other than or the same in existence as fuel*

[They reply by saying that] a person is not conceived in this way [in which milk is conceived], but rather in the way [in which] fire is conceived in reliance upon fuel.[17] [They say that] fire is conceived in reliance upon fuel, [and yet] it is not conceived unless fuel is present and cannot be conceived if it either is or is not other than fuel. If fire were other than fuel, fuel [in burning material] would not be hot,[18] [which is absurd.] And if fire were not other than fuel, what is burned could be the same as what burns it, [which is also absurd].[19]

2.1.4 *And that their theory is the middle way between the extremes of eternal transcendence and nihilism*

Similarly, [they contend,] a person is not conceived unless aggregates are present, [and] if he were other than aggregates, the eternal transcendence theory [that a person is substantially real] would be held, and if he were not other than aggregates, the nihilism theory [that a person does not exist at all] would be held.[20]

2.1.5 *But proper analyses of fire and fuel are inconsistent with both their fire and fuel reply and their theory that we are inexplicable*

They must explain, first of all, what fuel and fire are so we shall know how fire is conceived in reliance upon fuel. [They say that] fuel is what is burned and fire is what burns it. [But these are mere conventional definitions.] What is burned and what burns it are the very things we need to have explained [if it is to be known how they are in fact conceived].

It is commonly said that fuel is material[21] that is not burning, but can burn, and that fire is burning [material] that burns fuel.[22] A blazing and intensely hot fire, [it is commonly said,] burns or ignites fuel in that it brings about an alteration in its continuum. [But analysis shows that the] fire and fuel [of which these things are said] are composed of eight [elemental] substances,[23] and fire arises in dependence upon fuel in the way curds arise in dependence upon milk, and sour [milk] upon sweet [milk]. So we say [that fire is conceived] in reliance upon fuel, even though it is other than fuel by reason of existing at a different time [as a different collection of elements]. And [so] if a person arises in the same way in dependence upon aggregates, he must be other than them.[24] [Moreover, contrary to their view that a person is not impermanent,] he must also be impermanent, [since he arises in dependence upon aggregates].[25]

2.1.5.1 *Their reply, that fire is the heat present in burning material and that fuel is a collection of the three primary elements other than fire, is inconsistent with their fire and fuel reply and their theory of persons*

[The Pudgalavādins believe that they avoid these objections because] they assert that fire is the heat present in the above-mentioned burning material[26] and that [the] fuel [in reliance upon which fire is conceived] is comprised of the three elements [of earth, air, and water] that conjointly arise with it [in burning material].

[But according to this analysis] fire must still be other than fuel, since they will have different defining properties. Moreover, the meaning of "in reliance upon" must be explained, [since, according to their analyses of fire and fuel,] how is fire conceived in reliance upon fuel? For [if the analyses are correct, it is true not only that] fuel will not be a cause of fire, [but] also [that] it will not even be a cause of the conception of fire, since fire itself will be the cause of the conception [of fire].

If the meaning of "in reliance upon" is a support as inseparable concomitance,[27] then aggregates must also be said in the same way to be the supports or inseparable concomitants of a person, in which case they clearly must say that aggregates are other than a person, [since the supports and inseparable concomitants of something are other than it.] And [they must also say, contrary to their theory that a person does not exist in dependence upon the existence of aggregates, that] a person does not [in fact] exist unless aggregates exist,[28] just as fire does not [in fact] exist unless fuel exists.[29]

Finally, what does "hot" signify in their earlier assertion[30] that if fire were other than fuel, fuel [in burning material] would not be hot? If it signifies heat, then fuel itself is not hot, since it [is, according to their analysis, what] possesses the natures of the other [three] elements [rather than the nature of the fire whose presence in something is the cause of its heat. There remains the possibility that] what is hot, even if it is other than fire, which is hot by its own nature, can be shown to be hot in the sense that it can be combined with heat. [But] in this case fire being other than fuel is not a problem [for the view that fuel in burning material is hot].[31]

2.1.5.2 *Nor can the reply that burning material as a whole is the same in existence as fire and fuel, individually considered, be used to avoid the problems of the fire and fuel reply*

Should they say [in order to avoid the objection that fire is other than fuel] that burning material is as a whole both fire and fuel, they must explain what it can mean in this case to say [that fire is conceived] "in reliance upon" [fuel. For if burning material is as a whole both fire and fuel, fuel will be the fire, and that in reliance upon which fire is conceived will be the fire itself, which the Pudgalavādins deny]. Moreover, since aggregates themselves would also be the person, it follows that they could not avoid the theory that a person is not other than his aggregates.[32]

2.1.5.3 *So the fire and fuel reply is unsuccessful*

Therefore, they have not shown that a person is conceived in reliance upon aggregates in the way [in which they believe] that fire is conceived in reliance upon fuel.

2.2 If we are inexplicable phenomena we cannot be said to be or not to be a fifth kind of object known to exist

Since [the Pudgalavādins assert that a person is inexplicable,] they cannot say that a person is other than aggregates. [Hence,] they cannot say, [as they do,] that "there are five kinds of objects known to exist, [namely,] past, future, and present [causally conditioned phenomena], causally unconditioned phenomena, and the [persons that they call] inexplicable." For they cannot assert that an inexplicable [person] constitutes a fifth kind [of object known to exist, since if a person cannot be said to be other than aggregates, which are the three kinds of casually conditioned phenomena, he must be the same as them]. Nor [can they assert] that he does not constitute a fifth kind, [since in asserting that he is unexplicable they cannot say that he is the same as aggregates, and they do not believe that he is a causally unconditioned phenomenon. Hence, they cannot assert that a person is inexplicable.[33]]

2.3 Because we are conceived either after aggregates are perceived or after we are perceived we must either be the same in existence as collections of aggregates or not be conceived in reliance upon them

When conceived, is a person conceived after aggregates are perceived or after a person is perceived? If he is conceived after aggregates are perceived, [a person is not conceived after a person is perceived, and] the conception of a person refers only to them, since a person is not perceived. But if he is conceived after he himself is perceived, then how can a person be conceived in reliance upon aggregates, since then the person himself is the basis upon which he is conceived?

2.4 Their thesis, that we are conceived in reliance upon collections of aggregates because we are perceived when the aggregates are present, implies that a visible form is not conceived because it is perceived and that we are other than collections of aggregates

[They say that] a person is conceived in reliance upon aggregates because a person is perceived when aggregates are present. [But] in that case, since [if a person is conceived in reliance upon aggregates because a person is perceived when aggregates are present, and] a visible form is perceived when the eye, attentiveness, and light are present, they would have to say that a visible form is conceived in reliance upon them [rather than because of the visible form that is perceived]; and just as a visible form [is other than the eye, attentiveness, and light present when a visible form is perceived], clearly a person would be other [than aggregates present when a person is perceived].

2.5 The Pudgalavādins' account of how we are known to exist is that each of the six consciousnesses is aware of us and that we are neither other than nor the same in existence as its primary objects

They must state by which of the six consciousnesses a person is known to exist. They say that a person is known to exist by all six. They explain how [a person is known to exist by all six] by saying that if a consciousness is aware of[34] a person in dependence upon a visible form known to exist by means of the eye, it is said that a person is known to exist by means of the eye; but it is not said that a person is or is not the visible form [in dependence upon which the consciousness is aware of a person]. In the same way [they explain how a person is known to exist by each of the other five consciousnesses] up to [and including] the mental consciousness, [saying that] if a consciousness is aware of a person in dependence upon a phenomenon known to exist by means of the mental organ, it is said that a person is known to exist by means of the mental organ; but it is not said that a person either is or is not the phenomenon [in dependence upon which the consciousness is aware of a person].

2.5.1 *But in the same way each of four consciousnesses that perceives the elements of milk is aware of milk, yet milk is the same in existence as all of its elements as a collection*

But the same account can be given of [how] milk and other such things [are known to exist]. If a consciousness is aware of milk in dependence upon a visible form known to exist by means of the eye, it is said that milk is known to exist by means of the eye; but it is not said that milk either is or is not the visible form [in dependence upon which the consciousness is aware of milk]. For the same reason, if a consciousness is aware of milk in dependence upon objects known to exist by means of the nose, the tongue, and the body, it is said that milk is known to exist by means of these organs; but it is not said that milk is or is not [any one of] the objects [in dependence upon which the consciousness is aware of milk].

[It may be assumed that milk is not other than any one of the objects known to exist by the four consciousnesses aware of milk, since there is no awareness of milk that is not a perception of one of these objects.]

[Nor can milk be any one of these objects, for if it were any one of them it would be each of them, and if it were each of them, then since the objects known to exist by these four consciousnesses are of four different kinds] the absurd consequence follows that the milk would be of four different kinds.

[But if milk is known to exist by means of the eye, the nose, the tongue, and the body, and it neither is nor is not any one of these objects, then it must be all of them as a collection. And if milk is all of them as a collection, it must be all of them as a collection that are conceived as milk.] Therefore, just as [it must be all of] these very objects as a collection [that] are conceived as milk, in the same way, [it must also be all of the objects as a collection that are known to exist by the six consciousnesses that perceive a person that are conceived as a person. And since these very objects are aggregates,] it is established that aggregates are conceived as a person. [But if aggregates are conceived as a person, a person is aggregates. Therefore, the Pudgalavādins' account of how a person is known to exist by the six consciousnesses cannot be used to explain how an inexplicable person is known to exist.]

2.5.2 *Their account implies either that a visible form is not other than the other causes of the perception of a visible form or that we are either other than or the same in existence as a visible form*

Furthermore, what do they mean when they assert that [a person is known to exist if] a consciousness is aware of a person in dependence upon a visible form known to exist by means of the eye? Is [it meant that a person is known to exist if] a cause of a perception of a person is a visible form or is [it meant that a person is known to exist if] a person [is] perceived when a visible form is perceived?

If [they say that] a cause of a perception of a person is a visible form and [they also say that] a person cannot be said to be other than a visible form, they cannot say [as they do] that a visible form is other than light, the eye and attentiveness, since these are causes of a perception of a visible form.

If [they say that] a person is perceived when a visible form is perceived, a person is perceived by the same perception [by which a visible form is perceived] or by another perception. If a person is perceived by the same perception [by which a visible form is perceived, then since if one perception is the same as another, what is perceived by the one is the same in nature as what is perceived by the other], a person is the same in nature as a visible form and only it is to be conceived as that [person]. How, then, could a visible form be distinguished from a person? And if it cannot be distinguished in this way, how can it be asserted that both a visible form and a person [separately] exist, since it is on the strength of a [separate] perception of something that its [separate] existence is asserted? This same argument can be used [for objects perceived by the other five consciousnesses] up to [and including] a phenomenon [perceived by the mental consciousness]. If [a person is perceived] by a perception other than the one by which a visible form is perceived, then since he is perceived at a different time, a person must be other than a visible form, just as yellow is other than blue and one moment is other than another. This same argument can be used [for objects perceived by the other five consciousnesses] up to [and including] a phenomenon [perceived by the mental consciousness].

2.5.2.1 *Nor can the perception of ourselves be inexplicable, since a perception is a causally conditioned phenomenon*

[They reply that a person can be perceived when a visible form is perceived and yet the perception of a person and the perception of a visible form cannot be said either to be or not to be other than one another. But] if these perceptions, like [their objects,] a person, and a visible form, cannot be said either to be or not to be other than one another, they must contradict their own theory [that a perception is a causally conditioned phenomenon,] since [if a perception is inexplicable,] a causally conditioned phenomenon can then also be inexplicable, [which is absurd.]

2.5.2.2 *Because the Buddha teaches the doctrine of no-self they cannot say that our perceptions of ourselves are inexplicable in the way we ourselves are*

[The Pudgalavādins state that a perception of a person cannot be said either to be or not to be a perception of a visible form because] the person [perceived] exists and cannot be said either to be or not to be the visible form [perceived]. But if they hold this theory, [that a person exists and cannot be said either to be or not to be a visible form,] how can they explain the Bhagavān's teaching that a visible form and the other aggregates are selfless?

2.5.3 *Their account of how we are known to exist is also incompatible with the Buddha's teachings on perception*

Does an eye-consciousness that perceives a person arise in dependence upon visible forms, a person, or both? If it arises in dependence upon visible forms, then it cannot know to exist a person any more than it can know to exist a sound or the objects of the other consciousnesses, since a consciousness that arises in dependence upon a specific kind of object has only that kind of object as its supporting causal condition. If it arises in dependence upon a person or both visible forms and a person, the following sūtra, which states that [this] consciousness arises in dependence upon both [an eye and visible forms], is contradicted: "Bhikṣus, an eye is the cause, and visible forms are the causal condition, of the arising of an eye-consciousness, since every eye-consciousness arises in dependence upon an eye and visible forms."

Likewise, [contrary to their theory that a person cannot be said to be permanent or impermanent,] they must say that a person is impermanent, since in a sūtra it is said that "both the causes and causal conditions of the arising of a consciousness are impermanent."

[They say that their theory does not contradict these teachings, since] a person is not a causal support [or supporting causal condition] of a consciousness. But [in that case,] then a consciousness does not perceive a person.

Again, if they assert that all six consciousnesses perceive a person, then because an ear-consciousness perceives him, a person is other than visible forms, just as sounds are. And because an eye-consciousness perceives him, a person is other than sounds, just as visible forms are. This sort of reasoning can also be applied to [each of] the other [consciousnesses].

Their view [that each of the six consciousnesses perceives a person] is also contradicted by the passage in a sūtra that states, "Oh brāhmin, each of five organs encounters its own domain and objects. None encounters the domain and objects of another, neither an eye, ear, nose, tongue, or body. But a mental organ encounters the domain and objects of the five organs, which rely on a mental organ [to give rise to a conception of the objects they encounter]." [Therefore, since these five organs do not stray from their own domain and objects, and a consciousness perceives only the objects its organ encounters, a person is not perceived by all six consciousnesses.]

[They reply that] a person is not an object [encountered by an organ]. [But] if he is not an object [encountered by an organ], he will not be perceived [by a consciousness, and so will not be known to exist].

2.5.3.1 *The Pudgalavādins reply that our interpretation of scripture contradicts the Buddha's teaching that the mental organ encounters the objects encountered by the other five organs*

[They reply that] if this is the case, [that we can infer, from the Buddha's statement that each of five organs encounters its own domain and objects, that none of them strays from its own domain and objects,] then [it can be inferred, contrary to the passage just quoted, that] a mental organ also does not stray [from its own domain and objects, since] in the *Parable of the Six Animals*, it is said, "Each of the six organs seeks its own domain and objects."

2.5.3.2 *But the passage quoted by the Pudgalavādins does not contradict the Buddha's teaching*

[But we can in fact infer from the passage we cited that the five organs cannot stray from their own domains and objects, since] the organs mentioned in the passage [quoted by the Pudgalavādins] are not really organs. For the five organs do not seek to perceive [objects, since they are bodily forms, which cannot conceive an object and what cannot conceive an object cannot seek to perceive it]. Nor do the consciousnesses [to which the five sense-organs give rise seek to perceive the objects encountered by their organs insofar as they are mental organs, since in their capacity as mental organs they do not conceive an object encountered by their organs and what does not conceive an object does not seek to perceive it. Only a mental consciousness can seek to perceive an object its organ encounters.]

Therefore, [since each of the six organs mentioned in the passage cited by the Pudgalavādins is said to seek its own domain and objects, each must in fact be a mental consciousness. So it must be that] a mental consciousness produced through the influence of an organ is called an organ [because it is somehow like an organ. Moreover, although] a mental consciousness, which is produced because of the dominating influence of a mental organ, [seeks its own domain and objects, it] does not seek the domains and objects of the other organs. [Hence, it is said that each of these six organs seeks its own domain and objects.] So this [supposed consequence of our interpretation of the original passage, that a mental organ does not stray from its own domain and objects,] is not a fault [incurred by our view].[35]

2.5.4 *Their account of how we are known to exist is also incompatible with the Buddha's enumerations of phenomena known to exist*

The Bhagavān said, "Let me teach you, bhikṣus, the doctrine concerning all things of which you are to have comprehensive knowledge." Then he said, "You are to have comprehensive knowledge of an eye, visible forms, an eye-consciousness, a contact with an eye, a feeling that arises within oneself, whether pleasant, unpleasant, or indifferent, conditioned by the contact, . . ." [and so on, until] ". . . a feeling that arises because of a contact with a mental organ." He concluded, "These are all the things of which you are to have a full comprehensive knowledge." However, a person is not included among these phenomena of which he says we are to have comprehensive knowledge. Therefore, a person is also not an object of a consciousness, since the objects of wisdom [or knowledge] are the same as those of consciousnesses.

2.5.5 *Their account of how we are known to exist is incompatible with the Buddha's teaching on the selflessness of the organs of perception*

When the Pudgalavādins say that we see a person by means of an eye, they commit themselves to [what the sūtras show to be] the mistaken view that we see a self by means of what is selfless.[36] [This view is mistaken because an eye is said to be selfless in the sense that it is not something possessed by a self, and it is absurd to suggest that a self perceives itself by means of an organ it does not possess.]

2.6 The sūtras establish that persons are the same in existence as collections of aggregates rather than being inexplicable phenomena

In the sūtra, *On What A Human Being Is*, whose statements are to be understood literally, the Bhagavān said that what we call a person is simply the aggregates: "An eye-consciousness arises in dependence upon visible forms and an eye; and when there is a contact, which is the meeting of these three, there arises a feeling, a discrimination, and a volition.[37] These four non-bodily aggregates, along with an eye, [which is a bodily aggregate,] are called a human being. This [collection of aggregates] is called a sentient being, a man, a human being, an individual, a person, a living creature, and so on.[38] It is said to see visible forms by means of an eye.

The verbal conventions are adopted that he is venerable, has a certain name, belongs to a given caste, is a member of some family, eats food of a certain sort, is aware of pleasure and pain, lives for a while or for a long time, and lives to a certain age. Thus, bhikṣus, these are mere names or verbal conventions. All of these phenomena, which are impermanent and causally conditioned, are dependently arisen." And since the Bhagavān said to take refuge in sūtras whose statements are to be understood literally, this passage is not to be reinterpreted.

The Bhagavān said, "Oh brāhmins, all things [thus enumerated] exist, those up to and including the twelve bases [of perception]." And so if a person is not a basis [of perception], he does not exist, while if he is a basis [of perception], he is not [an] inexplicable [phenomenon]. This view, in fact, is expressed in sūtras accepted by the Pudgalavādins, where it is said, "Bhikṣus, the Tathāgata[39] teaches that all things exist to the extent that an eye, visible forms, [and so on] exist."

In the *Bimbisāra Sūtra*, the Bhagavān said, "Bhikṣus, common people, [who are] ignorant [of the teachings] and without wisdom, hold on to the conception of a self, [and suppose that the aggregates belong to this self]. But [if they should search among the phenomena in dependence upon which they are conceived, they would find that] there is no self or anything that belongs to a self [among them]; there exists [among them only the aggregates we call] this continuum of suffering."

The worthy, Śilā, is also reported to have said to Māra, "Do you, Māra, believe that a sentient being exists? [You should not,] for this is a mistaken view. This mass of [phenomena] causally conditioning [other] phenomena is empty [of selfhood]. No sentient being at all can be found among them. Just as we refer by name to a chariot on the basis of the collection of its parts, so, by convention, we speak of a sentient being in reliance upon aggregates."

In the *Kṣudraka* scriptures the following is also said to a mendicant brāhmin: "Listen attentively and with respect to the teaching that unties all knots [that bind us in *saṃsāra*]: [by the mistaken view of a self] the mind is contaminated and [by the knowledge of selflessness] the mind is purified. For a self does not exist; it is mistakenly mentally constructed. There is no self or sentient being here [to be found among the phenomena in dependence upon which a person is conceived]; there are only phenomena produced by causes. What exist are [the phenomena we call] the twelve constituents of [the process by which our] existence [is continued], the aggregates, the bases [of perception], and the elements, and when they are examined, no person is perceived. See internal [phenomena] to be empty [of self]; see external [phenomena] to be empty [of self]. Even the one who meditates on emptiness is not at all to be found."

As it was said, "The five evils of perceiving a self are that [1] one holds a mistaken view of a self," and so on, up to "[a mistaken view of] an individual, [2] one's mistaken view [of a self] is indistinguishable from that of

Tīrthikas, [3] one follows a wrong path, [4] one's mind does not seek emptiness, or become clear about it, or become established in it, or become inclined toward it, and [5] one fails to develop the pure qualities of the Āryas."[40]

2.6.1 *The Pudgalavādins should accept the authority of these sūtras*

These passages, however, are not recognized [by the Pudgalavādins] as authoritative because they are not included in their own [collection of] sūtras. But are only their own [collection of] sūtras authoritative? Or should what the Buddha said be the authority? If they accept only their own [collection of] sūtras, then the Buddha is not their teacher and they are not his followers. But if they accept the authority of what the Buddha said, they must accept the authority of these passages. For it is unreasonable to claim that these statements are not what the Buddha said simply because they are not included in their own collection of sūtras, since they are found in all other collections of sūtras and do not contradict [other collections of] sūtras or the truth. So it is overly bold of them to claim that our passages are not what the Buddha said because they are not included in their own collection of sūtras.

2.7 The doctrines expressed in the sūtras they accept as authentic contradict their theory of persons

Furthermore, do the sūtras accepted by them not include the teaching that all phenomena are selfless? [Why is this teaching included if a person is not one of these selfless phenomena? If] they say [that a person is not one of these selfless phenomena] because a person cannot be said either to be one of these phenomena or to be other than one, they must concede that a person cannot be perceived by a mental consciousness, [since] it is asserted [in a sūtra] that a consciousness arises in dependence upon both [an organ and an object of perception, each of which is a phenomenon said to be selfless].

In a sūtra [accepted by them as spoken by the Buddha] it is acknowledged [that the following statement is not to be interpreted]: "'What is selfless is a self' is a mistaken discrimination, a mistaken mind, a mistaken view." [If a person, according to the Pudgalavādins, is not one of these selfless phenomena, how can they say that the view that he is a self is mistaken?] The mistake [they say,] is not [to suppose, as they do,] that a self [or person] is a self, but [to suppose] that what is selfless is a self. [But] they will agree that "the aggregates, the bases of perception and the elements are selfless" [phenomena]; so [if they say that a person is not one of these selfless phenomena,] their earlier claim, that "a person neither is nor is not a visible form," is refuted.[41]

In another sūtra [in their collection] it is said, "Bhikṣus, those śrāmaṇas[42] and brāhmins who think that they perceive a self perceive only the five acquired aggregates." Thus all this is simply clinging to the selfless as a self.

[Finally, in one of the sūtras whose authority they accept] it is also said, "Whosoever has remembered, is remembering, or will remember his previous lives of many different sorts remembers only [the lives of] the five aggregates that have been acquired [as possessions of a self]."

[They reply that] if it were the case [that a person remembers the aggregates of previous lives when he remembers his previous lives,] it would not have been said [by the Buddha, upon recalling one of his past lives, that] "In a previous life I had a visible form."

[However, in saying, "In a previous life I had a visible form," the Buddha was merely following the convention according to which] those who remember past lives of certain kinds remember them in this way. Moreover, if [the Buddha's statement were to imply that] a person possesses a visible form, it would [also] imply [that he himself fell victim to] the mistaken view arising from a collection of perishable aggregates.[43] To avoid this consequence the Pudgalavādins would need to deny the authenticity of the passage [that occurs in their own collection of sūtras.]

Therefore, the person [mentioned in this passage] is real by way of a conception in the way a heap, [which is nothing but its parts as a collection,] and a stream, [which is nothing but its parts as a collection in a causal continuum], and other such things, are real by way of a conception.[44]

Section 3

Vasubandhu's replies to the objections of the Pudgalavādins

3.1 How, if we are the same in existence as collections of aggregates, a Buddha can be omniscient

[The Pudgalavādins object that] if this [view, that a person is like a stream, and is nothing but his parts as a collection in a causal continuum,] were correct, then the Buddha could not be omniscient. [They say that the Buddha's omniscience would then be the omniscience of a mind with its mental factors; and] because a mind with its mental factors[45] is momentary, it cannot know all things [unless it can know all things at once, and the Buddha rejected this view. They say that since the Buddha is] a person, [he] may [be said to] know all things [without implying that he knows everything all at once].

However, this [objection] commits them to the view that a person is permanent, since he does not perish when a mind [within the continuum of aggregates called a person] perishes.

We do not, of course, say that the Buddha is omniscient in the sense that he knows all things at one time, but in the sense that the Buddha, as a continuous series [of consciousnesses], can know, without error, anything he wants [to know] merely by directing his attention to it. And so it was said, "Just as a fire is thought to [be able to] consume all things one after another because there is [within its continuum] this capacity, so [the Buddha's] omniscience is asserted because there is [within his continuum the capacity for] knowledge of all things one after another."

It is known [that omniscience belongs to a continuum of consciousnesses, rather than to an inexplicable person,] because it was said, "The Buddhas of the past and the future, as well as the present Buddha, destroy the sufferings of the many." As they themselves claim, the aggregates exist [as causally conditioned phenomena] in the three times and a person does not.

3.2 Why, if we are the same in existence as collections of aggregates, we are said to be bearers of the burden

[The Pudgalavādins object that] a person cannot merely be the aggregates, since the Buddha would not have said, [in explanation of the problem of suffering and its solution,] "Bhikṣus, I will explain to you the burden, the taking up of the burden, the casting off of the burden, and what bears it." It is not reasonable, [they object,] that the burden be the same as its bearer, since the two are commonly recognized not to be the same.

But [if this objection is sound, we may infer that] it is also not reasonable that the inexplicable [phenomenon the Pudgalavādins call a person] exists, since it is commonly recognized not to exist. Moreover, [if the burden is not its bearer,] it follows that the taking up of the burden would not be included [by the Buddha, as we both agree it is, under the name, "grasping at existence,"] in the aggregates. [For if the burden not be its own bearer, the taking up of the burden would be part of the bearer of the burden rather than part of the burden.]

The Bhagavān spoke of the bearer of the burden with the intention that just this much should be understood: [that reference to it is a verbal convention, just as reference to a person is, when it is said, for instance, that] "he is venerable, has a certain name . . . lives for a while or for a long time, and lives to a certain age."[46] But it should not be understood to be permanent or inexplicable. Since the aggregates cause harm to themselves, the earlier are called a burden [to the later] and the later the bearer of the burden, since "burden" means "harm."[47]

3.3 Why, although we are not inexplicable phenomena, the denial of our spontaneous birth was said to be a mistaken view

[The Pudgalavādins also assert that it cannot be denied that] the [inexplicable] person really exists because [only an inexplicable person can be spontaneously born in another world, and in the sūtras] the view, "No sentient being can be spontaneously born [in another world]," was said to be mistaken. [What was said, they believe, shows that the denial of the existence of an inexplicable person is also a mistaken view.]

But this [inexplicable person with whom they identify a] sentient being is not [being said to be] spontaneously born. In the sūtra, *On What a Human Being Is*, the Bhagavān analyzed a sentient being [into aggregates in a causal continuum]. Someone denied that the aggregates in a causal continuum called a sentient being are spontaneously born in another world, and because aggregates are spontaneously born [in another world] this belief was declared to be false.

[Furthermore,] the denial of the existence of the [inexplicable] person is not a mistaken view, since it is not [a view that is] abandoned [on the paths of insight and meditation]. It is not reasonable [to assert] that this view is abandoned by insight and meditation, since the [inexplicable] person is not included among the realities [known to exist on these paths].

3.4 Why, if we are the same in existence as collections of aggregates, did the Buddha say that he is one person born into the world for the welfare of the many?

[They object that] a person is not aggregates because [in a sūtra] it is said [by the Buddha, in reference to himself], "One person is born into the world [for the welfare of the many]."[48] [The use of "one person" shows that the Buddha does not mean to refer to his aggregates.]

3.4.1 *We reply that the use of "one" in the passage is figurative*

[But in this passage the term,] "one," is applied figuratively[49] to a collection [of aggregates], just as [it is applied only figuratively to collections of elements when used in the expressions] "one sesame seed," "one grain of rice," "one heap," and "one word."

3.4.2 *And that the Pudgalavādins cannot explain the Buddha's reference in the passage to his birth*

Moreover, [if they accept this passage as a statement of doctrine that requires no interpretation,] they must, [contrary to their own view,] also admit that a person is [a] causally conditioned [phenomenon], since they will have agreed that he is born.

[They object that when it is said that a person is] born, [it is] not [meant that a person is born] in the way aggregates come to be, since a person does not come to be again after having ceased to be in the previous moment. A person is said to come to be, [they claim,] because different aggregates are acquired in the way, for instance, that a priest or a grammarian comes to be because knowledge is acquired, a monk or wanderer comes to be because the appropriate mark is acquired, or an old or diseased person comes to be because a different bodily condition is acquired.

But this [objection] is unacceptable, since it is contradicted by the Bhagavān in the sūtra, *Ultimate Emptiness*, in which he said, "Oh bhikṣus, there is action and its maturation, but no agent is perceived that casts off one set of aggregates and takes up another elsewhere apart from the phenomena agreed upon [by us to arise dependently]."[50] And since in the *Phālguna Sūtra*, it is said, "Oh Phālguna, I do not speak of [a person] acquiring [or casting off different aggregates]," there is nothing that acquires or casts them off.

Moreover, in these examples, to what are the Pudgalavādins referring when they speak of a priest [or grammarian, monk, or wanderer, and an old] or diseased person? [Each of the examples to which they refer must either be a person, a mind with its mental factors, or a body.] They cannot be referring to the [inexplicable] person, whose existence is not established;

nor to a mind with its mental factors, which come to be anew [each moment]; nor to a body, which also comes to be anew [each moment].

In addition, the aggregates would then be other than a person in the way that [the aforementioned] knowledge, appropriate mark, and bodily condition are other [than that from which they come to be]. And [we both believe, for instance, that] an old or diseased body is other than the body [before it comes to be old or diseased], since we have [both] rejected the Sāṃkhya's doctrine of [causality, according to which what comes to be is a] transformation [of that from which it comes to be, and thus is not other than that from which it comes to be]. So these are poor examples.

When [they claim that] the aggregates come to be anew [each moment] but a person does not, they have clearly shown, [contrary to their theory,] not only that a person is other than aggregates, but also that he is permanent.

3.4.3 *And if they reject our theory because we are one and aggregates are many, they must say that we are other than collections of aggregates*

[Finally,] if it is said that [a person is not aggregates because] there is one person and five aggregates, why is it not said that a person is other than aggregates?

[It may be replied that it is not said that a person is other than the aggregates, even though a person is one and the aggregates are five, since even Buddhadeva says[51] that] there is one visible form and four [primary] elements [that are its underlying support], even though the visible form is not other than these elements.

However, the thesis that a visible form is nothing but the four [primary] elements is a distortion [of the Buddha's teachings, according to which the four primary elements are separate substances,] and it is not accepted [by anyone except Buddhadeva. In any case, if the Pudgalavādins themselves should accept the thesis,] they must then also admit that just as a visible form is nothing but the [four primary] elements, a person, [contrary to their own theory,] is nothing but the aggregates.

3.5 Why, although we are the same in existence as aggregates as a collection, the Buddha did not answer the question of whether we are or are not other than our bodies

[They cannot object that] if a person were nothing but aggregates, the Bhagavān would have settled the question of whether an individual [or person] is or is not other than the body. [For he did not answer this question because] he took into consideration the questioner's intention [in asking the question]. The person who asked the question thought he was asking it about an individual that is one and is substantially real, namely, about a soul present within [the body]. Since an individual of this sort [does not exist, and so,] is not present in anything whatsoever, the Bhagavān declined to answer that it is or is not other [than the body]. To answer this question would be like answering the question of whether the hairs on a tortoise are hard or soft.

This knot has been untied by others before us. King Milinda[52] approached the Elder, Nāgasena, and said, "I would like to ask you a question, Venerable One. I know that śrāmaṇas like to talk a lot, [but] could you answer the very question I will ask?" "Ask your question," the Elder replied. And then he asked, "Is an individual this body [in which it is said to be present], or is it one thing and the body another?" The Elder replied, "This question cannot be answered." The king said, "But Venerable One, did you not promise a moment ago to answer the very question asked? Why then did you reply that the question cannot be answered?"

The Elder said, "I would like to ask you a question, great king. [I know that] kings like to talk a lot, [but] could you answer the very question I will ask?" "Ask your question," the king said. And so he asked, "Is the fruit on the mango tree in your inner court sour or sweet?" He replied, "There is no mango [tree] in my inner court." "But great king, did you not promise me a moment ago to answer the very question asked? Why then did you say that there is no mango tree?" The king said, "How can I answer that the fruit is sour or sweet if the mango tree does not exist?" The Elder replied, "Since, in the same way, great king, an individual does not exist, how can I answer that it is or is not other than its body?"

3.5.1 *Why, although the Buddha believed that persons of the sort the questioner was asking about do not exist, he did not answer the question by saying that they do not exist*

[They object that] the Bhagavān would have said that the individual [the questioner had in mind] does not exist [if it did not exist].

[We reply that] the Bhagavān [did not give this answer because he] took into consideration the intention of the questioner [in asking the question]. [If] the questioner, who was ignorant of the dependent arising of aggregates [on the basis of which the existence of the individual is asserted, were told that the individual does not exist, he] would have embraced the mistaken view that the continuum of aggregates called an individual does not exist, [since he would have adopted the extreme view that there is no individual at all,] and he was not capable of understanding the teachings on the dependent arising [of aggregates on the basis of which this nihilism extreme is avoided].

[That the Buddha did not want to mislead the questioner in] this [way] is made clear by the Bhagavān [himself], who said, "Oh Ānanda, when

Vatsagotra, the wandering ascetic, asked me [whether or not a self exists], would it not have been improper to reply that it does? [For] all phenomena are selfless. And would not Vatsagotra, the wandering ascetic, who was already confused, have become even more confused if I had replied that a self does not exist? [For] he would have then once thought that a self existed, and now [that a self] does not [exist]. Oh Ānanda, the belief that a self exists is the extreme of eternal transcendence, and the belief that a self does not exist is the extreme of nihilism."

And it has also been taught,[53] "The Jinas, who are aware of the wounds made by the teeth of mistaken views and by the abandonment of [virtuous] actions [and their results], teach the doctrine [with great care], just as a tigress carries her offsprings [in her teeth neither too tightly nor too loosely so they might not fall]. For one who accepts the existence of a self is pierced by the teeth of mistaken views and one who does not accept its conventional reality abandons the virtuous offsprings [that are its actions and their results]."[54]

Again, it was taught, "Because an individual does not exist, the Bhagavān did not say that it is the same as or other than [the body]. Nor did he say that an individual does not exist, lest [someone think that] it does not even exist by way of a conception. For the presence of [the aggregates that are the] good and bad results [of actions] in the continuum of aggregates is called an individual, and because he taught that an individual does not exist, [someone could think that he taught the view that] these results would not exist there. Nor did he teach anyone incapable of understanding emptiness that an individual is a mere conception for the aggregates. Likewise, he did not say, when questioned by Vatsagotra,[55] that a self does or does not exist, since he took into consideration the intention of the questioner [in answering the question]. Moreover, if a self exists, he would have said so."

3.5.2 *The Buddha also left unanswered the remainder of the fourteen questions because he took into consideration a false assumption of the questioner*

The Bhagavān also took into consideration the intention of the questioner [in asking the question] when he declined to say whether the world [of persons] is eternal, [not eternal, both, or neither. For the questioner would have equated the world of persons either with the totality of all selves or with the collections of aggregates that comprise the whole of saṃsāra, and] if he were to equate the world [of persons] with [a world in which a person is] a self, it would not be proper to answer with the four [that the world of persons is, is not, both is and is not, or neither is nor is not, eternal,] since a self does not exist. But if he were to equate the world [of persons] with [the collections of aggregates that comprise] the whole of saṃsāra, any one of these answers would again be improper. For if the world [of persons] were eternal, none [of the persons in it] could achieve the final nirvāṇa, and if it were not eternal, the whole [of saṃsāra] could cease [at some point, and all persons would effortlessly achieve the final nirvāṇa]. If the world [of persons] were both eternal [in some of its parts] and not eternal [in others], then some [persons] could [effortlessly] achieve the final nirvāṇa, and others could not achieve it at all. If the world [of persons] were neither eternal nor not eternal, then [since it could not exist,] there neither is nor is not a final nirvāṇa [for any person at all].

Thus, [it should be clear that] the question is not answered in any of these four ways because the final nirvāṇa depends upon [making an effort to traverse] the paths. This case is like that of the naked Jain mendicant and the sparrow. [When the mendicant asked the Buddha whether or not the sparrow he was holding in his hand behind his back is alive, the Buddha did not answer, since the bird's life depended upon the mendicant's decision to squeeze it to death if the Buddha answered that it is alive, and to spare its life if the Buddha said that it is dead].[56]

For the same reason, the Bhagavān did not answer the question of whether the world [of persons] does, [does not, both does and does not, or neither does nor does not,] come to an end. This four-part question has the same meaning [as the first]. For after the wanderer, Muktika, asked the same four-part question, [and was given the same response,] he again asked, "Will the whole world [of persons] or only a part of it be liberated by [making an effort to traverse] this path?" The Elder, Ānanda, said, "Muktika, you are now asking in a different way the very question you first asked the Bhagavān."

The question of whether the Tathāgata, does, [does not, both does and does not, or neither does nor does not,] exist after death was also not answered because the intention of the questioner was taken into consideration [in asking the question]. For the questioner assumed that the Tathāgata was a liberated self.

3.5.3 *The Pudgalavādins cannot account for the Buddha's silence about his existence after death*

The Pudgalavādins must explain why the Bhagavān said [in some circumstances] that a person, when alive, exists, but did not say, [when asked, with reference to himself, whether a person does, does not, both does and does not, or neither does nor does not, exist after death,] that a person exists after death. [They claim that the Bhagavān did not answer, when asked this question, that a person exists after death, because] the fault of [accepting] the eternal transcendence theory [of persons] is its consequence. [But if the Bhagavān's acceptance of the eternal transcendence theory of persons is a consequence of saying that a person exists after death,] he would not have said, "Maitreya, you will someday become an Arhat, a Tathāgata, and a Samyaksaṃbuddha."[57] Nor would he have said, about a disciple who had died, that in the past he was reborn in such and such a place. For in these cases also the eternal transcendence theory [of persons] would be a consequence.

3.5.3.1 *It is because the Buddha is omniscient that he did not answer the question about his existence after death*

If the Bhagavān has knowledge of [the existence of] a person before the person's final nirvāṇa, but not afterwards, he would not answer the question [of whether he does, does not, both does and does not, or neither does nor does not, exist after his final nirvāṇa] because he did not know its answer. Hence, [we must say either that] the teacher [did not answer the question because he] lacks omniscience, [which is heretical,] or [because] the person [about whom the questioner asked] does not exist. But if the Bhagavān has knowledge of the existence of the person [after his final nirvāṇa] and did not answer [this question], the eternal transcendence theory [of persons] would have been established [as true]. [But this theory is rejected by the Bhagavān. Hence, the only possible explanation of the Buddha not answering the question is that he knew that the person about whose existence after his final nirvāṇa the questioner was asking does not exist.]

Should they reply that it is not explicable that he does or does not know [that a person exists after the person's final nirvāṇa], then, in the same way, to say this they would have to say that the Bhagavān neither is nor is not omniscient, and it is to be said very quietly [because it is heretical].

3.6 Why, although we are not inexplicable phenomena, the Buddha declared false the denial of our existence

[The Pudgalavādins say that] the [inexplicable] person really exists because it is declared [in a sūtra] that "I am not in reality an enduring self" is a mistaken view.

But since [in the sūtras] the belief that a person exists is [also] said to be false, their claim is inadmissible. The Abhidharmikas[58] say that these mistaken views are, respectively, the extremes [called] the nihilism view and the eternal transcendence view. Their claim is quite reasonable, since in the *Vatsa Sūtra*, it is said, "Oh Ānanda, to claim that a self exists is to go to [the extreme of] eternal transcendence and to claim that it does not exist is to go to [the extreme of] nihilism."

3.7 How, even though we are not inexplicable phenomena, we wander in saṃsāra

[The Pudgalavādins object that] if the [inexplicable] person does not exist, there is nothing that wanders in saṃsāra. [They add that] saṃsāra itself, [which is nothing but a beginningless continuum of contaminated aggregates,] cannot wander in saṃsāra, and [that] the Bhagavān spoke of "sentient beings, obscured by ignorance, wandering in saṃsāra."

But how does the person they believe to exist wander in saṃsāra? It cannot be by taking up and abandoning different aggregates, since we have already replied to this view. On the contrary, just as we say that a momentary fire as a continuum moves about, so we say that the collection of aggregates called a sentient being wanders in saṃsāra on the basis of craving.

3.8 How, if we are the same in existence as collections of aggregates, references to ourselves in past lives are possible

[The Pudgalavādins object that] if a person were merely aggregates, the Bhagavān would not have said, "At that time and place I was the teacher called Sunetra," since the aggregates [of the Bhagavān] would be other than those [of Sunetra].

But it cannot be [to himself as] a person [that the Bhagavān refers], since he would then be committed to the eternal transcendence belief [that a person is a permanent phenomenon]. Therefore, [when the Bhagavān said, "I was the teacher called Sunetra,"] he was referring to a single [causal] continuum [of aggregates in dependence upon which, at one time, Sunetra was conceived, and now, Śakyamuni Buddha is conceived], just as when we say, "This same burning fire has moved" [from here to there, we are referring to a single causal continuum of a combination of elements in dependence upon which, at different times, fire is conceived].

3.9 Why, if we were inexplicable persons, there would be no liberation

[It is clear, therefore, that the Pudgalavādins are committed to the theory that a person is a self. But] if a self were to exist, only the Tathāgatas could clearly know it. And those who could know it would very powerfully cling to a self and become attached to it. Since in a sūtra it says, "When there is a self, there are things possessed by a self," their clinging to a self would also involve taking up the aggregates [as possessions of a self], and they would thus possess the mistaken view arising from a collection of perishable aggregates. And when there is the mistaken view of things possessed by a self, there is attachment to the things possessed by a self. Those who are fettered by strong attachment to a self and to the things possessed by a self are very far from liberation.

If the [Pudgalavādins'] view is that there is no attachment to a self, [but only to what appears to be, but is not, a self,] why should there be an attachment to what is not a self because it is believed to be a self unless there is an attachment to the self itself?

3.10 Our theory of persons is the middle way between the extreme theories propounded by the Pudgalavādins and Nāgārjuna

Therefore, a tumor of false theories [concerning the existence of a person] has grown within [the body of] the teaching [of the Buddha]. Some, [the Pudgalavādins,] cling to [the existence of] the [inexplicable] person, [and so accept the eternal transcendence extreme]. Others, [the followers of Nāgārjuna, who deny that the aggregates themselves exist, undermine the only foundation upon which persons can be said to exist. Hence, since they] cling to the non-existence of everything, [they accept the nihilism extreme.[59] Therefore, our view, that a person is real by way of a conception and yet is a collection of aggregates, is the true middle way.][60]

Section 4

Vasubandhu's replies to the objections of the Tīrthikas and objections to their arguments

4.0 Why Tīrthika views must be considered

In addition [to these views] there are [those of] the Tīrthikas, who propound the theory that a self is another substance [in addition to those that comprise the aggregates]. Here, also, the incorrigible fault [of this theory] is that there will be no liberation [for those who accept it].

4.1 How a memory of an object can occur if a self does not exist and minds are momentary phenomena

[Against our theory the Tīrthikas have objected that] if a self does not exist at all and minds [among the aggregates in dependence upon which we conceive a person] are momentary, there can be no memory or recognition of an object experienced in the past.

[This objection, however, is unwarranted, since according to our theory] an object is remembered because immediately before the memory [of it] occurs a special kind of mind arises that is [causally] connected to a [prior] discrimination of the object to be remembered. The special kind of mind after which this memory arises is a mind that is inclined toward the object to be remembered, is attended by a discrimination [of an object] associated with or like the object [to be remembered], and by other things [such as a resolution or a habit], and is not inhibited by grief, distraction, or any other such influence that would change the character of [the aggregates that are] its support.

Even if a mind is of this special sort, it cannot produce a memory of the object unless it is [causally] connected [to a prior discrimination of the object]. And should a mind be so connected, but not be of this special kind, it will not produce the memory. There are only [these] two possibilities. A memory is produced by this special kind of mind when it is [causally] connected to a discrimination of the object, since no other kind of mind is seen to have this power.

4.1.1 *Why this account of how a memory of an object occurs does not imply that one person remembers what another perceives*

[They say that if our account of how a memory of an object occurs is correct, what one mind perceives another mind remembers, and then object that] what one mind perceives another cannot remember, since [in that case, *per impossibile*,] what a mind of Devadatta would perceive, a mind of Yajñadatta could remember.

[However, this example cannot be used to reject our account of how a memory of an object occurs, for] there is no connection [of the appropriate sort between a mind in the continuum of Devadatta and a mind in the continuum of Yajñadatta], since these two minds are not related as cause to effect within one continuum.

Nor do we say [in our account] that one mind remembers what another perceives, but that a mind that remembers [an object] arises from another mind that perceives [it], just as we explained earlier in our discussion of developments within a continuum.[61] So there is no fault [of this sort in our account].

[Since] a recognition arises only from a memory, [our account of how a memory occurs suffices as an account of how a recognition of an object occurs.]

4.2 Why a self is needed neither as an agent of remembering nor as its cause

If a self does not exist, [they ask,] who remembers? [They claim that] what is meant by [saying that someone] "remembers" is [that an agent] "grasps an object [of perception] with [the help of] a memory [of the object]."

But is [an agent] grasping an object [in this case] anything other than [the occurrence of] a memory [in a continuum of consciousnesses? Surely it is not. No separate act of grasping is required, and consequently no self as the agent of this act is required, to explain the occurrence of a memory of an object. If they ask] what produces the memory [of the object if there is no self, we reply that] the producer of a memory, as we have [already] said, is the special kind of mind that causes a memory. Although we say that Caitra remembers, we say this because we perceive a memory that occurs in the continuum [of aggregates] we call Caitra.

4.3 Why a self is needed neither to possess a memory nor to possess a consciousness of an object

If a self does not exist, [they ask,] whose is this memory? [They say that] the meaning of the use of the possessive case [indicated by the use of "whose"] is ownership. It is the owner of a memory in the way that Caitra owns a cow. [In their view,] a cow cannot be used for milking or for carrying anything and so on unless it is owned, [and in the same way, a memory cannot be directed to an object unless it is owned.]

But where [and why] does the owner [of a memory] direct this memory, [the existence of] whose owner they seek in this way [to establish]? [They state that] it is directed [by its owner] to the object to be remembered and [that] it is so directed for the sake of remembering [that object].

But this is really well-said! For this [memory] itself [that is already possessed] must be directed [by its owner to the object to be remembered] for the sake of this [memory, which it already possesses, since the grasping of an object with the help of a memory of an object, as we have said, is nothing but the occurrence of the memory of the object].

And by way of what is a memory directed [to the object to be remembered]? [It must be directed] either by way of [its owner] producing [a memory of the object to be remembered] or by way of [its owner] sending [the memory to the object]. It must be by way of [its owner] producing [the memory], since a memory [that] does not move [cannot be sent to the object to be remembered]. But then an owner [of the memory] is merely its cause and the [memory] owned [by it] is merely an effect [of this cause], since a cause determines [what] its result [will be] and is said to have this [power to determine what its result will be] because of [its possession of] the result. A cause of a memory [is said to own the memory because it] is the cause of this [power to determine its effect].

[In your example,] what is called "Caitra" is called the owner of a cow because we are aware of a single continuum of a collection of [phenomena] causally conditioning [other] phenomena [within the same continuum] and assume a causal connection [of phenomena within this continuum] to the occurrence of changes of place of, and alterations in, [the continuum of the collection of phenomena we call] the cow. But there is no one thing called Caitra or a cow. Therefore, there is, [even in the Tīrthikas' example,] no relation between the owner and what it owns other than that between a cause and its effect.

We should explain, in the same way, what apprehends [an object] and what owns a consciousness, [what feels and what owns a feeling,] and so on. The only difference [in the explanations] is that, [for instance, in the case of an apprehension of an object] the parallel cause of this [effect] is [the presence of] an organ [of perception], an object, and attentiveness.

4.4 The Tīrthikas object that a consciousness of an object is an activity that exists in dependence upon a self

Some [Tīrthikas[62] would deny that we can explain apprehension of an object by reference to the presence of an organ of perception, an object, and attentiveness, since the existence of a self is also required. They] say that every activity [signified by an active verb] exists in dependence upon an agent [signified by a noun to which the active verb is attached],[63] since an activity [signified by an active verb] exists in dependence upon an agent [signified by a noun to which the active verb is attached]. [They argue that,] just as saying that Devadatta walks implies that walking, [which is] an activity [signified by the active verb, *gacchati*], exists in dependence upon Devadatta, a walker, so [saying that a person apprehends an object implies that] a consciousness [(*vijñāna*), which] is an activity [signified by the active verb, *vijānāti*, exists in dependence upon a self, which is the agent signified by a noun to which the active verb is attached]. Therefore, what apprehends[64] [an object] must exist [as a self].

4.4.1 *Their objection fails because their example either assumes that a self exists or it does not show that a self exists*

But what is [the nature of] this Devadatta [to whom they refer in the example]? If he is [assumed by them to be] a self, [how does the use of the example support the belief that there is a self, since] they will be assuming [the truth of] the very thing they seek to establish. If he is [assumed by them to be] what the world calls a man, [the example does not support the belief, since] he is not just one thing, but [a collection of phenomena] causally conditioning [other] phenomena [in the same continuum of the collection] to which this name, ["Devadatta,"] has been given. It is to these [phenomena] that we refer when we say that Devadatta moves or apprehends [an object].

4.5 How, although we are not selves, we can walk and apprehend an object

And how, [the Tīrthikas ask,] can Devadatta walk [if he is not a self]?

The Devadatta of whom common people speak is [a collection of] momentary [phenomena] causally conditioning [other] phenomena in an unbroken [causal] continuum. They grasp [this collection of phenomena] as one thing, a sentient being with a body, and they say that Devadatta walks because they think that they cause their own continua [of bodily aggregates as a collection] to arise in different places [at different times] and call this arising in different places "walking." [So they infer that Devadatta is a cause of the same sort and say that he too "walks."] They attribute change of place in the same way to the continua of [phenomena that as a collection comprise] both flame and sound.

For like reasons they also say that Devadatta apprehends [*vijānāti*], since they think that they cause a consciousness [(*vijñāna*) to arise in their own continua and call this arising "apprehending" an object]. These terms are also used, with their conventional meanings, by the Āryas.

4.6 How a consciousness, though not a self, can be said to apprehend an object

[Even] in [some passages in your own] sūtras, [they object,] a consciousness is said to apprehend [an object]. In such passages, [they ask,] is [not] a consciousness [being said to be a self that is] doing something?

[Although it is said to apprehend an object,] a consciousness does nothing at all. Just as we say that an effect, even though it does nothing, conforms to its cause because it receives a form like that of its cause, in the same way we say that a consciousness, even though it does nothing, apprehends an object because it receives a form like that of its cause. There is conformity [between the consciousness and the object of perception rather than between the consciousness and the organ of perception] because of the discernible form possessed [by the object]. Since the form a consciousness receives is the discernible form [of the object], the consciousness that arises because of an organ [of perception] is said to apprehend the object rather than to apprehend the organ.

[From another point of view,] there may be no fault [in the implication that a consciousness is an agent] when we say that a consciousness apprehends [an object], since in a continuum of consciousnesses a consciousness is a cause of a consciousness [that appears in the next moment], and its cause is [by some] called an agent. Similarly, [there may be no fault in the implication that a ring of a bell is an agent of a ring] when we say that a bell rings, [since in the continuum of its ringing a ring in one moment is a cause of a ring in the next, and its cause is by some called an agent.]

We might also say that a consciousness apprehends [an object] similar to the way in which a flame [of a butter lamp] moves. We figuratively apply the term, "flame [of a butterlamp]," to the continuum of flames and say that the flame moves to another place when a flame [at a later moment in its continuum] arises in another place. In the same way, we figuratively apply the expression, "a consciousness," to the continuum of consciousnesses, and say that a consciousness apprehends an object when an apprehension of a different object arises [at a later moment in the continuum].

And just as we can say that a bodily form arises and endures without implying that there is an agent apart from this [arising and enduring], so we can say this of a consciousness [that apprehends an object without implying that there is an agent apart from the consciousness that apprehends the object].

4.7 How, without a self, different kinds of mental phenomena can arise in the same continuum

[Some Tīrthikas[65] have objected that] if a consciousness arises not because of a self, but from a consciousness [that immediately precedes it in the same continuum], either exactly the same [kinds of] consciousnesses will always arise or different [kinds of] consciousnesses will [always] arise in a fixed order in the way, for instance, that a leaf arises from a stem and the stem from a sprout.

But [neither the same kinds of consciousnesses nor different kinds of consciousnesses in the same order always arise, since consciousnesses are causally conditioned phenomena and] it is a defining characteristic of causally conditioned phenomena to be different [in kind from moment to moment]. For if it were not the nature of causally conditioned phenomena necessarily to differ [in kind from moment to moment], then if we should achieve a perfect meditational equipoise, both body and mind would be the same [from moment to moment] and we could not emerge from it by ourselves, since there would be no difference between the first and last moment [of the meditational equipoise by reason of which we would emerge from the meditation after the last moment].

Moreover, there is a fixed order in the sequence of [kinds of] minds [that arise in the same continuum, but the order of the sequence is not so rigidly fixed as that of sprout–stem–leaf]. One [kind of] mind, [of course,] arises from another [of the kind] from which it is to arise, [yet] minds of the same kind can produce [different kinds of minds] because of different [kinds of] impressions [that may be present in different continua]. For instance, suppose that the idea of a woman arises [in the mental continuum of a bhikṣu and in the mental continuum of a lay person], and then immediately afterward there arises [in the bhikṣu's mental continuum] a repulsion to her body and [in the lay person's mental continuum] the idea of her husband and son. In these cases, if at a later time in the changing [mental] continuum [of the bhikṣu or lay person] there arises the idea of the woman, it can give arise, [in the case of the bhikṣu,] to a repulsion to her body, or [in the case of the lay person,] to the idea of her husband and son because of [the different kinds of] impressions [present in their mental continua]. Otherwise, [without different kinds of impressions of these sorts,] minds [of the same kind] could not [give rise to different kinds of minds].

Alternatively, [we may say that] although the idea of the woman may give rise to many different kinds of minds in different cases in succession, only those [kinds of] minds arise that, [in their association with the idea of the woman,] are very common, [very intense,[66]] or recent, since the impressions [produced by these means] are more powerful [than impressions produced by less common, intense, or recent associations]. The exception [to the rule] occurs when there is present a special bodily condition, [such as receiving a painful blow to the body,] or a special external condition, [such as encountering one's son, that inhibits the production of the mind associated in one of these ways with the idea of the woman.][67] This more powerful impression does not continually produce its [characteristic] result because [impressions are causally conditioned phenomena, and] it is a defining characteristic of causally conditioned phenomena to differ [in kind from moment to moment] and this difference favors a [different kind of] result to be produced [in the continuum of minds] from a different [kind of] impression.

This is just an indication of what can be known of all the workings of minds. A complete knowledge of the causes [of minds of different kinds] is the domain of the Buddhas. Thus it was said [by the Elder, Rāhula,[68]] that "Without omniscience we cannot know the great variety of causes of a single eye in a peacock's tail, [but] the Omniscient One can know this." How much more then [are we ignorant of the great variety of causes of] the different kinds of minds, which lack bodily form!

4.7.1 *Why certain Tīrthikas cannot explain how minds of different kinds arise from a self*

The above objection may be leveled against those Tīrthikas[69] who maintain that a mind arises from a self. For from [this view and] their view [that both a self and the internal organ are permanent] it follows that exactly the same [kinds of] minds will always arise or that different [kinds of] minds will [always] arise in a fixed order in the way, for instance, that a leaf arises from a stem and the stem from a sprout.

If [they say that exactly the same kinds of minds do not always arise] because [different kinds of minds arise from a self] in dependence upon [a self] being conjoined in different ways with an internal organ, [we object that a self and an internal organ, both of which are permanent, cannot be conjoined in different ways unless the conjunction between them is something other than them. But] they have not at all proved that a conjunction [between them exists that] is other [than the things conjoined]. Moreover, because two things that are conjoined are [in] separate [places] and they define conjunction as contact between things not previously in contact,[70] a self [and an internal organ] must be [in] separate [places, contrary to their theses that a self pervades the body and that an internal organ is present in the body]. And [consequently,] when the internal organ moves [from one place to another], a self either moves [out of its way], or it perishes, [since things that can exist in separate places cannot exist in the same place. This result is contrary to their view that a self is immovable and imperishable.]

Nor [can they say, in order to avoid these objections, that a different kind of mind arises from a self when an internal organ is] conjoined with a [different] part [of a self], since they do not admit that a self has parts. And even if there could be a conjunction [with a part of the self], how could the conjunction be different, since [the parts of the self are not different, and in their view] an internal organ is never different?

If they say [that the conjunction must be different] because a cognition [that] is different [in kind is produced by it], they must still face the same objection we raised earlier. How will these cognitions be different [in kind if they arise from a self and an internal organ that are permanent]?

If they say [that these cognitions will be different in kind] because between a self and an internal organ a conjunction arises under the influence of different [kinds of] impressions,[71] why not let these [different kinds of cognitions] arise from minds alone, [without a conjunction of a self and an internal organ,] under the influence of different sorts of impressions? For we do not at all perceive a power of a self [to produce different kinds of cognitions]. A self's power [to produce different kinds of cognitions] would be like the power of "*phūḥ svāha*" uttered by a charlatan [to cure someone] when in fact the effect [he claims that it produces] is produced by medicine.

Their claim that neither [minds nor impressions] can exist, unless a self exists, is mere words. They state that a self [must exist if they do, since it] is their underlying support. But it cannot be their underlying support in the way that a wall is an underlying support of a picture or a bowl is an underlying support of a piece of badara fruit, for it does not offer physical resistance to them or have a separate place.

If [it should be said that] it is an underlying support of them in the way earth is an underlying support of [its] odors and other sensible qualities,[72] we shall gladly accept the view, since we maintain that a self is not other [than minds and impressions] in just the way that earth is not other than [its] odors and other sensible qualities. For who could possibly discern earth that is other than [its] odors and other sensible qualities?

[It cannot be replied that if earth were not other than its odors and other sensible qualities, we would not distinguish it from them by saying that they are possessed by earth. For] we [do not] say that odors and other sensible qualities are possessed by earth [because earth is other than them, but] so that we can make a distinction [between the sensible qualities that comprise earth and the sensible qualities that comprise things such as fire]. For these very odors and other sensible qualities are called earth so that we can become conscious of them rather than conscious of [the odors and other sensible qualities that comprise] other things [such as fire]. In the same way, we say that a body is possessed by a wooden statue [when we wish to distinguish it, for instance, from the body of a baked clay statue, not because the wooden statue is other than its body, since the body possessed by the wooden statue, the Tīrthikas must agree, is not other than the wooden statue].

And if [they say that when the self is conjoined with an internal organ different kinds of cognitions arise from a self because the self is] under the influence of different kinds of impressions, why do not all [of the different kinds of] cognitions arise simultaneously? [For a permanent self would produce all of the cognitions for which the different kinds of impressions are present, and all of the different kinds of impressions are present.]

They cannot say that a stronger [impression] blocks [the influence of] the others [and so prevents the simultaneous arising of all of the different kinds of cognitions], for [from their theory it follows that] this stronger impression must then always produce its [own kind of] result [to the exclusion of any others].

Nor can they argue [that the stronger impression does not always produce its own kind of result because] it is the nature of impressions [to differ from moment to moment], as we argued [above, that stronger impressions do not always produce their own kinds of results because it is the nature of impressions to differ from moment to moment,[73] since] a self as conceived by them would be without a [causal] function [in the production of different kinds of cognitions].

4.8 Why a self is not needed as an underlying support of mental attributes

[The Tīrthikas say that] there must be a self, since a memory and other forms of cognition are attributes, attributes are in substances, and attributes [of this sort] cannot be in anything else [than the substance, a self].

However, the existence of attributes of this sort has yet to be established. In our theory, everything that exists is a substance, for it has been said, "The fruits of religious practice are [five uncontaminated aggregates and nirvāṇa,[74] which are] six kinds of substances." Nor can anyone prove that these [attributes, such as a memory and other forms of cognition,] are in a substance, since the notion of an underlying support of them has already been subjected to analysis [and rejected].[75] Therefore, nothing has changed.

4.9 How, without a self, there can be a reason to undertake an action, and why the object of the mind that conceives an "I" is known to be the same in existence as a collection of aggregates

[The Tīrthikas say that] if there is no self, there is no reason to undertake an action, [since an action is undertaken out of self-interest.]

[We agree that] the reason an action is undertaken is [expressed] in this way, "I would be happy and not suffer [if I should undertake this action]," but the "I" [to which we refer in this case] is the object of the mind that conceives an "I,"[76] and this object is the aggregates [as a collection].

The object of the mind that conceives an "I" [in this case] is known to be the aggregates because [an action undertaken out of self-interest arises from attachment to the object of the mind that conceives an "I" and] it is to the aggregates that we are [in fact] very attached, and [this object is not a self] because, when we conceive [the "I" as] fair-skinned, and so on, the subject [of the attributes of being fair-skinned, and so on,] is the same [as the object of the mind that conceives an "I." Thus, since we say,] "I am fair-skinned," "I am dark-skinned," "I am fat," "I am thin," "I am old," and "I am young," it is clear to us that, when we conceive [the "I" as] fair-skinned, and so on, the subject of these [attributes] is the same as this [object of the] mind that conceives an "I." These attributes are not recognized [by the Tīrthikas] to belong to a self. Therefore, it is known that this [mind that conceives an "I"] pertains to the aggregates.

4.9.1 *Why these Tīrthikas fail to explain away our ascriptions of the attributes of the body to ourselves*

[The Tīrthikas reject our counter-examples by saying that although "I" is in fact] a name for a self, [in "I am fair-skinned," and so on, it] is applied figuratively to a body that acts on its behalf [as its servant]. Similarly, [they maintain, "I" is figuratively applied by a master to a servant when he says,] "My servant is I myself [when he acts on my behalf]."

But [their objection fails. For] even if a name for a self is applied figuratively to what acts on its behalf, [it is] not [applied to the object of] the mind that conceives an "I."[77]

4.9.2 *How, without assuming that "I" is figuratively applied by a self to the body that acts on its behalf, we explain that the bodies of others are not objective supports for the minds that conceive an "I"*

[They object that] if the mind that conceives an "I" has [only] a body as an objective support, how is it to be explained that a body that is other [than one's own body] is not its objective support? [Must not the body belong to the very self that figuratively applies "I" to it?][78]

[But we can explain this,] since [we say that between the body of another person and the mind that conceives an "I"] there is no connection [on the basis of which the body becomes its objective support]. This mind that conceives an "I" arises only within [the continuum of] a body and mind related to it, and not elsewhere, since it is [the result of] a habit that exists in [the] beginningless saṃsāra [of that particular continuum]. The connection [in question] is that of cause to effect.

4.10 How, without a self to possess it, there can be a mind that conceives an "I"

[They say that] if there is no self, there is nothing to which the mind that conceives an "I" belongs [and without belonging to something it cannot exist]. [But] this question was already settled when we argued that there need be no self to which a memory belongs [in order to exist] because a memory has a cause other than a self.[79] The cause [of the mind that conceives an "I"] that is other [than a self] is a contaminated mind that has as its object its own continuum and is conditioned by a previous mind that conceives an "I" [in that same continuum].

4.11 How, without a self, there is an underlying support of feelings that come to be

[The Tīrthikas say that] if there is no self, there is no underlying support in which pleasure and pain come to be. [We reply that] there is an underlying support in which pleasure and pain come to be. They come to be in an underlying support in the way that flowers come to be in a tree and fruits come to be in a garden, [which are, as the underlying supports in which they come to be, merely collections of entities, not individual substances.] The underlying support [of pleasure and pain], as we have explained,[80] are the six bases of perception [that we call the organs of perception].

4.12 These Tīrthikas say that without a self there is no agent of actions or subject that experiences their results

[The Tīrthikas say that] without a self there can be no agent that performs actions or subject that experiences their results. But what is actually meant by "agent" [and "subject"] in this case? It cannot simply be said that an agent is what acts and a subject is what experiences a result [of actions], since these are synonyms rather than real meanings [of the expressions].

[They answer our question about the meaning of "agent" by saying that] the Lakṣaṇikas[81] [correctly] define an agent as [a causally] independent[82] [cause. So the reason there can be no agent without a self is that an agent, unlike other causes, is a causally independent cause and only a self is a causally independent cause. Moreover, they claim, we know that an agent is causally independent, since] the world recognizes that [causal] independence of this sort exists in relation to its various effects [when], for instance, [it recognizes that] Devadatta [exists] in relation to his bathing, eating, walking, and so on.[83]

4.12.1 *Why we need not accept their view that a self is needed as an agent of actions*

But in this example [of what the world recognizes], the term, "Devadatta," cannot [be assumed to] refer to a self, whose existence is at issue; and if it refers to the five aggregates, the aggregates become the only agent [of actions. Therefore, the Tīrthikas cannot support their thesis that a self exists by the above appeal to what the world recognizes about Devadatta.]

[Moreover, we can explain how actions arise without reference to a self. For] the three kinds of actions [that would be its effects] are those of body, speech, and mind. And among these, actions of body, first of all, are dependent upon an action of mind, and an action of mind that gives rise to the actions of body is dependent upon its own cause, [a prior mind that itself arises in dependence upon its causes, and so on. Actions of speech are also dependent in the same way upon an action of mind, which is dependent upon its own causally conditioned cause, and so on.] Since even an action of mind is dependent in this way [on its own causally conditioned cause], there is no [causal] independence among any of these [causes of actions of body, speech, or mind]. For all things, [including causes,] arise in dependence upon causal conditions.

Nor is the [existence of the causal] independence of a self that is [defined as a causally] independent [cause] established, since its causality cannot be assumed.[84] Therefore, the existence of an agent so defined is not established.[85]

But should the cause [of an action of body, for instance,] be called an agent, then since we do not at all perceive a self that is [such] a cause, a self is not even an agent in this sense. A self contributes nothing to the arising of an action [of body], for from a memory [of an object] a desire [to obtain the object] arises, [and this desire is the principal cause of an action of body. For] from this desire in turn arises a consideration [of how to satisfy the desire], and from this consideration there arises first an effort of the mind [to move the body for the sake of satisfying the desire], then [a movement in the] wind [channels], and [from this movement there arises,] finally, an action [of body].

4.12.2 *Why we need not accept their view that a self is needed as a subject that experiences the results of action*

[Nor is a self needed as a subject that experiences the result of actions, for] in what would a self's experience of the result consist? [They say that it consists in] a perception [of the result]; but that a self possesses a consciousness by means of which it perceives [anything] we have already refuted.[86]

4.13 Why the absence of a self is not needed to explain why beings not in saṃsāra do not accumulate merit and demerit

If there is no self, [they object, beings in saṃsāra do not exist. So if the existence of a self is denied and beings accumulate merit and demerit,] why don't beings not in saṃsāra accumulate merit and demerit?

[Our reply is that] beings not in saṃsāra [do not accumulate merit and demerit because they] lack an underlying support of the feelings [required in beings that accumulate merit and demerit]. The underlying support of them, as already stated, is the six [internal] bases of perception.[87]

4.14 How, even though a self does not exist, an action produces its result

[The Tīrthikas ask] how, if there is no self, can an action that no longer exists produce a result in the future? [Before we answer this question, however, let us ask, in turn,] how, if there is a self, can an action that no longer exists produce a result in the future? [They answer that it can produce a result in the future] because a self is an underlying support of the merit or demerit [produced by the action and directly causes the result]. But we have already pointed out that a self cannot be an underlying support of it.[88] Therefore, [since a result is produced and there is no self that provides an underlying support of merit or demerit,] it must be produced from the merit or demerit without an underlying support of it!

[Our answer to their question is that] we do not say that an action that no longer exists can produce a result in the future. [We say that] a result arises from an action because of a special development in the continuum of the action. In the same way, a fruit [arises] from a seed. We say that a fruit arises from a seed, but not that it arises from a seed that no longer exists or that a fruit arises immediately from the seed itself. A fruit arises from a seed because a special development arises in the continuum of the seed: a seed produces a sprout, a sprout a stem, a stem leaves, and leaves a flower, [which is the special development that produces the fruit]. Although a fruit arises from a flower, we say that it arises from a seed because the seed has indirectly transmitted to the flower the power [to produce the fruit]. For if the flower would not have obtained this power from the seed, it could not have produced a fruit of the same sort [as the fruit that produced the seed itself].

Similarly, we say that a result arises from an action, but not that it arises from an action that no longer exists or that a result arises directly from the action itself. A result arises from an action because a special development arises in the continuum of the action. This continuum is the occurrence of a sequence of minds that arises from the prior action, and a development in it is the production of a mind of a different character [from moment to moment]. Since [the mind with] the power to produce the result in the next moment is distinguished as the last development [in the production of the result], it is [called] the special development [in the continuum of an action].

For instance, at [the moment of] death a mind burdened with attachment has the power to produce a new life. [This mind is a special development in the continuum of a prior action.] Among the various kinds[89] of prior actions [with the power to produce a new life], the powers of the weighty, the recent, and the habitual [to produce a new life] dominate those of other kinds. Thus it has been said[90] that "Among actions [that produce rebirth] in saṃsāra, those that are weighty produce their results first, then those that are recent, those that are habitual, and finally those performed at an earlier time." The power of these actions to produce effects that require maturation is lost when they produce them.

[Effects that do not require maturation, but follow immediately upon their own causes, are themselves causes of effects like themselves. These effects may be afflicted or unafflicted.] The power of an afflicted [mind] to produce effects that are like itself [afflicted] is lost [when the afflictions are destroyed] by the antidotes [to the afflictions]. The power of an unafflicted [mind to produce effects like itself] is lost when final nirvāṇa is achieved, since [at that time] the continuum of minds is totally extinguished.

4.14.1 *Why another effect that requires maturation does not arise again from an effect that requires maturation*

[The Tīrthikas object that if a result arises from an action in the way a fruit arises from a seed] why doesn't another effect that requires maturation arise from an effect that requires maturation in the way that another fruit arises from a fruit as [from] a seed?[91]

In the first place, [it needs to be pointed out that] not everything [called an effect that requires maturation] is like the example [of a fruit, since not all effects that require maturation produce further effects that require maturation]. And even in this example another fruit does not arise again from a fruit [as from a seed], but from a special development [in the continuum of the fruit] produced by a special [sort of] decay. For this [development] is the [actual] seed that produces a sprout, [and so on, until another fruit is produced], not the other [so-called seed, which is in fact the fruit in whose continuum the actual cause of the next fruit appears]. The continuum [of the fruit] that [is called a seed and] precedes [this development] is called a seed because it gives rise to the [actual] seed or because it is similar in character to it.

In the same way, [a special development in the continuum of a result of an action is produced that causes another result, not the result itself. For instance,] a positive change in [the continuum of] a mind contaminated [by ignorance] may arise from an effect that requires maturation, [but] only if it arises from a special causal condition, such as hearing correct teachings [on virtue, which would be a special development in the continuum of the effect]. And a negative change in [the continuum of such] a mind may arise from an effect of this sort only if it arises from a special causal condition such as hearing incorrect teachings [on virtue, which would be a special development in the continuum of the effect]. In these cases another effect that requires maturation can again arise, but not otherwise. This is the similarity.

There is another way in which it can be understood [that it is not the result of an action, but a special development in the continuum of the result, that causes another result]. Just as from a mātuluṇga flower that has been stained by the red juice of a lākṣā plant, a red keśara fruit is produced by a special development in its continuum, yet from this fruit another [red keśara fruit] does not arise again, so from an effect requiring maturation produced by an action, [although another effect may be produced by a special development in its continuum,] another effect that requires maturation does not again arise.

This is a coarse explanation in accord with my [limited] understanding. How [the] continua [of aggregates], when perfumed by actions of different kinds and strengths, give rise to their [characteristic] results is understood [completely] only by the Buddhas. [For] it has been said, "An action, a development [in its continuum], the benefit of that [development], and the result of that [action] none but a Buddha with certainty knows fully."

Section 5

Concluding verses[92]

Those free from [the] blindness [of ignorance]
attain [nirvāṇa] by having heard the teachings of the Buddhas
on the nature of phenomena, [the teachings on selflessness
    that are] faultless
because well-formed on the path of reasoning,
and by rejecting the doctrines of Tīrthikas,
who are blind [with ignorance]
and put into practice in various ways false theories
    [of persons].[93]

Selflessness is the only road to the city of nirvāṇa;
it is illuminated by the shining words of the sun-like Tathāgata,
and traversed by a multitude of Āryas;
but the poor-sighted [Pudgalavādins and Tīrthikas]
are not inclined to see the [road of] selflessness that lies open
    [to all].[94]

What little is explained here [about selflessness
is drawn from the treatises on knowledge.
It] is for the very wise.
It is like a wound [that provides an opportunity]
for poison to spread [throughout the body] by its own power.
[So the doctrine of selflessness will prevent false views
from entering the body of our spiritual community.][95]

Notes

1 The additions made to the more literal translation are drawn from Yaśomitra's commentary, which refers the initial question back to the last part of the last verse of Ch. 8, in which Vasubandhu enjoins those who seek liberation to practice the teachings of the Buddha.

2 The term, "self" (*ātman*), in "conception of a self," is used here to refer to a person who is conventionally real. Everywhere else in the text Vasubandhu uses the term to signify a person who possesses an independent identity. An extension of his normal use is that which occurs in "selfless" (*anātman*) when used in the claim that the aggregates are selfless, for in this case the meaning is that the aggregates are not possessions of a self. The term has its normal use in the locutions, "mistaken view of a self" (*ātmadṛṣṭi*) and "clinging to a self" or "self-grasping" (*ātmagrāha*). Pruden, following La Vallée Poussin, and Stcherbatsky translate *ātman* as "soul," which has too many Christian connotations to be useful. Most translators now avoid "soul" as a translation.

Although *prajñapti*, which I have translated here as "conception," is used by Buddhists to signify either a conception or a name that expresses a conception, I shall render it consistently as "conception," with the understanding that for every conception there can be a name that expresses it. A conception, in the last analysis, is a consciousness that makes an object known (see p. 358 of Edgerton's *Buddhist Hybrid Sanskrit Dictionary* (Delhi, 1977)) by means of a mental image produced by direct perceptions or correct inferences. Pruden uses "metaphorical expression" and Stcherbatsky uses "conventional term," which call attention to the linguistic side of the meaning of *prajñapti*, but add to it an interpretation.

3 The "only" in this sentence is meant to exclude reference to an entity that can be identified independently of a collection of aggregates. Even though he says here that the conception of a self (i.e. person) refers to a continuum of aggregates, strictly speaking, his view is that it refers to a collection of aggregates that exist in a causal continuum powered by "actions" (*karma*-s) contaminated by the "mistaken view of a self" (*ātmadṛṣṭi*). The collection of aggregates to which the conception refers includes phenomena of two sorts, material and mental. These material and mental phenomena are called "aggregates" (*skandha*-s) primarily because they are not united in or by a substantially real underlying support.

4 Stcherbatsky loosely renders the technical term, *dravya*, as "a Reality" rather than as "a substance," and thereby conceals the exact nature of the Tīrthika claim.

5 "Direct perception" (*pratyakṣa*) and "correct inference" (*anumāna*) are two of the "valid cognitions" (*pramāṇa*-s) recognized by Vasubandhu, the third being cognitions based on "scripture" (*āgama*). Vasubandhu employs all three in the "Refutation." Yaśomitra claims that Vasubandhu does not mention cognitions based on scripture because it is included within correct inference. Pû-guâng believes that Vasubandhu does not mention it because he is addressing this argument to the Tīrthikas.

6 Yaśomitra suggests that Vasubandhu does not include a proof for the claim that the other cause of perception is a sense-organ because it has been established by the "great sages" (*maharṣi*-s) through one of the higher forms of knowledge (specifically, *praṇidhijñāna*) and because it has not been disputed by anyone.

7 Yaśomitra glosses *Vātsīputrīyā* as *Āryasaṃmatīyāḥ*. Here I have translated this term, along with *Paudgalika*, as "Pudgalavādins," which is the general term

used by the Indian Buddhists to refer to the followers of the Buddhist schools that advocate the existence of an inexplicable "person" (*pudgala*).

8 Stcherbatsky translates *pudgala* as "individual," while Pruden, like La Vallée Poussin, leaves the term untranslated. The Pudgalavādins distinguish a person (*pudgala*) from a self (*ātman*) and believe that a self, which does not exist, is a person that can be identified independently, while a person, which exists, exists by himself without possessing a separate identity. See the Introduction for an explanation of these terms. Vasubandhu here and elsewhere often uses *pudgala* as they do so that he may critique their theory as stated. In other contexts Vasubandhu uses it either to refer to a self or to a person that he believes to be real by way of a conception. The contexts of the three different uses of the term will make it clear in which sense it is being used.

9 Stcherbatsky translates *dravyatas* and *prajñaptitas* as "as a reality" and "as an existence merely nominal," while Pruden translates La Vallée Poussin's French translation of them as "as an entity" and "as a designation of a nominal existence" or simply "as a designation." My translation, I believe, makes room for what appears to be Vasubandhu's understanding of their meanings.

10 Jinamitra, whose translation into Tibetan is usually quite literal, understood the Sanskrit text he possessed to mean the following: "Consequently, if a person is substantially real, he will possess a different nature [than they possess]. So it must be said that he is other than aggregates. If he is other than aggregates in the way that each of them is other than the others, his causes should be explained." Although the Sanskrit text we have cannot be literally translated in this way, Jinamitra's translation correctly brings out the sense of the argument it contains. In any case, as my additions to the translation indicate, the Sanskrit text as we have it requires interpretation. The interpretation I have given it is based in part on Jinamitra's translation, which may be his attempt to make the argument clearer. The translations of the argument as a whole by Stcherbatsky and La Vallée Poussin do not represent the argument of Vasubandhu as it appears in the Sanskrit text we have.

11 Yaśomitra explains "does not function" by quoting a verse by Dharmakīrti to show that a person, like the sky, which is unaffected by rain or heat, would be unaffected by things in the world. Pû-guâng simply says that if a person is causally unconditioned, he is like space.

12 The exact meaning of *prajñapyate*, which I have translated here as "is conceived" is a matter of interpretation. In Prāsaṅgika philosophy it would seem to mean something more like "is a name or conception merely attributed [to something]," which many translators render as "is imputed." Vasubandhu, however, cannot be using the word in that same sense, since he thinks that the subjects to which he attaches the verb signify something whose reality is substantially established. (See the Introduction for details.) Technically, *prajñapyate* should be translated as "is conceived or named," but I have opted for the simpler translation of "is conceived," and leave it to the reader to infer that what is conceived is subsequently named.

13 A person is conceived in reliance upon [a collection of] aggregates (*skandān upādāya pudgalaḥ prajñapyate*) in the sense that he cannot, although perceived, be conceived on the basis of being perceived and must be conceived in dependence upon a collection of aggregates some of which are present when he is perceived. See the Introduction and Commentary for an explanation. Stcherbatsky's translation, "We give the name of an Individual to something conditioned by the elements," and Pruden's translation, "the designation *pudgala* occurs in necessary relationship to . . . *skandhas*," distort the grammar

and meaning of the claim. A person is not said to be conditioned by the aggregates, but conceived (and/or named) in reliance upon them, and there is no necessary relationship said to exist between the name of a person and the aggregates. Having misconstrued this central claim of the Pudgalavādins, Stcherbatsky, and La Vallée Poussin begin to systematically mistranslate and misinterpret their views and arguments.

14 Since all causally conditioned phenomena, even those not belonging to oneself, are included in the phenomena called the aggregates, aggregates that pertain to oneself (*adhyātmika*) are distinguished from those that do not.

15 The idea that the aggregates are acquired is often expressed in the Buddha's sūtras.

16 La Vallée Poussin thinks that this qualification of the aggregates in reliance upon which a person is conceived shows that the Pudgalavādins reject the existence of past and future aggregates. But in the *Sāṃmitīyanikāya Śāstra* and the *Tridharmaka Śāstra* the Pudgalavādins include past and future aggregates in the causal basis of the conception of a person. See the Commentary for a different interpretation.

17 Yaśomitra seems to think that this example is used by the Pudgalavādins as part of an explanation of how a person is substantially real. But in Section 2.1 Vasubandhu represents them as denying that a person is substantially real. Yaśomitra may be attributing this view to them under the assumption, which is shared by Vasubandhu, that their theory of persons commits them to it. He also tells us that their view is that a person is conceived "in reliance upon what he acquires for himself" (*svam upādānam upādāya*), just as a fire is conceived in reliance upon the fuel it ignites. We are to understand that since persons cannot be said to be other than or the same in existence as the collections of aggregates they acquire, they are like fire, which also takes possession of fuel when it ignites it and yet cannot be said to be other than or the same in existence as the fuel it ignites. Stcherbatsky, I believe, misunderstands Yaśomitra's comment because he translates it as a person's existence being "conditioned by the existence of its own causes – the elements."

18 If fire were other than fuel, fire could not cause fuel to be hot by uniting with it, and if fire could not cause fuel to be hot by uniting with it, fuel could not be hot, since fuel is not by its own nature hot. See the Commentary.

19 Pû-guâng attributes to the Pudgalavādins the view that fire cannot be said to be the same as fuel because an agent cannot be the same as the object upon which it acts.

20 That the reference here is to the existence of persons rather than to their identity over time or unity may be inferred from the fact that the issue being discussed is in what way persons exist rather than in what way they are the same over time or one. The question of whether the identity over time and unity of persons can be explicated in terms of a collection of aggregates entering into a causal continuum and arising together arises in Sections 3.1, 3.4, 3.7, 3.8, 4.1, and 4.2.

21 Here and elsewhere what literally means "wood, etc." I have translated as "material."

22 Following Yaśomitra and Fâ-bâu, rather than Pû-guâng, who attributes what is expressed in this and the next two sentences to the Pudgalavādins, I attribute it to Vasubandhu, who is giving reasons why the Pudgalavādins cannot identify fuel and fire with what he himself takes to be the conventional realities commonly called fuel and fire. Stcherbatsky and La Vallée Poussin follow Pû-guâng's interpretation. The Pudgalavādins do not ascribe to the views, which

are presented in these sentences, that fire and fuel are made up of the eight elements and exist at different times.

23 The eight elements of which bodies are composed are the four "primary elements" (*mahābhuta*-s), called fire, air, water, and earth, and four secondary elements (*bhautika*-s) that comprise what we call the sensible qualities of such bodies and are perceived by means of an ear, nose, tongue, and body. The defining properties of the four elements are themselves counted as objects of the body as an organ of tactile perception. If and when a body makes a sound, it will also contain momentary elements that comprise its sound and will be perceived by means of an ear. According to Vasubandhu, every body is composed of at least the first eight, all of which exist apart from a mind that perceives or conceives them. See the Introduction for more information.

24 The point is that, even though, by convention, fire is what burns fuel, analysis shows that, from the point of view of ultimate reality, it is other than fuel.

25 According to the Pudgalavādins, the view that we are impermanent phenomena is a nihilism extreme, and the view that we are permanent phenomena is an eternal transcendence extreme. Vasubandhu's assumption, that our attributions of sameness over time to ourselves can be explained in terms of the causal continuity of the impermanent aggregates in the collection of aggregates in dependence upon which we are conceived, would be rejected because it too falls to the nihilism extreme.

26 The Pudgalavādins avoid identifying fire, as an agent of change, with the substance that Vasubandhu himself calls the fire-element and claims to be present in all bodies, since this element is no more an agent of change than are the other three elements present in all bodies. Stcherbatsky translates *auṣyam* as "the caloric element" rather than as "heat," and accepts Vasubandhu's assumption that the Pudgalavādins identify fire with the substance he calls the fire-element. The heat to which the Pudgalavādins refer here is not even the defining property of the fire-element. It is, as I have added to the Translation, what is *commonly called* heat, and is in fact an inexplicable phenomenon that, by its presence in burning material, is said to cause its fuel to burn.

27 According to Vasubandhu, the four primary elements support the existence of one another in the sense of being inseparably concomitant. He brings up this meaning of "in reliance upon" because he assumes in the argument that the Pudgalavādins have identified fire with the fire-element as he himself construes it in the *Treasury*.

28 Stcherbatsky's interpretative translation obscures the point of Vasubandhu's argument because it attributes to the Pudgalavādins the claim that a person does not exist unless his aggregates exist. Vasubandhu in fact represents them as claiming that a person cannot be conceived unless his aggregates are present, not that he cannot exist if they do not exist.

29 Whether or not the Pudgalavādins believe that fire exists apart from fuel is not clear. See the Commentary for a discussion.

30 See Section 2.1.3.

31 Stcherbatsky believes that in this sentence the Pudgalavādins are claiming that there is no problem with the theory that the fire-element is other than the other three elements, since the fuel is hot by being combined with the fire-element. He then interprets the next sentence as Vasubandhu drawing the conclusion, from their explanation of how fuel can be burned, that they have identified both fire and its fuel with burning material. However, the use of *atha punaḥ* in the next sentence strongly suggests that an alternative interpretation of fire and fuel is being presented.

32 Although Vasubandhu writes "is not other than," what he means can only be "is," since the Pudgalavādins hold the view that a person is not other than his aggregates.

33 Stcherbatsky is alone in supposing that in Section 2.2 Vasubandhu is claiming that the Pudgalavādins must accept the idea that persons belong to a fifth category of things known to exist.

34 My translation of *prativibhāvayati* as "is aware of" calls for comment. According to volume two of Edgerton's *Buddhist Hybrid Sanskrit Dictionary* (Delhi, 1953, p. 368), in the *Lankavatāra Sūtra* the verb means "considers thoroughly" or "considers individually." Since no other meanings or citations are given I assume that its use in Buddhist texts is unusual. Stcherbatsky translates it in *The Soul Theory of the Buddhists*, p. 21, as "indirectly cognizes." In the last volume of his *L'Abhidharmakośa de Vasubandhu* (Paris, 1931, p. 239), La Vallée Poussin translates it as "discerne en seconde ligne," which Pruden translates, in his English translation of La Vallée Poussin's French translation, as "indirectly discerns."

But the Pudgalavādins probably believe, as Vasubandhu does, that a mental consciousness can indirectly perceive objects directly perceived by the six consciousnesses. So it seems better not to employ in the translation above an expression which should be used to translate another idea altogether. I believe that the Pudgalavādins' use of this unusual verb for a perception of ourselves may be attributed to the fact that it is not like the perception of a visible form, yet is some form of perception. The Pudgalavādins have already stated in their explanation of aggregate reliance that a person "is perceived" (*upalabhyate*) when aggregates are present, which clearly indicates that *prativibhāvayati* signifies a kind of perception. I shall employ the least interpretative way to deal with the problem of translating the verb, by translating it by "is aware of," which calls the reader's attention to the fact that it is a kind of perception.

35 The extensive additions to the argument in this section are based on the commentary of Yaśomitra.

36 According to Xúanzàng, who is followed by La Vallée Poussin, the thought expressed in this sentence is that the Pudgalavādins err when they say that an eye sees a person because then it must see a self "in" (*yu*) what is selfless, since a visible form, which is what is seen by means of an organ of sight, is selfless. But the Sanskrit text we have says, and this is confirmed by Yaśomitra's commentary, that the erroneous implication of the Pudgalavādins' statement is that we see a self "by means of what is selfless" (*ānātmanā*). So the error thought to be entailed is that an eye is not selfless. My addition to the translation is based on one of the senses in which "selfless" is used in scripture. See the Commentary for an explanation.

37 The text lists *cetanā* as the fourth aggregate rather than *saṃskāra*-s, which is usually employed as the name of the fourth aggregate. Perhaps Vasubandhu substitutes the former for the latter because it heads the list of the *saṃskāra*-s.

38 The list contains Sanskrit words not all of which have English equivalents, so I have omitted a few.

39 "Tathāgata" is an epithet applied to the Buddha that means "He who is thus gone."

40 "Āryas" literally means "Superior Ones," "Higher Beings," or Worthy Ones," none of which is self-explanatory. Technically, an Ārya is one who has traversed the "path of insight" (*darśanamārga*) on which the four realities have been nondually realized. Persons are called Āryas because they have actually begun to eliminate the mental afflictions. Before that path is directly realized, the mental afflictions are merely suppressed.

41 Vasubandhu here renders the Pudgalavādins' view, that a person is neither a visible form nor other than a visible form, as the view that he neither is nor is not a visible form. Vasubandhu's assumption, that not to be a visible form is to be other than a visible form, is rejected by the Pudgalavādins, who do not think that not to be a visible form is to be a different substance.
42 A śrāmaṇa is a mendicant monk who listens to teachings.
43 See the *Treasury* and *Commentary*, Ch. VII, verse 1 for the account of *satkāyadṛṣṭi* on the basis of which I translate it as "mistaken view arising from a collection of perishable aggregates."
44 Yaśomitra says that these examples are meant to illustrate that a person is real by way of a conception both at a given moment and also from moment to moment. Fâ-bâu says that both together illustrate that a person is nothing but his aggregates.
45 Here and elsewhere I render *cittacaitta*-s as "a mind and its mental factors."
46 The same quotation is employed in Section 2.5.
47 La Vallée Poussin follows the interpretative translation of Xúanzàng, who makes the earlier set of aggregates the carrier of the burden and the later set the burden, since they are contaminated by the earlier. The Sanskrit text and Yaśomitra's commentary support the translation I have given.
48 My completion of the quotation is drawn from the *Anguttara Nikāya*, I, 22, where the Buddha is referring to himself in the context of enumerating things that are one.
49 What exactly it means for a term to be applied figuratively is not clear. It at least means that the term is not applied according to its literal meaning. Vasubandhu's point, however, is clear. He believes that the term, "one," is applied, according to its literal meaning, to a substance, but when applied to a collection of substances, is applied to it according to the convention that this collection of substances is a single entity of some sort.
50 Here I follow Yaśomitra's interpretation, which glosses *anyatra dharmasamsetād* as *prati pratītyasamutpādalakṣanāt*. La Vallée Poussin also follows this interpretation, in opposition to Paramārtha's view.
51 Identified by Yaśomitra.
52 Here I use the better known name of this king, "Milinda," rather than "Kaliṇga," which is found in the text.
53 Identified by Yaśomitra as Bhantakumāralāta. La Vallée Poussin and Stcherbatsky call him Kumāralābha. He belongs to the Sautrāntika school.
54 The additions to his paragraph are based on Yaśomitra's commentary.
55 Here I translate *vātsena*, which is the reading of another manuscript. See the *Index to the Abhidharmakośabhāṣya, Part One, Sanskrit–Tibetan–Chinese* (Daizo Shappan: Tokyo, 1973, p. 437), for the correction to the edition of Pradhan.
56 The story is told by Yaśomitra.
57 An Arhat is someone who has achieved nirvāṇa, a Tathāgata is one who has thus gone (an epithet for the Buddha) and a Samyaksaṃmbuddha is one who is a perfectly accomplished Buddha.
58 The Abhidharmikas would seem simply to be Buddhist scholars of the Abhidharma.
59 The reference is to the thesis of Nāgārjuna. It is not clear why Vasubandhu omits a discussion of his thesis that not even aggregates ultimately exist.
60 Unlike Stcherbatsky, La Vallée Poussin, and the Chinese commentators, who assume that the debate with the Pudgalavādins is continuing, I see here the end of Vasubandhu's consideration of their objections to his theory of persons. The Pudgalavādins may have been convinced by some of the objections of the

Nyāya-Vaiśeṣikas to reject the theory of persons held by the orthodox Vaibhāṣika schools, and so may have used some of these very objections. But since none of the views expressed or implied by Vasubandhu's adversaries after this point presupposes a Buddhist framework, I shall suppose that the objections and arguments of the Nyāya-Vaiśeṣikas are now to be taken up. A sign that this change has in fact taken place is that the term "self" is hereafter used in place of "person" in statements of the opponent's theories and objections, and the Pudgalavādins have to this point been represented primarily as presenting and defending the view that a person exists, but a self does not. Although he takes the Pudgalavādins' theory that persons are inexplicable phenomena to imply that a self exists and criticizes their theory on that basis, Vasubandhu usually avoids the use of the term, "self," in direct statements of their theory. It is also significant that the set of objections to which Vasubandhu now turns concern memory, which the Nyāya-Vaiśeṣikas repeatedly claim cannot be explained without reference to a self.

61 In his commentary on Book II, verse 36c, Vasubandhu rejects the orthodox Vaibhāṣika view that there are special substances, called possession (*prāpti*) and nonpossession (*aprāpti*), the first of which binds causes and effects into a single continuum, and the second of which prevents them from being members of any other continuum. His own view is that the causal relationships between the members of a continuum are sufficient to bind them together and prevent them from being members of other continua.

62 The Vaiyākaraṇas seem to be identified by Yaśomitra as Vasubandhu's opponents here. Stcherbatsky assumes the opponents to the Pudgalavādins. La Vallée Poussin does not commit himself to a view on the matter. I believe the opponents to be the Vaiśeṣikas.

63 Exactly what *bhāva* and *bhāvitār* mean in this objection is not clear. I do not follow Stcherbatsky in simply taking them to mean "action" and "agent," respectively. Pruden, following La Vallée Poussin's lead, translates them as "an existence" and "an existing being," respectively. The Sanskrit terms in question admit of a great variety of different translations, and since no one has yet found a textual source for the objection, it seems that the translator is left to his wits in developing the translation. I have arrived at my translations of *bhāva* as "an activity [signified by a verb]" and of *bhāvitr* as "an agent [signified by a noun attached to this verb]" on the basis of an analysis of the conditions under which the argument makes most sense. See the Commentary for my interpretation.

64 The verb, *vijānāti*, is grammatically understood to signify an activity performed by an agent signified by a noun to which the verb is attached. It is the verbal expression of *vijñāna*, which is translated as "a consciousness." Stcherbatsky translates it as "cognises," I believe, in order to capture its role as an active verb. Although its etymological connection to the noun, *vijñāna*, suggests the translation "is conscious of," I have elected instead to translate it as "apprehends" for the same reason Stcherbatsky translates it as "cognises," even though its etymological connection with "consciousness" is lost.

65 Stcherbatsky believes these Tīrthikas to be the Sāṃkhyas. Yaśomitra believes them to be the Vaiśeṣikas.

66 The text used by Yaśomitra contains "very intense" (*patutaram*) at this point.

67 The examples are from Fâ-bâu.

68 Identified by Yaśomitra.

69 Identified by Yaśomitra as the Vaiśeṣikas.

70 This is the definition given in the *Padārthadharmasaṃgraha* of Praśastapāda rather than the one given in the *Vaiśeṣika Sūtras*, Book VII, Part 2, verse 9.

71 When *saṃskāra*-s is used in the Vaiśeṣika philosophy I translate it as "impressions."

72 Although Vasubandhu says in the text, "odors, etc.," I render this more freely as "odors and other sensible qualities" in order to convey the Nyāya-Vaiśeṣikas' own view that odors, etc. are sensible qualities of physical substances. Even when "odors, etc." is used by Vasubandhu I keep this translation, since even though he believes that sensible qualities, as defined by the Nyāya-Vaiśeṣikas, do not ultimately exist, he does believe that they are real by convention.

73 See Section 4.7.

74 From Yaśomitra's commentary.

75 See Section 4.7.1.

76 The Sanskrit term, *ahaṃkāra*, literally means "I-maker," which Vasubandhu believes to be what the consciousness that conceives an "I" is. I translate it as "mind that conceives an 'I' " in order to convey the idea that the consciousness that conceives the "I" causes the "I" to exist in relation to the aggregates. This is why Vasubandhu believes that a person, the object of the conception of ourselves, is real by way of a conception. Stcherbatsky translates the term as "self-perception," which omits the conceptual nature of the idea of *ahaṃkāra* and the implication that the mind that conceives an "I" is creating what it conceives in dependence upon its apprehension of the aggregates.

77 The exact meaning of the Sanskrit is difficult to make out at this point. Stcherbatsky translates it as "Indeed, a useful thing might be metaphorically called a Self, but not self-perception itself!" Pruden's English translation of La Vallée Poussin's French is "So be it: one metaphorically calls what is used by the 'I' by the name of 'I.' But one cannot explain in this manner the consciousness that says 'I' (with regard to the body, sensations, consciousness, etc.)." I cannot make sense out of either of these translations. But Vasubandhu's point, I believe, is simply that his opponents' account of the figurative use of "I" assumes that "I" is a name of the self, which has not yet been established.

78 In the translation I made for the *Journal of Indian Philosophy* I interpreted this objection differently. I thought that, contrary to the interpretation of Stcherbatsky, the objection was to be interpreted as the claim that Vasubandhu could not explain why "I" was not applied to bodies other than the bodies of persons, since he did not recognize the existence of selves to which bodies belong. After considerable reflection, I now think that his interpretation is correct.

79 See Section 4.1.

80 In Vasubandhu's commentary on Book I, verse 45, it is said that the six internal bases of perception, i.e. the six organs of perception, are the underlying supports for their associated consciousnesses of objects, since the consciousnesses are different when their respective objects are different. Since a different organ of perception will also produce a different feeling in the corresponding consciousness, that organ is said to be its underlying support.

81 Yaśomitra identifies the Lakṣaṇikas as the Vaiyākaraṇas.

82 See Pāṇini's *Aṣṭādhyāyī*, 1.4.54. Stcherbatsky, I believe, distorts Pāṇini's definition of an agent when he translates it as "what is endowed with a free will." This rendering makes it appear that the issue at hand is freedom of the will rather than the existence of a self that is an agent of actions.

83 In other words, the Vaiśeṣikas claim that the existence of a self cannot be denied since the world says that Devadatta prays, eats, walks, and so on, and in saying this it acknowledges the existence of an independent or first cause.

84 See Section 4.7.1 for a closely related argument. There Vasubandhu argued that a permanent self could not cause different minds to arise, while here he is arguing that a self that exists without causes and conditions cannot be assumed to cause actions to arise.

85 Literally, "no agent so defined is perceived." But Stcherbatsky seems to be right to take this to mean that an agent of action "is not to be found," i.e. is not established to exist by means of direct or indirect perception.

86 See Section 4.3.

87 See Section 4.11.

88 See Section 4.8.

89 Here I read *vividha* for *trividha* because the Chinese and Tibetan translations seem to have assumed the latter, and this reading makes more sense of the thought of the passage.

90 According to Yaśomitra it was said by the Elder, Rāhula.

91 In my original translation, published in the *Journal of Indian Philosophy*, I interpreted the compound, *bījaphalād*, to mean "from the fruit-seed" instead of "from a fruit as from a seed," and then interpreted most later references to *phalām* to be references to an effect rather than to a fruit. (The same word means both "fruit" and "effect" or "result.") These interpretations led, I now realize, to a mistranslation of the entire section. The present translation most closely resembles that of La Vallée Poussin.

92 Vasubandhu concludes the "Refutation" with the following three verses, for which I do not provide a separate commentary. He concludes that we can become free from suffering in saṃsāra if we reject the Tīrthikas' theory of a self and internalize the Buddha's teachings on selflessness, that only the Buddha's teachings on selflessness, which he implies have been misunderstood by the Pudgalavādins, can free us from suffering, and that he hopes that what he has explained in the "Refutation" about our selflessness will spread by its own power among those wise enough to comprehend and practice it. Since the only readers Vasubandhu has in mind for the "Refutation" are other Buddhists, it is clear that he means that he wishes that what he has explained will lead the Buddhists who study the "Refutation" to abandon the Pudgalavādins' theory of persons. The three verses as a whole make it clear that his purpose in composing the "Refutation" is to clear away impediments to liberation from suffering in saṃsāra caused by the false beliefs about persons presented by the Pudgalavādins and Tīrthikas.

93 Although in this first verse Vasubandhu calls upon all of us to reject the doctrines of the Tīrthikas, the implication is that the Pudgalavādins are Buddhists who have accepted their doctrine in a slightly different form. The Pudgalavādins, like the Tīrthikas, he believes, will not be liberated from suffering because their theory that we exist without dependence upon the collection of our aggregates entails the Tīrthikas' theory that we are separate substances. So he is claiming that if the Pudgalavādins base their meditations on selflessness on their theory of persons, they will not become free of suffering in saṃsāra in spite of the fact that they have studied the teachings of the Buddha. But if the Pudgalavādins' interpretation of the selflessness of persons thesis is the same as that of Vasubandhu, as I have suggested above it is, can Vasubandhu's claim be true? Is it true that if we base our meditations on selflessness on their theory, we will not become free from suffering in saṃsāra, but if we base our meditations on his theory, we will become free? At first sight, it seems that it is not true, since, strictly speaking, they believe, as he does, that the realization that we cannot be independently identified is what destroys our

assent to our false appearance of being independently identifiable. In the end, however, if Vasubandhu is correct in his assumption that there is no entity without a separate identity, it would seem that when the Pudgalavādins assert that we can exist apart from our aggregates they would be committed to the view that we are independently identifiable. So from Vasubandhu's point of view, at least, we could not become from free suffering in saṃsāra if we base our meditations on the theory of persons of the Pudgalavādins.

94 It may be implied in the second verse that it is the failure of the Pudgalavādins to understand the Buddha's doctrine of selflessness that has led them astray. Their failure, in this case, would be the failure to realize that the absence of independent identifiability implies the absence of separate existence, not the failure to realize that we cannot be independently identified.

95 The poison to be spread by the study of Vasubandhu's treatise would seem to be the realization of selflessness. Why does he call it poison? Perhaps he thinks it to be a poison of the sort that will immunize the body of the spiritual community from being affected by a worse poison, the acceptance of the false theories of persons presented by the Pudgalavādins or by the Tīrthikas.

3

COMMENTARY ON SECTION 1

Vasubandhu's theory of persons

§ 1.1 Vasubandhu's theory of persons and the problem of suffering

Vasubandhu begins the "Refutation" by claiming that there is no liberation from suffering for those with the mistaken view of a self. He thinks that the mistaken view of a self is an assent to a naturally occurring false appearance of ourselves being identifiable independently of our aggregates. But according to Yaśomitra, Vasubandhu's reference to those for whom there is no liberation is a reference to the Tīrthikas, who believe that liberation from suffering is attained by coming to realize that we are selves, which they believe to be persons who are in fact separate substances. Although Vasubandhu does not believe that the acceptance of the Tīrthikas' theory of persons is the root cause of our suffering, I have incorporated Yaśomitra's suggestion as an implication of Vasubandhu's initial claim into the translation within brackets, since it explains why he goes on to say of those for whom there is no liberation that "they believe that a self is a separate substance."

Vasubandhu does not think that our mistaken view of a self is a view of a self of the sort the Tīrthikas' claim we are. For he believes that we suffer even if we do not in fact adopt this theory. He seems to have two reasons for bringing up the theory of the Tīrthikas when talking about the mistaken view of a self. The first reason is that the self the mistaken view of which is the cause of all suffering is a person who can be independently identified and that if a person can be independently identified he must be a separate substance. The second reason is that the acceptance of the separate substance thesis of the Tīrthikas' theory of persons will reinforce the mistaken view of a self, since it amounts to an attempt to provide it with a metaphysical justification.

In Section 2 of the "Refutation" Vasubandhu assumes, when he presents objections to the Pudgalavādins' theory of persons, that we ultimately exist, and that since we ultimately exist, we must be either other than collections of aggregates in the sense of being separate substances, or the same in existence as these collections. Hence, he assumes, since the Pudgalavādins reject the view that we are the same in existence as collections of aggregates, they too are committed to the Tīrthikas' theory that we are separate substances. Hence, we may assume that Vasubandhu believes that those who adopt the Pudgalavādins' theory will not be able to free themselves from suffering.

§ 1.2 Vasubandhu's middle way argument

Vasubandhu's statement of the argument for his theory of persons

In Section 1.2 Vasubandhu presents an abbreviated statement of the central argument for his theory of persons. Literally, he says, "It is known that the expression, 'self,' refers to a continuum of aggregates and to nothing else because there is no direct perception or sound inference." Although he says in this argument that the expression, "self" (*ātman*), is known to refer to a continuum of aggregates and to nothing else, Vasubandhu normally uses "self" to refer to a person who can be identified independently of the aggregates. In presenting Vasubandhu's own views I shall use "self" in this more restricted sense. In keeping with this usage, let us substitute "person" for "self" in his claim that the expression, "self," refers to a continuum of aggregates and to nothing else. When Vasubandhu says that the term refers to "nothing else" than a continuum of aggregates, he means that it does not refer to a self. He cannot mean that it does not refer to a person, who he believes to be a conventional reality. He means that the term, which refers to a person, refers to a continuum of aggregates rather than to a self. He believes this, of course, because he thinks that a person is the same in existence as a continuum of aggregates rather than being the same in existence as a self.

Although Vasubandhu says that it is to a continuum of aggregates, rather than to a self, that the term, "person," refers, his view, strictly speaking, is that it refers to a collection of aggregates. The collection includes all of the aggregates in a beginningless causal continuum perpetuated by the mistaken view of a self. He normally simply says that it is to the aggregates that the term also refers. It is when he is concerned with the question of how to explain the convention that we are the same over time that he most often calls attention to the fact that the aggregates in the collections in dependence upon which we conceive ourselves exist in a causal continuum. The fact that our aggregates exist in a causal continuum of this sort, he believes, explains why we can continue to refer to ourselves as the same person from moment to moment in spite of the fact that the aggregates in the collection in dependence upon which we conceive ourselves are different from moment to moment. By convention, a collection of aggregates is the causal basis of the conception of ourselves. By contrast, the cause of the application of the conception in a particular instance is simply the occurrence of some of the aggregates in the collection. For instance, when thinking occurs at a particular time within the collection in dependence upon which I conceive myself, the mind in this collection that conceives the "I" thinks "I think" at that time. Since the causal basis of the conception of ourselves, and hence, the general causal basis of reference to ourselves is a collection of aggregates, let us paraphrase Vasubandhu's claim as the claim, "It is known that the expression, 'person,' refers to a collection of aggregates rather than to a self."

We need to be clear that to say that the expression, "person," refers to a collection of aggregates is not to say that the aggregates as a collection are what a person is, i.e. what the object of the conception of a person is. According to Vasubandhu, the object of the conception of a person is a conventional reality. A person as a person is not just a collection of aggregates. A person and a collection of aggregates, he believes, are the same in existence, and so, when reference is made to a person, reference is made to a collection of aggregates rather than to a self. So that we may be clearer that Vasubandhu does not mean to suggest that a collection of aggregates is the object of the conception of a person, let us paraphrase what he says as the statement that "It is known the expression, 'person,' which refers to a person, refers to a collection of aggregates rather than to a self."

Finally, we should notice that since Vasubandhu believes that terms like "person" are linguistic expressions of conceptions, Vasubandhu's statement may also be paraphrased as, "It is known that the conception of a person, which refers to a person, refers to a collection of aggregates rather than to a self."

The reason Vasubandhu gives in support of his conclusion is that "there is no direct perception or correct inference." The claim that there is no direct perception or correct inference is obviously used to support the conclusion that it is known that the conception of a person does not refer to a self. In other words, he is claiming that it is known that a person is not a self, since a self, which is a person who can be independently identified, is not known to exist among the phenomena that are the causal basis of the conception of a person. But Vasubandhu is surely also implying in his argument that it is known by direct perception or correct inference that the conception also refers to a collection of aggregates. He does not explain how direct perception or correct inference enable us to know that the conception of a person refers to a collection of aggregates or how the absence of direct perception and correct inference enables us to know that the conception does not refer to a self.

In order to understand Vasubandhu's argument, therefore, we must unearth the unstated premises upon which he relies in drawing its two-sided conclusion. What these premises are can easily be determined on the basis of the consideration that he believes that in meditation on the selflessness of persons an attempt is being made to determine whether or not we are selves. But in Buddhist meditation, in order to determine whether or not we are selves, it is necessary to analyze the object of the conception of ourselves to determine whether or not the conception has a self as its causal basis. If the conception of ourselves is found to have a causal basis, Vasubandhu believes, we can be sure that its object exists. The principle he employs here is that an object of a conception is the same in existence as its causal basis. But apart from determining that the conception of ourselves has a causal basis, and so, that its object exists, we also need to examine its causal basis to determine whether or not it or any or all of the phenomena in it is a self. If the causal basis of the conception neither is nor contains a self, we may conclude that we are not the same in existence as a self.

In preparation for meditation on the selflessness of persons we need to determine what the phenomena are in dependence upon which we conceive ourselves. These are found to be collections of aggregates. The meditation begins with an attempt to determine exactly how we appear to our minds when we conceive ourselves. For Vasubandhu this step yields the result that when we are conceived we appear to our minds to be identifiable independently of our aggregates. In other words, we appear to be selves. When it is found that none of the aggregates, individually or as a collection, are the persons we appear to be when we conceive ourselves, it is concluded that we are not selves.

Nonetheless, Vasubandhu believes, we do not exist solely in dependence upon being conceived, since the causal basis of the conception of ourselves is comprised of a collection of aggregates that ultimately exist. If conceiving ourselves were to have no causal basis, he assumes, we would not exist at all. In order to avoid the conclusion that we do not exist at all, he thinks, we need to establish our existence as conventional realities. We may draw the conclusion that we are conventional realities, according to Vasubandhu, because the object of the conception of ourselves is, by convention, composed of substances the collection of which is the causal basis of the conception. Since our existence is the same as the existence of a collection of substances, we possess substantially established reality. Therefore, we may also conclude that we ultimately exist, since a substantially established reality ultimately exists.

So what are the roles played in Vasubandhu's two arguments by direct perception and/or correct inference? The absence of a direct perception of a self or correct inference to the existence of a self in the causal basis of the conception of ourselves, it is assumed, proves that there is no self present in the causal basis of the conception. About this assumption I shall have something to say below. The direct perception of the phenomena in the causal basis of the conception or correct inference to the existence of the phenomena in the causal basis of the conception, it is clear, is used to prove that the object of the conception possesses ultimate existence.

So Vasubandhu's argument is in fact two arguments. The conclusion of the first argument is that we are not selves, and the conclusion of the second is that we ultimately exist. The first is the argument that the object of the conception of ourselves is known not to be a self because no phenomenon in the collection of phenomena that causes us to be conceived is known, by means of direct perception or correct inference, to be a self. I shall call this the "no-self argument" (hereafter, NSA). The purpose of the NSA is to bring us to the realization that, even though we falsely appear to be selves, we are not selves, since the causal basis of the conception of ourselves is not known to contain selves. It is not known to contain selves because if it did contain selves, selves would be directly perceived or could be correctly inferred to exist among the phenomena in dependence upon which we are conceived, and there is no direct perception of selves and no correct inference that show that they must exist among these phenomena.

The second argument is that the object of the conception of ourselves is known to exist because the phenomena in the collection of aggregates that is its causal basis are known to exist by means of direct perception or correct inference. I shall call this the "ultimate existence argument" (hereafter, UEA). The purpose of the UEA is to show that, although we are not selves, we do exist, since we are the same in existence as collections of aggregates. In this argument Vasubandhu assumes that if we do not possess either substantial reality or substantially established reality we do not exist at all. But we do exist, he believes, since not only is our reality substantially established, but the denial of our ultimate existence is held by the Buddha to be a mistaken view.

Vasubandhu believes that he avoids an eternal transcendence theory of persons by the use of the NSA. We know that we are not selves, he believes, because selves cannot be found among the phenomena in the causal basis of the conception of ourselves. He believes that he avoids a nihilism theory of persons by the use of the UEA. Although we are not selves, he thinks, we ultimately exist, since we know that the conception of ourselves has ultimately existent phenomena as causal basis. Because Vasubandhu assumes his argument to provide a middle way between the extremes of eternal transcendence and nihilism, I shall call his argument as a whole the "middle way argument" for his theory of persons.

In the NSA, Vasubandhu assumes, first of all, that (I) we are the objects of the conception of ourselves. Then he argues that (II) if we are selves, selves are the causal basis of the conception of ourselves. But according to the causal reference thesis, (III) the objects of the conception of ourselves are the same in existence as the causal basis of the conception. So from (II) and (III), we may infer that (IV) if we are selves, selves are the same in existence as the causal basis of the conception of ourselves. Vasubandhu also believes that (V) the causal basis of the conception of an object is an object of direct perception or correct inference in dependence upon which the conception is formed or a collection of such objects that is the basis upon which the conception is formed. Therefore, from (IV) and (V), we may infer that (VI) if we are selves, selves are objects of direct perception or correct inference in dependence upon which the conception is formed or collections of such objects that are the basis upon which the conception is formed. In accord with the results of meditation in which the causal basis of the conception of ourselves is checked to determine whether or not it is or contains selves, we may assert that (VII) selves are not the objects of direct perception or correct inference in dependence upon which the conception of ourselves is formed or collections of such objects on the basis of which the conception is formed. Therefore, from (VI) and (VII) we may infer that (VIII) we are not selves. So from (I) and (VIII) we may infer that (IX) the objects of the conception of ourselves are not selves.

To explain the UEA, we need to add the premise that (X) collections of aggregates are the collections of objects of direct perception or correct inference that are the basis upon which the conception of ourselves is formed. From (V) and (X) we may infer that (XI) collections of aggregates are the causal basis of the conception of ourselves. Therefore, from (II), which is the causal reference thesis, and (XI), we may infer that (XII) the objects of the conception of ourselves are the same in existence as collections of aggregates. Therefore, from (I), (XI), and (XII) we may infer that (XIII) we are the same in existence as collections of aggregates. He draws this conclusion so that we will infer that we ultimately exist. The steps needed to draw this conclusion, using our knowledge of the theses of his theory of persons, are that (XIV) if we are the same in existence as collections of aggregates, we are conventional realities, that (XV) if we are conventional realities, we possess substantially established reality, and that (XVI) if we possess substantially established reality, we ultimately exist. Therefore, from (XIII), (XIV), (XV), and (XVI) we may infer that (XVII) we ultimately exist.

The truth of the causal reference thesis that is employed in the NSA and occurs again in the UEA is rejected by both the Pudgalavādins and Candrakīrti. The causal reference thesis will in fact be the main target of the Pudgalavādins' replies to Vasubandhu's first set of objections to their theory of persons. Nor do the Pudgalavādins or Candrakīrti accept the truth of (XII), (XIV), (XV), or (XVI). The truth of (X), (XI), (XII), and (XIV), moreover, is not accepted by the Indian Buddhist philosophers who claim or imply that we are the same in existence as subtle forms of our mental consciousnesses in a causal continuum.

Vasubandhu's defense of the no verification criterion of nonexistence

In the NSA Vasubandhu in effect assumes that if something is not known to exist by means of perception or correct inference, it is known not to exist. For an abbreviated statement of the NSA is that it is known that a person is not a self because a self is not known to exist by means of direct perception or correct inference. Immediately after presenting the NSA,

Vasubandhu attempts to defend this assumption, which may be called "the no verification criterion of nonexistence." (This is not, by the way, to say that something being known not to exist *means* that its existence is not verified by direct perception or correct inference.) The criterion itself is subject to interpretation, since the natures of direct perception and correct inference may be variously interpreted and the nonexistence that is to be verified by the absence of direct perception and correct inference may be variously interpreted. Nonetheless, apart from these different interpretations, the criterion itself calls for comment. Why is something that is not known to exist by means of direct perception or correct inference known not to exist?

That Vasubandhu should assert the criterion at all, in fact, seems problematic, since he himself says elsewhere that there are some things that are known to exist by means of scripture. Perhaps he thinks, for instance, that the existence of the law of actions and their results is known only by means of scripture, since we most certainly do not directly perceive it, and it is difficult to imagine a correct inference to its existence on a par with a correct inference of the sort Vasubandhu himself cites in this very section for the existence of a sense-organ. This difficulty is not avoided, therefore, by Yaśomitra's suggestion that Vasubandhu includes knowledge of the existence of something by means of scripture under guise of knowledge by correct inference. And even if Pû-guâng is right, that Vasubandhu does not mention knowing that something exists by means of scripture because he is addressing the NSA to the Tīrthikas, the problem remains, since if knowledge of the existence of something by means of scripture is a way of knowing something to exist that is not known to exist by the other means, the no verification criterion of nonexistence is incorrect.

Perhaps the way out of this last problem is to claim that only for beings other than Buddhas is knowledge of the existence of something by means of scripture the only way in which it is known to exist, since for Buddhas all things are known to exist by means of direct perception or correct inference. Or perhaps the no verification criterion of nonexistence should be amended to include no verification by means of scripture.

In any case, Vasubandhu's justification of the criterion is to assume that all phenomena known to exist are included in the twelve bases of perception and then to argue that the twelve bases of perception are known to exist either by means of direct perception or by means of correct inference. This argument, however, will not satisfy the Tīrthikas or the Pudgalavādins, who probably also believe that everything that exists is known to exist, but deny that only the twelve bases of perception are known to exist. The Tīrthikas deny this because they believe that selves, which are not included in the twelve bases of perception, are separate substances. The Pudgalavādins deny it because they believe that persons, who are not the same in existence as anything included in the twelve bases of perception, ultimately exist.

Perhaps Vasubandhu accepts the view that the twelve bases of cognition include all phenomena that are known to exist on the basis of his beliefs that the Buddha asserted it or implied that it is true and that what the Buddha asserts or implies is true, is true. However, if this is his view, in the very argument he uses to prove that what is not known to exist is known not to exist, he would be assuming that it is by means of scripture that he knows that all phenomena known to exist are included in the twelve bases of perception! Even if we overlook this difficulty, the reliance upon scripture shifts the problem of justifying his version of the no verification criterion of nonexistence to the equally difficult problems of justifying the claim that Vasubandhu's interpretation of what the Buddha asserted is correct and justifying the claim that what the Buddha asserts or implies is true, is true.

The denial of a correct inference to the existence of a self

In explanation of his claim that there is no correct inference to the existence of a self Vasubandhu presents an illustration of the sort of correct inference he believes would be required. The causal nature of his illustration, as well as his attempts in Sections 3 and 4 of the "Refutation" to defend his theory of persons against objections, suggests a picture of what he believes will count as a correct inference to the existence of a self and how we are to go about objecting to such an inference. The illustration suggests that the only sort of correct inference Vasubandhu would deem acceptable to prove that a self exists is one in which it is proved that a self is needed as an extra cause, besides the twelve bases of perception, of the perception of an object, just as it is proved that a sense-organ is needed as an extra cause, besides the others needed, of a perception of a sensible object. Many of the objections to his own theory, moreover, are claims to the effect that unless a self exists, perception, memory, and other such phenomena cannot be explained. This is particularly true of the objections posed by the Nyāya-Vaiśeṣikas, who are made to object that Vasubandhu cannot explain the occurrence of a memory of an object, a consciousness of an object, the accumulation of merit and demerit, etc. Vasubandhu's replies to these objections almost always include an attempt to explain how, without a self as a cause, they are caused. Does this mean that when Vasubandhu claims that there is no correct inference to the existence of a self he is simply presenting a generalization on the basis of the failure of the Tīrthikas to show that a self is needed as an extra cause of the occurrence of the aggregates? Does this provide us with a clue to discovering the form that this part of the NSA takes? Does he simply mean, when he implies that the absence of correct inference to the existence of self entails the nonexistence of the self if there is no direct perception of a self, that he has proved that all arguments thus far used to prove the existence of a self are unsound?

If Vasubandhu's rejection of a correct inference to the existence of a self takes this form, it would be a very elaborate form of argument indeed, and would not in fact fully support the premise he needs. Perhaps, then, this is not the form Vasubandhu intends this part of the NSA to have. What is needed is an argument to the effect that the very idea of a self as a cause of the occurrence of perception, memory, etc. is incoherent or self-contradictory. Does Vasubandhu have such an argument?

Vasubandhu does have such an argument in the "Refutation." But because it is an argument used by all Indian Buddhist philosophers against the Tīrthikas' theory of persons, and the primary target of the "Refutation" is the Pudgalavādins' theory of persons, Vasubandhu mentions it only in passing in Section 2.1, where he says that if persons are causally unconditioned phenomena, they are without a causal function. The thrust of this argument, which is a standard Buddhist objection to the Tīrthikas' theory of persons, is that by making the self a causally unconditioned phenomenon the Tīrthikas have undercut any attempt they might make to argue that its existence explains the occurrence of the aggregates, since what is causally unconditioned neither produces anything else nor is affected by anything else, including the aggregates. A causally unconditioned self can no more explain the occurrence of perception, memory, etc. than space can explain the occurrence of bodies within it. An argument closely related to this argument is used in Section 4.7.1 against the Nyāya-Vaiśeṣika view that minds arise from a self.

But how can this standard objection to the Tīrthika theory of persons be used to refute the Pudgalavādins' theory of persons, since they also reject the view that persons are causally unconditioned phenomena? Vasubandhu believes that the NSA is also applicable to the Pudgalavādins' theory. He assumes that even though they deny that we are causally unconditioned phenomena, they imply that we are causally unconditioned phe-nomena when they deny that we are the same in existence as the causally conditioned phenomena in dependence upon which we are conceived and assert that we ultimately exist. This implication, he would undoubtedly say, exists because all phenomena that ultimately exist are either causally conditioned or causally unconditioned. So their theory implies that we are other than collections of aggregates, which comprise all causally conditioned phenomena.

But the Pudgalavādins, we must note, do not accept the view that all phenomena that ultimately exist are either causally conditioned or causally unconditioned, since persons, they believe, ultimately exist and yet are neither causally conditioned nor causally unconditioned phenomena. Hence, they would deny that the standard Buddhist argument against the Tīrthikas' theory of persons can be used against their theory of persons.

4

COMMENTARY ON SECTION 2

Vasubandhu's objections to the Pudgalavādins' theory of persons

§ 2.1 Vasubandhu's statement of the Pudgalavādins' existence thesis and objection to it from the two realities

Vasubandhu has just argued that liberation from suffering is not possible for the Tīrthikas, since their belief that we are other than collections of aggregates will prevent them from abandoning the grasping at a self which causes them to suffer. He has also argued that we are not selves, but the same in existence as collections of aggregates. This last argument sets the stage for his introduction of the Pudgalavādins' theory of persons.

"They assert," he says, "that a person exists" (*pudgalaṃ santam icchanti*). For both Vasubandhu and the Pudgalavādins, a person is a conventional reality that ultimately exists. They think that a conventional reality ultimately exists in the sense that it exists apart from being conceived. However, according to the Pudgalavādins, a person ultimately exists without being the same in existence as a collection of aggregates, and according to Vasubandhu, a person ultimately exists only insofar as he is the same in existence as a collection of aggregates. So when Vasubandhu raises his question about the Pudgalavādins' claim, that we exist, and lays out what he believes are the only two ways he believes that we can ultimately exist, he is actually raising an objection to their thesis that we ultimately exist without being the same in existence as collections of aggregates. Let us call this objection his "two realities objection," since it is based upon the Buddha's doctrine of the two realities as it is interpreted within the orthodox Vaibhāṣika school.

The question Vasubandhu raises is whether in saying that a person ultimately exists they are claiming that a person is "substantially real" (*dravyataḥ asti*) or is "real by way of a conception" (*prajñaptitaḥ asti*). What is substantially real, which he also calls an "ultimate reality" (*paramārthasatya*), is an object of knowledge whose identity cannot be eliminated by analysis. What is real by way of a conception, which he also calls a "conventional reality" (*saṃvṛtisatya*), is an object of knowledge whose identity can be eliminated by analysis. Nonetheless, what is real by way of a conception ultimately exists, since it is the same in existence as a collection of substances in dependence upon which it is conceived. What is real by way of a conception, in other words, is a substantially established reality. The objection is formulated in the form of an argument to the effect that if we exist, we must be one of these two realities, and since the Pudgalavādins do not believe that we are substantial realities, they must agree that we are substantially established realities.

In the objection Vasubandhu states that if we are substantial realities, we are other than collections of aggregates, since we will possess a different nature than is possessed by any of the aggregates. The nature to which he refers is an identity that we would possess by ourselves, apart from any and all of the aggregates in the collections in dependence upon which we conceive ourselves. But why it should be true, that if we are substantial realities we possess a different nature than possessed by any of our aggregates, he does not explain. We need to understand what his explanation would be if we are to assess properly his two realities objection.

Vasubandhu assumes that if we are substantial realities, we possess an identity that cannot be eliminated by analysis and that this identity is not possessed by any of our aggregates, individually or as a collection. But why would he assume this? The answer lies in his belief about what this identity would be if we were substantial realities. The identity he believes we would need to possess by ourselves if we were substantial realities is that of being owners or possessors of aggregates that use them to perceive objects, think thoughts, perform actions, have feelings, remember objects, etc. For this is the identity that by convention we are assumed to possess when we use the conception of ourselves to refer to ourselves and that our aggregates do not possess, either individually or as a collection. Vasubandhu therefore says, on the assumption that we are substantial realities if and only if we possess such a separate identity, that if we are substantial realities, we possess a different nature than possessed by our aggregates, individually or as a collection. On the basis of these assumptions Vasubandhu states that if we are substantial realities we possess a different nature than possessed by our aggregates.

Vasubandhu also assumes that if we are other than our aggregates, we are either causally conditioned phenomena or causally unconditioned phenomena. Since the Pudgalavādins claim that we are not causally conditioned phenomena, they provide no account of how we are causally conditioned. So in his explanation of the two realities objection Vasubandhu does not elaborate on the possibility that we are causally conditioned phenomena. Moreover, he assumes that the Pudgalavādins, like all other Buddhists, reject the Tīrthikas' view that we are causally unconditioned phenomena. This view is rejected by all on the ground that if we were causally unconditioned phenomena, we could not, as we can, be "affected by anything or produce effects" (*niṣprayojanatva*). So Vasubandhu believes that the Pudgalavādins accept, for instance, the argument that we are not causally unconditioned phenomena because we suffer in saṃsāra. It follows, therefore, that we are not substantial realities, but instead, substantially established realities, and hence, are the same in existence as collections of aggregates. The argument in the text ends at this point. Vasubandhu has in effect argued that the Pudgalavādins must accept the thesis that we are substantially established realities, since they believe that we ultimately exist. The Pudgalavādins, accordingly, are then represented as denying that we are either substantial realities or substantially established realities, and Vasubandhu objects to their reason for this denial.

But their denial that we are either one of these two realities is a variant of their denial that we are either other than or the same in existence as collections of aggregates. In other words, the denial amounts to the assertion of their inexplicability thesis, which becomes the target of Vasubandhu's next set of objections.

§ 2.1.1 *The Pudgalavādins' reply from aggregate-reliant identity*

The Pudgalavādins' answer to Vasubandhu's question, which is equivalent to the question of whether we are other than or the same in existence as collections of aggregates, is to say that we are neither of the two realities as he has explained them. This answer may be interpreted as the Pudgalavādins' reply to Vasubandhu's implicit objection to their theory of persons. They claim that we are neither substantial realities nor substantially established realities, since we conceive ourselves in reliance upon collections of aggregates that pertain to us, are acquired and exist in the present. Let us set aside for the moment a discussion of the three attributes they believe the collections of aggregates to possess so we may first come to an understanding of what the Pudgalavādins mean by "in reliance upon" (*upādāya*) in the claim that we conceive ourselves in reliance upon collections of aggregates. The view that we conceive ourselves in reliance upon collections of aggregates may be called "the aggregate-reliant identity thesis" of their theory of persons.

The aggregate-reliant identity thesis, we can be sure, is not the simple thesis that we are conceived in dependence upon collections of aggregates. For Vasubandhu himself accepts that thesis. What must mark off aggregate-reliant identity from aggregate-dependent identity is that in the first case the person ultimately exists without being the same in existence as a collection of aggregates, and in the second case, he ultimately exists because he is the same in existence as a collection of aggregates. The problem, of course, is that this difference is not made clear simply by introducing the term "in reliance upon" to mark it. So let us attempt to unpack the meaning of the term so that we may better understand the series of objections that

Vasubandhu is about to bring to the aggregate-reliant identity thesis and the Pudgalavādins' replies to these objections.

First of all, we need to be clear that the Pudgalavādins themselves believe that we are conventional realities without being substantially established realities. We are persons who are conventionally real and inexplicable. We are not conventional realities in the way milk is, which is by being a collection of elements for which an identity has been mentally constructed, but in the way fire is. Both fire and persons, the Pudgalavādins believe, are entities without separate identities and possess identities only insofar as their identities are mentally constructed in dependence upon collections of phenomena. Like milk, we ultimately exist, but not because we are collections of elements in dependence upon which we are conceived. So it must be the denial that we are conventional realities of the sort milk is that is built into the claim that we are conceived "in reliance upon" (as opposed to "in dependence upon") collections of aggregates. This means, in the end, that our being conceived in reliance upon collections of aggregates implies that, although we are conceived in dependence upon them, we do not exist in dependence upon them. Let us explore this view further. On what basis do the Pudgalavādins hold the view?

The Pudgalavādins will claim in Section 2.5 that we are known to exist by means of perception. In Vasubandhu's objection to this claim he will assume that a perception that establishes the existence of an object of a conception always includes a discrimination of a character the object possesses by itself. Only if such a character of the object of a conception is discriminated when the object is perceived, he assumes, can the existence of the object be established by means of perception, since what exists apart from being conceived must possess by itself a character that can be discriminated. Let us call a perception of this sort a "discriminative perception" of an object of a conception.

But the Pudgalavādins do not believe that when we perceive ourselves a character we possess by ourselves is discriminated. Nonetheless, they believe, our existence is established by such a perception. How is this possible? How can a perception establish our existence if it does not include a discrimination of a character we possess by ourselves? It is possible, they believe, if we conceive ourselves not on the basis of a discriminative perception of ourselves, but on the basis of discriminative perceptions of aggregates that are always present when we perceive ourselves. Since we do not by ourselves possess a character that can be discriminated when we perceive ourselves, the conception of ourselves must be formed on the basis of a discriminative perception of the aggregates that are present when we perceive ourselves.

But if we perceive ourselves when our aggregates are present, we are present when they are. How exactly are we to understand our being present when they are? The Pudgalavādins make it clear in Section 3.4.2 that we are present when our aggregates are present similar to the way in which the Nyāya-Vaiśeṣikas say that a substance is present when its attributes are present, as their "underlying support" (*āśraya*). But the Nyāya-Vaiśeṣikas and Pudgalavādins do not have the very same conception of an underlying support. For the Pudgalavādins, the underlying support is an entity without a separate identity rather than a substance, and the phenomena for which it is an underlying support are aggregates rather than attributes. Nonetheless, the underlying support, in both cases, is that which performs the functions of providing a common subject in which all of the supported phenomena inhere and of persisting through the momentary coming to be and passing away of the phenomena that inhere in it. The perception of ourselves, the Pudgalavādins believe, is the perception of an inexplicable underlying support for our aggregates. Since we lack a character by ourselves that can be discriminated when we are perceived, we must be conceived in reliance upon the aggregates for which we are the underlying support.

But how can this be? Do not all Buddhists, as our secondary sources often tell us, reject the idea that we are underlying supports for our aggregates? There need be no problem for the Pudgalavādins, I believe, since a more accurate statement of what all Buddhists reject is that we are substantially real underlying supports for our aggregates. What is objectionable about our being substantially real underlying supports for our aggregates is that we would then be other than our aggregates, and hence, subject to all of the arguments used to refute the thesis that we are separate substances. The Pudgalavādins do not believe, of course, that the view, that we are inexplicable underlying support for our aggregates, is subject to this objection.

According to the Pudgalavādins, therefore, we nondiscriminatively perceive ourselves when our aggregates are present, and we are inexplicable underlying supports for our aggregates. The means by which it is known that we are inexplicable underlying supports for our aggregates, we may assume, is that we repeatedly nondiscriminatively perceive ourselves when the aggregates in the collections in dependence upon which we conceive ourselves are present to our minds. Moreover, it is surely because we are the inexplicable underlying supports for collections of aggregates that we are conceived in reliance upon them. So we are now in a better position to define aggregate-reliant identity. We possess aggregate-reliant identity just in case we are inexplicable underlying supports for the aggregates in the collections of aggregates in dependence upon which we are conceived.

The simplest form we may give to a reconstruction of the Pudgalavādins' reply from aggregate-reliant identity begins with the statement of the Pudgalavādins' aggregate-reliant identity thesis, which is that we conceive ourselves in reliance upon collections of aggregates. Let us now assume that we are conceived in reliance upon collections of aggregates just in case we are inexplicable underlying supports for the aggregates in the collections. On this basis, we may infer that we are inexplicable underlying supports for the aggregates in the collections in dependence upon which we conceive ourselves. To reach the conclusion that we are neither substantial realities nor substantially established realities we need only add that if we are inexplicable underlying supports then we are neither substantial realities nor substantially established realities. Hence, Vasubandhu's two realities objection, the Pudgalavādins believe, does not show that we do not ultimately exist without being the same in existence as collections of aggregates.

In Section 2.1.2, Vasubandhu will liken our conceiving ourselves in reliance upon collections of aggregates to the way in which milk is conceived in dependence upon the collection of substances of which it is composed. The aggregates in the collections of aggregates in reliance upon which we conceive ourselves, according to this comparison, are the substances of which we are composed. Vasubandhu assumes in both cases that the objects of the conception of ourselves are the same in existence as the collections of aggregates in dependence upon which the objects are conceived. This assumption is an application of the causal reference principle, which is the principle that the object of a conception is the same in existence as the causal basis of the conception. This is the principle that the Pudgalavādins will try, in Section 2.1.3, to undermine.

The attributes of the aggregates in reliance upon which we conceive ourselves

The attributes the Pudgalavādins assign to the collection of aggregates in reliance upon which a person conceives himself are that they "pertain to oneself" (*ādhyātmika*), are "acquired" (*upātta*), and "exist in the present" (*vartamāna*). The collection of aggregates that the Pudgalavādins believe to pertain to oneself seems to be the collection in reliance upon which we conceive ourselves as opposed to collections in reliance upon which we conceive other persons and other phenomena. Vasubandhu himself uses *ādhyātmika* to refer to internal aggregates (sense organs and mental phenomena) as opposed to external aggregates. But because the Pudgalavādins are using the term here to signify the collections of aggregates in reliance upon which we conceive ourselves, and we conceive ourselves in reliance upon our bodies as a whole, not just in reliance upon our sense-organs, I assume that the collections of aggregates that pertain to us include all of the elements of our own bodies. This characterization of the collections of aggregates in reliance upon which we conceive ourselves gets its point, if I am right about this, due to the fact that a collection of aggregates, *qua* aggregates, can be any collection of substances conceived as a single entity of some sort, and the Pudgalavādins wish to call attention to the fact that we do not conceive ourselves in reliance upon collections of aggregates that belong to other persons or other objects.

When the Pudgalavādins say that the collection of aggregates in reliance upon which a person conceives himself is "acquired" (*upātta*), what do they mean by *upātta*? In Monier Williams' *Sanskrit–English Dictionary* *upātta* is rendered as "appropriated," but the definition of the term that seems best to fit the sort of use the Pudgalavādins make of it, is "acquired," as in a part of a whole being acquired. If this definition captures the sense of the Pudgalavādins' use of the term, *upātta*, the Pudgalavādins are implying that we are properly conceived as "acquirers" (*upādātā*-s) of aggregates in the sense that, at every moment, we acquire different aggregates in the collections in dependence upon which we conceive ourselves. Once acquired, of course, the aggregates are owned or possessed, if only for a moment, and the aggregates are used at that moment to perceive an object, to think a thought, to have a feeling, to remember an object, etc. Hence, the implication of the Pudgalavādins' claim, that the collections of aggregates in reliance upon which we conceive ourselves are acquired, seems also to imply that we are owners or possessors of the aggregates in the collections of aggregates in dependence upon which we conceive ourselves. So let us assume, and I think it is a safe assumption, that the Pudgalavādins think that, from the conventional point of view, we are what acquire and then possess the different aggregates in the collections that are the causal basis of the conception of ourselves.

It is not clear to me how Vasubandhu would interpret the Pudgalavādins' use of *upātta* in this passage. In Edgerton's *Buddhist Hybrid Sanskrit Dictionary*, the dominant meaning of *upādāna*, which is based on the same verbal root as *upātta*, seems to be "clinging" or "grasping," since it is listed as one of the twelve links of "dependent origination" (*pratītyasamutpāda*). The twelve links of dependent origination were set out by the Buddha to explain how we are propelled from one rebirth to another. In this context, the Buddha said that in dependence upon "craving" (*tṛṣṇā*), clinging or grasping arises. In this context, *upādāna*, which is the ninth link, seems to mean clinging to saṃsāra. Perhaps, then, when the Pudgalavādins refer to the collection of aggregates in reliance upon which we conceive ourselves as *upātta*, Vasubandhu took this reference to mean that the aggregates are the objects of the clinging that is the clinging to saṃsāra. Another possibility, which I sketched in the Introduction, is that Vasubandhu took it to be a reference to a whole that acquires and possesses different parts. For one or the other of these reasons, I believe, Vasubandhu does not find fault with the Pudgalavādins' claim that the aggregates in the collections of aggregates in reliance upon which we conceive ourselves are *upātta*.

When the Pudgalavādins say that we conceive ourselves in reliance upon collections of aggregates that exist in the present I believe that they mean that the collections of aggregates in reliance upon which we conceive ourselves are, in the most basic way, those that exist at the time we conceive ourselves. Hence, they can allow for less basic ways in which we conceive ourselves, as they do in the *Sāṃmitīyanikāya Śāstra* and the *Tridharmaka Śāstra*. On this interpretation, for instance, at the present moment, as I am writing this sentence, and I think, "I am writing this sentence," I am conceiving myself as "I" in reliance upon a collection of aggregates that exists at this moment, as I am writing this sentence. In general, whenever I formulate a thought in which I am the subject of the thought, I am conceiving myself in reliance upon a collection of aggregates that exists at the moment I am formulating the thought. This will be true not only of thoughts about myself that are expressed in the present tense of verbs, but also of thoughts about myself that are expressed in the past or future tenses of verbs. "I wrote this sentence yesterday," for instance, is used to conceive me, now, as the person thinking this thought and expresses the idea that I am the same person that wrote the sentence yesterday. An aggregate in reliance upon which I conceive myself as "I" in the case of "I wrote this sentence yesterday" is the present memory of the writing of the sentence yesterday. Similarly, an aggregate in reliance upon which I conceive myself as "I" in the case of "I shall write another sentence tomorrow" is the present intention to write another sentence tomorrow. Although I am also conceiving myself in the last two cases in dependence upon past and future aggregates, I am also conceiving myself in dependence upon my present aggregates. Hence, conceiving myself in dependence upon present aggregates is the basic way, which is present even in the cases in which I extend reference to myself to the past or the future.

In the *Tridharmaka Śāstra*, a Pudgalavādin account of how persons are conceived is also presented. It is much more elaborate than the account in the "Refutation," but does not seem to be inconsistent with that account. It may be helpful, in fact, to explain the account in the *Tridharmaka Śāstra*, since it may provide us with a better understanding of the account in the "Refutation." My explanation of that account is based on my interpretation of Priestley's translations, in *Pudgalavāda Buddhism*, of the relevant passages in the two different Chinese translations of the *Tridharmaka Śāstra* (pp. 56–60). I have, however, substituted "acquisition" for his "appropriation," "in dependence upon" for his "based on" and "according to," and "their own" for his "internal."

According to Sanghadeva's Chinese translation of the *Tridharmaka Śāstra*, the first way in which persons are said to be conceived is in dependence upon the acquisition of aggregates. According to Kumārabuddhi's translation, the first way in which persons are conceived is in dependence upon the acquisition of aggregates that are present and acquired as their own. Kumārabuddhi's version, although similar to the account Vasubandhu provides in the "Refutation," is quite different. The basic similarity between the two accounts is that in both it is being explained how it is possible for persons, who ultimately exist but have no identity of their own, to be conceived. However, for persons to be conceived in dependence upon the *acquisition* of aggregates that are present and acquired as their own is not the same as persons being conceived in reliance upon *aggregates* that are present and acquired as their own. The account presented in the "Refutation" is meant to explain why persons are neither substantial realities nor substantially established realities, while the account in *Tridharmaka Śāstra* is not. The work done by the account in Vasubandhu's "Refutation" is done by "in reliance upon" (*upādāya*), while the work done by the account in Kumārabuddhi's account, is done by "acquisition" (*upādāna*). (Although it is possible that the Chinese translation was meant to convey the idea of "in reliance upon," I am not in a position to explore this possibility here.) The difference between the two accounts, so understood, is to be explained by the fact that the first of the three accounts presented in the *Tridharmaka Śāstra* is meant to be contrasted to the other two accounts, while the account in the "Refutation" is not. The first account presented in Kumārabuddhi's interpretation of the *Tridharmaka Śāstra* may be contrasted to the second account, according to which persons are conceived in dependence upon the repeated acquisition of the aggregates in the temporally ordered collections of aggregates on the basis of which persons are conceived, and to the third account, according to which persons are conceived because these same aggregates are no longer being acquired. These contrasts, in fact, are what mark off the three accounts in the *Tridharmaka Śāstra*.

The second way in which persons are conceived, according to Kumārabuddhi's translation of the *Tridharmaka Śāstra*, is said to be in dependence upon approach or skillful means, which is explained as being conceived in dependence upon past, present, and future aggregates. Past aggregates are the aggregates in dependence upon whose acquisition in the past persons are conceived, present aggregates are these same aggregates insofar as they are continuously being acquired every moment, and future aggregates are these same aggregates insofar as they have not yet been acquired.

There seems to be no way to decide with certainty whether Sanghadeva's version of this second account, according to which persons are conceived in dependence only upon past aggregates, or Kumārabuddhi's version, according to which persons are conceived in dependence upon past, present, and future aggregates, is correct. But it seems that Kumārabuddhi's version is more likely to be the correct one. First of all, it is not clear why, if persons can be conceived in dependence upon past aggregates, they cannot also be conceived in dependence upon future aggregates. So Sanghadeva's version is rather puzzling in this regard. Second, Kumārabuddhi's account of the second way in which persons are conceived is virtually the same as the account to be found in the *Sāṃmitīyanikāya Śāstra*.

Although his account of the second way in which persons are conceived may seem to be inconsistent with the account given in the "Refutation" of how persons are conceived (or at least with my interpretation of that account), it is not. For Kumārabuddhi's account, as his examples make clear, is actually an account of how conventionally real persons are conceived to be the same persons over time. The example of conceiving persons in dependence upon past aggregates is, "In a former life, I was king Kuśa," and the example of conceiving persons in dependence upon future aggregates is, "In the future, he will be called Ajita." The meaning of the first example, surely, is, "I am the same person that existed in a former life, and in that life I was called king Kuśa." The meaning of the second example is, "He is the same person that will exist in a future life, and in that life he will be called Ajita." The idea is that, in dependence upon the aggregates acquired at different times, i.e. a temporally ordered collection of aggregates, we conceive ourselves as existing at different times. This interpretation accords with the account, presented in the *Sāṃmitīyanikāya Śāstra*, of the second way in which persons are conceived. According to that account, persons are conceived in dependence upon transition, which is the passing over to another existence. Once again, the examples cited in the text confirm this interpretation. This second way of conceiving persons, therefore, would seem to be a reference to our conceiving persons, who are conventional realities, as the same over time. It is said that since conventionally real persons are conceived in dependence upon the past, present and future of the aggregates, the nihilism view, that we do not receive the results of the actions we performed in the past, is avoided.

The third way in which persons are conceived, according to both the *Tridharmaka Śāstra* and the *Sāṃmitīyanikāya Śāstra*, is in dependence upon the cessation of aggregates, which is explained in terms of aggregates no longer being acquired. In both texts the example used to illustrate a person being conceived is "The Fortunate One has attained final release from saṃsāra." The idea is that reference to a person in this case depends upon the continuum of aggregates (those in dependence upon whose acquisition ultimately existent persons are conceived) no longer being acquired. We might notice that we can only conceive other persons in this third way, since the collections of aggregates that are the causal basis of conceiving oneself as "I," according to the statement itself, no longer exist.

In the *Sāṃmitīyanikāya Śāstra*, the account of three ways in which persons are conceived is called an account of three kinds of persons. The account of the first kind is that persons are conceived from a basis. It is then argued that persons are neither other than nor the same as the aggregates, which are the basis in dependence upon which they are conceived, and that persons come to be and cease to be when the bases upon which they are conceived do. When it is said that persons come to be and cease to be when the bases upon which they are conceived do, the meaning seems to be that conventionally real persons are said to be born when they acquire the collection of aggregates by which they are identified as the persons of that life and are said to die when they lose that collection of aggregates. Hence, it would seem that, according to the *Sāṃmitīyanikāya Śāstra*, the first kind of person is a person who is conceived in dependence upon the collection of aggregates by which he is identified as the person of that life. By contrast, it seems that the second kind of person is a person who is conceived in dependence upon the collection of aggregates by which he is identified as living more than one life, and the third kind is a person who is conceived in dependence upon the collection of aggregates whose causal continuum has ceased to exist. Although somewhat different in formulation, this account is enough like the account in the *Tridharmaka Śāstra* to be taken as an alternative attempt to explain the different ways in which persons are conceived.

In the "Refutation" these elaborations of the Pudgalavādins' theory of persons are ignored, since Vasubandhu's concern is to show that persons, as conventionally real phenomena, cannot be inexplicable. When in Section 2.1.1 the Pudgalavādins say that persons are conceived in reliance upon aggregates, they mean to be claiming that, since persons cannot be conceived on the basis of a character they possess by their own natures, they must be conceived in reliance upon aggregates in such a way that persons, so conceived, are neither other than nor the same in existence as their aggregates.

§ 2.1.2 *Vasubandhu's objection from the causal reference principle*

Vasubandhu's objection to the reply from aggregate-reliant identity takes the form of providing an account of the meaning of "in reliance upon" that contradicts their claim that if we conceive ourselves in reliance upon aggregates, we are neither substantial realities nor substantially established realities. The claim is false, he argues, since we conceive ourselves either in dependence upon aggregates in the collections of our aggregates having been perceived or simply in dependence upon the collections of our aggregates, in which case we are substantially established realities, since we are then the same in existence as collections of aggregates. The distinction Vasubandhu draws between the alternative ways in which we conceive ourselves does not mark a real difference in his view, since the aggregates in the collections in dependence upon which we conceive ourselves, he assumes, are present to consciousnesses as objects of perception. He is arguing that if collections of aggregates are the causes of our conceiving ourselves, the conception of ourselves refers to us in dependence upon referring to collections of aggregates rather than to an inexplicable person.

He can draw this conclusion only if he assumes the truth of the causal reference principle. This principle is not accepted by the Pudgalavādins, whose aggregate-reliant identity thesis implies that it is false. Vasubandhu supports his use of the causal reference principle with the example of how milk is conceived. Since milk is conceived in reliance upon the collection of its elements, he argues, the conception of milk refers to milk in dependence upon referring to the collection of elements of which milk is composed; likewise, if we conceive ourselves in reliance upon a collection of aggregates, the conception of ourselves refers to us in dependence upon referring to collections of aggregates rather than to inexplicable entities. Finally, Vasubandhu concludes his objection with the statement that "the difficulty is the same." The difficulty to which I believe he alludes is that the Pudgalavādins are committed to his version of the view that we are substantially established realities, and hence, that we are the same in existence as collections of aggregates.

§ 2.1.3 *The Pudgalavādins' fire and fuel reply*

The Pudgalavādins' reply begins with the denial that we conceive ourselves in the way milk is conceived. They mean that we are not conventional realities in the way milk is, but in some other way. Instead of explaining the difference between these two different kinds of conventional realities, they simply say that we conceive ourselves in reliance upon collections of aggregates in the way fire is conceived in reliance upon fuel. In saying that fire is conceived in reliance upon fuel without being the same in existence as fuel the Pudgalavādins are attempting to produce a counter-example to Vasubandhu's causal reference principle, and so, to undermine this argument that persons ultimately exist in the way milk does.

In making this comparison the Pudgalavādins need not be implying that the relation of fire to fuel is in all respects the same as the relation of ourselves to the collection of our aggregates. It need not be implied, for instance, that fire is known to exist in the same way that we are known to exist, which they believe to be by means of perception. Although it is possible that the Pudgalavādins think that fire is known to exist by direct perception, it is not likely. But the comparison would seem to imply that fire exists apart from fuel, since even though the Pudgalavādins are not here arguing that we exist apart from aggregates, the idea of our aggregate-reliant identity, we have found, implies that we do. So what is implied by the comparison is (1) that the fire conceived in dependence upon fuel exists apart from the fuel, (2) that the fire is not other than this fuel, and (3) that fire is not the same in existence as fuel. For the purpose of refuting the causal reference principle, all three of these implications are required.

The Pudgalavādins' reply to Vasubandhu's causal reference objection requires arguments for the theses that fire ultimately exists, that fire is not conceived unless fuel is present, that fire is not other than fuel, and that fire is not the same in existence as fuel, and it will imply that collections of aggregates are the causal basis of conceiving ourselves and that we are not

Pudgalavādins agree with Vasubandhu's characterization of what is commonly said about the activity of fire, just as they do in the case of what is commonly said about the activities of persons. How would they explain the alteration that is commonly said to occur in the continuum of fuel by the action of fire?

We may be sure that the Pudgalavādins do not believe that the alteration caused by fire in the continuum of fuel is a change of some sort in a substance, since no Indian Buddhists accept the idea of a substance that undergoes change. The key to understanding the nature of this alteration, from their point of view, is that the analogy they make to persons and their aggregates implies that its cause, fire, is not other than the collection of the earth-, air-, and water-elements in whose continuum the alteration is produced. For if fire is not other than fuel, we may assume, it is without a separate identity. What this implies, in turn, is that fire is capable of an inexplicable union with fuel in such a way as to provide an explanation of why fire is said to cause fuel to burn. An inexplicable union would be a union that is not other than what is united nor the same in existence as what is united. It is precisely such an inexplicable union, they may think, which would be required to explain how it is possible for fuel, which is not hot by itself, to be said to become hot by the action of fire. For fuel, they believe, cannot become hot by itself. So let us assume that in burning material, according to the Pudgalavādins, there is present fire or heat that is acting upon fuel to cause the fuel to burn. But in what does the burning of the fuel consist if fire is inexplicably united with it?

An account of the burning of fuel that is at least consistent with what we know of the Pudgalavādins' cosmology is that it consists in the moment by moment destruction of the parts of fuel with which fire is inexplicably united, until the continuum of fuel ceases to exist as a continuum called fuel. In this case, there is no substantially real entity in fuel that undergoes a change of any sort, but the continuum of the substantially real elements of which fuel is composed burns in the sense that the number of its combined elements decreases moment by moment, until the continuum called fuel ceases to exist. For this reason, they seem to believe, fuel is said to be consumed by the fire with which it inexplicably unites. The fire that is inexplicably united with fuel in burning material, moreover, can be said to continue to be known to exist until it consumes the fuel, since so long as fuel is burning it may be inferred that fire is inexplicably united with it and provides a rationale for saying that fire causes it to burn. This fire will be inexplicably the same over time in the way the Pudgalavādins seem to believe that a person is inexplicably the same over time. It remains the same over time without being a permanent phenomenon and without being a causal continuum of impermanent phenomena.

It should be clear that the Pudgalavādins believe that the definitions of fire as what causes fuel to burn and of a person as what acquires and possesses different aggregates are not definitions based on characters they possess by themselves. They must be definitions formed on the basis of the invariable presence of fuel and aggregates when fire and a person, respectively, are known to exist. So when I say that they believe that fire consumes its fuel I mean that fire, insofar as it is what is conceived in reliance upon fuel, is what consumes fuel. Nonetheless, apart from being so conceived, they imply, fire ultimately exists without being other than or the same in existence as the fuel in reliance upon which it is conceived. Similarly, they believe that we are, by convention, what acquire and possess different aggregates, but do not acquire and possess them by virtue of a character we possess by ourselves. But apart from being so conceived, they imply, we exist without being the same in existence as the causal basis of the conception of ourselves. What the Pudgalavādins believe, surely, is that their theory of persons better explains the convention that we acquire and possess different aggregates than does the theory of Vasubandhu; likewise, they think, their theory of fire better explains the convention that it burns fuel than does the theory of Vasubandhu.

But exactly how do the theories of the Pudgalavādins better explain these conventions than do the theories of Vasubandhu? They would seem to believe that we are inexplicably united with different aggregates as their inexplicable underlying supports, and that, because we lack separate identities, we can say that we acquire and possess different aggregates without being other than them or the same in existence as them. Basically, they are committed to the thesis that our acquisition and possession of different aggregates are inexplicable in the sense that we do not acquire and possess them in the way that a substantially real phenomenon might be said to acquire and possess different parts or in the way that collections of such phenomena might be said to acquire and possess different parts. This thesis, that our acquisition and possession of aggregates is inexplicable, is an alternative to what would seem to be Vasubandhu's thesis, which is that we acquire and possess different aggregates in the way that a collection of substances like milk or a pot acquires and possesses different parts.

Moreover, the Pudgalavādins' analogy to fire points in the same direction. Just as fire can be conceived to be what causes fuel to burn because it is an inexplicable underlying support for burning fuel, so we can be conceived to be what acquire and possess different aggregates because we are inexplicable underlying supports for aggregates. My point is that the Pudgalavādins' theory of persons and use of fire as an analogy may be based on a carefully worked out metaphysical explanation of our conventional views concerning the natures of ourselves and of fire. Particularly important, I believe, is the view that the possession of ultimate existence without possessing a separate identity is what makes it possible for a person to be inexplicably united with aggregates and fire with fuel as inexplicable underlying supports. If they did not possess ultimate existence, there would not be anything at all that unites with aggregates and fuel, and if they possessed a separate identity, their union with aggregates and fuel would be impossible, since they would be separate substances.

The Pudgalavādins' view, that fire is what causes the fuel with which it is inexplicably united to burn, enables us to understand their arguments for the theses that fire is not other than fuel and that fire is not the same in existence as fuel. The first argument consists simply of the statement, "if fire were other than fuel, fuel would not be hot." We can now take the premise of this argument to be grounded in the assumption that if the fire were other than fuel, it could not unite with it and be the underlying support for the perceptible heat in fuel. The second argument consists of the statement, "if fire were not other than fuel, what burns and what causes it to burn would be the same." Since they present this statement as part of an argument for the conclusion that fire is not the same in existence as fuel, we may assume that they take it for granted that what burns and what causes it to burn cannot be the same in existence. But fire, they have assumed, is what causes fuel to burn. So what they deem to be the impossible consequence of fire being the same in existence as fuel is that fuel causes itself to burn. The principle employed in this argument, therefore, is that nothing can produce an effect in itself. In other words, the Pudgalavādins are assuming that a cause of an effect in the continuum of fuel cannot be the same in existence as that in which it causes its effect.

Vasubandhu would agree that fire is not the same in existence as fuel, but not for the reason given by the Pudgalavādins. He believes that fire is not the same in existence as fuel because fire and fuel are composed of elements of different intensities or of elements differently configured. Hence, although he disagrees with the reason the Pudgalavādins have for denying that fire is the same in existence as fuel, he does not comment on this part of their argument.

We are ready now to reconstruct the Pudgalavādins' arguments for the three basic theses of their account of why fire is conceived in reliance upon fuel. In this reconstruction I shall follow Vasubandhu's practice of retaining the Pudgalavādins' use of "in reliance upon," but without the special meaning they gave to it in their reply from aggregate-reliant identity. The reply, in its full form, is made up of four component arguments. The first is an argument that is not actually formulated in the text, but may be assumed on the basis of the replies the Pudgalavādins' will make to Vasubandhu's objections to the reply. This is the simple argument that since fire is what causes fuel to burn, it is conceived in reliance upon fuel. The premise established by this argument I shall call the fuel-reliant identity premise of their reply.

In support of the view that fire is not other than fuel the Pudgalavādins argue that if fire is other than fuel, fuel is not hot. The meaning of this statement, their analysis of fire and fuel in Section 2.1.5 will make clear, is that if fire is other than fuel, fuel *in burning material* is not hot. Since the Pudgalavādins assume that fuel in burning material is hot, they would have us conclude that fire is not other than fuel. The full argument for this conclusion is that if we assume (I) that fire is other than fuel, fire does not inexplicably unite with fuel in burning material, (II) that if fire does not inexplicably unite with fuel in burning material, fuel in burning material is not hot, and (III) that fuel in burning material is hot, we may conclude (IV) that fire is not other than fuel. In support of the thesis that fire is not the same in existence as fuel the Pudgalavādins assume that if fire is what causes fuel to burn and fire is the same in existence as fuel, then fuel causes fuel to burn. Since fuel does not cause fuel to burn, it follows that fire is not the same in existence as fuel. At this point the Pudgalavādins' reply has provided an example of something besides a person that is conceived in dependence upon something else without being other than it or the same in existence as it.

To show exactly how the reply answers the causal reference objection we need to add one further argument. From the premises that fire is not the same in existence as fuel and that if fire is not the same in existence as fuel, the conception of fire does not refer to fuel, the Pudgalavādins would have us infer that the conception of fire does not refer to fuel. But they believe that if fire is conceived in reliance upon fuel, fuel is the causal basis of the conception of fire. Therefore, they would have us infer that fuel is the causal basis of the conception of fire and the conception of fire does not refer to fuel. But if fuel is the causal basis of the conception of fire and the conception of fuel does not refer to fuel, it is clear that the object of the conception of fire is not the same in existence as its causal basis. This is the logical structure of the argument they use to provide a counter-example to the causal reference principle used by Vasubandhu in his causal reference objection to their reply from aggregate-reliant identity.

§ 2.1.4 *The Pudgalavādins' middle way argument*

The Pudgalavādins' fire and fuel reply is primarily used to show that the object we are conceived to be need not be the same in existence as the causal basis of our being conceived. Immediately after replying to Vasubandhu's causal reference objection, they introduce premises analogous to those used in the reply to formulate their main argument for the view that we are inexplicable phenomena. This argument, I believe, is based on the assumption that we are what acquire different aggregates and, having taken possession of them, use them to perceive objects, etc. The conclusion of the argument is that the Pudgalavādins' theory of persons is the middle way the Buddha taught exists between eternal transcendence and nihilism theories. Although the Pudgalavādins in this argument implicitly appeal to the Buddha's rejection of extreme theories of persons in order to argue that we are ultimately existent inexplicable persons, they probably believe, as Vasubandhu does, that separate philosophical arguments are to be used to reject these extreme theories.

Since conceiving ourselves in reliance upon collections of aggregates is meant to be analogous to conceiving fire in reliance upon fuel, it is reasonable to assume that the Pudgalavādins' middle way argument is predicated on a definition of ourselves, just as their fire and fuel reply is predicated on a definition of fire. The definition required by their argument is that we are what acquire and possess different aggregates and use them to perceive objects, etc. What makes it possible for us to acquire and possess different aggregates, and thereby to be said to possess attributes of the aggregates we acquire, I assume they believe, is that we are the ultimately existent inexplicable underlying supports for aggregates. Because we acquire and possess different aggregates we are not the same in existence as the collection of the different aggregates we acquire and possess, and because we are not separate substances, we are not other than this collection, and so do not possess by ourselves the attributes ascribed to us. Moreover, if we ultimately exist without separate identities, we cannot, from an ultimate point of view, be said to cease to exist when the continuum of the collection of our aggregates ceases to exist at the time of our "final release from saṃsāra" (*parinirvāṇa*) or be said not to cease to exist at that time. Whether or not we cease to exist at that time is a question we are not in a position to answer from an ultimate point of view.

At the most fundamental level, the Pudgalavādins' argument for their theory being a middle way between the extremes of eternal transcendence and nihilism, I shall assume, relies on the definition of ourselves as acquirers and possessors of different aggregates, etc. They believe, if this is correct, that since we are what acquire and possess different aggregates, and could not acquire and possess them unless we are ultimately existent inexplicable phenomena, we must be ultimately existent inexplicable phenomena. The Pudgalavādins do not explicitly formulate this argument or its conclusion, but it is reasonable to assume that the argument they do present is based on it.

The first part of their argument is that we are not other than collections of aggregates, since if we were other than these collections, we would be committed to the eternal transcendence theory of persons rejected by the Buddha. The theory rejected here, of course, is that we are separate substances. Indian Buddhists offer a variety of arguments to show that we are not separate substances. The very simplest of these arguments we could use in this context is that we cannot be separate substances, since we conceive ourselves in reliance upon collections of aggregates. So the simplest form of argument is that if we are separate substances, we would not, as we do, conceive ourselves in dependence upon these collections.

Since the conclusion of this argument is not disputed by Vasubandhu, we need not discuss it further.

The second part of the Pudgalavādins' argument is that if we should say that we are the same in existence as collections of aggregates, we would be committed to a nihilism theory of persons. The form of the nihilism theory to which the Pudgalavādins believe we would be committed, I assume, is the theory that we do not ultimately exist. For if we are the same in existence as collections of aggregates, which lack the unity and identity over time required by the referent of "I," which is what performs contaminated actions, suffers the results of these actions, and can, through sufficient effort, become free from suffering by extinguishing the continuum of the aggregates in dependence upon which it is conceived, then we do not perform contaminated actions, etc. If we do not perform contaminated actions, etc. we are not persons at all. In other words, it follows that persons do not ultimately exist. Hence, since the eternal transcendence extreme, that we are other than collections of aggregates, and the nihilism extreme, that we are the same in existence as collections of aggregates, are abandoned, their own theory, that we are ultimately existent inexplicable persons, is the middle way.

Unfortunately, in the "Refutation" Vasubandhu does not discuss the Pudgalavādins' middle way argument, and the Pudgalavādins, for the most part, are made simply to assume the truth of the premises of their own middle way argument in their objections to Vasubandhu's theory, just as Vasubandhu assumes the falsity of their premises in his objections to their theory. So what the Pudgalavādins' statement of their middle way argument accomplishes, in its occurrence in the "Refutation," is simply a reformulation of their theory of persons that fits with the Buddha's claim that his own theory of persons is a middle way between extreme theories.

§ 2.1.5 *Vasubandhu's call for analyses of fire and fuel and his first three objections to the fire and fuel reply*

Vasubandhu's critique begins with a request for explanations of fire and fuel that will enable him to determine whether its fuel-reliant identity premise represents how fire and fuel are in fact conceived. This request is motivated, surely, by Vasubandhu's belief that if fire is conceived in reliance upon fuel, it is not conceived in the way milk is conceived, which is in dependence upon the collection of elements of which it is composed, since fuel is not a collection of elements of which fire is composed. Hence, if it is known that fire is conceived in reliance upon fuel, it is not in the same way as milk is known to be conceived in dependence upon the collection of its elements.

The Pudgalavādins first advance the view that the fuel-reliant identity premise is known to be true because of the way in which fire is conventionally defined. The definition of fire as what burns fuel shows immediately that fire is conceived in reliance upon fuel. But Vasubandhu objects that the conventional definitions of fire and fuel require an explanation in terms of an analysis of fire and fuel that reveals in what form they ultimately exist. I shall call the analysis of the sort he demands a "causal basis analysis," since its purpose is to determine in what the ultimate existence of a object of a conception consists by analyzing the object into the phenomena that are the causal basis of the conception. A causal basis analysis is required, he assumes, if it is to be known whether or not fire being conceived in reliance upon fuel implies that it is neither other than nor the same in existence as fuel. Even if fire is by convention defined as what burns fuel, a causal basis analysis may show that it does not in fact burn fuel, and so is conceived in reliance upon fuel merely by convention. Vasubandhu believes that such an analysis will show that, from an ultimate perspective, fire does not burn fuel, that fire is other than fuel and that fire is impermanent. When the Pudgalavādins object to the analysis Vasubandhu gives by presenting a different sort of analysis of fire and fuel, Vasubandhu argues that the statement of their own analysis implies that fire is other than fuel, that fuel is not a cause of fire, that fire is not conceived in reliance upon fuel, and that fire can cause fuel in burning material to be hot even if it is other than fuel. To determine whether or not he is successful in the arguments he uses to support these beliefs is the main objective of my commentaries on his critique of their fire and fuel reply.

Vasubandhu presents three objections to the Pudgalavādins' fire and fuel reply on the basis of his own causal basis analysis of fire and fuel. In the first, Vasubandhu argues that even though fire is conceived in reliance upon fuel from the point of view of its conventional definition, a causal basis analysis of fire and fuel shows that fire is other than fuel. Vasubandhu acknowledges that in our everyday lives we define fire as what causes fuel to burn and conceive of burning as an alteration in the continuum of elements of which fuel is composed. Because we conceive fire and fuel in this way, he grants, fire is said to be conceived in reliance upon fuel. But he does not thereby commit himself to the view that fire is in fact conceived in reliance upon fuel. A causal basis analysis of fire and fuel, he believes, shows that fire does not in fact burn fuel. This does not mean that he believes that the definition of fire they use is not the one conventionally employed. The implication is that he rejects the Pudgalavādins' assumption, that since fire is by convention conceived in reliance upon fuel, we may infer that it is an ultimately existent inexplicable entity.

When in this objection Vasubandhu grants that the fuel-reliant identity premise is true, he must be assuming that, although we do by convention conceive fire in reliance upon fuel, fire, as it actually exists, does not burn fuel. Because he does not make explicit in his objection his belief that the conventional definition used by the Pudgalavādins falsely portrays it as an agent that produces a change in fuel, his statement of the objection hides the fact that he does not believe the definition to be correct. According to Vasubandhu, the conventional definition of fire is based on a false view of its nature as an agent that produces a change in an object, and so cannot be used by the Pudgalavādins in an argument to overturn the principle that the object of a conception is the same in existence as the causal basis of the conception. In spite of its conventional definition, fire arises in dependence upon fuel rather than being an agent that causes a change in fuel. But if fire arises in dependence upon fuel, he concludes, fire must be other than fuel.

Vasubandhu illustrates how fire arises in dependence upon fuel by reference to how curd arises in dependence upon milk and to how sour milk arises in dependence upon sweet milk. In the illustration, reference to curd, milk, sour milk, and sweet milk is made according to what Vasubandhu assumes to be the causal bases of their conceptions. Hence, it is implied that, from the perspective of the causal basis of its conception, fire is no more a cause of an alteration in fuel than curd is a cause of an alteration in milk or sour milk is a cause of an alteration in sweet milk. It is also implied, of course, that although by convention fire is conceived in reliance upon fuel, it should not, from an ultimate perspective, be so conceived any more than curd should be conceived in reliance upon milk, etc. from that perspective. He believes that fire arises in dependence upon fuel in the way that one collection of momentary substances arises in dependence upon another. He assumes that what arises in dependence upon something else must be other than that in dependence upon which it arises, since he adopts the theories that all causally conditioned phenomena are momentary and that momentary phenomena, even those within a single causal continuum, are other than one another.

Vasubandhu's objection, therefore, simply assumes the correctness of his own causal analysis of fire and fuel. Moreover, since the Pudgalavādins' fire and fuel reply omitted an argument for the ultimate existence of fire as an agent that causes fuel to burn, Vasubandhu simply assumes the truth of his own theory of causality in this first objection to their reply. The Pudgalavādins' actual reply to the objection is to challenge the correctness of Vasubandhu's causal basis analysis of fire and fuel. Without an argument for the correctness of this analysis, Vasubandhu cannot be said to have established that fire is other than fuel. Moreover, their reply will imply that Vasubandhu's implied rejection of their definition of fire is question-begging, since it is based on his own causal basis analysis of fire and fuel.

In Vasubandhu's second objection to the fire and fuel reply on the basis of his causal basis analysis of fire and fuel he argues that since he has shown that fire arises in dependence upon fuel, it follows, if the Pudgalavādins' analogy is correct, that we arise in dependence upon collections of aggregates. But since what arises in dependence upon something else is other than it, he concludes, we will be other than collections of aggregates.

Vasubandhu's third objection is that another consequence of the fire and fuel reply, if the causal basis analyses of fire and fuel are correct, is that we are impermanent phenomena. He is minimally arguing that the Pudgalavādins must abandon the thesis that we are not impermanent phenomena, since fire, their analog, arises in dependence upon fuel, and all dependently arising phenomena are impermanent. But the argument may also be understood to be directed to the Pudgalavādins' thesis that we are neither permanent phenomena nor causal continua of impermanent phenomena.

§ 2.1.5.1 *The Pudgalavādins' reply, that fire is the heat present in burning material and that fuel is the collection of three primary elements that exist in burning material, is inconsistent with both their fire and fuel reply and their theory of persons*

Vasubandhu has thus far argued that, according to his causal analysis of fire and fuel, the fire and fuel reply fails to accomplish its purpose of providing an analog of how we are conceived in dependence upon aggregates without being either other than or the same in existence as them. So he now represents the Pudgalavādins as presenting an analysis of their own that they believe will accomplish this purpose.

The analysis that the Pudgalavādins use is not what we might have expected in the light of their view that a person, the analog to fire, is an ultimately existent inexplicable entity. They are represented as saying that the fire that is defined as what causes fuel to burn is the heat that is present in burning material. I shall try to explain why they say this in a moment. Before I do that, I want to introduce and comment on their analysis of fuel, which is that fuel is the collection of earth-, air-, and water-elements that are present in burning material. This analysis is peculiar in three ways. The first peculiarity is that it does not indicate whether fuel can exist when not present in burning materials. The second is that it omits reference to the fire-substance that the orthodox Vaibhāṣikas believe needs to be present, along with the other three primary substances, in every inseparable combination of substances of which bodies are composed. The third is that by omitting reference to a fire-substance in the analysis of fuel the impression is created that the heat that is present in burning material and is identified with fire is the fire-substance itself, since no mention is made of a fire-substance in the analysis of fuel. This third point is especially important, since it provides Vasubandhu with the opportunity to identify the heat that the Pudgalavādins claim is fire with the fire-substance. Whether or not this identification is correct will become apparent as I explain the second of the three peculiarities, and will become central to an appraisal of Vasubandhu's objections. The first peculiarity, perhaps, can be explained as the result of a view the Pudgalavādins actually hold, and can be summarily set aside. They may believe that something is not actually fuel until it is present in burning material and being burned. Before that point, they may say, it is only potential fuel.

The second peculiarity is not so easily explained. There is an interpretation of the Pudgalavādins' theory of fire and fuel that seems to explain why reference to a fire-substance is omitted in the analysis of fuel. It can also explain a number of other claims they make. This interpretation includes five parts. The first is that the fire-element, which Vasubandhu believes to be a substance, has been replaced in the Pudgalavādins' system, by a fire-element that is an inexplicable conventional reality. The second part of the interpretation is that, although this inexplicable fire-element is, just as the substantially real fire-element was said to be, present in every conventionally real body, along with the other three primary elements, the Pudgalavādins do not believe that it is present in fuel, since fuel is not by itself a conventionally real body, but that aspect of a conventionally real body by virtue of which it is said to be burning when the inexplicable fire-element present in it is causing its burning. The third part is that although an inexplicable fire-element is present in every conventionally real body, they believe that it causes fuel to be hot similar to the way in which the substantially real fire-element is said by Vasubandhu to cause a conventionally real body of which it is a constituent to be hot, which is by somehow "dominating" the other elements present in the body. The fourth part of this interpretation is that the Pudgalavādins think that fuel, unlike fire, is not an inexplicable entity, since it is a collection of three substantially real primary elements. Although it is not a conventional reality in the way in which Vasubandhu defines a conventional reality, it is the collection of the remaining three primary elements that are present in the burning material in which fire and fuel are present. Finally, the fifth part of the interpretation is that the Pudgalavādins regard burning material as a conventional reality that differs from a conventional reality as conceived by Vasubandhu insofar as its fire-element is an ultimately existent inexplicable entity.

The Pudgalavādins' identification of fire with the heat present in burning material does not contradict this interpretation, since the identification need not mean that fire is present only in burning material. Its more likely meaning, in fact, is that the ultimately existent inexplicable fire-element present in all conventionally real bodies, is, when it is in burning fuel, called the heat that is present in the burning material. On this interpretation of the Pudgalavādins' theory of fire and fuel, fire, like a person, is an ultimately existent inexplicable entity. In what follows I shall use this interpretation of their theory of fire and fuel to explain how the Pudgalavādins think that the presence of an ultimately existent inexplicable fire-element in bodies can explain the burning of fuel.

The Pudgalavādins' analysis of fire and fuel is explicitly comprised of the identification of fire with the heat present in burning material, and a fuel analysis, which is that fuel is the collection of the earth-, air-, and water-elements that conjointly arise in burning material when fire is present. Exactly how this analysis is supposed to enable the Pudgalavādins to avoid Vasubandhu's objections is not stated. Hence, we shall need to reconstruct how they believe it will enable them to do so.

One clue to how this analysis is to be used to avoid Vasubandhu's objections to the fire and fuel reply is to show how it factors into their use of the conventional definition of fire to prove that fire is conceived in reliance upon fuel. The fire and fuel analysis is meant to give support to this conventional definition. How they do so is easy to explain: to support the definition we need only to add to their fire and fuel analysis what may be called "the causality assumption," which is that the heat present in burning material is what causes fuel to burn. So from the fire and fuel analysis and this assumption we may derive the conventional definition of fire. Hence, it is clear how the Pudgalavādins' analysis of fire and fuel is meant to be an explanation of why fire is conceived in reliance upon fuel: it is an attempt to explain why fire is defined as what causes fuel to burn by identifying fire with what it is in burning material that is said to cause the fuel in burning material to burn.

The Pudgalavādins' identification of fire with the heat present in burning material, we may notice, is not, in spite of being an answer to Vasubandhu's request for an analysis, an account of fire that reveals in what form it ultimately exists. Even if we add the causality assumption to their account of fire, something important is missing. The form in which fire ultimately exists, in their view, is as an entity without a separate identity. So the account of fire they provide is not a statement of the form in which fire ultimately exists, but a statement of what it is called when it is actually burning fuel. Moreover, the causality assumption itself needs to be explained by an account of the way in which this "heat" causes fuel to burn. No such account is provided. But if the analogy between a person and fire is any indication, the account would take the form of treating fire as an inexplicable underlying causal support for fuel that is burning. So once again, the Pudgalavādins are represented as failing to respond to one of Vasubandhu's objections in a straightforward and complete fashion. Nonetheless, we shall now see, even Vasubandhu's critique of their incomplete analysis does not completely succeed.

Vasubandhu presents three arguments that purport to show that if the Pudgalavādins' analysis of fire and fuel is correct, one of the premises of their fire and fuel reply is false. Vasubandhu's first argues that even according to their own analysis of fire and fuel, fire will be other than fuel, since the analysis implies that fire and fuel have different defining properties. Vasubandhu does not mean to imply, when he says that fire and fuel have different defining properties, that fuel has a defining property in the way that fire does. His meaning is that the defining property of fire is other than those of the other elements of which fuel is composed. But he does not explain why he believes that fire as analyzed by the Pudgalavādins must possess a different defining property than possessed by the other three elements.

It is clear that this objection is based on the assumption that the fire to which the Pudgalavādins refer is a substantially real fire-element, and that for this reason it possesses a different defining property than that possessed by the other three elements. His reason for making this assumption may be that he believes that fire could not cause fuel to be hot, and so, to burn, unless fire were hot by its own nature and that the fire-element is precisely that which is hot by its own nature. The Pudgalavādins, of course, do not believe this. Their view seems to be that heat is by convention taken to be what causes fuel to burn, but fire, apart from being conceived as fire, cannot be said to possess heat. It cannot be known what fire is, apart from being conceived as fire, and therefore, apart from being conceived in dependence upon fuel.

Vasubandhu's first objection is based on the assumption that (I) if fire is the heat present in burning material, fire is the substantially real fire-element. But according to the Pudgalavādins, (II) fire is the heat present in burning material. Therefore, from (I) and (II) we may infer that (III) fire is the substantially real fire-element. But since the four primary substantially real elements have different defining properties, Vasubandhu assumes that (IV) if fire is the substantially real fire-element, then the defining property of fire is other than the defining properties of the other three elements. Therefore, from (III) and (IV) we may infer that (V) the defining property of fire is other than the defining properties of the other three elements. But according to the Pudgalavādins, (VI) fuel is the same in existence as the other three elements. Hence, from (V) and (VI) we may infer that (VII) the defining property of fire is other than the defining properties of fuel. According to Vasubandhu, (VIII) if the defining property of fire is other than the defining properties of fuel, then fire is other than fuel. Therefore, from (VII) and(VIII) we may infer that (IX) fire is other than fuel.

Although no reply to the objection from defining properties is presented in the text, it is clear that the Pudgalavādins would have a reasonable reply. They could simply deny that heat being present in burning material implies that a substantially real fire-element is present, since the heat present in burning material does not, as a substantially real fire-element does, possess by itself a character on the basis of which it can be conceived. Even if they should say that fire has heat as a defining property, they would not say that this character belongs to fire by itself. If the defining property of fire does not belong to fire by itself, then even if fire has heat as a defining property, it does not follow that fire is other than any other phenomenon. Since the Pudgalavādins clearly do not identify fire with a substantially real fire-element, Vasubandhu's objection from defining properties is based on a misinterpretation of their analysis of fire.

Vasubandhu's second objection to the fire and fuel reply based on their analysis of fire and fuel is that the analysis implies that the fuel-reliant identity premise of the reply is false. He calls attention to the fact that if the Pudgalavādins' analysis of fire and fuel is correct, fuel is not a cause of fire, but in doing so he is not presenting an objection to the fire and fuel reply based on their own analysis. Rather, he is pointing out that an implication of their analysis is the denial of a thesis he himself believes to be true on the basis of his own causal basis analysis of fire and fuel and its causal implication. Not only is this implication true, he is saying, but there is an implication that contradicts the fuel-reliant identity premise of their fire and fuel reply.

Vasubandhu's objection is that since, according to their own analysis of fire and fuel, fire is present in burning material, fire is not conceived in reliance upon fuel; for if fire is present in burning material, fire is the causal basis of the conception of fire. Vasubandhu assumes that if fire is the causal basis of the conception of fire, fire is not conceived in reliance upon fuel.

The obvious reply the Pudgalavādins can make to this objection is to argue that it is not true that if fire is present in the burning material, fire is the causal basis of the conception of fire, since the fire present in burning material does not possess a character of its own on the basis of which it can be conceived. So it cannot be the causal basis of the conception of fire. No such reply is made in the text.

Vasubandhu's objection from the presence of fire took the form of saying that the meaning of "in reliance upon" must be explained, since the Pudgalavādins' analysis of fire implies that fire itself is the causal basis of the conception of fire. He then takes up an explanation according to which the phenomena upon which something relies are its support in the sense of being its inseparable concomitants. He has two objections to this definition. The first is that it implies that a collection of aggregates is other than a person, since things that support one another in this way are other than one another, which would imply that a person is other than a collection of aggregates. The second is that it implies that a person does not exist unless a collection of aggregates exists, since inseparable concomitants, although other than one another, always occur in combination with one another. This explanation of the meaning of "in reliance upon," of course, is suggested to Vasubandhu by his identification of the inexplicable fire-element of the Pudgalavādins with a substantially real fire-element. According to the *Treasury*, each of the primary elements has as its supports or inseparable concomitants the other three.

This explanation of "in reliance upon" could not possibly have been suggested by the Pudgalavādins, because fire is an inexplicable phenomenon. What value this objection has lies in the fact that it confirms the fact that a central thesis of the Pudgalavādins' theory of persons is that we exist apart from our aggregates. Since Vasubandhu draws the consequence, from the supposition that "in reliance upon" means inseparable concomitance, that a person would not exist unless the aggregates do, and expects this to contradict one of the Pudgalavādins' theses, it is clear that he believes that one of their theses is that a person exists apart from his aggregates.

Vasubandhu's third objection to the fire and fuel reply based on the Pudgalavādins' own analysis of fire and fuel is explicitly directed against their argument that if fire were other than fuel, fuel in burning material would not be hot. The objection turns on an alleged ambiguity in the premise that the fuel in burning material is hot. Vasubandhu assumes in the objection that the heat present in fuel is either a substantially real fire-element or its defining property, that if this heat is the defining property of a substantially real fire-element, what is combined with the defining property of the fire-element is combined with the fire-element, and that phenomena that are combined are other than one another. Whether or not the heat is interpreted as a substantially real fire-element or as its defining property does not matter to the argument, since Vasubandhu assumes that a substantially real phenomenon and its defining property are not other than one another. These are assumptions that he believes to be true and that he needs in order to infer, at different points in his objection, that fuel is not hot if "hot" in "Fuel in burning material is hot" signifies heat, and that fire is other than fuel if "hot" in "Fuel in burning material is hot" signifies what is combined with heat.

Vasubandhu's objection begins with the premise that (I) "hot" signifies heat or "hot" signifies something that is combined with heat. If we assume that Vasubandhu identifies heat with the defining property of a substantially real fire-element, the objection continues with the assumption that (II) if "hot" signifies heat, "hot" signifies the defining property of a substantially real fire-element. But (III) if "hot" signifies the defining property of a substantially real fire-element, "hot" does not signify a defining property that belongs to the earth-, air-, or water-elements. The Pudgalavādins' fuel analysis, Vasubandhu assumes, is that (IV) fuel is the same in existence as the earth-, air-, and water-elements. Therefore, from (II), (III), and (IV), he believes, we may infer that (V) if "hot" signifies heat, "hot" does not signify a defining property that belongs to fuel. However, (VI) if "hot" does not signify a defining property that belongs to fuel, fuel in burning material is not hot. But the Pudgalavādins assume, when they argue that fire is not other than fuel, that (VII) fuel in burning material is hot. Hence, from (V), (VI), and (VII) he thinks that we may infer that (VIII) "hot" does not signify heat. Therefore, from (I) and (VIII) we may infer that (IX) "hot" signifies something that is combined with heat.

But what is the implication of the thesis that "hot" signifies something combined with heat? Vasubandhu assumes that what combines with the defining property of the fire-element combines with the fire-element. So he would have us infer that (X) if "hot" signifies something combined with heat, then "hot" signifies something combined with the fire-element. Therefore, from (IX) and (X) we may infer that (XI) "hot" signifies something combined with the fire-element. However, (XII) if fuel in burning material is hot and "hot" signifies something combined with the fire-element, fuel in burning material is combined with the fire-element. Therefore, from (VII), (XI), and (XII) we may infer that (XIII) fuel in burning material is combined with the fire-element. But phenomena that can combine, Vasubandhu assumes, are other than one another. In other words, (XIV) if fuel in burning material is combined with the fire-element, fire is other than fuel. Therefore, from (XIII) and (XIV) we may infer that (XV) fire is other than fuel. If (XV) is true, the premise in the fire and fuel reply, that fire is not other than fuel, is false. Hence, Vasubandhu would have us conclude, it is not true that if fire is other than fuel, fuel in burning material is not hot, since it has just been demonstrated that fuel can be hot in spite of being other than fuel.

The Pudgalavādins are not made to formulate a reply to Vasubandhu's objection. Nonetheless, we can formulate a reasonable reply for them. Their reply would be to deny the truth of both (II) and (IX) on the ground that "hot" in "Fuel in burning material is hot" does not signify the defining property of a substantially real fire-element or something that is combined with fuel in the way a substantially real element would be combined with it. It does not signify the defining property of a substantially real fire-element, since a substantially real fire-element does not exist in fuel, which contains only the other three elements. "Hot" does not signify something that is combined with fuel in the sense that a substantially real fire-element combines with fuel, since "hot" in "Fuel in burning material is hot," from the Pudgalavādins' perspective, need not signify something that combines with fuel. We need to recall, first of all, that the heat conventionally attributed to fuel is not the same as the heat that causes the fuel to be hot. The latter is an effect produced by the former. But how does it produce this effect, and where does the effect occur?

The Pudgalavādins do not answer these questions, but answers in agreement with their other theses can be ventured. I believe that they would say that "hot" in "Fuel in burning material is hot" signifies an effect produced in the fuel that is being caused to burn by fire. The burning itself is the moment by moment destruction of many of the elements in the collection of elements of which fuel is composed. The so-called heat of the fuel, as an effect produced in the fuel by burning, therefore, does not "combine" with fuel in the way Vasubandhu construes a combination. What exactly is the heat of fuel? Perhaps it is the power of the fuel to provide, when in proximity with the body organ, a sensation of heat. What fire causes in fuel is not heat, but burning, which causes the fuel to cause a sensation of heat. Although we cannot be sure that the Pudgalavādins held this view, that they may have held it shows that Vasubandhu's objection is not conclusive.

§ 2.1.5.2 *The burning material analysis of fire and fuel*

When Vasubandhu presented his causal basis analysis of fire and fuel, he identified fire and fuel with different collections of elements and argued that since fire, so construed, arises in dependence upon fuel, fire is other than fuel. In effect, he interpreted fire as burning material and fuel as material in dependence upon which fire can arise. When the Pudgalavādins presented their own analysis, Vasubandhu thinks, they interpreted fire as one part of burning material and fuel as another part. But from this analysis, Vasubandhu concluded, it still follows that fire is other than fuel. Now that Vasubandhu believes he has shown that neither his analysis nor theirs is consistent with the thesis that fire is not other than fuel, he considers and rejects one last attempt that might be made to avoid this inconsistency. Perhaps both fire and fuel may be analyzed not as burning material and material in dependence upon which burning material arises, or as different parts of burning material, respectively, but as each being the same in existence as the burning material as a whole.

He expresses this view as the thesis that "burning material as a whole is fire and fuel." Although this thesis might be taken to mean that fire and fuel together are the same in existence as burning material as a whole, we can be sure that it does not. For Vasubandhu is surely assuming that this analysis means that fire and fuel, individually considered, are the same in existence as the burning material as a whole. If the meaning were that fire and fuel together are the same in existence as burning material as a whole, what is said would be a paraphrase of Vasubandhu's understanding of the Pudgalavādins' own analysis, since according to him their analysis is that fire is one part of burning material and fuel is another part. But it is doubtful that this third analysis is meant simply to be a rephrasing of the second.

The idea of fire and fuel, individually considered, being the same in existence as burning material as a whole, of course, is obviously flawed, but it may, nonetheless, be a reasoned view. It might be said that certain kinds of parts of wholes exist in dependence upon the wholes of which they are parts, rather than, as Vasubandhu would have it, that wholes of parts exist in dependence upon their parts. Such would be the case if the parts are intrinsic parts of a whole, i.e. are defined in terms of the wholes of which they are parts. In this view, both fire and fuel exist in dependence upon burning material, since fire is not fire, i.e. the cause of the burning of fuel, unless it is by definition a part of burning material, and fuel is not fuel unless it is by definition a part of burning material. So in this case, neither exists apart from burning material. Neither fire nor fuel, so understood, is other than the burning material of which it is a part, since each is just the burning material being described from a different perspective. Hence, it may be said that each is the same in existence as the whole of which it is a part. This analysis of fire and fuel, it seems, does not give rise to the objection, as did both of the previous two analyses, that fire is other than fuel. Although we cannot be sure that this is the sort of analysis meant, I shall assume that it is, since I cannot think of a better alternative. Let us call it the burning material analysis of fire and fuel.

We can be sure that the Pudgalavādins themselves would not resort to this analysis in order to avoid the consequence that fire is other than fuel, since they would not, as we have seen, agree that the previous analysis is inconsistent with any of the premises of their fire and fuel reply or with any of the theses of their theory of persons. Vasubandhu includes this third analysis, we may assume, so that he may block an attempt the Pudgalavādins might make to save the fire and fuel reply by propounding an analysis of fire and fuel that cannot possibly give rise to the objection that fire is other than fuel.

In Vasubandhu's first objection to the fire and fuel reply based on the burning material analysis of fire and fuel he claims that if burning material as a whole is both fire and fuel, individually considered, then the fuel-reliant identity premise of the fire and fuel reply has lost its meaning. In suggesting that the fuel-reliant identity premise has lost its meaning, of course, Vasubandhu means that it is false. The intervening steps of the objection are easily supplied. First of all, a clear implication of the analysis is that fuel is the same in existence as fire, since if the whole is the same in existence as each of its parts, the parts are the same in existence as each other. Second, Vasubandhu reasons, if, therefore, fuel is the same in existence as fire, and fire is conceived in reliance upon fuel, as the Pudgalavādins claim it is, then fire is conceived in reliance upon fire. But the Pudgalavādins imply that fire is not conceived in reliance upon fire when they assert that it is conceived in reliance upon fuel. Therefore, Vasubandhu concludes, if burning material as a whole is the same in existence as both fire and fuel, individually considered, the fuel-reliant identity premise of the fire and fuel reply is false.

Vasubandhu's second objection concerns a consequence of employing both the fire and fuel analogy and the burning material analysis of fire and fuel. It is the objection that since the analysis implies that fuel is the same in existence as fire, we may infer, by the Pudgalavādins' own analogy, that collections of aggregates are the same in existence as persons, which is inconsistent with their claim that we are not the same in existence as collections of aggregates. When Vasubandhu says in the text that the

Pudgalavādins could not avoid the theory that we are not other than collections of aggregates, he must be using "not other than" to mean "the same in existence as," since the thesis that we are not other than collection of aggregates is a part of their theory of persons. Vasubandhu is arguing that the burning material analysis implies the falsity of their thesis that we are not the same in existence as collections of aggregates, since by analogy from the fire and fuel reply it can be used to infer that we are the same in existence as collections of aggregates.

§ 2.1.5.3 *The conclusion of Vasubandhu's critique*

Vasubandhu concludes, on the basis of his critique of the fire and fuel reply, that the Pudgalavādins have failed to provide an analogy that shows that we can be conceived in dependence upon collections of aggregates without being other than the collections or the same in existence as them. In other words, he has argued that the fire and fuel reply does not provide another example of a phenomenon that is conceived in dependence upon a collection of substances without being either other than this collection or the same in existence as it.

It might be thought that Vasubandhu's critique takes the form of assuming that fire and fuel must be subject either to causal basis analysis, to the Pudgalavādins' own analysis, or to the burning material analysis, and proceeds by arguing that, according to each, either some of the premises of the fire and fuel reply are false or some of theses of their theory of persons are false. But is this assumption correct? To decide whether or not this assumption is correct would take more space and time than available here. In any case, I doubt that Vasubandhu makes this assumption, since he need only assume that just the causal basis analysis and Pudgalavādins' analysis are pertinent to a consideration of the fire and fuel reply. Since the Pudgalavādins surely would agree with this assumption, we need not attempt to justify it. The burning material analysis of fire and fuel, if this interpretation is correct, is added simply for the sake of blocking a path of retreat the Pudgalavādins might be tempted to take once it has been shown that neither causal basis analysis nor their analysis is consistent both with the premises of the fire and fuel reply and with the theses of their theory of persons. Hence, it seems best to construe Vasubandhu's critique of the fire and fuel reply as an argument to the effect that the Pudgalavādins must abandon the fire and fuel reply, since regardless of whether fire and fuel are analyzed as he does or as the Pudgalavādins do, some of the premises of the fire and fuel reply are false or some of the theses of their theory of persons are false.

§ 2.2 Vasubandhu's objection, that if we are inexplicable, we cannot be said either to be or not to be a fifth kind of object known to exist

Vasubandhu's second objection to the Pudgalavādins' theory of persons is that it implies that they cannot assert or deny that we are a fifth kind of object known to exist. Stcherbatsky believes that Vasubandhu is arguing in this objection that the Pudgalavādins are committed to the idea that persons belong to a fifth category of objects known to exist, even though they deny that they are. He is alone in adopting this analysis among the sources I have consulted. (In fact, Thích Thiên Châu reports, in the *Personalists*, pp. 91–2, that in the *Tridharmaka Śāstra* the Pudgalavādins claim that these are the five kinds of objects that are known to exist.) The argument of Vasubandhu's objection is condensed and my translation of it is supplemented by bracketed words, phrases, and sentences that I believe will help the reader to understand its underlying logical structure. In this objection, I believe, Vasubandhu needs to make the six assumptions that I have added to the translation in brackets.

The first assumption is that the Pudgalavādins accept the view that objects known to exist include three kinds of causally conditioned phenomena, causally unconditioned phenomena, and phenomena that are inexplicable. Since he refers to the three kinds of causally conditioned phenomena as past, future, and present phenomena, it would seem that the Pudgalavādins accept the Vaibhāṣika view that causally conditioned phenomena possess substantial reality in the three times. Since these same phenomena are, in the context of an analysis of persons, classified as the five aggregates, he also assumes that if we are not other than collections of aggregates, we are not other than the three kinds of causally conditioned phenomena.

Vasubandhu's third assumption is that the inexplicable phenomenon said to be the fifth kind of object known to exist is a person. This assumption is an oversimplification, since the Pudgalavādins would seem to recognize fire as an inexplicable phenomenon. Since the objection can easily be rewritten to include other inexplicable phenomena, the oversimplification is unimportant. His fourth assumption, without which he cannot infer that the Pudgalavādins must deny that an inexplicable person constitutes a fifth kind of object known to exist, is that if we are not other than the three kinds of causally conditioned phenomena, we are the same in existence as them. His fifth assumption is that if we are inexplicable, we are not only not the same in existence as the three kinds of causally conditioned phenomena, but we are also not causally unconditioned phenomena, since they are other than the three kinds of causally conditioned phenomena. Finally, he assumes that since the Pudgalavādins' theory implies that it cannot be asserted or denied that we are a fifth kind of object known to exist, the theory is false.

Although the Pudgalavādins assert that we are a fifth kind of object known to exist, the target of Vasubandhu's objection is not this assertion, but the thesis that we are inexplicable phenomena. The objection begins with the statement that (I) if we are inexplicable phenomena, then we are not other than collections of aggregates. Vasubandhu then assumes that (II) aggregates are the three kinds of causally conditioned phenomena, that (III) if we are not other than the three kinds of causally conditioned phenomena, then we are the same in existence as the three kinds of causally conditioned phenomena, and that (IV) if we are the same in existence as the three kinds of causally conditioned phenomena, then it cannot be asserted that we are a fifth kind of object known to exist. From (I)–(IV) Vasubandhu infers that (V) if we are inexplicable phenomena, then it cannot be asserted that we are a fifth kind of object known to exist. The second part of Vasubandhu's objection begins with the statement that (VI) if we are inexplicable phenomena, then we are not the same in existence as a collection of aggregates and we are not causally unconditioned phenomena. Vasubandhu assumes that the Pudgalavādins must admit that (VII) if we are not the same in existence as the three kinds of causally conditioned phenomena and we are not causally unconditioned phenomena, then it cannot be denied that we are a fifth kind of object known to exist. So from (VI) and (VII) he infers that (VIII) if we are inexplicable phenomena, then it cannot be denied that we are a fifth kind of object known to exist. From (V) and (VIII) it follows that (IX) if we are inexplicable phenomena, then it cannot be asserted that we are a fifth kind of object known to exist and it cannot be denied that we are a fifth kind of object known to exist. Vasubandhu believes that it is undeniable that (X) it must be asserted that we are a fifth kind of object known to exist or denied that we are a fifth kind of object known to exist. Therefore, from (IX) and (X) he assumes that we shall infer, contrary to the Pudgalavādins' theory of persons, that (XI) we are not inexplicable phenomena. In other words, he would have us conclude that we are either other than or the same in existence as collections of aggregates. And since, as Buddhists, they must assert that we are not other than our aggregates, Vasubandhu implies, they must assert that we are the same in existence as collections of aggregates.

The Pudgalavādins are not made to reply to this objection, but a reply is easily supplied on the basis of our reconstruction of their theory. Their reply would be to deny that (III) is true on the ground that it assumes that we are not inexplicable phenomena. If Vasubandhu expects his readers to accept this objection, he cannot assume in it that we are not inexplicable phenomena. From another point of view, we can say that Vasubandhu's objection is vitiated by an ambiguity in the idea of a fifth kind of object known to exist. If the criterion of difference in kind is otherness, the Pudgalavādins can say that we are not a fifth kind of object known to exist, since we are not other than the three kinds of causally conditioned phenomena. In this case they can say that the objection is unsound because (VIII) is false. But if the criterion of difference in kind is separate ultimate existence, they can say that we are a fifth kind of object known to exist, since we are ultimately existent without being other than either causally conditioned phenomena or being causally unconditioned phenomena. So they can reply that the argument is unsound because either (III) or (VIII) is false. Hence, it cannot be said that Vasubandhu has succeeded in showing in this objection that the Pudgalavādins' theory of persons is logically incoherent.

§ 2.3 Vasubandhu's perceptual dilemma objection

Vasubandhu's third objection to the Pudgalavādins' theory of persons is based on a consideration of the perceptual conditions of our being conceived. It will be easier to understand this objection if we restate it with a more precise terminology consistent with the terminology we have developed.

First of all, when Vasubandhu refers to our being conceived after aggregates are perceived or after we are perceived, what he means to convey is the idea that the perception of aggregates establishes our existence or the perception of ourselves establishes our existence. He mentions only perception as the means by which our existence is established, I believe, since he is anticipating the Pudgalavādins' assertion that we are known to exist by perception. The second change of terminology concerns Vasubandhu's reference to the basis upon which we conceive ourselves and to that in reliance upon which we conceive ourselves. According to the terminology we have developed, he is referring in each case to what he elsewhere calls the cause of the conception of ourselves.

When paraphrased in accord with this terminology, we may say that in this objection Vasubandhu begins by asserting that if we conceive ourselves, either the perception of aggregates in the collections in dependence upon which we conceive ourselves establishes our existence or the perception of ourselves establishes our existence. He believes that the Pudgalavādins must choose just one of these alternatives, since they believe that we are not the same in existence as collections of aggregates. His argument is that since both alternatives are inconsistent with their theory of persons and they cannot deny that we conceive ourselves, their theory of persons is logically incoherent.

He first argues, on the assumption that we are not the same in existence as collections of aggregates, that if perception of aggregates in these collections establishes our existence, a perception of ourselves does not, and if it does not, the conception of ourselves refers to collections of aggregates, not to ourselves. Then he argues that if a perception of ourselves establishes our existence, we are the cause of the conception of ourselves, and that if we are the cause of the conception of ourselves and are not the same in existence as collections of aggregates, collections of aggregates are not the cause of the conception of ourselves. Here he expects the reader to realize that if collections of aggregates are not the cause of the conception of ourselves, we are not conceived in reliance upon collections of aggregates. Therefore, the implication of the objection is that the Pudgalavādins' theory of persons cannot be reconciled with the perceptual conditions of our being conceived.

The premise of the objection with which the Pudgalavādins would most obviously disagree, of course, is that if a perception of ourselves establishes our existence, we are the cause of the conception of ourselves. If asked how he knows that we are the cause of the conception of ourselves if a perception of ourselves establishes our existence, Vasubandhu will argue that if a perception of ourselves establishes our existence, we are the object of the conception of ourselves, and if we are the object of the conception of ourselves, we are the same in existence as the cause of the conception of ourselves. So Vasubandhu is assuming in the second premise of this argument the truth of the causal reference principle, that a conception's object is the same in existence as its causal basis. Vasubandhu has already assumed its truth in his causal reference objection to their reply to his objection from the two realities. The point of their fire and fuel reply, I have already argued, is to show that this principle is false. But since Vasubandhu believes that he has already shown their fire and fuel reply to be logically incoherent, he assumes that he can continue to employ the causal reference principle in his objections. But I have already shown that Vasubandhu's objection to the Pudgalavādins' fire and fuel reply fails to show that it is logically incoherent.

The Pudgalavādins are not made in our text to offer a reply to Vasubandhu's objection. Instead, they are made simply to state a thesis concerning why we conceive ourselves in reliance upon a collection of aggregates. But their reply, I believe, is buried within the statement of this thesis. The above reconstruction of Vasubandhu's perceptual dilemma objection enables us to see that the premise of the objection to which the reply would be directed is once again the causal reference principle.

§ 2.4 The Pudgalavādins' explanation of aggregate-reliant identity and Vasubandhu's objections to it

The Pudgalavādins' explanation of aggregate-reliant identity

The Pudgalavādins' explanation of why we conceive ourselves in reliance upon collections of aggregates is now presented and criticized. They say that we conceive ourselves in reliance upon collections of aggregates because we are perceived when any of the aggregates in the collections are present. But how is our being perceived when these aggregates are present supposed to explain why we conceive ourselves in reliance upon collections of aggregates? Since the Pudgalavādins are claiming that we are perceived, it is clear that of the two perceptual conditions Vasubandhu has just set out in his perceptual dilemma objection the Pudgalavādins choose that according to which the perception of ourselves establishes our existence. Their explanation adds to this choice the view that we are perceived when some of our aggregates are present. The addition, of course, is made in order to indicate that we conceive ourselves because of the presence of aggregates when we perceive ourselves rather than because we perceive ourselves. But what do they mean by saying that we are perceived and why does the presence of some of our aggregates when we are perceived show that we conceive ourselves in reliance upon collections of aggregates? I have already anticipated the Pudgalavādins' answer to these questions in my account of their reply to Vasubandhu's two realities objection. Here I shall give a more detailed answer, which will show how their explanation of aggregate-reliant identity enables them to escape the dilemma posed by Vasubandhu.

It is clear that the Pudgalavādins assert that we are perceived because they believe that a perception of ourselves establishes the existence (but not the identity) of the object of the conception of ourselves. Let us call the view that a perception of ourselves establishes the existence of the object of the conception of ourselves the perceptual verification thesis. But the perceptual verification thesis by itself is not sufficient to distinguish the Pudgalavādins' view from that of Vasubandhu, who can agree that it is true on the ground that since we are the same in existence as collections of aggregates, a perception of ourselves is a perception of any of our aggregates. It follows, he can add, that a perception of ourselves shows that the conception of ourselves refers to collections of aggregates, even though the collections of aggregates are not the immediate objects of the conception of ourselves. (The immediate objects are the conventionally real persons, who are objects, Vasubandhu believes, only because they are the same in existence as collections of aggregates, which are the basis of reference to conventionally real persons.) So the Pudgalavādins' claim that we are perceived must also be meant to imply, if it is to distinguish their view from that of Vasubandhu, that a perception of ourselves is not a perception of one or more of our aggregates and that the conception of ourselves does not refer to collections of aggregates. Moreover, the Pudgalavādins surely believe that the claim, that we are perceived when aggregates are present, implies that we are not the same in existence as the cause of the conception of ourselves. In what follows I shall try to explain why the Pudgalavādins believe that their explanation of aggregate-reliant identity implies that a perception of ourselves is not a perception of one or more of our aggregates, and so, that the conception of ourselves does not refer to a collection of aggregates, and that we are not the causal basis of the conception of ourselves. In this way, it will be shown why the Pudgalavādins believe that the causal reference principle is false.

When in their explanation of aggregate-reliant identity the Pudgalavādins claim that a person "is perceived" (*upalabhyate*) they cannot mean that he is perceived in the way that a substantial reality or a substantially established reality is perceived. They claim that we are perceived, of course, in order to make it clear that the object of the conception of ourselves exists. For it is held by both the orthodox Vaibhāṣikas and the Pudgalavādins that a perception of an object of a conception establishes its existence, since the object, as a cause of its perception, must exist. What is peculiar to the Pudgalavādins, as I explained earlier, is the view that a perception of ourselves, unlike a perception of a substantial reality or a substantially established reality, is nondiscriminative in character. It is nondiscriminative in character because we, unlike these other phenomena, possess ultimate existence without possessing separate identities. This belief does not imply that the Pudgalavādins reject Vasubandhu's thesis that discrimination is one of the mental factors that accompany every mind or consciousness. For their account in Section 2.5 of how we are known to exist by the six consciousnesses, we shall see, implies that the consciousness that perceives us also knows to exist its own special object by means of a discrimination of a character possessed by this object, and for this reason, the consciousness that perceives us is in fact accompanied by a discrimination of a character possessed by an object.

Let us call the belief, that the perception that establishes our existence does not include a discrimination of a character we possess, the nondiscriminative perception verification thesis. One implication of the nondiscriminative perception verification thesis is that a perception of ourselves is not a perception of a substantial reality or a substantially established reality. A second implication is that the conception of ourselves cannot refer either to a substantial reality or to a substantially established reality. A third implication is that we cannot be the causal basis of the conception of ourselves, since we do not possess a character on the basis of whose discrimination a conception of ourselves can be formed. A fourth implication is that we are the same in existence as the entity nondiscriminatively perceived when aggregates in the collections in dependence upon which we are conceived are present.

So that all four of the implications the Pudgalavādins intend their explanation of aggregate-reliant identity to have may become more evident, let us formulate it as the aggregate-reliant identity explanation, which is that we conceive ourselves in reliance upon collections of aggregates because we are nondiscriminatively perceived when one or more of the aggregates in the collections are present and the characters these aggregates possess by themselves are discriminated. The aggregate-reliant identity explanation implies not only that we are the object of the conception of ourselves without being the same in existence as its causal basis, but also that a collection of aggregates is the causal basis of the conception in spite of the fact that the conception does not refer to them. Hence, the Pudgalavādins' aggregate-reliant identity explanation, properly understood, implies that the causal reference principle is false. It also follows that, since the perceptual dilemma objection is not sound unless the causal reference principle is true, and the causal reference principle is false if the aggregate-reliant identity explanation is correct, the Pudgalavādins' explanation of aggregate-reliant identity implies that Vasubandhu's perceptual dilemma objection is unsound. So although the Pudgalavādins' reply to Vasubandhu's perceptual dilemma objection is not spelled out in the text, it can be reconstructed on the basis of uncovering the meaning of their explanation of aggregate-reliant identity.

Vasubandhu's objections to the Pudgalavādins' explanation of aggregate-reliant identity

Vasubandhu's objections to the Pudgalavādins' explanation of aggregate-reliant identity take advantage of its incompleteness. It is incomplete because it does not explain why the perception of ourselves when one or more of our aggregates are present implies that the conception of ourselves does not refer to a collection of aggregates or why we ourselves are not the same in existence as the causal basis of the conception of ourselves. He construes the perception of ourselves as a discriminative perception and the presence of our aggregates when we are perceived as the presence of the external supports of a perception. The external supports of a perception are those phenomena that are other than the object perceived and yet must be immediately present if the perception of it is to occur. The external supports of the perception of a visible form he mentions are the eye, attentiveness, and light. On this basis, he argues, first of all, that if collections of aggregates cause the conception of ourselves because we are perceived when one or more of our aggregates are present, then we may infer that the eye, attentiveness, and light rather than visible form cause the conception of a visible form, since a visible form is perceived when the eye, attentiveness, and light are present. But it is false, he objects, that the eye, attentiveness, and light rather than visible form cause the conception of visible form. Second, he argues that it also follows that just as a visible form is other than the eye, attentiveness, and light, so we will be other than our aggregates. But according to the Pudgalavādins, he objects, we are not other than our aggregates. Vasubandhu would have us infer that the Pudgalavādins must abandon their explanation of aggregate-reliant identity because it commits them to these two unwanted consequences.

Although the Pudgalavādins are not made to reply to these objections, their proper reply would clearly be to deny that we are perceived when any of our aggregates are present in the same way that a visible form is perceived when an eye, attentiveness, and light are present. They would deny that this is true because they do not believe that we possess by ourselves characters that are discriminated when we are perceived or that aggregates are the external supports of the perception of ourselves. We can be sure of this because they deny that we are other than or the same in existence as the aggregates that are present when we are perceived. So it is clear that Vasubandhu's objections to their explanation of aggregate-reliant identity do not show it to be unreasonable. He has shown at most that the Pudgalavādins' explanation of aggregate-reliant identity, due to its incomplete formulation, can be interpreted to be inconsistent with both their explanation of why a visible form is conceived and their thesis that we are not other than collections of aggregates.

§ 2.5 Vasubandhu's statement of the Pudgalavādins' account of how we are known to exist by the six consciousnesses

The Pudgalavādins have claimed that inexplicable persons are perceived when any of their aggregates are present, but they have not explained the work this perception does in their system of thought. The work it does is to justify the claim that inexplicable persons are known to exist. (The question of whether or not the Pudgalavādins believe that we are known to exist by a correct inference does not arise in the text. In what follows I shall ignore this possibility.) Since the Buddha said that what is known to exist is known to exist by one or more of the six consciousnesses, the Pudgalavādins must say that a person is perceived by one or more of the six consciousnesses. He also said that each of the six consciousnesses knows to exist its own special objects, which are the objects in the domains of the organs of cognition after which they are named. The special objects each of the six consciousnesses knows to exist may be called the primary objects of each consciousness. The Pudgalavādins claim that we are perceived by each of the six consciousnesses that know its primary objects to exist and that we are neither other than these primary objects nor the same in existence as them.

To make my discussion somewhat less cumbersome and easier to follow I shall employ a generalization based on Vasubandhu's statement of the Pudgalavādins' account of how we are known to exist by the six consciousnesses. I shall also paraphrase his statement that an object is known to exist by means of an organ of perception by saying that the consciousness named after that organ knows its primary object to exist. Vasubandhu's statement of their account of how an inexplicable person is known to exist by the six consciousnesses may then be said to consist of (1) "the knowledge thesis," which is that we are known to exist by each of the six consciousnesses if we are perceived by each in dependence upon a primary object it knows to exist, (2) "the primary object nonotherness thesis," which is that we are not other than any one of the primary objects known to exist by the six consciousnesses that perceive us, and (3) "the primary object nonsameness thesis," which is that we are not the same in existence as any one of the primary objects known to exist by the six consciousnesses that perceive us. The primary object nonotherness thesis and primary object nonsameness thesis are closely related to the theses that we are neither other than nor the same in existence as collections of aggregates. For the primary objects that are known to exist by the six consciousnesses that perceive us include the aggregates that are present when we are perceived and are in the collections of aggregates in dependence upon which we are conceived. But the primary objects known to exist by each of the six consciousnesses need not include these aggregates.

Readers may notice that I say that the knowledge thesis, the primary object nonotherness thesis and the primary object nonsameness thesis are a reconstruction of Vasubandhu's statement of the Pudgalavādins' account of how we are known to exist by the six consciousnesses. A full reconstruction of their account, I believe, would need to include a thesis not explicitly presented in the account. For we shall see that the account as stated by Vasubandhu is incomplete. Moreover, we shall see, the account as represented by Vasubandhu is ambiguous. Hence, it is not likely that Vasubandhu's statement of the account represents a complete and adequate statement of it.

There are four features of Vasubandhu's statement of the Pudgalavādins' account of how we are known to exist by the six consciousnesses we need to discuss if their exchange about it is to be properly understood and assessed. The first is that the knowledge thesis may be interpreted in three different ways. According to the first, the knowledge thesis is true because a perception of ourselves is nothing but a perception of one of the primary objects known to exist by the six consciousnesses. In other words, the thesis means that we are known to exist by each of the six consciousnesses if a primary object it knows to exist causes a perception of itself. Let us call this "the naïve interpretation" because it is obviously not what the Pudgalavādins mean. For in this case, since in their view we are not the same in existence as any of the primary objects known to exist by the six consciousnesses, we would no longer cause the perception of ourselves, and if we were no longer to cause the perception of ourselves, we could not be the object of the perception. Although the Pudgalavādins deny that the object of the conception of ourselves is the same in existence as the cause of the conception, they cannot deny that the object of the perception of ourselves is the same in existence as the cause of the perception, since if they did, they could not claim that the perception of ourselves establishes our existence.

The second way to interpret the knowledge thesis is that it means that we are known to exist by each of the six consciousnesses if a primary object it knows to exist causes a perception of ourselves in the way an external support of a perception of an object causes the perception of this object. Let us call this "the external support interpretation." That this is not the correct interpretation of the knowledge thesis is clear because an object of a perception is other than the external supports of the perception of the object, and the object of the perception of ourselves, the Pudgalavādins claim, is not other than any one of the primary objects known to exist by the six consciousnesses that perceive us. In other words, this interpretation is inconsistent with the primary object nonotherness thesis.

The third interpretation of the knowledge thesis is that it means that we are known to exist by each of the six consciousnesses if a primary object it knows to exist is an incidental cause of its perception of ourselves. A primary object a consciousness knows to exist is an incidental cause of a perception of ourselves in the sense that it causes the consciousness to arise that knows that it exists and this consciousness also happens to perceive us. According to this interpretation, which we may call "the incidental cause interpretation," even though we cause a perception of ourselves, we do not cause the consciousness that perceives us to arise; the cause of its arising is the primary object known to exist by it, since it is caused to arise as a consciousness that knows that the object exists. We are, consequently, incidental objects of the six consciousnesses. Because we do not cause the consciousnesses to arise, we are not their primary objects, but we are objects of these consciousnesses, whose awareness of us, we may say, is incidental. This is the correct interpretation of the knowledge thesis, since it is the only one of the three consistent with their theory of persons. In Vasubandhu's first objection to the Pudgalavādins' account of how we are known to exist, we shall see, he adopts the naïve interpretation, while his second objection is based on a distinction he makes that amounts to a distinction between the external support and incidental cause interpretations.

The second feature of Vasubandhu's statement of the Pudgalavādins' account of how we are known to exist by the six consciousnesses we need to discuss, if their exchange about it is to be properly understood and assessed, is that the knowledge thesis, as stated, does not explicitly include the Pudgalavādins' view that we are perceived by the same consciousnesses that know to exist the primary objects in dependence upon which we are perceived. This omission will enable him to entertain the possibility of the external support interpretation of the knowledge thesis in his second objection to their account. In this objection he will consider the possibility that a visible form is a cause of a perception of ourselves in the way an external support of a perception of a visible form is a cause of a perception of a visible form. But he could not have considered this to be a possibility if his statement of their knowledge thesis had included the view that we are perceived by the same consciousnesses that know to exist the primary objects in dependence upon which we are perceived. For no Buddhist accepts the view that one consciousness can both know that an object exists and perceive the external support of its knowledge of the object.

The third feature of Vasubandhu's statement of the Pudgalavādins' account of how we are known to exist by the six consciousnesses is that it does not include an explanation of why we are perceived by the same consciousnesses that know to exist the primary objects in dependence upon which we are perceived. It should be clear that in making this claim the Pudgalavādins are assuming (1) that when we apprehend objects we are simultaneously aware that we exist, and (2) that this awareness of our own existence does not include a discrimination of a character we possess by ourselves. The Pudgalavādins seem to be redescribing this self-awareness in the form of a thesis about a consciousness of a primary object. They are claiming that when a consciousness knows to exist its primary object it is simultaneously aware of the existence of the owner or possessor of this consciousness. This explanation of why the Pudgalavādins believe the knowledge thesis to be true also explains to a great extent why they believe that we are nondiscriminatively perceived and that we do not possess separate identities. For the self-awareness that seems to attend apprehension of objects does not have an object that possesses by itself a character that is discriminated when the awareness occurs.

If the Pudgalavādins had explained why they believe that the six consciousnesses that know their primary objects to exist also know a person to exist, Vasubandhu would not have been able to advance the naïve interpretation of the knowledge thesis. For in this interpretation, the primary objects known to exist by the six consciousnesses are identified with the aggregates present when we are perceived. This identification confuses the primary objects perceived by a consciousness with the aggregates that as a collection are the causal basis of the conception of ourselves. Once again the incompleteness of the Pudgalavādins' statement of a view they hold will enable Vasubandhu to construe it in a way that lends itself to the charge of logical incoherence.

There is a fourth feature of Vasubandhu's statement of the Pudgalavādins' account of how we are known to exist by the six consciousnesses to which attention should be paid in order to understand and assess properly the subsequent exchange between them. This is the feature that the thesis, that we are not the same in existence as the collections of primary objects known to exist by the six consciousnesses that perceive us, is not included in the statement of their account. This thesis is not explicitly included, I believe, because the Pudgalavādins think that it is an implication of the primary object nonsameness thesis. Nevertheless, because it is not included, and Vasubandhu identifies the objects of the six consciousnesses with the aggregates in dependence upon which we are conceived, he is able to adopt the naïve interpretation of their knowledge thesis in his first objection and to argue that their account of how we are known to exist does not exclude the view that we are the same in existence as all of our aggregates.

What about the thesis that we are not other than all of the objects as a collection that are known to exist by the six consciousnesses? Is it included? This thesis is included because it is entailed by the primary object non-otherness thesis. If we are not other than any one of the primary objects known to exist by the six consciousnesses, we are not other than all of these objects as a collection.

§ 2.5.1 *Vasubandhu's first objection to the account: the objection from knowledge of the existence of milk*

In his first objection Vasubandhu assumes that the Pudgalavādins' account of how a person is known to exist by the six consciousnesses is comparable to his own account of how a conventional reality such as milk is known to exist by four consciousnesses. (Although in the text Vasubandhu says that it is milk *or water* known to exist by the four consciousnesses, in my translation and discussion I shall abbreviate it as an account of how milk is known to exist by the four consciousnesses.) He argues on this basis that it is compatible with the view that a collection of aggregates is conceived as a person. The view that a collection of aggregates is conceived as a person is a paraphrase of his view that the object of the conception of a person is the same in existence as a collection of aggregates. So the point of the argument, it seems, is that since their account of how we are known to exist is comparable to his own, it cannot be used to support their belief that inexplicable persons exist.

The account Vasubandhu gives of how milk is known to exist by the four consciousnesses is surely his own. He believes that milk is known to exist by the eye-consciousness, the tongue-consciousness, the nose-consciousness, and the body-consciousness, since each perceives milk in dependence upon an element in the milk it knows to exist. (Milk may also be known to exist by the ear-consciousness, but only if it happens to emit a sound.) Because some of the elements in milk are known to exist by perception, Vasubandhu thinks that milk is known to exist by perception. So milk, in his view, is perceived when any of its elements are perceived. Hence, in likening the Pudgalavādins' account of how we are known to exist by the six consciousnesses to his own account of how milk is known to exist by four consciousnesses, Vasubandhu is assuming the truth of the naïve interpretation of the knowledge thesis. According to this interpretation, the knowledge thesis is true because a perception of ourselves is nothing but a perception of one of the primary objects known to exist by the six consciousnesses.

Vasubandhu's account of how milk is known to exist by the four consciousnesses may be reconstructed simply by replacing "us" by "milk," "we are" by "milk is," and "six" by "four" in the three explicit theses of my reconstruction of his statement of the Pudgalavādins' account of how we are known to exist by the six consciousnesses. The substitutions yield the theses that (I) milk is known to exist by each of the four consciousnesses if milk is perceived by each in dependence upon an object it knows to exist, that (II) milk is not other than any one of the primary objects known to exist by the four consciousnesses that perceive milk, and that (III) milk is not the same in existence as any one of the primary objects known to exist by the four consciousnesses that perceive milk. On the assumption that (I), (II), and (III) are comparable to the knowledge thesis, the primary object nonotherness thesis, and the primary object nonsameness thesis, Vasubandhu will now argue that the Pudgalavādins' account of how we are known to exist by the six consciousnesses fails to support their claim that inexplicable persons exist.

Vasubandhu's argument is that, even though (I), (II), and (III) are true, the collection of primary objects known to exist by the four consciousnesses that perceive milk is conceived as milk, and this implies, by analogy, that a collection of aggregates is conceived as a person. His argument, as stated, is condensed. In it he (1) assumes that we know why he thinks that (II) is true, (2) states the reason why he thinks that (III) is true without stating that it is his reason for thinking that it is true, (3) infers from (I)–(III), without stating the other premises needed for the inference, that the collection of primary objects known to exist by the four consciousnesses is conceived as milk, (4) assumes that the milk perceived by each of the four consciousnesses in dependence upon a primary object it knows to exist must either be the same in existence as any one of the objects perceived by these four consciousnesses, other than any one of them, or the same in existence as all of them as a collection, (5) assumes that the objects known to exist by the six consciousnesses are the aggregates in dependence upon which we are conceived, and (6) assumes that we shall realize that the implication of his conclusion, that a collection of aggregates is conceived as a person, is that the Pudgalavādins' account of how we are known to exist cannot be used to explain how a person is known to exist. In the translation I help the reader gain an idea of how his argument actually works by supplying these missing premises in brackets.

As I have interpreted the argument, Vasubandhu does not even bother to argue that (II) is true because he takes it for granted that a perception of milk is nothing but a perception of one of its elements. But he does explicitly mention what he takes to be an absurd consequence of denying that (III) is true, since he wants to call attention to its limited scope, and thereby, to the possibility that milk exists if it is the same in existence as the collection of the primary objects known to exist by the four consciousnesses that perceive milk. To conclude that this last possibility should be chosen, I believe that Vasubandhu assumes that since milk exists and it has been shown that milk is neither other than nor the same in existence as any one of the primary objects known to exist by the four consciousnesses that perceive milk, it must be the same in existence as the collection of these objects. He expresses this conclusion by saying that the collection is conceived as milk. Then on the assumption that the collection of primary objects known to exist by the six consciousnesses that perceive us is the collection of aggregates in dependence upon which we are conceived, he infers that, since his account of how milk is known to exist by the four consciousnesses has the same form as the Pudgalavādins' account of how we are known to exist by the six consciousnesses, we may conclude that collections of aggregates are conceived as ourselves. This conclusion, of course, is a version of Vasubandhu's thesis that we are the same in existence as collections of aggregates.

In the text the Pudgalavādins do not reply to this objection. But we may imagine that they could admit that since their knowledge thesis is ambiguous and their account of how we are known to exist by the six consciousnesses is incomplete, the naïve interpretation of the knowledge thesis is possible. Nonetheless, they could say, Vasubandhu has not succeeded in demonstrating that their account, when unambiguously and fully stated, does not support their claim that inexplicable persons exist. First of all, the Pudgalavādins would reject the view that what is perceived by each of a number of consciousnesses in dependence upon a primary object it knows to exist must either be other than any one of the primary objects known to exist, the same in existence as one of these objects, or the same in existence as all of them as a collection. But their rejection of this view does not mean that the Pudgalavādins would reject Vasubandhu's account of how milk is known to exist by the four consciousnesses that perceive milk. In fact, they seem to accept his view that milk is the same in existence as the collection of primary objects known to exist by the four consciousnesses that perceive milk. What the Pudgalavādins most certainly do not accept are the naïve interpretation of the knowledge thesis and the identification of collections of primary objects known to exist by the consciousnesses that perceive us with collections of aggregates in dependence upon which we conceive ourselves. But perhaps Vasubandhu knows this to be so, since in his second objection to the Pudgalavādins' account of how we are known to exist by the six consciousnesses he in effect distinguishes the external support and incidental cause interpretations and treats them as exhaustive of its meaning. The point of his first objection may therefore be that because the Pudgalavādins' account of how we are known to exist by the six consciousnesses is ambiguous and incompletely stated, it can be made to be compatible with his own account of how we are known to exist, and hence, with his own theory of persons. As such it cannot be used to support their claim that inexplicable persons exist. If this be his intent, the objection works; but it still does not show that their actual account cannot be used to support the claim that inexplicable persons exist.

Independent confirmation of the Pudgalavādins' rejection of Vasubandhu's analogy between how milk is conceived and how persons are conceived can be found in the *Sāṃmitīyanikāya Śāstra*. In this work, as I explained in the Introduction, the Sāṃmitīyas, who are Pudgalavādins, mention two different ways in which conventional realities are conceived. These are the ways in which milk is conceived and in which fire is conceived. Although the differences between these two examples in particular are not explained, it is reasonable to suppose that persons are believed to be conceived in the way fire is conceived rather than the way in which milk is conceived. Immediately after the statement of these two examples, the Sāṃmitīyas argue that bodily forms and the persons that acquire them are neither other than one another nor the same in existence. Since this argument parallels the argument, in Section 2.1.2 of the "Refutation," that fire is neither other than nor the same in existence as the fuel in dependence upon which it is conceived, we may be sure, I believe, that the Sāṃmitīyas would reject Vasubandhu's assimilation of the ways in which milk and persons are conceived.

§ 2.5.2 *Vasubandhu's second objection to the account: the objection to the knowledge thesis*

Vasubandhu's second objection to the Pudgalavādins' account of how we are known to exist by the six consciousnesses relies on the formulation of the knowledge thesis in its application to a visible form. He argues that in this application it can be interpreted in two different ways, neither of which has a consequence acceptable to them. I assume that the upshot of the objection is once again that the Pudgalavādins should abandon the account, in which case they could no longer use it to support their claim that inexplicable persons exist. Specifically, I interpret him to be arguing that on the external support interpretation it implies that a visible form is not other than light, the eye, and attentiveness, and that on the incidental cause interpretation it implies that either the primary object nonotherness thesis or the primary object nonsameness thesis is false. He begins the objection with the assumption that this application of the knowledge thesis to a visible form can be interpreted in just one of these two ways. It can be interpreted to mean either that we are known to exist by the eye-consciousness if a visible form causes a perception of ourselves or that we are known to exist by the eye-consciousness if we are perceived when a visible form is perceived.

These two interpretations of the meaning of this application of the knowledge thesis are based in part on two different ways in which "in dependence upon" (*pratītya*) might be used in it. According to the external support interpretation, "in dependence upon" is used to signify the causal dependence of a perception of ourselves upon a visible form in the same way that a perception of a visible form is causally dependent upon its external supports. This is the interpretation made possible because Vasubandhu's statement of this application of the Pudgalavādins' knowledge thesis does not include their view that we are perceived by the same consciousness that perceives a visible form. But even so, the interpretation is made impossible by the primary object nonotherness thesis of their theory of how we are known to exist. According to the incidental cause interpretation, "in dependence upon" is used to signify an incidental causal dependence of a perception of ourselves upon a visible form. The idea is that since a visible form causes a perception of a visible form by a consciousness and this consciousness also perceives us, a visible form may be said to cause the perception of ourselves.

Vasubandhu's formulation of the incidental cause interpretation of the knowledge thesis in its application to a visible form is tailored to the objection he is about to formulate. It does not include the Pudgalavādins' view that we are perceived by the same consciousness that perceives a visible form. Nor can it be generalized and extended to all other applications of the thesis. In particular, it cannot be extended to the case of a perception of ourselves by a consciousness that knows that a sense-organ exists, since a sense-organ is not perceived by the consciousness that knows that it exists except in the sense that the perception in question is indirect (i.e. is a correct inference rather than a direct perception). What is perhaps most peculiar about it is that rather than stating that a visible form perceived by a consciousness that perceives us is an incidental cause of the perception of ourselves, it merely states the conditional relation that obtains between the perception of ourselves and the perception of a visible form because a visible form incidentally causes the perception of ourselves. Nonetheless, Vasubandhu's tailored formulation of the incidental cause interpretation of this application of their knowledge thesis does not seem to force upon them a view they do not hold. Its use merely serves to more easily set up his statement of the second half of his objection to the knowledge thesis.

Vasubandhu first considers the thesis on the assumption that the external support interpretation is correct. This part of his objection clearly rests on his assumption that a visible form is a cause of a perception of ourselves in the same way that light, the eye, and attentiveness are causes of a perception of a visible form. This assumption enables him to infer that when the Pudgalavādins say that we cannot be said to be other than a visible form, which they say is a cause of a perception of ourselves, they imply that a visible form cannot be said to be other than light, the eye, and attentiveness, which are causes of the perception of a visible form. But in that case, he objects, they are committed to the false view that a visible form is not other than light, the eye, and attentiveness. The unstated conclusion in this part of his objection is that since this interpretation of this application of the knowledge thesis has this consequence, the thesis on this interpretation cannot be used to support the claim that inexplicable persons exist.

In the next part of the objection he takes up his own version of the incidental cause interpretation of the application of the knowledge thesis to a visible form. The objection, like so many of the others he makes to the Pudgalavādins' theses and replies to objections, is condensed. Vasubandhu first argues that if a perception of ourselves is the same in existence as a perception of a visible form, what is perceived by the first perception is the same in existence as what is perceived by the second, which implies that the Pudgalavādins' primary object nonsameness thesis is false. He supports this argument by saying that the Pudgalavādins cannot claim that we and a visible form are distinguishable unless it is said that we and a visible form are perceived by perceptions that are other than one another. He generalizes this result for the perception of ourselves and the perceptions of the primary objects known to exist by the other five consciousnesses. Then he argues that if a perception of ourselves is other than a perception of a visible form, it must occur at a different time, and that if it occurs at a different time, what is perceived by the first perception must be other than what is perceived by the second perception. But if what is perceived by the first perception is other than what is perceived by the second perception, he concludes, the Pudgalavādins' primary object nonotherness thesis is false, since a person will be other than a visible form. Then he generalizes this result for the perception of ourselves and the perception of primary objects known to exist by the other five consciousnesses.

Why does Vasubandhu claim that if a perception of ourselves and a perception of a visible form are other than one another they must occur at different times? I believe that he thinks that since the Pudgalavādins assume that these perceptions belong to the same continuum of aggregates, they must admit that they occur at different times if they are other than one another. This interpretation of the missing argument in the text has the advantage that the Pudgalavādins would probably find the argument to be unobjectionable.

Why does Vasubandhu claim that if these perceptions occur at different times their objects must be other than one another? His own reason for making this claim, I believe, is that he assumes that because the Pudgalavādins deny that both we and visible forms are permanent phenomena, they are committed to the view that we and visible forms are momentary in existence. They are committed to this view, he thinks, since according to the theses he has already established in the *Commentary*, (1) if we are not permanent phenomena, we must be impermanent phenomena, and (2) all impermanent phenomena are momentary in existence. But if we and visible forms are momentary in existence, we and visible forms must be other than one another if perceived at different times. Although this interpretation of why Vasubandhu makes his claim is based on views that Vasubandhu himself holds, it has the disadvantage that the Pudgalavādins would reject an assumption of the argument it contains, since they deny that all phenomena that are not permanent are impermanent. My reconstruction of Vasubandhu's objection can side-step the need to import into it an assumption the Pudgalavādins would clearly reject. For it is clear that the Pudgalavādins would accept as a replacement for the two arguments Vasubandhu actually uses the simple argument that if a perception of ourselves is other than a perception of a visible form, we are other than a visible form.

In outline, Vasubandhu's objection is that of the two possible interpretations of the Pudgalavādins' knowledge thesis in its application to a visible form, the external support interpretation implies the falsehood that a visible form is not other than light, the eye, and attentiveness, and the incidental cause interpretation is inconsistent with either the primary object nonsameness or primary object nonotherness thesis. He leaves it to his readers to draw the conclusion that since the Pudgalavādins must abandon the knowledge thesis, they lose their justification for claiming that inexplicable persons are known to exist.

To the first half of Vasubandhu's objection the Pudgalavādins are not made to reply in the text. Their reply, of course, would have been to deny the correctness of the external support interpretation of their knowledge thesis. They do not believe that a visible form is a cause of a perception of ourselves in the way that an external support of a perception of a visible form is one of its causes. They could have shown that this is a misinterpretation by pointing out that the visible form in dependence upon which we are perceived is itself perceived by the same consciousness that perceives us, while an external support of a perception of a visible form is not perceived by the same consciousness that perceives a visible form.

§ 2.5.2.1 *The Pudgalavādins' reply from inexplicable perception and Vasubandhu's objection from the causal conditionedness of perception*

The reply Vasubandhu implies that the Pudgalavādins do give to his objection to the knowledge thesis is to claim that it is false that if we are perceived when a visible form is perceived, then a perception of ourselves is either other than a perception of a visible form or the same in existence as a perception of a visible form. Specifically, he implies that they reply that this view is false because the perception of ourselves that occurs when a visible form is perceived is neither other than nor the same in existence as the perception of the visible form. He immediately objects that this reply contradicts their own theory.

The Pudgalavādins' reply, when generalized and filled out, takes the form of what may be called "the inexplicable perception thesis," which is that the perception of ourselves, which occurs when a primary object known to exist by each of the six consciousnesses is perceived, is neither other than nor the same in existence as the perception of the object. Since the inexplicable perception thesis is true, the Pudgalavādins believe, it is false that if we are perceived when a visible form is perceived, then a perception of ourselves is either other than a perception of a visible form or the same in existence as a perception of a visible form. And if this view is false, the argument of Vasubandhu's objection to the knowledge thesis is unsound.

Vasubandhu's objection to the Pudgalavādins' inexplicable perception reply is that the inexplicable perception thesis contradicts one of their own views. The view they would be contradicting, his argument makes clear, is that a perception is a causally conditioned phenomenon. Vasubandhu implies that since a causally conditioned phenomena is not inexplicable and a perception is a causally conditioned phenomenon, a perception of ourselves is not inexplicable.

The obvious reply the Pudgalavādins could give to Vasubandhu's objection is not presented by Vasubandhu on their behalf. It is the reply that they do not contradict their own theory, which is that only discriminative perceptions are causally conditioned phenomena, and perceptions of ourselves are not discriminative perceptions. The Pudgalavādins could argue, I surmise, that causally conditioned phenomena are phenomena that possess substantial reality or substantially established reality, but perceptions of ourselves are neither substantial realities nor substantially established realities. Moreover, they could add, all causally conditioned phenomena are directly caused by other phenomena that are causally conditioned, and perceptions of ourselves are not directly caused by such phenomena. For even though we are causes of perceptions of ourselves, we are not causally conditioned phenomena. Again, unlike a visible form, which causes a perception of itself by causing a consciousness that perceives it to arise, we do not cause a perception of ourselves by causing the consciousness that perceives us to arise. Nonetheless, since we do cause the perception by the consciousness caused to arise by a visible form, we are the object of its perception of ourselves. And although a perception of ourselves is incidentally caused by a visible form, an incidentally caused phenomenon is not a causally conditioned phenomenon. By presenting these arguments on behalf of the Pudgalavādins, I do not mean to imply that their view, that perceptions of ourselves are not causally conditioned phenomena, is without its problems. I merely want to point out that it is highly unlikely that they believe, as Vasubandhu believes they do, that a perception of ourselves is a causally conditioned phenomenon.

Vasubandhu could, in turn, ask the Pudgalavādins how an inexplicable perception of ourselves is known to exist. If it is known to exist by means of inexplicable perceptions, how in turn would these inexplicable perceptions be known to exist, etc.? Since an infinite regress of inexplicable perceptions would be required, it could not then be said that it is known that inexplicable perceptions exist by perception. If the Pudgalavādins claim that an inexplicable perception of ourselves is known to exist by a consciousness that has inexplicably correctly inferred its existence, in reliance upon what would its inexplicable correct inference be known to exist? Ultimately, once again, the Pudgalavādins will be forced into an infinite regress. Hence, Vasubandhu might conclude, the Pudgalavādins' appeal to inexplicable perceptions of ourselves is illegitimate, since it cannot be known that there are inexplicable perceptions of ourselves.

But the above objection may not be as strong as it at first sight appears to be. For the Pudgalavādins may deny that a correct inference by which it is known that an inexplicable perception of ourselves exists need itself be inexplicable. To be sure, the object that would be known to exist by correct inference would in this case be inexplicable, but why should the inference itself be inexplicable? They may say that an inexplicable perception of ourselves is known to exist on the basis of the correct inference, that since it is the same consciousness that is aware of its primary object and is aware of ourselves, and this is not possible unless the awareness of ourselves is inexplicable, an inexplicable perception of ourselves exists. The premise, that a consciousness is incidentally aware of its possessor when it is aware of its primary object, they may say, is true by convention. Although the conclusion concerns an inexplicable phenomenon, they may then claim, the inference itself is not inexplicable.

Vasubandhu might also object that if the Pudgalavādins claim that a perception of ourselves is inexplicably related to a perception of an object in the way we are inexplicably related to our aggregates, they are committed to the view that a perception of ourselves exists without dependence upon the perception of an object in the way we exist without dependence upon our aggregates. But the Pudgalavādins surely do not believe that we exist without dependence upon our aggregates because we are inexplicably related to them. Rather, they believe that if we do not exist apart from aggregates, we do not, for instance, survive the cessation of the causal continuum of our aggregates. There is no comparable reason the Pudgalavādins have to believe that a perception of ourselves can exist without dependence upon a perception of an object.

§ 2.5.2.2 *The Pudgalavādins' argument for inexplicable perception and Vasubandhu's objection to it*

The Pudgalavādins are not made to reply to Vasubandhu's objection. Instead of arguing that they do not believe that all perceptions are causally conditioned, as I have argued they could do, they are made simply to state that we exist and yet are inexplicable phenomena. In this context their statement is an argument for the truth or possible truth of the inexplicable perception thesis instead of an objection to Vasubandhu's objection to it. As an argument for its truth, its meaning is that if we exist and are inexplicable, the perception of us must exist and be inexplicable. As an argument for its possible truth, its meaning is that if we exist and are inexplicable, there is no reason why a perception of ourselves cannot exist and be inexplicable. Both versions of the argument have their problems. The second version does not establish what needs to be proved, which is the existence of an inexplicable perception of ourselves, and the first version would seem to be a rather weak argument. The first version not only assumes that inexplicable persons exist and are perceived, but also does not explain why they must be perceived by means of an inexplicable perception if they exist. If we grant, for the sake of the argument, that we exist as inexplicable entities and that we are perceived, why must we be perceived by means of inexplicable perceptions? Although the Pudgalavādins assert that we are perceived by means of inexplicable perceptions in order to avoid Vasubandhu's objection to the knowledge thesis, to have a way to avoid that objection is not the same as having an account of why inexplicable persons are perceived by means of inexplicable perceptions. If the second version of the argument is intended, therefore, much more needs to be said.

A difficulty Vasubandhu might raise against the Pudgalavādins' theory, that there are inexplicable perceptions that establish our existence, is that if there is an inexplicable perception that establishes our existence, it does not possess existence in the way we do, since it surely cannot exist independently of a perception of a primary object by a consciousness in the way we exist independently of collections of aggregates. As a perception by a consciousness, it cannot exist apart from the consciousness whose perception it is, and this consciousness, it would appear, does not exist unless it is perceiving a primary object of that consciousness. Hence, strictly speaking, Vasubandhu might object, the Pudgalavādins can hardly believe that inexplicable perceptions of ourselves can or must possess existence in the way we do.

But this objection, I believe, is bogus. For the ultimate existence of perceptions of ourselves is not their existence apart from perceptions of primary objects, but their existence apart from being conceived. Moreover, although perceptions of ourselves are not the same in existence as perceptions of primary objects, they are the same in existence as consciousnesses that perceive primary objects. Hence, although, unlike persons, who are not the same in existence as any substantial reality or substantially established reality, perceptions are the same in existence as the substantially real consciousnesses that perceive their primary objects.

Vasubandhu's own objection is that the Pudgalavādins' argument for the inexplicable perception thesis fails because in the Buddha's sūtras a visible form and the other aggregates are said to be selfless. He assumes, of course, that what the Buddha said implies that we cannot both exist and be inexplicable. So his objection, I believe, is that the Pudgalavādins cannot claim that a perception of ourselves exists and is inexplicable because we are, since scripture implies that we cannot both exist and be inexplicable.

How does this scriptural teaching imply that we cannot both exist and be inexplicable? Vasubandhu seems to assume here that the Pudgalavādins themselves are willing to identify an inexplicable person with a self, and that since the Buddha said that the aggregates are selfless, what the Buddha said implies that there are no inexplicable persons. Hence, Vasubandhu believes that since the Buddha's claim that the aggregates are selfless implies that there are no inexplicable persons, it certainly implies that there are no inexplicable perceptions of inexplicable persons.

But the quotation used by Vasubandhu can also be interpreted as the Pudgalavādins would interpret it. They too believe that the aggregates are selfless in the sense that they are not possessions of a person with a separate identity, but they do not believe, as Vasubandhu does, that an inseparable identity implies an inseparable existence. Hence, according to the Pudgalavādins' own interpretation, the quotation does not contradict their view that we are ultimately existent inexplicable phenomena.

Vasubandhu's use of this scriptural teaching against the Pudgalavādins' theory raises a perplexing question. Why does he think that the Pudgalavādins would be willing to accept the idea that a person is a self? In order to conform verbally to the Buddha's teaching that there is no self they would most certainly deny that there is a self. The self whose existence they deny, we have seen, is the same as the self whose existence Vasubandhu denies. Both believe that a self is a person who possesses a separate identity. On what ground then does Vasubandhu presume to use the Buddha's denial of the existence of a self against the views expressed by the Pudgalavādins?

Part of the answer, surely, is that Vasubandhu assumes that we possess separate identities if and only if we possess separate existence. Hence, by implying that we possess separate existence, Vasubandhu believes, the Pudgalavādins are also committed to the view that we possess separate identities, and hence, to the view that we are separate substances. To further complicate the issue, it is clear that in many scriptures accepted as authentic discourses of the Buddha the term "self" is used with different meanings. It is used not only to signify persons who are separate substances and persons who possess separate identities, but also persons who are conventional realities. Therefore, it may very well be the case that the Pudgalavādins were at times willing to use the term "self" to refer to a person who is an inexplicable conventional reality. That the scriptures accepted as authentic by the Pudgalavādins contain the use of "self" to signify an inexplicable person is strongly suggested by Vasubandhu's representation in Section 2.7 of the Pudgalavādins' acceptance of this usage in their own scriptures. If this is correct, they will be somewhat handicapped in their replies to Vasubandhu's use of scriptural references to "self" and "selfless" because of the chronic ambiguity of such terms in their own scriptures. Nonetheless, it is difficult to believe that the Pudgalavādins did not carefully distinguish these different uses of "self." How exactly this ambiguity plays out in their replies to Vasubandhu's objections based on their own scriptures I shall discuss in the Commentary on Section 2.7.

At this point in his critique of the Pudgalavādins' theory of persons Vasubandhu has begun to base his objections on scripture. He will go on in Sections 2.5.3, 2.5.4, and 2.5.5 to argue that their account of how we are known to exist by the six consciousnesses contradicts the Buddha's teachings on perception, teachings on objects known to exist, and teachings on the selflessness of the eye as an organ of perception. He concludes his objections to the Pudgalavādins' theory of persons in Sections 2.6, 2.6.1, and 2.7 by citing an assortment of scriptural passages that he believes contradict their theory, by arguing that they should not reject the authority of the passages he cites, and by presenting an assortment of passages from scriptures whose authority they do accept and that he believes contradict their theory of persons. Then he begins in Section 3 his own replies to the Pudgalavādins' objections to his own theory of persons.

§ 2.5.3 *Vasubandhu's objection to the account from its incompatibility with the Buddha's teachings on perception*

Four objections to the Pudgalavādins' account of how we are known to exist are put forward in Section 2.5.3, all of which deal with, or presuppose the truth of, scriptural teachings on perception. I shall call these "the objection from the supporting causal condition," "the objection from the impermanence of the supporting causal condition," "the objection from the otherness of the objects of the different sense-organs" and "the objection from organ encounters." In the first, second, and fourth of these objections passages from the sūtras are employed, and in the third the validity of doctrines expressed in those passages is assumed. The second and fourth objections are followed by one-sentence replies and are set aside by one-sentence objections by Vasubandhu. Although these four objections are appeals to the authority of a teaching of the Buddha, they are philosophical to the extent that the teaching upon which they are based is a philosophical analysis of perception. Each of the objections is directed against the view that a person is known to exist by all six consciousnesses by means of perception. In this section "person" is used to signify an ultimately existent inexplicable person. The first three of these objections are straightforward and easy to understand. Since the fourth objection occasions a subtle reply by the Pudgalavādins and an objection to this reply, I shall more closely examine the entire exchange for the sake of clarity and an objective assessment.

The objections from the supporting causal condition and the impermanence of the supporting causal condition

These two objections begin with the premise that if an eye-consciousness that perceives a person arises, it must arise in dependence upon a visible form, a person, or both a visible form and a person. Vasubandhu assumes that an object in dependence upon which a consciousness arises is its supporting causal condition. So the question he asks is whether the supporting causal condition of an eye-consciousness that perceives us is a visible form, a person, or both a visible form and a person. His first argument is that if a visible form is the supporting causal condition of an eye-consciousness, the eye-consciousness does not know that a person exists by means of perception. He assumes that what an eye-consciousness knows to exist by means of perception can only be an object that is its supporting causal condition. This assumption is made on the basis of the scriptural teaching that the eye-consciousness cannot, by means of perception, know the objects of the other five consciousnesses to exist. Then he argues that the view, that an eye-consciousness arises in dependence upon a person or both a person and a visible form as its supporting causal condition, is inconsistent with the Buddha's teaching that it arises in dependence upon an eye, as its cause, and a visible form, as its supporting causal condition. Vasubandhu adds the objection that if a person were to be a supporting causal condition of an eye-consciousness, a person would, as scripture confirms, be impermanent, and the Pudgalavādins deny that a person is impermanent. Therefore, he would have us conclude, an eye-consciousness does not know that a person exists by means of perception.

The reply to these first two objections presented on behalf of the Pudgalavādins is that they do not claim that a person is a supporting causal condition of an eye-consciousness. The implication of the reply is that a person is perceived by an eye-consciousness and yet is not its supporting causal condition. Their view, we have seen, is that a visible form is indeed the supporting causal condition of an eye-consciousness that incidentally perceives a person. Another implication of the reply may be that the Buddha did not mention a person in the quotation about the cause and supporting causal condition of an eye-consciousness because he was explaining why an eye-consciousness arises rather than explaining what it perceives. They might say that Vasubandhu erroneously assumes, without scriptural support, that the only object perceived by an eye-consciousness is its supporting causal condition. Although it is true that the Buddha denied that an eye-consciousness perceives an object perceived by an ear-consciousness or by any other kind of sensory consciousness, he did not explicitly deny that it can perceive an object that is not its supporting causal condition.

Vasubandhu's objection to the Pudgalavādins' reply is that a person who is not a supporting causal condition of a consciousness is not perceived by the consciousness. But this objection begs the question, since what is actually at issue is whether or not a consciousness can perceive an object that is not its supporting causal condition. Vasubandhu may be assuming that the silence of the Buddha about anything other than the supporting causal condition of an eye-consciousness being perceived by this consciousness is sufficient ground for denying that he held such a view. But this assumption, in turn, involves argumentation not presented in the text. To be sure, once again, the Pudgalavādins' reply by itself is not sufficient to overturn Vasubandhu's initial two objections, but we need not conclude, on this basis, that their account of how we are known to exist has been conclusively refuted. Since the objection from the impermanence of the supporting causal condition is based on these same illegitimate assumptions, it too is inconclusive.

The objection from the otherness of the objects of different sense-organs

Vasubandhu's third objection is that since an object perceived by means of one kind of sense-organ is other than an object perceived by means of another, we too must be other than the objects perceived by means of the other four if we are perceived by means of any one of these kinds of sense-organs. The upshot, of course, is that the Pudgalavādins' doctrine, that we are not other than any one of these objects, is inconsistent with their view that we are perceived by the six consciousnesses.

The Pudgalavādins can easily reply to this objection, but a reply is not presented on their behalf. The reply is that in Vasubandhu's objection it is mistakenly assumed that only the mutually exclusive objects of the five sense-organs are perceived by means of them and that we are the same in existence as one of these objects. This latter assumption, which the Pudgalavādins reject, enables Vasubandhu to identify us with each of the objects of the five sense-organs.

The objection from organ encounters

The fourth objection Vasubandhu presents to the Pudgalavādins' account of how we are known to exist occasions a reply by the Pudgalavādins in Section 2.5.3.1, which in turn is rejected by Vasubandhu in Section 2.5.3.2. The objection is that since the Buddha taught that each of the five sense-organs encounters its own domain and objects and not those of the others, a person is not known to exist by the six consciousnesses. Let us call the passage quoted by Vasubandhu in support of this objection "the sense-organs passage."

In the statement of the objection it is said that both the domain and objects of an organ are encountered by the organ. What exactly this means is not clear. I shall take it to mean that an organ encounters the objects in its own domain. The objection, we may notice, does not include an explanation of how an organ encountering its own domain and objects is connected to a consciousness perceiving the objects encountered by its organ. So I will need to supply this connection. With this change and addition, we may say that the objection begins with the statement that (I) each of the five sense-organs encounters the objects in its own domain. In the sense-organ passage this statement is followed by the statement, that none of the five organs encounters the objects in the domains of the others, which seems to be regarded as the implication of the first statement. So let us add that (II) if each of the five sense-organs encounters the objects in its own domain, none of the five sense organs encounters the objects in the domains of the others. Therefore, it is said, in accord with (I) and (II), that (III) none of the five sense-organs encounters the objects in the domains of the others. Vasubandhu leaves it to his readers to realize that (IV) if none of the five sense-organs encounters the objects in the domains of the others, a sense-organ does not encounter anything other than the objects in its own domain. This assumption, as the Pudgalavādins will point out, involves an unwarranted jump from the denial that no sense-organ encounters the objects of another to the denial that it encounters anything other than its own object. Vasubandhu would have us infer, from (III) and (IV), that (V) a sense-organ does not encounter anything other than the objects in its own domain. The objection also assumes that (VI) if a sense-organ does not encounter anything other than the objects in its own domain, a consciousness that arises in dependence upon a sense-organ does not perceive anything other than the objects in the domain of the sense-organ. But if the Pudgalavādins are correct in their belief that we are not the same in existence as any of the objects in the domains of the six organs, Vasubandhu assumes, they must assert that (VII) if a consciousness that arises in dependence upon a sense-organ does not perceive anything other than the objects in the domain of the sense-organ, we are not perceived by a consciousness by means of its sense-organ. But (VIII) if we are not perceived by a consciousness by means of its sense-organ, we are not perceived by all the six consciousnesses. Therefore, from (V)–(VIII), we may infer that (IX) we are not perceived by all the six consciousnesses. If (IX) is true, the Pudgalavādins' account of how we are known to exist is false.

The Pudgalavādins' one-sentence reply is that the Buddha's teaching in the sense-organ passage does not imply that we are not perceived by all six consciousnesses, since we are not objects in the domains of the sense-organs. How can we be objects in the domains of any of the sense-organs, they may ask, since objects in the domains of the sense-organs possess separate identities, but we do not? A sensory consciousness that perceives us, of course, arises in dependence upon one of the sense-organs, but its perception of ourselves only incidentally arises in dependence upon it.

Hence, they reply that Vasubandhu's objection from organ encounters is not relevant to their claim that we are known to exist by all six consciousnesses.

Vasubandhu's one-sentence objection to the Pudgalavādins' one-sentence reply is that if we are not objects in the domains of the sense-organs, we are not perceived. The implication is that we cannot be known to exist by means of a perception by a consciousness named after one of these sense-organs. But since he simply assumes in this objection that objects not in the domains of the sense-organs are not perceived by the consciousnesses to which the organs give rise, and the Pudgalavādins obviously do not believe this assumption to be true, it cannot be said that his objection to their reply succeeds. So he has not yet refuted their theory of how we are known to exist by reference to the sense-organs passage. Vasubandhu has shown at best that the Pudgalavādins' theory of how we are known to exist is inconsistent with the theory of perception he himself ascribes to the Buddha.

§ 2.5.3.1 *The Pudgalavādins' reply to the objection from organ encounters*

In Section 2.5.3.1 the Pudgalavādins present a more extensive reply to Vasubandhu's objection from organ encounters. The brevity of expression in this section and the next section would render them unintelligible without Yaśomitra's extensive explanation. From him we learn that the Pudgalavādins are replying that the sense-organs passage cannot be interpreted in the way Vasubandhu interprets it, since the same interpretation, if given to the passage they cite, which I shall call "the six organs passage," contradicts the Buddha's teaching that the mental organ encounters the objects in the domains of the five sense-organs. They are arguing that Vasubandhu has misinterpreted the sense-organs passage, which does not in fact imply that we cannot be perceived by all six consciousnesses.

The Pudgalavādins seem to be correct in replying that Vasubandhu draws an unwarranted conclusion from the sense-organs passage. For it is clear that his argument involves a jump from a qualified claim about what the sense-organs encounter to an unqualified claim. But how exactly the six organs passage shows this to be so is not clear. We will also see that Vasubandhu's attempt to interpret the six organs passage so that it does not contradict his interpretation of the sense-organs passage is at best rather implausible. The philosophical interest of the dispute lies in what it reveals about the extent to which Vasubandhu thinks he can use philosophical considerations to stretch the meaning of a scriptural passage to defend his own interpretation of passages against objections. To understand the argument of this dispute we need to understand the Buddhist teachings that each of the six organs has its own domain of objects it alone encounters and that the mental organ encounters both the objects in its own domain and the objects in the domains of the five sense-organs.

When a sense-organ and an object it alone encounters come into contact, a consciousness of the object arises within the same continuum of aggregates in which the organ is present. The consciousness that arises is named after the sense-organ that causes it and is said to perceive directly the object encountered by the sense-organ. A mental organ is a consciousness that produces a mental consciousness of an object. It is called an organ of perception because, like a sense-organ, which causes an object it alone encounters to be directly perceived by a sensory consciousness, it causes an object it alone encounters to be perceived directly by a mental consciousness. But a mental consciousness not only can directly perceive the immediately preceding consciousness and its mental factors; it can also indirectly perceive the object of the immediately preceding consciousness. In this case, an indirect perception of an object is a perception of an object by means of a mental image formed on the basis of the discrimination that attends the immediately preceding consciousness. Although the object and organ of perception are the same entity in the case in which a mental organ produces, in the next moment, a direct perception of itself, it is said that the direct perception arises in dependence upon an encounter between an object and an organ in order to conform to the general doctrine that a consciousness arises from an encounter between an organ and an object. (This is the Buddhist version of the idea that the mind is the organ of its own perception.) The mental organ is said to encounter not only the mental phenomena whose direct perception it produces, but also to encounter the objects whose indirect perception it produces. Hence, a mental organ is said to encounter the same objects encountered by the five sense-organs in addition to encountering its own objects. The five sense-organs rely upon a mental organ in order to give rise to an indirect perception of the objects they encounter. An indirect perception of these objects is a conception of them.

In the present section of the text the Pudgalavādins are claiming that Vasubandhu cannot infer, from the passage in which it is said that each of the five sense-organs encounters the objects in its own domain, the conclusion that each of the five sense-organs does not stray from the objects in its own domain. For they believe that we must then be able to infer, from the six organs passage, in which it is said that each of the six organs seeks the objects in its own domain, the false conclusion that the mental organ does not encounter anything other than the objects in its own domain. The Pudgalavādins assume that, although in the six organs passage each of the organs is said to "seek" the objects in its own domain, the implication of what is said is that each "encounters" the objects in its own domain. If each of the six organs encounters the objects in its own domain, the mental organ encounters the objects in its own domain. When the Pudgalavādins say that Vasubandhu's interpretation of the sense-organs passage commits him to the view that the six organs passage implies that a mental organ does not "stray" from the objects in its own domain, they mean that it commits him to the view that a mental organ does not encounter anything other than the objects in its own domain. But the mental organ does encounter objects that are not in its domain, since it encounters the objects in the domains of the sense-organs. Hence, Vasubandhu cannot assume that if a sense-organ encounters the objects in its own domain it cannot encounter anything other than the objects in its own domain.

The six organs passage is a statement of the standard Buddhist doctrine that all six organs encounter the objects in their own domains. The Pudgalavādins cite the passage in an attempt to show Vasubandhu that his interpretation of the sense-organs passage, if applied to theirs, contradicts one of the doctrines expressed in his own passage, that a mental organ can encounter the objects in the domains of the sense-organs.

§ 2.5.3.2 *Vasubandhu's rejection of their reply*

In Section 2.5.3.2, Vasubandhu gives an interpretation of the six organs passage that he believes absolves his interpretation of the sense-organs passage from the charge that it implies, when applied to the six organs passage, the falsehood that a mental organ does not stray from the objects in its own domain. In the six organs passage, Vasubandhu claims, the expression "the six organs" is used to refer to six kinds of mental consciousnesses, since only a mental consciousness can conceive an object and only a consciousness that can conceive an object can "seek" an object. Consequently, he claims that the six organs passage, if interpreted along the same lines as he interpreted the sense-organs passage, does not imply the falsehood that a mental organ does not encounter anything other than the objects in its own domain, but rather implies the truth that these six kinds of mental consciousnesses seek the objects in their own domains.

In favor of Vasubandhu's interpretation is the fact that if it were correct, it would resolve the inconsistency between his interpretation of the sense-organ passage and what is said in the six organs passage. But there surely are passages in the sūtras that express the doctrine to which the Pudgalavādins mean to call attention and do not include the term "seek." Moreover, Vasubandhu's construal of the six organs as six kinds of mental consciousnesses is at best strained. In the first place, nowhere else is there expressed, at least to my knowledge, a Buddhist doctrine that there are six kinds of mental consciousnesses each of which seeks the objects in its own domain. Second, his claim about the implications of the use of the term "seek" in the six organs passage is not very convincing, since it is much more plausible to suppose that the use of "seek" is metaphorical than to suppose that a technical expression like "organ" is metaphorically used.

The Pudgalavādins could just as easily, and more persuasively, argue that in the six organs passage the Buddha uses the term "seek" metaphorically to signify the encounter of the six organs with the objects in their domains.

§ 2.5.4 *Vasubandhu's objection to the account from its incompatibility with the Buddha's enumerations of objects that are known to exist*

In this section, Vasubandhu quotes a part of a passage in the whole of which the Buddha catalogs all objects that are known to exist. Since the phenomena that are listed all possess ultimate existence, we may construe the objection to mean that the Buddha did not list inexplicable persons among the phenomena known to possess ultimate existence. If they are not known to possess ultimate existence, they are not known to exist by all six consciousnesses, as the Pudgalavādins say they are. The Pudgalavādins can reply that the Buddha's catalog is meant to include only phenomena that possess substantial reality, in which case, the fact that persons are not listed can be explained away.

§ 2.5.5 *Vasubandhu's objection to the account from its incompatibility with the Buddha's teaching on the selflessness of an organ of perception*

Vasubandhu's last scriptural objection to the Pudgalavādins' account of how we are known to exist concerns the specific claim that we know that we exist because we see a self by means of an eye, but it can of course be generalized to cover the perception of a self by means of the other five organs.

There has been some confusion about what his argument is. The translations of La Vallée Poussin and Stcherbatsky do not convey the meaning of the Sanskrit text we have. La Vallée Poussin's translation makes Vasubandhu's point to be that since a visible form, which is known to exist by means of an eye, is said in scripture to be selfless, we cannot see a self by means of an eye, since a self cannot be seen in what is selfless. In this interpretation the meaning is that since a visible form is without a self, no self can be seen in a visible form. But the Sanskrit text clearly means that "a self cannot be seen by means of what is selfless." So what is being assumed is that the eye by means of which it is seen is selfless, not that what is seen, a visible form, is selfless. Hence, this interpretation cannot be correct. Stcherbatsky's translation, by contrast, is vague and is highly interpretive. He has Vasubandhu say that the Pudgalavādins' view that a real self has an eye by which it sees other selves is called "Wrong Personalism." How exactly this renders the meaning of the text I cannot say.

Vasubandhu, I believe, is objecting that the Pudgalavādins' account of how we are known to exist implies that we see a self by means of an eye that is selfless in the sense that the eye is not owned or possessed by a self. The implication is that an eye not owned or possessed by a self is used to see the self that is its possessor. If this is the correct interpretation, Vasubandhu is arguing that since the Pudgalavādins claim that we see a person by means of an eye, they are committed to the view that we see a self by means of an eye not owned or possessed by a self, and thereby not used by a self to see itself. The bite of the argument comes from the paradoxical idea that an eye not possessed by a self is used by a self to see itself.

On any of the above three interpretations of this objection Vasubandhu fails to bring a telling point against the Pudgalavādins' account of how we are known to exist. For they make a distinction between a self that is a person who possesses a separate identity and a self that is an inexplicable person who possesses ultimate existence. Their account, correctly expressed, is not that a self is perceived by means of what is selfless, but that an inexplicable person is perceived by means of an organ that is not possessed and used by a self. Indeed, as we have seen, they believe that our aggregates, including the organs of perception, are acquired by us.

§ 2.6 Vasubandhu's scriptural objections to the Pudgalavādins' theory of persons

In Section 2.6 Vasubandhu cites seven passages from the Buddha's sūtras. The first passage would seem to provide the strongest scriptural support for his own theory of persons and his rejection of the Pudgalavādins' theory of persons, since it seems to convey the idea that we are the same in existence as collections of aggregates. It is literally taught in this passage that a collection of aggregates is called a person and that the attributes of a person are mere names or verbal conventions. Let us call this passage "the aggregates passage." Vasubandhu claims that this passage occurs in a sūtra whose statements are to be interpreted literally. We shall need to discuss this passage in some detail.

The second and third passages, which we may call "the twelve bases passages," are taken by Vasubandhu to be statements to the effect that every phenomenon that exists is either one, some or all of the twelve bases of perception. The third passage, which is said to belong to the collection of sūtras accepted by the Pudgalavādins themselves, is used to support the authenticity of the teaching taught in the second passage. Vasubandhu believes that these passages show either that a self does not exist or that if it does, it is the same in existence as one, some or all the twelve bases of perception. But the twelve bases passages can just as well be interpreted by the Pudgalavādins to show only that every substance is either one, some, or all of the twelve bases of perception.

The fourth passage, which may be called the "*Bimbisāra* passage," basically expresses the doctrine that aggregates are selfless. It is clear that this is a theory that the Pudgalavādins do not deny. In the fifth passage, which may be called the "*Śīla* passage," it is said that no sentient being is found among the collection of aggregates in dependence upon which he is conceived, just as no chariot is found among its parts, which are the phenomena in dependence upon which it is conceived. It is concluded that just as, in dependence upon the collection of its parts we refer to a chariot, so in dependence upon a collection of aggregates, we refer to a sentient being. Vasubandhu believes that this passage can be used to establish his own theory of persons and to refute the Pudgalavādins' theory of persons. We shall need to investigate whether or not it can.

In the sixth passage, which may be called the "*Kṣudraka* passage," it is in effect said that when we search for a self we find only aggregates, none of which is a self or a possession of a self. In reply the Pudgalavādins could say that since the search is a search for a self among the collection of aggregates in dependence upon which we are conceived, and a self is a person who possesses a separate identity, what is found, of course, is only aggregates. The passage, they may say, concerns only the proof that there is no person who possesses a separate identity. The passage, therefore, does not prove that there is no person who possesses a separate existence. The seventh passage, which may be called the "five evils passage," simply lists the evils of having a mistaken view of a self and cannot be said to support his own theory over against theirs.

Rather than discuss all of these passages individually, I shall discuss the doctrines they express or presuppose that are most relevant to an appraisal of Vasubandhu's use of them to support his own theory of persons and refute that of the Pudgalavādins as correct interpretations of the Buddha's own theory. The doctrines that I shall discuss are those expressed in the aggregates passage, the *Bimbisāra* passage and the *Kṣudraka* passage. The doctrines are (1) that some passages are not to be interpreted, but understood literally, while others are to be interpreted, (2) that collections of aggregates are called persons and the attributes of persons are mere names or verbal conventions, and (3) that the aggregates in the collections of aggregates in dependence upon which we conceive ourselves are selfless.

The use of literal and interpretable sūtras and its implications

Vasubandhu twice mentions in his discussion of the aggregates passage that the passage comes from a sūtra whose statements are to be understood according to their literal meaning rather than from a sūtra whose statements are to be given an interpretation that explains away and corrects what they seem to mean literally. It was a standard practice among Indian Buddhist philosophers to distinguish between the statements of the Buddha that are to be accepted as true in their literal meaning and those that require interpretation. They accepted the view that the Buddha, through his omniscience, knew what doctrines the disciples he happened to be teaching at any given time were capable of understanding and accepting as true, and taught them only what they could understand and accept at the time they were being taught. To those disciples not yet ready to accept the correct theory he taught theories they could understand and accept, and, although actually false, helped them to abandon theories even more seriously mistaken. Later he would teach the correct theory to them if they had developed their understanding to a point at which they could accept it. All of these theories, or at least as many as his followers managed to commit to memory, are believed to be preserved in the sūtras. Because most Indian Buddhist philosophers held this view of the provisional status of parts of the Buddha's teachings, they were forced to decide, on the basis of their own independent philosophical reasonings, which of the various competing theories taught in scriptures are correct and which are incorrect. It is of course true that these philosophers tended to accept the interpretations of their own teachers, but there was no prohibition against formulating objections to the interpretations of their teachers if they were supported by cogent reasons.

The belief in literal and interpretable scriptures fostered an amazing variety of interpretations of the Buddha's teachings. Because of this belief the same sūtras were made compatible with the views held in the different Indian Buddhist philosophical schools. In the last analysis, what is necessary for a theory to be attributed to the Buddha is for there to be a passage that, when interpreted literally, presents that theory. All Indian Buddhist philosophers, I have already mentioned, accepted, as classifications of phenomena, the five aggregates, the twelve bases of perception, the eighteen elements, and the twelve links. But the interpretation of what the Buddha said about these phenomena was debated by the Indian Buddhist philosophers on the basis of independent reasoning. Hence, although the Indian Buddhist philosophers are constrained by their commitment to the sūtras to use these classifications, they had considerable freedom in the interpretation of them. If we add to this consideration the fact that the determination of the literal meaning of Sanskrit words in the sūtras is not always a simple matter, since so many of them have a great variety of meanings in different contexts and change their meanings over time, it is easy to see why the Indian Buddhist philosophers' interpretations of passages in the sūtras can also vary considerably. To some extent, moreover, differences of interpretation of passages in the sūtras may involve appeals to different conventional usages of the same terms. The difficulty of determining the meaning of Sanskrit terms, of course, is alleviated to a great extent by definitions provided by the Buddha in the sūtras, but an understanding of these definitions is still tainted by different meanings that may be assigned to the terms used in the definitions. If we add all this together, we can see why an argument based on a passage from the sūtras is a very complicated and slippery move in a dispute between Indian Buddhist philosophers. We have already seen just how complicated and slippery it can be in our analysis of the dispute between Vasubandhu and the Pudgalavādins in Sections 2.5.3.1 and 2.5.3.2 about the meaning of the six organs passage.

Therefore, when Vasubandhu claims for the sūtra on *What a Human Being Is* the status of a sūtra whose statements are to be understood literally, the final basis upon which he makes his claim is that he believes, according to his own understanding of the literal meaning of the statements in this sūtra, that these statements are philosophically sound and defensible. Since what counts as being philosophically sound and defensible in the context of the scriptural debate between Vasubandhu and the Pudgalavādins is problematic, their claims for the truth of a passage in its literal meaning are equally problematic. The detailed reasoning that stands behind their claims needs to be presented to, and withstand the examination of, the opponent before they can bear any weight whatsoever. In the present context, moreover, it must in the end be the philosophical merit of the individual passages being presented, not that of the entire sūtra from which they are drawn, that should be decided, since only the correctness of these passages is at issue. In any case, the philosophical worthiness of a sūtra as a whole must be decided by an examination of its individual passages, including the one at issue.

In Section 2.6.1 the Pudgalavādins are made to challenge Vasubandhu's use of sūtras whose passages are cited in Section 2.6. But they are not made to question whether the quoted passages are to be accepted as true in their literal meaning, but rather whether they come from genuine sūtras, which are authentic reports of what the Buddha said. This is, of course, a different issue, and I shall discuss it in my comments on Section 2.6.1, where that issue is addressed.

A collection of aggregates is called a person, whose attributes are mere names or verbal conventions

Vasubandhu apparently believes that the aggregates passage directly supports his theory that persons are the same in existence as collections of aggregates. Whether or not it does so unequivocally I will try to determine. What is literally said in the passage is that a collection of aggregates is called a person, that the verbal conventions are adopted that a person has the various attributes enumerated in the passage, and that these attributes are mere names or verbal conventions. The passage begins with an account of a perceptual situation that gives rise to calling a collection of aggregates a person and ends with the conclusion, "all of these phenomena, which are impermanent and causally conditioned, are dependently arisen." What exactly do these statements mean?

The claim that a collection of aggregates is called a person does seem to support Vasubandhu's view that a person is the same in existence as a collection of aggregates. This claim, along with the claims that the verbal conventions are adopted that a person has the listed attributes and that these attributes are mere names or verbal conventions, surely suggests to Vasubandhu that a person does not, apart from being conceived in dependence upon a collection of aggregates, possess these attributes. The dependently arisen phenomena mentioned in the conclusion of the passage, he probably thinks, include the person. The implication of saying that the person arises dependently, he might say, is that the identity of the person, as set out in the list of its attributes, depends upon being conceived on the basis of a collection of aggregates.

Although it is not literally so stated, the passage implies that not only the attributes assigned to persons, but also persons themselves, are mere names or verbal conventions. Vasubandhu, of course, thinks that this is a way of saying that persons and their attributes are real by way of a conception. But another interpretation of the claim that persons and their attributes are mere names and verbal conventions is possible. This is the interpretation of Candrakīrti, according to whom persons and their attributes are mere names or verbal conventions in the sense that they possess both existence and identity in dependence upon our convention of conceiving persons and their attributes when collections of aggregates are present. If this is the correct interpretation, it would seem to follow, if it is assumed, as Vasubandhu does, that the aggregates ultimately exist, that the passage implies that persons are not the same in existence as collections of aggregates, since persons will not possess ultimate existence. Similarly, the statement that the attributes ascribed to persons are mere names or verbal conventions seems to imply, on the same assumption, that persons have no attributes at all, since they will not possess ultimate existence.

In the *Śīla* passage, moreover, it is said that by convention we speak of ourselves in reliance upon our aggregates in the way we refer by name to a chariot on the basis of the collection of its parts. But here, again, it is not said that a chariot is the same in existence as the collection of its parts or that persons are the same in existence as the collections of their aggregates. In fact, since the comparison of a person to a chariot is made immediately after the claim that there is no sentient being to be found among our aggregates, the point of the passage could be interpreted to be that we are assigned names even though we do not possess ultimate existence. The explanation is that, even though we are not by ourselves objects to which reference can be made, reference to ourselves occurs in dependence upon the convention that we exist when aggregates are present in the way we refer to a chariot on the basis of the convention that it exists when its parts are present. Indeed, this is how Candrakīrti in the *Madhyamakāvatāra* understands the *Śīla* passage, for he quotes it in Chapter 6 to show that we are not the same in existence as collections of aggregates. Candrakīrti's interpretation does not explain why the Buddha said in the aggregates passage that a collection of aggregates is called a person, since this statement seems to imply that a collection of aggregates is that to which we refer when we speak of ourselves. Candrakīrti would need to claim, it seems, that the statement was made to disciples incapable of understanding and accepting the theory that that to which we refer when we speak of ourselves is a dependently real person rather than a collection of aggregates.

Similarly, the Pudgalavādins might interpret the claim that a collection of aggregates is called a person as being addressed to those who were incapable of understanding and accepting the theory that the conventionally real person to whom we refer when we refer to ourselves is an inexplicable phenomenon that possesses ultimate existence. In fact, both the aggregates passage and the *Śīla* passage could be rejected by them on the ground that they require an interpretation. But what is said in Section 2.6.1 suggests that they might reject the scriptures from which the aggregates passages come as unauthentic.

But how could the Pudgalavādins interpret the claim that persons and their attributes are mere names or verbal conventions? Surely they would say that it means that persons and their attributes, insofar as they are conceived, are mere names or verbal conventions, since persons do not possess separate identities on the basis of which they are conceived, and so do not by themselves possess the attributes ascribed to them. It is because we assume that we possess separate identities, they believe, that we suffer. They can similarly interpret the *Śīla* passage to be conveying both the doctrine that reference to ourselves by means of discourse or thought depends in part upon the presence of aggregates when we are perceived, and the doctrine that when it is said that we are not found among the phenomena in dependence upon which we are conceived, it is implied that we do not possess separate identities, not that we do not possess separate existence. Hence, Vasubandhu's use of the aggregates passage and the *Śīla* passage, I conclude, would not seem to be a conclusive scriptural refutation of the Pudgalavādins' theory of persons.

The selflessness of the aggregates

In the *Bimbisāra* and *Kṣudraka* passages there is expressed the doctrine that the phenomena in dependence upon which we conceive ourselves are selfless. I have already pointed out that Vasubandhu cannot, at least without further argument, use these passages against the Pudgalavādins' theory that we are ultimately existent inexplicable phenomena. They identify a self with a person who has a separate identity, and a self of this sort, they agree, is most certainly not found among the phenomena in dependence upon which we conceive ourselves.

Vasubandhu might still contend that if persons were inexplicable phenomena, these passages ought to be saying that persons, not the phenomena in dependence upon which persons are conceived, are selfless. If, as they claim, persons rather than collections of aggregates wander and suffer in cyclic life, act to free themselves, and are finally liberated, it must be the realization that persons are selfless that frees them from suffering, not the realization of the selflessness of the phenomena in dependence upon which they are conceived. Vasubandhu can argue that the passage confirms his own view that we are the same in existence as collections of these phenomena precisely because in these passages it is shown that the realization of the selflessness of these phenomena frees us from suffering. The Pudgalavādins can reply that in these passages phenomena are said to be selfless in the sense that they are not possessed by a self and that it is implied, therefore, that the possessor of these phenomena is not a self. In any case, they can say, the claim that a person is not a self would have been too confusing for the Buddha to have made, since "person" and "self" can be used as synonyms.

Finally, in the *Kṣudraka* passage, in which it is said that "there is no person or sentient being here, there are only phenomena produced by causes," the terms, "person," and "sentient being," the Pudgalavādins might claim, are used to signify a substance that exists apart from causally conditioned phenomena. This teaching, they can say, was intended for those who were not ready for the teaching that a person is an ultimately existent inexplicable phenomenon. They might also claim that the teaching according to which persons and their attributes are mere names is intended only for disciples who are not ready to distinguish inexplicable persons from selves, and that it means that persons, insofar as they are seen as selves, are mere names.

§ 2.6.1 *The Pudgalavādins should not reject the authenticity of these sūtras*

In Section 2.6.1, Vasubandhu states that the Pudgalavādins cannot reject the authority of the passages he cites on the ground that they are not included in the collection of sūtras they accept as genuine reports of what the Buddha said. If the Pudgalavādins actually argued that these passages are not acceptable because they are not in their own collection of sūtras, Vasubandhu is quite right about this. The passages are not unacceptable simply because not accepted by the Pudgalavādins. But Vasubandhu's argument for the statement that they cannot reject these passages for this reason is unconvincing. He argues that the Pudgalavādins cannot reject the authority of the passages cited simply because they are not included in their own collection of sūtras, since either the sūtras accepted by the Pudgalavādins as genuine are authoritative or what the Buddha said is authoritative, and if the former is true, they are not Buddhists, and if the latter is true, they must accept the authority of the passages cited against their theory, since they are found in the sūtras accepted by all others and are not inconsistent with other sūtras or the truth.

This argument, of course, does not show that the Pudgalavādins should accept the authority of the passages in question, since it simply assumes that the sūtras accepted by the Pudgalavādins are not the entirety of what the Buddha said, that the entirety of what the Buddha said is determined by consensus, that the passages in question are not contradicted by other passages in these scriptures, and that the passages are not inconsistent with the truth. It is clear that the authenticity of sūtras is not in the end to be determined by either consensus or the consistency of the passages in these sūtras, or even by both together. And even if we give Vasubandhu the benefit of the doubt concerning the acceptance by all other Buddhists of the authority of the sūtras from which the passages quoted come, we are still left with the question of what reasons the Pudgalavādins already have for rejecting the authority of the sūtras from which they come. It is in the end the evaluation of these reasons that would seem to be most decisive in deciding the validity of their rejection. The question is further complicated by Vasubandhu's rejection of the authenticity of the Mahāyāna sūtras, since his own reasons for this rejection, insofar as he adopts the Sautrāntika point of view in the *Commentary*, are not irrelevant to the appraisal of a critique he might make of the Pudgalavādins' actual reasons for rejecting the authenticity of the passages being discussed.

Vasubandhu's claim that the doctrines expressed in the passages he quotes do not contradict the doctrines expressed in other sūtras will not be judged here. A proper evaluation would be a very complicated affair and would also be rendered exceedingly interpretative by the vagueness of the reference to other scriptures. It is not clear whether his claim that those passages do not contradict the truth means that they do not contradict the final truth as expressed by the Buddha or contradict the truth as it is revealed by independent investigation. Needless to say, Vasubandhu's argument in this section fails to show that the Pudgalavādins should accept the authority of the sūtras from which the passages he cited come.

§ 2.7 The charge of inconsistency with doctrines in sūtras they themselves accept as authoritative

Vasubandhu argues in Section 2.7 that the Pudgalavādins' theory of persons is also inconsistent with doctrines presented in the sūtras they themselves accept as genuine reports of the Buddha's teachings. The teachings in their sūtras with which he claims it is inconsistent are that all phenomena are selfless, that the mind that believes that what is selfless is a self is mistaken, that those who think that they perceive a self perceive only the five aggregates, which are selfless phenomena, and that those who remember previous lives remember only the lives of the five aggregates. Let us call these objections, respectively, "the selfless phenomena objection," "the mistaken view objection," "the aggregate-perception objection," and "the aggregate-remembrance objection." To the first, second, and fourth of these objections the Pudgalavādins are represented as offering replies, which are in turn rejected by Vasubandhu.

In the selfless phenomena objection Vasubandhu simply states that the sūtras accepted as genuine by the Pudgalavādins contain the teaching that all phenomena are selfless. He seems to assume that the Pudgalavādins hold the view that an ultimately existent inexplicable person is a self and that this view is inconsistent with the teaching in their own sūtras that all phenomena are selfless. But why exactly he assumes that they hold the view that an ultimately existent inexplicable person is a self is not clear. It may be, as I suggested earlier, that the Pudgalavādins did in fact use "self" in two different senses and simply assumed that it would be known in which of the two senses they were using the terms in any given case. They may have said both that an ultimately existent inexplicable person is not a self, meaning that he is not a person who possesses a separate identity, and that an inexplicable person is a self, meaning that he is a person who possesses ultimate existence. Accordingly, the teaching that all phenomena are selfless, we may suppose, they would interpret to mean that no phenomenon is a person who possesses a separate identity. Hence, we should expect the Pudgalavādins to reply to Vasubandhu's selfless phenomena objection by stating that in the sense in which all phenomena are selfless, persons too are selfless.

But the Pudgalavādins are made to give what at first glance seems to be a surprising reply to this objection. The reply is that the teaching that all phenomena are selfless does not contradict their theory that a person is not a selfless phenomenon because a person cannot be said to be either other than or the same in existence as any selfless phenomenon. The intent of this inexplicability reply is clear. It is that persons are not said to be selfless phenomena because the selfless phenomena in question are substantial realities or substantially established realities, and persons are neither other than nor the same in existence as any substantial reality or substantially established reality. The inexplicability reply, in other words, is used to defend the view that a person is not a substantial reality or substantially established reality rather than to point out that a person is selfless for the same reason that all other phenomena are selfless. Although it is assumed in the question and its reply that the selfless phenomena at issue are either substantial realities or substantially established realities, the reply does not call attention to this assumption. The reply also fails to include the Pudgalavādins' teaching that persons are selfless in the sense that they lack separate identities. We may conclude that neither Vasubandhu's selfless phenomena objection nor the Pudgalavādins' inexplicability reply are successful as they are formulated.

Vasubandhu's objection to the inexplicability reply is that if persons are neither other than nor the same in existence as any selfless phenomenon, they cannot be perceived by means of a mental organ. He thinks that they cannot be perceived by a means of a mental organ, since in scripture it is said that every consciousness arises in dependence upon an organ of perception and an object of perception, each of which is said to be a selfless phenomenon. The point, it seems, is that since the Pudgalavādins claim that a person is not a selfless phenomenon, they cannot say, since the objects perceived by the six consciousnesses are said to be selfless phenomena, that he is perceived by a mental consciousness any more than that he is perceived by the other five consciousnesses. This objection is another variation on the objection made in Section 2.5.3. In that section it is simply assumed that an object that is not a supporting causal condition of a consciousness is not perceived by it. The Pudgalavādins, of course, do not accept this assumption. Since Vasubandhu believes that their knowledge thesis has been refuted, he may think that he is entitled to make this assumption.

In the mistaken view objection Vasubandhu argues that the Pudgalavādins' theory of persons is inconsistent with their own scriptural teaching that it is a mistake to view what is selfless as a self. He assumes that the Pudgalavādins are committed to the view that it is not a mistake to view what is selfless as a self, since they both deny that a person is selfless and assert that he is a self. He thinks that they deny that a person is selfless because they deny that he is either other than or the same in existence as selfless phenomena and that they assert that he is a self because they assert that he exists apart from all selfless phenomena. In reply, the Pudgalavādins could have said that since in this objection "what is selfless" means "substantial realities or substantially established realities that are not selves or possessions of self," and "self" means a "person that possesses a separate identity," it is true that it is a mistake to view what is selfless as a self. Vasubandhu, therefore, is himself mistaken in thinking that they think that the quotation means that a person, who is not selfless, is a self. But instead of the reply I just supposed they would make to this objection Vasubandhu has them reply that the passage does not contradict their view, since the passage pertains to the mistaken view that what is selfless is a self, not to their own view that a self is a self. When they are made to claim that the view, that a self is a self, is correct, the first "self" in the claim is surely used to signify a person who is the object of the conception of ourselves, the second "self" used to signify an ultimately existent inexplicable person, and "is" used to mean "is the same in existence as."

Vasubandhu ignores the Pudgalavādins' claim, that their view is that a self is a self, and instead focuses on their view that a person is not the same in existence as selfless phenomena. He objects that if they accept this view and also admit that visible forms, which are included in the five aggregates, the twelve bases of perception, and the eighteen elements, are selfless phenomena, then they must also admit that their view, that persons neither are nor are not visible forms, is mistaken. How, Vasubandhu wonders, can persons not be other than visible forms if persons are not the same in existence as selfless phenomena and visible forms are selfless phenomena? The Pudgalavādins are not made to reply to this objection, but what their reply would be is clear. Vasubandhu is assuming that if persons are not the same in existence as selfless phenomena, they must be other than selfless phenomena. This assumption, they believe, is false.

In Vasubandhu's aggregate-perception objection to the Pudgalavādins' theory of persons he cites a passage in which it is said that śrāmaṇas and brāhmins who think that they perceive a self actually perceive only the five aggregates, and concludes, on this basis, that the mistaken view of a self amounts to believing that what is selfless is a self. If those who think that they perceive a self actually perceive the five aggregates, he implies, persons are the same in existence as the five aggregates, since persons who are perceived are the same in existence as these aggregates, not the same in existence as selves. Hence, persons cannot be inexplicable phenomena, as the Pudgalavādins claim they are.

No response is given to this last objection, but a response can be devised on behalf of the Pudgalavādins based on the claims and arguments already attributed to them. They can say that the passage does not require the interpretation Vasubandhu gives to it. The passage, they might add, is addressed to those not ready to accept the existence of an inexplicable person. Alternatively, they may say that the meaning of "perceived" in the passage is "perceived with discrimination," in which case only the five aggregates are perceived. The point of the passage, they could then conclude, is to refute the view that a person is a self in the sense of being a separate substance. Since it is śrāmaṇas and brāhmins who think they perceive a self, and these are the sorts of teachers in India who in fact believe that we are separate substances, this interpretation would seem to be plausible.

In Vasubandhu's aggregate-remembrance objection he cites a passage from the Pudgalavādins' sūtras in which the Buddha is reported to have said that one who remembers his past lives remembers only the past lives of the five aggregates. Since he thinks that the passage clearly implies that we are the same in existence as collections of aggregates, he does not bother to say that it refutes the Pudgalavādins' claim that we are not the same in existence as collections of aggregates.

The Pudgalavādins are made to reply that this passage cannot be interpreted in this way, since when the Buddha remembered a past life, what he remembered he expressed by saying, "In a past life I possessed a visible form." The Pudgalavādins argue that this passage implies that what he remembered was that a person, not a collection of aggregates, possessed a visible form. The Pudgalavādins' reply fails to explain exactly how they would interpret the aggregate-remembrance passage cited by Vasubandhu. What could be meant by the claim that a person who remembers his past lives remembers only the lives of the five aggregates if it does not imply that the person is the same in existence as a collection of aggregates? It is doubtful that the Pudgalavādins could interpret the aggregate-remembrance passage to mean that we do not retain a memory of our lives as persons because only explicable phenomena can be remembered, since such an interpretation would seem to be incongruent with their theory that persons are conceived because they are perceived when their aggregates are present. If persons are perceived and conceived, why can they not be remembered?

Perhaps the Pudgalavādins meant to use their reply to support the claim that the aggregate-remembrance passage reflects the Buddha's practice of giving a provisional teaching to those who were capable only of accepting the thesis that a person is the same in existence as a collection of aggregates. So by pointing out that the Buddha also said that he remembers having possessed a visible form, they might have meant to imply that the aggregate-remembrance passage is a provisional teaching, while the passage in which he is saying that he remembers having possessed a certain visible form contains a teaching meant to be taken literally. But they do not make this move in Vasubandhu's text.

By failing to make this move, the Pudgalavādins enable Vasubandhu to make it. He says that in the passage cited by them the Buddha was simply following the conventional way of speaking, which requires an interpretation in terms of the causal basis form of analysis used to determine the mode of existence a phenomenon possesses. He adds that if this passage were interpreted in the way the Pudgalavādins interpret it, either it does not contain a teaching of the Buddha, which they do not admit, or the Buddha himself fell victim to the mistaken view arising from a perishable collection of aggregates (*satkāyadṛṣṭi*), which they cannot accept. He concludes that the Buddha, who is the person mentioned in the passage quoted by the Pudgalavādins, must be like a heap or a stream insofar as he is real by way of a conception, and is not, as the Pudgalavādins claim he is, an inexplicable phenomenon. We are supposed to conclude, of course, that the passage quoted by the Pudgalavādins cannot be used to undermine Vasubandhu's interpretation of the claim that he who remembers his past lives remembers only the lives of a collection of aggregates.

It is curious that the Pudgalavādins do not reply that Vasubandhu is simply superimposing his own thesis, that a person is the same in existence as a collection of aggregates, upon the passage they quote. Should Vasubandhu object that his point is that their own interpretation of the passage is not the only one possible and so cannot be used to undermine his claim that the aggregate-remembrance passage implies that a person is the same in existence as a collection of aggregates, the Pudgalavādins could respond by reminding him that, after all, the passage that has the Buddha remember possessing aggregates comes from their own scriptures. Nonetheless, the Pudgalavādins would actually need to show that Vasubandhu's interpretation of the passage they quote is incorrect if they are to counter his point successfully. But it is difficult to see how they might show this unless they can provide a plausible explanation of why the Buddha would say that persons who remember their past lives remember only the lives of collections of aggregates. Such an explanation, as I said above, would require them to explain away the passage as a provisional teaching meant for those without the intelligence to understand the final doctrine.

Of some interest in this last argument is Vasubandhu's use of a heap and a stream as illustrations of things that are like us insofar as they are real by way of a conception. Yaśomitra takes Vasubandhu's point in mentioning a heap and a stream here to be to illuminate two different ways in which we are said to be real by way of a conception. Indeed, Vasubandhu seems to be indifferent to whether his theory is to be expressed by saying that we are the same in existence as collections of aggregates or by saying that we are the same in existence as causal continua of aggregates. His ambivalence to the differences between these formulations of his theory, I believe, reflects the fact that his primary concern in the "Refutation" is to refute the view that a person is a self rather than to refute the views that a person is a unitary or partless self, that a person is a permanent self, or that a person is a permanent and partless self. He assumes that if a person is a self, a person possesses a separate identity, and that the person who possesses a separate identity must be a separate substance. The permanence and partlessness of a separate substance do not seem to become issues in the "Refutation" except when the arguments for the existence of a self rely on the assumption that a self is a permanent or partless separate substance. We shall see that arguments of this sort appear in Section 4, in which the Tīrthikas' view, that we are in fact partless and permanent separate substances, comes into play.

Since Vasubandhu believes that the Pudgalavādins' theory of persons implies that persons are selves, he also believes that the facts that persons are impermanent and have parts show that their theory is false. But he does not usually raise objections to their theory of persons on the basis of these "facts." The reason he does not, perhaps, is that they claim that persons are neither permanent nor impermanent, nor with or without parts, in the way substantial realities or substantially established realities are. Nonetheless, Vasubandhu sometimes illegitimately argues or assumes that their theory of persons implies that we are permanent phenomena, since they deny that we are impermanent phenomena.

5

COMMENTARY ON SECTION 3

Vasubandhu's replies to objections by the Pudgalavādins

Introductory note

In Section 3 of the "Refutation" Vasubandhu for the most part presents the Pudgalavādins' objections to his own theory of persons and his replies to them. In their objections, all of which make reference to scriptural teachings, they call attention to what they believe to be five undesirable consequences of Vasubandhu's theory and three undesirable consequences of his denial of their own theory of persons. In Section 3.4.2, Vasubandhu presents objections to the Pudgalavādins' theories of how persons are born and in Section 3.5.3 he argues that they cannot explain why the Buddha did not answer, when asked whether he exists after death, that he continues to exist. In Section 3.9 he rounds off his discussion of the Pudgalavādins' objections to his own theory of persons with the claim that the acceptance of their theory of persons is not the means by which liberation from suffering can be obtained. His conclusion, expressed in Section 3.10, is that his own theory is the middle way between the eternal transcendence theory of the Pudgalavādin schools and the nihilism theory of Nāgārjuna, according to which no phenomena possess independent reality. Since the topics of dispute in Section 3 do not seem to be organized in any systematic fashion, I shall simply discuss them as they arise and label them according to their most distinctive features.

Although all of the Pudgalavādins' objections make reference to scripture, not all need to be interpreted merely as scriptural objections, since some rely on passages in which the Buddha attributes to persons attributes Indians commonly attribute to them. This is true, for instance, of the passages cited in Sections 3.4, 3.7, and 3.8, in which the Buddha says or implies, respectively, that a person is one, wanders in saṃsāra and is the same person in different lives. It is also true of their claim in Section 3.4.2 that a person comes to be in the way a grammarian comes to be. In these cases the Pudgalavādins are relying on the common understanding of what these statements mean rather than on the fact that the Buddha made these statements. Hence, their objections to Vasubandhu's theory of persons would seem to appeal not only to the authority of scripture, but also to the conventions of the world and to logical coherence.

§ 3.1 The objection from the impossibility of omniscience and Vasubandhu's reply

The Pudgalavādins begin by objecting that if we are the same in existence as collections of aggregates in the way a stream is the same in existence as the collection of its parts, a Buddha, who Vasubandhu admits to be an omniscient person, cannot be omniscient. Although this objection is formulated in the text by reference to the impossibility of the Buddha's knowledge of all things, the point of the objection is that if persons are the same in existence as collections of aggregates, they cannot possess knowledge of all things. It is assumed that the aggregates in these collections are momentary and exist in a causal continuum. It is also assumed that although the Buddha knows all things one after another, he does not know all things all at once. This second assumption is based on statements made by the Buddha himself that are accepted as genuine and true, as literally interpreted, by both the Pudgalavādins and Vasubandhu. The Pudgalavādins' objection, therefore, may be paraphrased as the claim that if the Buddha is the same in existence as the collection of his momentary aggregates in a causal continuum, he cannot, as he said he could, know all things, since he would then know them all at once, and he denied that he knew them all at once. They add that according to their own theory of persons, on the contrary, there is no conflict with the Buddha's teaching, that a person can be omniscient without knowing all things at once, since it is not claimed that a person is the same in existence as a collection of aggregates. Since the Buddha is not, as the collection of his mental aggregates is, momentary in existence, he can be said to be omniscient without knowing all things at once.

Vasubandhu responds first to the Pudgalavādins' claim, that they avoid a conflict with the doctrine of the Buddha's omniscience, and then to their claim, that his own theory of persons conflicts with it. He objects that the price they pay to avoid the conflict is too high, since it implies that a Buddha is permanent in the sense that he continues to exist without coming to be and passing away from moment to moment. Vasubandhu assumes that if the Pudgalavādins' view, that a Buddha does not pass away when his mental aggregates pass away, is true, he must be other than his mental aggregates, and therefore, that if he continues to exist when they pass away, he must be permanent. But the Pudgalavādins deny that a Buddha is permanent. Therefore, Vasubandhu concludes, their attempt to avoid a conflict with the doctrine of omniscience contradicts their view that we are inexplicably the same over time.

But the Pudgalavādins are not, as Vasubandhu claims they are, committed to the view that a Buddha is permanent when they claim that he does not pass away when his mental aggregates pass away. Since one part of their view, that we are inexplicably the same over time, implies that a Buddha is not permanent in the way causally unconditioned phenomena are permanent, how are they committed to the thesis that a Buddha is permanent? They can point out that their attribution of omniscience to a Buddha does not commit them to the existence of a simultaneous knowledge of all things, since they deny that a Buddha is impermanent in the way his mental aggregates are. And since they also deny that persons are permanent, their claim that a Buddha is not impermanent does not entail that he is permanent. Perhaps Vasubandhu here assumes that he has already shown that there are no inexplicable persons, but if that is so, the present objection has no separate force whatsoever.

To the objection that his own theory of persons has the consequence, that a Buddha cannot know all things without knowing them all at once, Vasubandhu replies by denying that a Buddha's mental aggregates at any given moment must know all things if they know all things and are momentary in existence. He implies, when he says that his view is that knowledge of all things is attributed to the continuum of a Buddha's mental aggregates, that the Pudgalavādins' objection is based on the false assumption that if the mental aggregates of a Buddha know all things, this knowledge of all things must be attributed to his mental aggregates each and every moment. His view, strictly speaking, is that a Buddha continues to exist so long as the collection of his aggregates continues to exist in a causal continuum, and that his omniscience is attributed to him because he can know all things, one thing at a time, merely by directing his attention to what he wants to know.

Vasubandhu's reply to the Pudgalavādins' objection from the impossibility of omniscience also includes the denial that he asserts that the Buddha knows all things at once. In support of this denial he quotes a passage from the sūtras in which it is said that knowledge of all things is attributed to the Buddha because of his capacity to know all things one after another. Then he quotes another passage to justify his claim that this capacity belongs to the Buddha's continuum of mental aggregates rather than to a Buddha who is an inexplicable phenomenon. The justification, apparently, is that when in the passage the Buddhas of the three times are said to destroy the sufferings of the many, it is implied that they do this by reason of their capacity to know all things; but if this capacity belongs to the Buddhas of the three times, it must belong to the Buddha's continuum of mental aggregates rather than to Buddhas who are inexplicable phenomena, since in Section 2.2 the Pudgalavādins themselves imply that inexplicable persons do not exist in the three times. Hence, they must agree, he claims, that the Buddha's knowledge of all things must be attributed to a continuum of mental aggregates.

But how exactly is the second passage quoted by Vasubandhu supposed to imply that the capacity to know all things one after another must be attributed to the Buddha's continuum of mental aggregates? In the passage itself the reference to Buddhas of the three times is a reference to Buddhas of the past, future, and present ages, not to the past, future, and present times of a single Buddha. Nor is it stated in the passage that each of these Buddhas belongs to the three times. Perhaps the problem Vasubandhu sees is that an inexplicable Buddha cannot be said to exist in any of the three times, since he is not a causally conditioned phenomenon, but the passage he quotes does not support the claim that a Buddha exists in the three times.

What do the Pudgalavādins mean if they claim, as Vasubandhu says they do, that we do not exist in the three times? If Section 2.2 of the "Refutation" is any indication, they mean that we are not the same in existence as any of the causally conditioned phenomena of the past, present, or future, not that we are without a past, present, or future in any sense. If they mean that we cannot, by ourselves, apart from being conceived in reliance upon collections of aggregates, be said to exist in the three times, they can still say that we exist in the three times in dependence upon the three times in which the aggregates in the collections in dependence upon which we are conceived exist.

We might also ask whether Vasubandhu is entitled to claim that knowledge of all things is to be attributed to the continuum of the Buddha's mental aggregates. For Vasubandhu himself surely does not believe that the continuum of the Buddha's mental aggregates is an entity that exists apart from the momentary mental aggregates within the continuum. How then can he attribute to it a capacity none of its members possesses? Faced with such an objection, Vasubandhu could reply that his view is to be more precisely expressed by saying that a Buddha's knowledge of all things is not to be analyzed as a capacity possessed by his continuum of mental aggregates, but as a capacity of each mental aggregate in his continuum of aggregates to produce in the next moment in that continuum, if the mere desire to do so is present, a knowledge of any object. In this way, Vasubandhu can argue that all objects can be known to exist by a Buddha without attributing to him a simultaneous knowledge of all things. It cannot be said, therefore, that the Pudgalavādins' objection from the impossibility of omniscience conclusively shows that the Buddha, a person, is not the same in existence as a collection of aggregates. But this is so, not because of the reply Vasubandhu actually gives, but because of a more accurate statement of his view.

§ 3.2 The Pudgalavādins' second objection, from the passage on the bearer of the burden, and Vasubandhu's reply to it

The Pudgalavādins now point out that the Buddha said that we take up aggregates, which are a burden to us, and that we can solve this problem by casting them off. The Buddha would not have said that aggregates are a burden we bear, they object, if we are the same in existence as collections of aggregates, since a burden and its bearer are commonly recognized not to be the same in existence.

The assumptions of the objection are easy to supply. It is assumed (1) that the Buddha rejects as false what is commonly recognized to be false, (2) that what the Buddha says is true, is true, and (3) that what the Buddha says is false, is false. Since the meaning of "commonly recognized" (*dṛśyate*) plays a crucial role in the objection and is not explained, we must make an attempt to fix its meaning in order to be in a better position to assess the Pudgalavādins' objection and Vasubandhu's replies to it.

Since we do not to my knowledge have preserved in our sources the Pudgalavādins' own account of what it means for something to be commonly recognized, let us take the next best available path, which is to base our interpretation upon what Vasubandhu seems to understand it to mean. When judged from this perceptive, what is commonly recognized is a convention of the sort that needs to be accepted in order to practice the paths of morality and concentration. It is a common belief that enables us to perform the functions persons need to perform in order to perpetuate their existence in saṃsāra, to suffer as a result of their contaminated actions and to become free from these results by purifying the mind of contamination. In spite of the fact that such conventions carry with them the false appearance of being true independently of our adoption of them, they are valid insofar as they have proven themselves to be causally efficacious. Let us call them valid conventions. One of the most important of these valid conventions, according to the Buddha himself, is that persons ultimately exist. The view that what is commonly recognized is a valid convention explains why Vasubandhu, in his reply to the Pudgalavādins' objection, does not challenge the truth of the claim that the Buddha rejects as false the views that are not commonly recognized to be true.

The Pudgalavādins would seem to believe that a burden and its bearer not being the same in existence is a valid convention. It is a convention, presumably, that is grounded in two others. The first is that a burden is related to its bearer as a thing owned or possessed is related to its owner or possessor, and the second is that an owner or possessor is not the same in existence as what it owns or possesses. The primary source of the Pudgalavādins' objection would therefore seem to be the valid convention that we are owners or possessors of aggregates. The unstated upshot of the Pudgalavādins' objection is that since we know, on the authority of the Buddha, that by convention we own or possess aggregates, which are a burden to us, we cannot be the same in existence as collections of aggregates, and since we are certainly not other than collections of aggregates, yet ultimately exist, we must be inexplicable persons who do not exist in dependence upon these collections.

The Pudgalavādins' objection begins with the claims that (I) the Buddha says that we are bearers of a burden and that aggregates are the burden we bear, and that (II) if the Buddha says that we are bearers of a burden and that aggregates are the burden we bear, we are bearers of a burden and aggregates are the burden we bear. Therefore, from (I) and (II) we may infer that (III) we are bearers of a burden and aggregates are the burden we bear. The Pudgalavādins now assume that (IV) it is commonly recognized that the bearers of a burden are not the same in existence as their burden. On the authority of the Buddha, the Pudgalavādins assume that (V) if it is commonly recognized that the bearers of a burden are not the same in existence as their burden, the bearers of a burden are not the same in existence as their burden. Therefore, from (IV) and (V) we may infer that (VI) the bearers of a burden are not the same in existence as their burden. Therefore, from (III) and (VI) we may infer that (VII) we are not the same in existence as our aggregates. Moreover, according to the Buddha, (VIII) we are not other than our aggregates. Therefore, from (VII) and (VIII) and the fact that inexplicability in this case is being not other than or the same in existence as our aggregates, we may infer that (IX) we are inexplicable phenomena. Hence, the Buddha's statement that we bear aggregates as a burden shows that we are inexplicable phenomena.

There are three arguments that Vasubandhu presents in response to the Pudgalavādins' objection. The first of the three is very tersely worded. He simply says, "But it is also not reasonable that the inexplicable exists, since it is commonly recognized not to exist." Vasubandhu here seems to be arguing that if what is commonly recognized can be used to show that we are not the same in existence as collections of aggregates, it can also be used to show that we are not inexplicable phenomena, since the view that there are inexplicable phenomena contradicts one of the valid conventions of the world. The valid convention he believes to be contradicted, apparently, is that things that ultimately exist must be either other than or the same in existence as the phenomena in dependence upon which they are conceived.

But if part of the point the Pudgalavādins are making in their objection is that the Buddha would have been misleading his disciples by using the analogy to a burden and its bearer if he taught the doctrine that we are the same in existence as collections of aggregates, Vasubandhu's retort in no way meets this point, since there is nothing about the analogy in question that would similarly mislead his disciples if he taught the doctrine that we are inexplicable phenomena. Moreover, the Pudgalavādins have a ready response to the implied charge that they are contradicting the valid convention that things that exist must be either other than or the same in existence as the phenomena in dependence upon which they are conceived. This convention, in fact, is a more elaborate statement of the causal reference principle against which the Pudgalavādins have already argued. So they would deny that this view is a well-established convention.

The second reply Vasubandhu presents to the burden and bearer objection is even more terse than the first. He says, "Moreover, it follows that the taking up of the burden would not be included in the aggregates." That the taking up of the burden would not be included in the aggregates is taken to be an undesirable consequence of one or more of the premises of the Pudgalavādins' objection. Vasubandhu believes that the consequence, that the taking up of the burden is not included in the aggregates, is undesirable because the taking up of the burden is the same in existence as grasping (*tṛṣṇā*), which is the functioning of a mental affliction that the Buddha includes among our aggregates. It is not explained from what premise or premises of the burden and bearer objection this undesirable consequence is supposed to follow or what we are supposed to conclude from the fact that this premise or these premises have this undesirable consequence. The most likely interpretation is that Vasubandhu is arguing that if the bearer is not the same in existence as the collection of aggregates that is the burden, the taking up of the burden is not an activity of one of the aggregates, which it is, and that since the taking up of the burden is an activity of one of the aggregates, the bearer of the burden is also included in the aggregates in the collection. If this is his reply, Vasubandhu is ignoring an objection the Pudgalavādins could make. They could object that the taking up of the burden is included as an activity of one of the aggregates in the collection because a person does not, of his own nature, take up the burden; he is said to take up the burden in reliance upon the presence of the activity of taking up the burden in the collection of aggregates in dependence upon which he is conceived. A person is said both to be a bearer of a burden and to take up the burden in reliance upon the collection of aggregates in dependence upon which he is conceived.

Vasubandhu's most straightforward reply to the Pudgalavādins' objection is the third. He prefaces the reply with the statement that the Buddha's reference to the bearer of a burden is a concession to a verbal convention, not to a permanent self or to an inexplicable person. In fact, he argues, the Buddha's distinction between a burden and its bearer does not contradict his claim, that a person is the same in existence as a collection of aggregates, because it is a distinction between aggregates at different times in the causal continuum to which they belong. The earlier aggregates within a continuum, he believes, are called a burden to the later, which bears the burden, because an action belonging to the earlier collection of aggregates brings about, as its result, the suffering in the later collection. Understood in this way, the Buddha's reference to the bearer of a burden, Vasubandhu implies, is like his reference to persons. Both are based on the verbal convention of giving a single name to what is, from its own side, only a collection of entities. Attributing something to the bearer of the burden, like attributing something to a person, is a further verbal convention, built on the foundation of the first.

But Vasubandhu's ingenious response does not seem to work. For if the Buddha had intended to have his disciples identify the bearer of the burden with a collection of aggregates that is "harmed" by the earlier collection within the same continuum, why did he refer to the later collection as a person and to the earlier as a collection of aggregates? Why did he mark off the later collection, but not the earlier, as ourselves? Would not the Buddha then at least be misleading his disciples when he referred to one collection of aggregates as a collection of aggregates and not to the other as a collection of aggregates? Vasubandhu might reply that the Buddha was not so much misleading his disciples as protecting them, since the parable of the burden was presented to disciples not capable of comprehending and accepting the truth of his theory of persons. In other words, he might say that the Buddha purposely hid the deeper meaning of the parable so that its proper interpretation would not interfere with their acceptance of the message he was most concerned at the time to convey.

The heart of the burden and bearer objection lies in its assumption that the owner or possessor of a collection of aggregates is not the same in existence as the collection of aggregates owned or possessed, since he is the underlying support of the collection. Vasubandhu does not challenge this assumption. He does not even broach the question of whether or not the bearer of a burden is an owner or possessor of a burden or whether or not it is an underlying support for it. Insofar as the Pudgalavādins have failed to bring this issue out into the open in their objection, it has failed. Nor has Vasubandhu dealt adequately with it without touching upon this issue.

§ 3.3 The Pudgalavādins' objection, from spontaneous birth, and Vasubandhu's reply

If we judge the Pudgalavādins' objection in Section 3.3 by Vasubandhu's response to it, it is the objection that Vasubandhu cannot claim that it is a mistaken view that we are inexplicable phenomena, since the Buddha implies that we are inexplicable phenomena when he says that the denial of our spontaneous birth in another world is a mistaken view. To be spontaneously born in another world is to be born in that world with all of our faculties fully developed. The Buddha says that we are born in this way, for instance, into the god realms. In this objection the Pudgalavādins are assuming that we can be spontaneously born in another world only if we are inexplicable phenomena that at birth acquire a new set of fully developed aggregates. They believe that the passage implies that we are inexplicable phenomena, since if we were other than collections of aggregates, we could not acquire the aggregates in the collections in the way that makes them "ours," and if we were the same in existence as collections of aggregates, it makes no sense to say that we acquire aggregates. They conclude that if we are not inexplicable phenomena, we cannot be spontaneously born at all.

Vasubandhu replies that in the very scripture from which the Buddha's statement about spontaneous birth is taken persons are analyzed into a continuum of aggregates, and it is said, about the persons so analyzed, that the denial of their spontaneous birth in another world is a mistaken view. This reply amounts to the claim that in their objection the Pudgalavādins cite a passage from a scripture that confirms Vasubandhu's own theory of persons.

Vasubandhu then argues that if it were a mistaken view to deny that we are inexplicable phenomena, inexplicable persons would be, though they are not, listed among the realities known to exist on the Buddhist paths of insight and meditation. The realities known to exist on these paths, he assumes, are either causally conditioned phenomena into which the Buddha analyzed substantially established realities or causally unconditioned phenomena. Simply put, his point seems to be that only if we are one of these substances, or by implication, collections of them conceived as single entities of a certain sort, would it be a mistaken view to deny our existence, and since an inexplicable person is not listed as one of these realities, it is not a mistaken view to deny the existence of an inexplicable person.

The Pudgalavādins are not made to reply, but they could reply, I believe, that the Buddha never meant conventional realities to be included among the realities to be known on the paths of insight and meditation. In the *Tridharmaka Śāstra*, conventional realities are in effect distinguished from the four realities known to the Āryas on the paths of insight and meditation. Some of these conventional realities, they seem to concede, are the same in existence as collections of causally conditioned phenomena, but not all. If some conventional realities, persons included, are inexplicable and still ultimately exist, inexplicable persons would not be included among the four realities. In particular, the Pudgalavādins can say that it is not necessary for us to realize that we are inexplicable in order to complete the path of insight, and continue on the path of meditation, only to realize that we do not possess separate identities. And since the realization that we do not possess separate identities requires only that we do not find, among the phenomena in dependence upon which we are conceived, a single phenomenon that possesses all of the attributes by reference to which we are conceived as persons, we need not realize that we are inexplicable phenomena in order to enter the path of insight and continue on the path of meditation.

Vasubandhu's objection might be taken to be predicated on the assumption that an inexplicable person is a separate substance. On this assumption, the fact that the Buddha did not include an inexplicable person among the substances that comprise the four realities could be used to deny that it is a mistaken view to deny the existence of an inexplicable person. However, in this case, Vasubandhu's objection is predicated on a false assumption.

§ 3.4 The Pudgalavādins' one and many objection

In Section 3.4 the Pudgalavādins argue that because the Buddha refers to himself as one person when saying that he was born into the world for the welfare of the many, a person cannot be the same in existence as a collection of aggregates, which is many things. The Pudgalavādins, apparently, believe that a person is inexplicably one in the sense that he is not one in the way a substantial reality is one or one in the way a substantially established reality is one. Hence, when the Buddha refers to himself as one person, they believe, he is saying that he is inexplicably one. But if he is inexplicably one, he cannot be the same in existence as a collection of aggregates. However, they present no evidence for the claim that the Buddha himself meant to ascribe inexplicable unity to himself, and in fact do not explicitly include in the objection the premise that a person or the Buddha is inexplicably one.

But even if we ignore the omission of the premise, that a person is inexplicably one, crucial premises of the Pudgalavādins' objection are missing. The key premise that is missing is that if persons are one they cannot be the same in existence as many things. Their objection, which I shall call the one and many objection, begins with the argument that if it is true that (I) the Buddha says that he is one and that (II) if the Buddha says that he is one, the Buddha is one, then it follows that (III) the Buddha is one. Vasubandhu must agree that (IV) a collection of aggregates is many things. Yet, (V) what is one is not the same in existence as many things. Therefore, from (III), (IV), and (V) we may infer that (VI) the Buddha is not the same in existence as a collection of aggregates.

§ 3.4.1 *Vasubandhu's reply from unity by way of a conception*

In Section 3.4.1 the primary target of Vasubandhu's reply is the claim that what is one is not the same in existence as many things. Vasubandhu replies that what is one can be many, since "one" can be figuratively applied to a collection of things, as it is in our references to one sesame seed, one grain of rice, one heap, and one word, which are, nonetheless, many different things. Hence, there is no incompatibility between these things being both one and many. Vasubandhu's reply would seem to be sound, since they have failed to rule out his interpretation of the Buddha's statement. But if we assume that the Pudgalavādins' objection is based on the assumption that what is inexplicably one is not the same in existence as many things, Vasubandhu's reply does not work. Nonetheless, in this case, he has the option of pointing out that the Buddha did not actually say that he is inexplicably one. For this reason, he may reply, the objection of the Pudgalavādins begs the question.

§ 3.4.2 *Vasubandhu's second reply and the debate about the birth of persons*

In Section 3.4.2 Vasubandhu presents a second reply to the Pudgalavādins' objection. It is that the quotation from the sūtras implies that we are born, and if we are born, we are causally conditioned phenomena, which the Pudgalavādins themselves deny. A subtler implication of the reply is that if the Buddha's claim that he is one person is to be taken literally, then so is his claim that he is born, which the Pudgalavādins cannot interpret literally. Hence, the Pudgalavādins cannot adopt a literal interpretation of his claim that he is one person. This subtler implication is not taken up in the subsequent discussion.

The Pudgalavādins are made to object to Vasubandhu's assumption, that we are born in the way aggregates come to be, which is by coming to be from a cause that has ceased to exist at the time its effect is produced. We are said to come to be, they object, because we acquire a different set of aggregates, just as a priest or grammarian, a bhikṣu or śrāmaṇa, and an old or diseased body are said to come to be, because a person acquires a different set of aggregates. A grammarian, for instance, is said to come to be because a person acquires the grammatical knowledge that entitles him to be called a grammarian, not in the sense that this knowledge is produced from antecedent conditions that cease to exist just before the knowledge is produced.

What is involved in the Pudgalavādins' belief that we are said to come to be in the way a grammarian, for instance, is said to come to be? In both cases, the attributions of coming to be, they surely believe, are made in dependence upon the convention that persons acquire attributes not previously possessed. What comes to be are the persons who by convention possess just these attributes. The Pudgalavādins' explanation of this convention, of course, is that inexplicable persons acquire different sets of aggregates on the basis of which they are conceived differently. Just as a grammarian can be said to come to be because the aggregates that constitute grammatical knowledge are acquired by a person, so a person can be said to come to be because the aggregates that constitute a new birth are acquired by the person. In the first case a person who was previously not called a "grammarian" is so called, and in the second case a person previously not called "Vasubandhu," for instance, comes to be called "Vasubandhu." The meaning is that we, who were once conceived as one person in reliance upon aggregates we possessed in a previous lifetime, are now conceived to be born as a different person in reliance upon having lost that set of aggregates and having acquired a different set that constitutes the body and mind of a newborn person. The only relevant difference in the cases of the coming to be of a grammarian and the coming to be of a person is the difference between the sets of aggregates that appear before and after the two comings to be.

Because persons are not by their own natures born, the Pudgalavādins believe, they do not actually undergo any change in themselves when born; they are simply conceived to be born in reliance upon the acquisition of the aggregates that constitute the body and mind of a newborn person and are given a new name in dependence upon those new aggregates. We may call this "the inexplicable birth thesis." What makes this theory possible for them is that they believe that a person is an inexplicable underlying support for the aggregates that come to be and pass away. This theory is comparable to the Nyāya-Vaiśeṣika theory that a self is a underlying support for the various attributes that come to be and pass away in it, but with the differences that a person who is the underlying support is an inexplicable conventionally real entity rather than a substance and that what comes to be and passes away in it are aggregates rather than attributes. The Pudgalavādins' view, that a person is an inexplicable underlying support for the aggregates that come to be and pass away in him, we may call "the inexplicable underlying support thesis."

Vasubandhu replies that the Pudgalavādins' inexplicable birth thesis should not be accepted for four different reasons. The first reply is that both the acquisition and loss of aggregates are explicitly denied by the Buddha. The second reply is that their examples of what come to be cannot be used to give independent support to the view that we come to be, since the examples must be examples of either inexplicable persons, minds and their mental functions, or bodies, but they cannot be examples of inexplicable persons, since in that case what is to be proved is assumed to be true, and they cannot be examples of minds and their mental functions or of bodies, since in that case what is to be proved is disproved. The third reply is that their use of these examples implies, since they do not accept the Sāṃkhyas' view that what comes to be is a transformation of that from which it comes to be, that we are other than our aggregates. The fourth reply is that if, as they claim, we do not, but aggregates do, arise anew every moment, then, contrary to their theory of persons, we are not only other than our aggregates, but also permanent. Let us call these, respectively, "the scriptural reply," "the illegitimate examples reply," "the otherness reply," and "the permanence reply."

The scriptural reply

In the scriptural reply Vasubandhu quotes two passages. In the first the Buddha is quoted as denying that we acquire a new set of aggregates after having lost another set. The quotation does not, therefore, overturn the Pudgalavādins' view if it is interpreted to mean that an independently identifiable person cannot acquire a new collection of aggregates after having lost another collection. In the quotation it is literally said that no agent "is perceived" that casts off one collection of aggregates and takes up another elsewhere. But the Pudgalavādins could reply that what is said not to be perceived is an agent that is independently identifiable as an agent. In the second quotation the Buddha simply says that he does not speak of acquiring aggregates. However, since the quotation does not include the reason the Buddha gives for not speaking of acquiring aggregates, it does not by itself imply that the Buddha rejects the view that an inexplicable person acquires different aggregates, since it may only mean that he rejects the view that an independently identifiable person acquires different aggregates. Moreover, the Buddha does in fact often say that the aggregates are "acquired."

The illegitimate examples reply

Vasubandhu's other three replies are more philosophical in nature. The illegitimate examples reply may be formulated in terms of their example of a grammarian coming to be. The reply is that the example does not support their view that an inexplicable person comes to be, since they cannot assume that the grammarian is an inexplicable person, that he is his mind with its mental functions or that he is his body. We may take these last two alternatives to be equivalent to the assumption that the grammarian is the same in existence as the collection of his aggregates. Hence, the reply would seem to be predicated on the assumption that (I) if the example of a grammarian coming to be can be used to support the view that an inexplicable person comes to be, then it is being assumed either that the grammarian is an inexplicable person or that he is the same in existence as a collection of aggregates. But (II) if it is assumed that the grammarian is an inexplicable person, the existence of an inexplicable person must have been independently established. Vasubandhu objects that (III) the existence of an inexplicable person has not been independently established. Therefore, from (II) and (III) we may infer that (IV) it is not being assumed that the grammarian is an inexplicable person. But the Pudgalavādins agree that (V) it is not being assumed that the grammarian is the same in existence as a collection of aggregates. Therefore, from (I), (IV), and (V) we may infer that (VI) the example of a grammarian coming to be cannot be used to support the view that an inexplicable person comes to be.

To this reply, I believe, the Pudgalavādins could object that (I) is false, since they need not assume that a grammarian is either an inexplicable person or the same in existence as a collection of aggregates in order to use the example of a grammarian coming to be to support the view that an inexplicable person comes to be. In the first place, they would not themselves assert that a grammarian is either an inexplicable person or the same in existence as a collection of aggregates. They would assert that a grammarian is an inexplicable person who is conceived in reliance upon the aggregates that constitute grammatical knowledge. Second, and more importantly, they may say, the example can be used to support their view that an inexplicable person comes to be, since it is a well-established convention, apart from any analysis that may be made of the convention, that a grammarian comes to be when a person acquires grammatical knowledge. For this reason, in their example of a grammarian, a grammarian is not being assumed to be an inexplicable person or to be the same in existence as a collection of aggregates.

Although the Pudgalavādins themselves explain how a grammarian can be said to come to be in terms of an inexplicable person acquiring the aggregates that constitute grammatical knowledge, this explanation is not what gives their example its logical point. Part and parcel of many of their objections to Vasubandhu's theory of persons are appeals to well-established conventions of the world about ourselves that the Buddha said were not to be abandoned. In the present case, they are arguing that the well-established convention, that a grammarian comes to be when a person acquires grammatical knowledge, is used to support their denial that a person comes to be in the way that the aggregates come to be. Vasubandhu's illegitimate examples reply, therefore, does not succeed.

The otherness reply

In the otherness reply Vasubandhu argues that the Pudgalavādins' examples of what comes to be are subject to causal analysis that makes them be other in existence than that from which they come to be. In each of the examples, he believes, the Pudgalavādins must admit, since all Buddhists reject the Sāṃkhyas' theory that what comes to be is a transformation of that from which it comes to be, that what comes to be is other than that from which it comes to be. (If what comes to be is a transformation of that from which it comes to be, what comes to be and that from which it comes to be are not other than one another.) For instance, he says, a Buddhist must say that a diseased body that comes to be from a body is other than the body from which it comes to be. The implication is that if the Pudgalavādins say that a person comes to be in the way that a diseased body comes to be, they must say that it comes to be from that which is other than itself, which, presumably, is from a collection of aggregates of a previous life. The unstated upshot of the reply is that since it is the person who comes to be in a birth, and he comes to be from a collection of aggregates of a previous life, which must be other than what comes to be from them, the person that comes to be in the new birth will be other than this collection of aggregates.

The Sāṃkhyas' view to which Vasubandhu alludes here is that what comes to be must come to be from a substantially real cause that continues to exist when it produces its effect, which is a modification of this cause. If the substantially real cause did not continue to exist when its effect begins to exist, they reason, the effect is without a cause. That Vasubandhu rejects this view is shown by his argument in Section 4.7.1, where he argues that a permanent phenomenon cannot be a cause of an effect, and even if it could, its effect would also need to be a permanent phenomenon. By denying the existence of a permanent cause, he believes, the extreme view of permanence is avoided. But to deny that a cause of any sort exists, he believes, is to go to the opposite extreme view of causal nihilism. The middle way between these extremes, they believe, is to deny that a substantially real cause is permanent, since it ceases to exist when its effect is produced, and to assert that a substantially real phenomenon can be a cause, since it has an effect that arises after the cause has ceased to exist. This is the rationale for Vasubandhu's claim that cause and effect are other than one another.

Although the Pudgalavādins seem to follow the Vaibhāṣikas' view that among causally conditioned phenomena cause and effect are other than one another, they surely do not believe that inexplicable phenomena are effects produced by causes that are other than their causes. Vasubandhu assumes that because they reject Sāṃkhyas' view, that cause and effect are not other than one another, they must accept the view that they are other than one another. But since the Pudgalavādins claim that persons are not causally conditioned or causally unconditioned phenomena as defined by Vasubandhu, they reject the Sāṃkhya view that all phenomena that come to be come to be from a permanent cause, as well as the Vaibhāṣika view that all phenomena that come to be come to be from a cause that has already ceased to exist. A person, apart from being conceived, cannot be said to come to be. A person is said by convention to come to be and neither Sāṃkhyas nor the Vaibhāṣikas have a correct explanation of this convention. The Pudgalavādins' view is that a person is not, according to its own nature, born, and hence, from this point of view, cannot be said to come to be from anything at all. It is the collection of aggregates with which a person unites, they can say, that comes to be from a collection of aggregates that is other than itself. It is in reliance upon the coming to be of a collection of aggregates from another collection that the person of that new life is conceived to be born.

The permanence reply

Vasubandhu's final reason for rejecting the Pudgalavādins' inexplicable birth thesis is the permanence reply. It is the reply that from their denial of our momentariness and their affirmation of the momentariness of the aggregates, it follows, contrary to their doctrine, not only that we and our aggregates are other than one another, but also that we are permanent. In this case, once again, Vasubandhu employs a premise the Pudgalavādins reject. Since they deny that we are other than collections of aggregates, which are momentary, they are not committed, when they deny that we are momentary, to the view that we are permanent phenomena. They deny not only that we are momentary phenomena, but also that we are permanent phenomena.

The exchange between Vasubandhu and the Pudgalavādins concerning the birth of persons has provided us with more information about the Pudgalavādins' view of persons as inexplicable underlying supports of their aggregates. Specifically, it has turned up their general explanation of how it is possible for us to ascribe changes of all kinds to an inexplicable person in dependence upon the different kinds of aggregates that are produced in the collection of aggregates in reliance upon which he is conceived.

§ 3.4.3 *Vasubandhu's third reply and the Pudgalavādins' response*

Vasubandhu's third reply is that if the Pudgalavādins are correct, that we are not the same in existence as our aggregates by reason of our being one and they being many, then we must be other than our aggregates. The meaning of the reply is that the Pudgalavādins' use of this objection is inconsistent with their thesis that we are not other than our aggregates.

The major problem with Vasubandhu's reply is that the Pudgalavādins do not accept the thesis that if one thing is not the same in existence as another it is other than it. Nor does the objection take account of what the Pudgalavādins may mean when they allude to the unity of a person. They surely hold the view that we are inexplicably one in the sense that we are neither substantially one nor one in the way a substantially established phenomenon is one.

Instead of objecting that Vasubandhu's third reply is based on a thesis that they reject, the Pudgalavādins are made to argue that our being one and the aggregates being five does not imply that we are other than our aggregates any more than a visible form being one and the primary elements in dependence upon which it is conceived being four implies that the visible form is other than these elements. Vasubandhu presents two replies to the objection. The first is that, according to most other Buddhists, a visible form is other than the four elements, and the second is that if a visible form were not other than the four primary elements in dependence upon which it is conceived, the Pudgalavādins would commit themselves, by citing this analogy, to the view that we are the same in existence as the five aggregates.

In this final exchange, Vasubandhu's two replies to the Pudgalavādins' objection are no better than the objection itself in the form in which it is stated. The Pudgalavādins' objection, as stated, is problematic. How can they claim that there is one visible form that is not other than the four primary elements in dependence upon which it is conceived? For it is clear that they cannot in fact believe that this claim is true. For if they did believe it to be true, they would be committed to the theory that a visible form, like a person, is an inexplicable phenomenon, and they surely do not hold such a theory. Vasubandhu's replies to the objection do not fare much better. His first reply, which is that most other Buddhists do not accept this view, does not show that it is wrong. And his second reply, which is that their use of the objection implies that they believe that we are the same in existence as our aggregates, makes an assumption not acceptable to the Pudgalavādins. Since they believe that what is not other than something can also not be the same in existence as it, it does not follow, from the claim that a visible form is not other than the four primary elements in dependence upon which it is conceived, that it is the same in existence as them. Hence, by analogy, it does not follow that they are committed to the view that we are the same in existence as the five aggregates.

The most perplexing aspect of the exchange is that it seems to imply that the Pudgalavādins believe that a visible form is related to the four primary elements in the same way we are related to our aggregates. We should be able to infer, if this were so, that a visible form is conceived in reliance upon the four primary elements and that it is an inexplicable phenomenon. But if they were to accept this view, their earlier argument in Section 2.5 for the view that we and visible forms are not perceived in the same way, would be undermined. So it does not seem likely that they would accept this view. Nor is it likely that Vasubandhu would represent them in the "Refutation" as making this reply had they not done so. Why then do the Pudgalavādins call on this view in their reply?

The answer, I believe, is that the Pudgalavādins do not mean to be implying that this is a view they actually hold. We know that Buddhadeva held the view in question, and it seems that the Pudgalavādins are putting forward Buddhadeva's view in order to show that they are not alone in denying that a difference in number implies otherness. Accordingly, I have added to the translation, in brackets, the idea that the Pudgalavādins are claiming that they need not say that we are other than aggregates in dependence upon which we are conceived because we are one and the aggregates are five any more than certain other Buddhists needed to say that a visible form is other than the elements in dependence upon which it is conceived because a visible form is one and these elements are four.

§ 3.5 The Pudgalavādins' objection, from the Buddha's rejection of the otherness and sameness question, and Vasubandhu's reply

The Pudgalavādins in Section 3.5 object that we are not the same in existence as collections of aggregates, since if we were, the Buddha would not have left unanswered the question of whether we are other than our bodies or the same in existence as them. Let us call this pair of questions the "otherness and sameness question." It is the first of four composite questions, the other three of which comprise four questions each, which make up what has come to be known as the fourteen unanswered questions.

Vasubandhu replies that the Buddha did not answer the otherness and sameness question because he realized that in asking the question the questioner was assuming that we are individuals and that individuals are persons who in ultimate reality are separate substances. Since such individuals do not exist and things that do not exist cannot be said to be other than or the same in existence as anything else, the Buddha did not answer the question. Vasubandhu quotes, in support of his interpretation, a story about king Milinda and the Elder Nāgasena. When the king asked Nāgasena whether an individual is other than the body or the same in existence as it, Nāgasena asked the king, whose inner court did not contain a mango tree, whether the fruit on the mango tree in his inner court was sour or sweet. He was driving home the point that since an individual, like the mango tree, does not exist, it cannot be said that it is other than the body or the same in existence as it.

A variety of theories have been suggested by both the Indian Buddhists themselves and Western scholars about why the Buddha did not answer the otherness and sameness question and the remaining twelve of the fourteen questions the Buddha left unanswered. I shall not attempt here to reproduce these theories or to determine the correctness of one or another of them, since the attempt would take us well beyond what needs to be said for our purposes. But I can say the following: if Vasubandhu's interpretation of the Buddha's silence on the otherness and sameness question is correct, the Buddha would appear to be right in avoiding a direct answer to the question, since the question is based on the false assumption that the subject about which the question is asked exists. To answer the otherness and sameness question in the terms in which it is asked would surely imply that the subject exists and that would mislead the person who asked the question.

The Pudgalavādins surely have their own version of why the Buddha did not answer this question. Although it is not presented in this text, their view, I believe, is that the Buddha did not answer the question because he took it into consideration that the questioner, like Vasubandhu himself, believes that if we are neither other than our bodies nor the same in existence as them, we do not exist. Hence, since the Buddha holds the view that inexplicable persons exist, he could not answer that we are other than our bodies, which is false, or that we are the same in existence as our bodies, which is false. Nor could he have given the correct answer, which is that we are neither other than nor the same in existence as our bodies, since it would have led the questioner to falsely conclude that we do not exist. It would seem that a Pudgalavādin account of this sort is as plausible as that put forward by Vasubandhu.

§ 3.5.1 *The Pudgalavādins' objection to Vasubandhu's reply and Vasubandhu's reply to their objection*

The Pudgalavādins object that if the Buddha thought that the questioner had in mind a separate substance when he asked whether we are other than or the same in existence as our bodies, he would have answered the question by saying that the individual does not exist. Vasubandhu replies that the Buddha did not say that the individual does not exist because it would have led the questioner to the mistaken view that there is no person at all, even though a person is the same in existence as a collection of aggregates, which does exist. The questioner would have been led to this mistaken view, it is said, because he was unfamiliar with, and unable to accept, the view that the aggregates dependently arise. (The view that the aggregates dependently arise is the view that they arise in dependence upon causes and conditions.) If this consideration is to explain why he was led to this mistaken view, Vasubandhu must be assuming here that persons exist in dependence upon the dependent arising of aggregates. The idea, in this case, is that if the questioner were to accept the view that substantially real persons did not exist and were ignorant about, and unable to accept, the view that persons exist by reason of the dependent arising of the collection of aggregates in dependence upon which they are conceived, he would think that persons do not exist at all. So when Vasubandhu says that "the questioner would have embraced the mistaken view that the continuum of aggregates called an individual does not exist," he does not mean to imply that a continuum of aggregates is what a person is, but that the existence of a person, who is conceived in dependence upon a continuum of aggregates, is the existence of the continuum of aggregates in dependence upon which it is conceived. He means that the questioner would have embraced the mistaken view that no person, not even a person who is conceived in dependence upon a continuum of aggregates, possesses any existence. Moreover, although he says that the continuum of aggregates is called a person, strictly speaking, he believes that a person is conceived in dependence upon a collection of aggregates that exist in a causal continuum. The fact that the aggregates in such a collection exist in a causal continuum is what explains our practice of assuming that a person is the same over time.

Vasubandhu supports his interpretation of the Buddha's avoidance of denying that an individual exists by citing a passage from a sūtra in which the Buddha says that to answer the question of whether or not a self exists would mislead a questioner, Vatsagotra, into thinking that we do not exist at all. But the quotation, which is concerned with a different question, has only indirect bearing, and does not by itself support Vasubandhu's claim that the Buddha could not have answered the otherness and sameness question by saying that the individual does not exist. The passage stresses the care the Buddha took not to mislead Vatsagotra by answering his question of whether or not a self exists. Since there is no self, the Buddha could not have said that a self exists. But to say that there is no self would only have confused Vatsagotra. His confusion, it seems, would have been to jump to the conclusion that, if the eternal transcendence view, that a self exists, is false, then the nihilism view, that a person does not exist at all, must be true. Vasubandhu also cites a pair of passages from a work by a highly respected scholar, Kumāralābha. The first passage simply presents Kumāralābha's illustration of how careful the Buddha is to teach the middle way between the extreme views that we exist as separate substances and that we do not exist at all. The second passage is basically a summary of the account Vasubandhu has given in Sections 3.5 and 3.5.1. This passage also contains a revealing statement of Vasubandhu's theory of persons. In the passage the aggregates are identified as the results of previous actions. The idea is that our aggregates continue to arise as they do because of contaminated actions performed in the past. These quotations from Kumāralābha's work are probably among the sources of the views Vasubandhu is presenting here.

Of special interest in the quotation from Kumāralābha's work are (1) the implication that another form of nihilism entailed by the denial of the existence of the conventionally real person is the denial of the existence of the results of prior actions in the continuum of aggregates, (2) the apparent implication that what Vasubandhu called the inability to understand dependent arising Kumāralābha calls the inability to understand emptiness, and (3) the statement that the inability to understand emptiness prevents one from understanding that an individual "is a mere conception for the aggregates." The view implied in (1), of course, is held in all Indian Buddhist schools, with the possible exception of the Pudgalavādin schools. But even they will say that, insofar as persons are conceived in dependence upon aggregates, they are the results of prior actions in the continuum of aggregates. If the apparent implication mentioned in (2) is real, it would seem that for both Vasubandhu and Kumāralābha emptiness is the absence of phenomena arising without causes and conditions. In their version of this view, the causes and conditions for the arising of phenomena are other than the phenomena that arise. In this respect, their view is rejected by Candrakīrti, who denies the independent reality of phenomena, and probably also rejected by the Pudgalavādins, for whom persons and fire would seem to be inexplicable agents that cause phenomena to arise. Finally, the statement mentioned in (3), in the light of the implication mentioned in (2), would seem to imply that Vasubandhu and Kumāralābha believe that the emptiness of persons is the absence of their existence apart from being conceived in dependence upon the arising of collections of aggregates.

Vasubandhu does not say in this section that the Buddha did not answer the otherness and sameness question because he assumed that nothing can be said of what does not exist. Indeed, the claim that nothing can be said of what does not exist is self-defeating, since it itself is saying of what does not exist that nothing can be said of it. He is either unaware of, or perhaps dismisses as false, the view that we cannot speak of what does not exist. This need not mean that he believes that reference can be made to what does not exist. In fact, if our prior analysis is correct of his motivation for adopting the view, that we are the same in existence as collection of aggregates, he most certainly does not hold this belief. For in Section 1.2 he rejects the view that the conception of ourselves can refer to a self on the ground that it is not known to exist among the phenomena in dependence upon which we are conceived. Moreover, if my interpretation is correct, Vasubandhu believes that we can refer to persons in dependence upon their being the same in existence as collections of aggregates.

Do all Buddhists believe that reference to phenomena requires their existence? The answer to this question depends upon what is meant by "existence." Since Vasubandhu believes that everything that exists possesses substantial reality or substantially established reality, he believes that reference to phenomena requires their ultimate existence. But the Pudgalavādins, apparently, believe that what exists possesses either substantial reality, substantially established reality, or ultimate existence without a separate identity. Hence, for them too whatever exists ultimately exists. Candrakīrti believes that what exists cannot exist apart from being conceived, and for this reason he denies that reference to phenomena requires their ultimate existence. It would seem that it is because Vasubandhu believes that reference to ourselves is not possible unless we possess ultimate existence that he argues that we are the same in existence as collections of aggregates. Candrakīrti in fact assumes that reference to anything that possesses ultimate existence is impossible, since he believes that no phenomena possess ultimate existence. Nonetheless, he too believes that reference to phenomena requires their existence, except, in his case, reference to what exists requires only the dependent existence of the object of reference. He believes that the conception of ourselves refers to persons who exist in dependence upon being conceived in reliance upon aggregates and that a self, the mistaken view of which is the cause of suffering, is a person who possesses ultimate existence. Nonetheless, Candrakīrti, like Vasubandhu and the Pudgalavādins, seems to think that we can deny the existence of a phenomenon without making reference to it. None of the three, to my knowledge, attempt to provide an account of how this is possible.

§ 3.5.2 *Vasubandhu's account of the Buddha's silence on the remainder of the fourteen questions*

In Section 3.5.2 Vasubandhu extends to the remainder of the fourteen questions unanswered by the Buddha the general principle that when the Buddha does not answer a question it is because he takes into consideration what the questioner intends to be asking. He first explains why the question of whether the world is eternal, not eternal, both, or neither is not answered. Then he claims that this same explanation is applicable to the Buddha's avoidance of an answer to the question of whether the world has an end, does not have an end, both does and does not have an end, or neither does nor does not have an end. Finally, he explains why the Buddha did not answer the question of whether a Buddha exists after death, does not exist after death, both does and does not exist after death, or neither does nor does not exist after death. Among these the first explanation is the most complicated, and a detailed examination of it will suffice to give us a general idea of Vasubandhu's approach.

The world about which the Buddha was asked whether it is eternal, not eternal, both eternal and not eternal, or neither eternal nor not eternal, Vasubandhu implies, was assumed by the questioner either to be a self or to be the whole of saṃsāra. What exactly does this assumption mean? According to the logic of the argument Vasubandhu will use in his explication of why the Buddha did not answer the four questions, the world being a self can only mean that the world is composed of selves and the world being the whole of saṃsāra can only mean that the world is composed of persons who are the same in existence as collections of aggregates. In line with this interpretation of the assumption, let us simplify the assumption by saying that it is assumed that the world is composed of selves or of "aggregate-persons." Vasubandhu first argues that if the world is composed of selves, the world cannot be said to be either eternal, not eternal, both eternal and not eternal, or neither eternal nor not eternal, since there are no selves. The argument continues on the supposition that the questioner might believe that the world is composed of aggregate-persons. First of all, Vasubandhu argues, if the world is composed of aggregate-persons, then if the Buddha answered the question by saying that the world is eternal, he would be implying, contrary to fact, that no aggregate-persons would achieve final release from saṃsāra by making the effort to do so, since the continua of their aggregates would never come to an end. Had the Buddha answered that the world is not eternal, Vasubandhu continues, he would have implied that all aggregate-persons could effortlessly achieve final release, since the continua of their aggregates would eventually cease to exist. This implication is also false. Had the Buddha answered that the world is both eternal and not eternal, he could only have meant that it is in part eternal and in part not eternal, since nothing could be unqualifiedly both eternal and not eternal. Hence, had he answered that the world is both eternal and not eternal, he would have implied the falsehood that some aggregate-persons (those that are eternal) would never achieve final release no matter how much effort they exerted and others (those who are not eternal) would achieve it effortlessly. In this case, the implication obtains because the answer would mean that some of the aggregate-persons in it are eternal and others are not eternal. Had the Buddha answered by adopting the final alternative, that the world is neither eternal nor not eternal, Vasubandhu says, the falsehood would be implied that aggregate-persons neither can nor cannot obtain release from saṃsāra. The meaning, it seems, is that if the world of aggregate-persons were neither eternal nor not eternal, it could not exist at all, since what possesses neither of two contradictory attributes cannot exist. Hence, since aggregate-persons could not exist in that world, they could neither obtain final release from saṃsāra nor not obtain it. But it cannot be denied that aggregate-persons can or cannot obtain final release from saṃsāra. So we may infer that if the world is composed of aggregate-persons, then the world cannot be said to be neither eternal nor not eternal.

Therefore, regardless whether the world is composed of selves or of aggregate-persons, we may infer that it cannot be said to be either eternal, not eternal, both eternal and not eternal, or neither eternal nor not eternal. This interpretation of why the Buddha did not answer the four questions about the eternity of the world, although convoluted, would at least seem to be self-consistent. How the Pudgalavādins might interpret the Buddha's silence is not easy to reconstruct, since we do not know what they might claim the questioner had in mind in asking the question. Perhaps they would have supplemented Vasubandhu's own interpretation by adding that the same consequences would have been implied if the world were composed of inexplicable persons. I shall not try to reconstruct their interpretation.

The next set of four questions among the fourteen, Vasubandhu says, is the same as this first set of four, except that they are rephrased as whether the world has an end, does not have an end, both does and does not have an end, or neither. The reconstruction of the argument concerning the Buddha's reasons for not answering the first four questions would seem to be applicable, *mutatis mutandis*, if this second set of four questions is just a different way of asking again the first set. A third set of four questions addressed to the Buddha is whether or not he himself exists after death, does not exist after death, both does and does not exist after death, or neither. In this case the questioner, according to Vasubandhu, presumed that the Buddha was a self, which does not exist. Hence, the question cannot be answered straightforwardly. Moreover, if the Buddha were to respond that this self does not exist, Vasubandhu implies, the questioner, who was incapable of believing that the Buddha is the same in existence as a collection of aggregates, would draw the false conclusion that the Buddha does not exist at all.

§ 3.5.3 *Vasubandhu's objection, that the Pudgalavādins cannot account for the Buddha's silence about his existence after death*

Immediately after calling attention to the Buddha's leaving unanswered the questions of whether the Buddha does, does not, both does and does not, or neither does nor does not exist after death, Vasubandhu develops, in Section 3.5.3, the objection that the Pudgalavādins themselves cannot explain why, if persons exist apart from their aggregates, the Buddha did not answer this question by saying that the Buddha exists after death. The form in which the objection is given is based on taking the Buddha as an example of a person. Why, Vasubandhu wants to know, did the Buddha not answer the question by saying that he exists after death, since in other circumstances he admits that a person exists when alive? The Pudgalavādins are made to respond that the Buddha thought that the answer implies the acceptance of an eternal transcendence theory of persons, which he does not accept. Vasubandhu, in turn, rejects this response on the ground that if it were correct, the Buddha would not have predicted what will happen to Maitreya after his death or what had happened to one of his disciples after he died in a past rebirth.

Vasubandhu's rejection of the response is applicable only if the Pudgalavādins' response is interpreted to mean that the Buddha, independently of any assumption made by the questioner, thought that to answer the question by saying that the Buddha exists after death would imply that he is a separate substance. But it is highly unlikely that the Pudgalavādins believe that the Buddha thought that his reply would have such an implication independently of what the questioner had in mind in asking the question. Rather, the meaning of their response is surely that the Buddha did not answer, that he exists after death, because he realized that the person who asked the question was assuming that the Buddha was a separate substance. Hence, their view is that the Buddha did not answer the question by saying that the Buddha exists after death because he realized that the questioner believed that the Buddha was a separate substance and would have thought that the Buddha as a separate substance existed after his death. Once again, it seems, Vasubandhu has taken advantage of a reply that is incomplete in formulation. So I do not think that we can in the end accept his rejection of the Pudgalavādins' reply.

§ 3.5.3.1 *Vasubandhu's demonstration that the Buddha did not answer the question concerning his existence after death because the questioner assumed that he was a self*

In Section 3.5.3.1, Vasubandhu presents an argument whose relevance to the previous discussion is difficult to make out, since the topic of discussion appears to have changed and what the argument is supposed to establish is not clear. The topic of discussion is surely the same as that which was introduced at the end of Section 3.5.2 and was continued in Section 3.5.3. This is the topic of why the Buddha did not answer the set of four questions about his existence after death. Although the argument in Section 3.5.3.1 is concerned with a person's "final release from saṃsāra" (*parinirvāṇa*), while the discussion at the end of Section 3.5.2 and in Section 3.5.3 is concerned with the Buddha's existence after death, the topic has not changed, since the death of a Buddha constitutes a person's final release from saṃsāra. So in Section 3.5.3.1 the person being discussed is the Buddha and the discussion still pertains to his failure to answer the set of four questions about his existence after death. Let us call the Buddha's death a person's final death.

A second and much more difficult problem with the argument in Section 3.5.3.1 concerns what exactly Vasubandhu is trying to establish. In this section he presents a dilemma. If the Buddha knows that a person exists before his final death, but not after his final death, and does not answer the question about his existence after his final death, either the Buddha lacks omniscience or a person does not exist. But if the Buddha knows that a person exists after his final death and does not answer this question, an eternal transcendence theory of persons must be true. What are we to make of this argument? Although a variety of interpretations seem to be possible, I think the following is the most plausible.

The argument, I believe, is an attempt to demonstrate the correctness of Vasubandhu's own account of why the Buddha does not answer the question concerning whether he does, does not, both does and does not, or neither does nor does not exist after his final death. Vasubandhu assumes that the Buddha knows that we exist while alive, since to deny this would be to adopt the nihilism view of persons. The question he raises, on this assumption, is that he either does not know that we exist after our final death or he does know this. If he does not know that we exist after our final death, then he did not answer the question about our existence after our final death either because he is not omniscient, which cannot be correct, or because he knew that the person *about whom the questioner was asking* did not exist, in which case, no answer was possible. In this first part of the argument, then, Vasubandhu is arguing that if the Buddha did not know whether or not a person exists after his final death, his silence in response to the question of whether he exists after his final death shows that the Buddha knew that the questioner was assuming that the Buddha was a liberated self, and since a liberated self does not exist, and what does not exist cannot be said to exist, not exist, both exist and not exist, or neither exist nor not exist, after its final death, any one of these answers would have implied that a self exists.

In the second part of the argument Vasubandhu assumes that if the person about whom the questioner asks his question exists after his final death, he must be other than a collection of aggregates. Since the view that a person is other than a collection of aggregates, Vasubandhu believes, is an eternal transcendence theory of persons, he concludes that if the Buddha knows that the person about whom the questioner asks exists after his final death, he accepts an eternal transcendence theory of persons. But it is absurd that the Buddha accepts such a theory. Therefore, the Buddha does not know that the person about whom the questioner asked exists after his final death. But it has already been established that if the Buddha does not know that the person about whom the questioner asked exists after his final death, it can only be because he knows that the person about whom the questioner asked does not exist. Hence, the Buddha did not answer the question because the questioner assumed that the person about whom he asked the question is a liberated self, which does not exist at all. The overall interpretation of Vasubandhu's argument, therefore, is that since the Buddha is omniscient, he did not answer this question because it cannot be known that a self, which does not exist, either does, does not, both does and does not, or neither does nor does not, exist after its final death.

Vasubandhu then considers a reply the Pudgalavādins might make to this argument. It is the reply that the Buddha cannot be said either to be or not to be omniscient. He objects that such a reply would be heretical. That the Pudgalavādins would give such a reply, I believe, is unlikely. They would not claim that the Buddha neither is nor is not omniscient, since they believe that omniscience is attributed to him in dependence upon the presence of omniscience in the continuum of his aggregates.

What the Pudgalavādins' reply would be to the argument from the Buddha's omniscience, though not presented in our text, is clear. They would deny that if the person about whom the questioner asked the question exists after his final death, he must be a person who is other than a collection of aggregates. Hence, even if the Buddha knows that a person exists after his final death, he need not accept an eternal transcendence theory of persons. The Pudgalavādins might not say that the Buddha can know that a person exists after his final death, since they may believe that the only way a person can be known to exist is by a perception that occurs when the aggregates exist and after the person's final death the aggregates no longer exist. But according to the *Tridharmaka Śāstra* and the *Sāṃmitīyanikāya Śāstra*, persons are also conceived in dependence upon the cessation of their aggregates. It is likely, therefore, that they believe that persons can be known to exist by an inference to the existence of persons whose aggregates have ceased to exist. If so, a Buddha can know that persons exist after their final death. Alternatively, they might also claim that just because Buddhas are omniscient, they can, while we cannot, know that persons exist after their final deaths. In any case, it is clear that the Pudgalavādins are not committed to the view that if the Buddha knows that persons exist after their final deaths, persons are other than collections of aggregates.

In my commentary on Section 3.5.3 I suggested that the Pudgalavādins would in fact agree with Vasubandhu's contention, made at the end of Section 3.5.2, that the Buddha did not answer the question of whether he does, does not, both does and does not, or neither does nor does not exist after his final death because he realized that the question concerned a self, which does not exist. So now, in Section 3.5.3.1, when Vasubandhu argues that his contention must be true, he is not arguing for a conclusion that the Pudgalavādins do not accept as true.

It is peculiar that Vasubandhu should present an argument for a conclusion that the Pudgalavādins themselves accept. Does Vasubandhu not realize that they would agree that the Buddha did not answer the question because it would have led the questioner to believe that a person is other than a collection of aggregates? Or does he realize this, but assumes that, since they did not actually assert this view, but only the view that the Buddha would not answer the question because he thought it would imply that he was a separate substance, they need to be convinced that the Buddha did not answer because he took into consideration the fact that the questioner assumed that the Buddha could exist after his final death only if he was a separate substance? My best guess is that Vasubandhu is reporting an exchange with the Pudgalavādins and is once again playing the part of a 'hard-nosed' debater who attacks what the opponents actually say rather than what they meant to say. This is one way, indeed, in which to force the opponents to say what they mean. But Vasubandhu's argument at this point, nonetheless, appears to be a rather too clever defense of a view that needed no defense. The so-called Pudgalavādin reply, that the Buddha neither is nor is not omniscient, I assume to be Vasubandhu's playful attribution of a possible reply they might attempt.

§ 3.6 The Pudgalavādins' objection, from the Buddha's rejection of nihilism, and Vasubandhu's reply

The Pudgalavādins are made finally to resort to an appeal to the Buddha's rejection of the nihilism theory that persons do not exist in order to support their theory that we are inexplicable phenomena. But their appeal, as Vasubandhu implies, begs the question insofar as they fail to substantiate the assumption that the Buddha's rejection is a rejection of the denial of the existence of an inexplicable person. This is the implication of his claim that their theory of persons is false because the Buddha rejects eternal transcendence theories of persons. In other words, he simply assumes, as they do, that his own interpretation of the Buddha's words is correct, and concludes that the Pudgalavādins' theory of persons is false on this assumption. This exchange, though perhaps necessary for the purpose of each side clarifying what its own view is of the Buddha's rejection of nihilism, establishes nothing.

§ 3.7 The Pudgalavādins' objection, from the need for an underlying support for the coming to be and passing away of aggregates

The Pudgalavādins are made in Section 3.7 to argue that we cannot wander in saṃsāra if we are not inexplicable phenomena. To live in saṃsāra, they seem to be assuming, is to possess contaminated aggregates that continuously come to be and pass away. So in this objection we are being assumed to be the inexplicable underlying supports for the contaminated aggregates that come to be and pass away. Since we wander in saṃsāra, the Pudgalavādins believe, and neither the Tīrthikas' separate substance thesis nor Vasubandhu's substantially established reality thesis can explain how this is possible, we must be inexplicable underlying supports for the contaminated aggregates that come to be and pass away. We cannot be the same in existence as collections of aggregates, they believe, since collections of contaminated aggregates cannot be the underlying supports for the aggregates in them. The Pudgalavādins are implying that the reduction of our existence to that of collections of contaminated aggregates that continuously come to be and pass away violates the well-established convention of the world that we wander in saṃsāra, since an underlying support cannot be the same in existence as that which comes to be and passes away in it. The Pudgalavādins are also made to claim that since the Bhagavān said that we wander in saṃsāra, our rebirth must be that of inexplicable persons. This is possible, they were made to say in Section 3.4.1, only if we take on new aggregates and cast off old ones.

Vasubandhu replies by pointing out that he has already shown, in Section 3.4.1, that we cannot acquire and lose aggregates, and by providing an account of how collections of aggregates can be said to wander in saṃsāra. The account is that we wander in saṃsāra in the way fire moves about, even though the existence of the fire is the same as that of a continuum of momentary fires. (Momentary fires, he assumes, are also the same in existence as the momentary collections of their elements.) The point of his account, it seems, is to show that even though we, as conventional realities, are said to wander in saṃsāra, from the point of view of our existence, we, like fire, are collections of substances that come to be and pass away continually in a causal continuum.

Vasubandhu's analogy to how fire moves would not be acceptable to the Pudgalavādins, since they would argue that fire, which is not the same in existence as fuel, is said to move only because the fuel it ignites is in different places at different times. (In other words, the movement of fire is inexplicable.) Persons are said to wander in saṃsāra, they believe, because the aggregates that come to be and pass away in them come to be and pass away in different places at different times. Their ability to interpret Vasubandhu's example from their own perspective shows that the example fails to support this account of how, even though we say that we wander in saṃsāra, we come to be and pass away continuously in a causal continuum.

Similarly, since Vasubandhu rejected the Pudgalavādins' theory that we wander in saṃsāra by taking up and casting off different aggregates by claiming that the Buddha denied this theory, the Pudgalavādins could always counter by reinterpreting the Buddha's denial of the theory as directed to those who were incapable of understanding it or by interpreting it as the denial of the theory that independently identifiable persons take up and cast off different aggregates. In other words, the arguments and counter-arguments used in the exchange do not establish the correctness of one or the other of their accounts of how wandering in saṃsāra is possible.

Nevertheless, in this objection the Pudgalavādins are simply assuming, without argument, that what is said to wander in saṃsāra is an underlying support for the coming to be and passing away of contaminated aggregates. Hence, when Vasubandhu replies that wandering in saṃsāra can be interpreted in the way he interprets fire to move, which is according to a causal basis analysis, he in effect challenges that assumption, and thereby manages to show that the objection is inconclusive.

§ 3.8 The Pudgalavādins' objection, from the Buddha's reference to himself in a past life, and Vasubandhu's reply

In Section 3.8 the Pudgalavādins are made to follow up on their claim that Vasubandhu cannot account for the rebirth of persons. They say that if persons are the same in existence as collections of aggregates, then the Buddha would not have referred to himself as the person, Sunetra, when he spoke of one of his past lives, since the collection of aggregates of the Buddha and the collection of the aggregates of Sunetra are other than one another. If these collections of aggregates are other than one another, and the Buddha and Sunetra are the same in existence as their respective collections of aggregates, the Pudgalavādins reason, the Bhagavān and Sunetra have to be two different persons.

Vasubandhu responds by saying that the Pudgalavādins' interpretation of the Buddha's reference to himself as Sunetra commits them to the eternal transcendence theory that persons are permanent phenomena. He thinks that if they say that the Buddha is not other than Sunetra they must say that he and Sunetra are the same person, even though they exist at different times, and hence, that the Buddha is a permanent phenomenon. The Pudgalavādins, of course, are not committed to this consequence, since they deny that the Buddha is the same person as Sunetra in the way a permanent phenomenon is the same phenomenon at different times. A permanent phenomenon is the same phenomenon at different times in the sense that it is the same substance at two different times. Vasubandhu's reply ignores the fact that the Pudgalavādins believe that persons possess inexplicable identity over time.

Vasubandhu's second reply is that when the Buddha said, "I was the teacher called Sunetra," the "I" to which he was referring is the collection of aggregates that, at one time in its causal continuum, was called Sunetra, and now, at a different time, is called the Buddha. Similarly, he says, when we say, "this same fire has moved," we are referring to a collection of elements that, at one time in its causal continuum, was said to be here, and now, at a different time, is said to be there. In other words, Vasubandhu claims that even though the aggregates in the collection in dependence upon which a person is conceived are continually being replaced, we say that the same person continues to exist because the aggregates in the collection exist in a causal continuum.

The Pudgalavādins, as I have suggested above, would have a different account of the way in which the same fire moves about. Just as persons remain inexplicably the same over time while their aggregates continually come to be and pass away, so fire remains inexplicably the same over time while its fuel continuously comes to be and passes away in different places. But the fact that the Pudgalavādins have their own account of these phenomena does not obviate the point of Vasubandhu's reply, which is that what the Buddha said need not be interpreted so as to contradict the substantially established reality thesis of his theory of persons.

§ 3.9 Vasubandhu's objection, that the Pudgalavādins' theory of persons makes liberation impossible, and his rejection of a reply to this objection

In Section 3.9 Vasubandhu presents his last objection to the Pudgalavādins' claim that persons are inexplicable phenomena. It is not so much an objection as it is Vasubandhu's summary statement of what he believes to be the most heretical consequence of the Pudgalavādins' theory of persons. The most heretical consequence of the theory, Vasubandhu thinks, is that there will be no liberation from suffering even for the Buddhas, since the theory implies that there is a self and that the attachment to it that causes suffering is not mistaken. This objection is patently question-begging insofar as it assumes that the theory that persons are inexplicable phenomena is tantamount to the theory that they are selves. Vasubandhu objects that if persons, as the Pudgalavādins believe, are selves, the Buddhas would contradict themselves and so not in fact be liberated from suffering. The Buddha said that we suffer because we have a mistaken view that arises from a collection of impermanent aggregates. This mistaken view is our attachment and/or assent to the naturally occurring false appearance of ourselves as selves and of our aggregates as possessions of selves. Because this false appearance arises in dependence upon a collection of impermanent aggregates, the mistaken view is called the mistaken view that arises from a collection of impermanent aggregates. But if the Buddhas know that a self exists, he says, they have a mistaken view that arises from a collection of impermanent aggregates. Hence, the Buddhas will not be free of suffering.

Vasubandhu considers a possible reply to his objection. The reply he considers would seem to be based on a reply the Pudgalavādins might in fact have given to his objection. This is the reply that there is no attachment to a self. If the Pudgalavādins gave this reply, the self to which they refer, of course, is a person as he ultimately exists, as opposed to his appearance of possessing a separate identity. In his objection to the reply Vasubandhu assumes that the Pudgalavādins are committed to the belief that we are attached to a self because we confuse ourselves with a self. He then asks why attachment to a self would arise from this confusion unless we are attached to ourselves as we ultimately exist, and this attachment is transferred to the selves we appear to be. But if there is attachment to ourselves as we ultimately exist, he implies, it is this attachment that is the cause of suffering.

The Pudgalavādins would agree that we suffer because we are attached to ourselves as selves, but they do not believe that this attachment arises because we are attached to ourselves as we ultimately exist and transfer this attachment to the selves we appear to be. Their view, surely, is that attachment to an entity without a separate identity is not possible, and that attachment to a self arises from the fact that it is, as an object of consciousness, something that appears to possess a separate identity because it is conceived in dependence upon a collection of aggregates. Vasubandhu seems to have interpreted the Pudgalavādins' reply, that there is no attachment to ourselves as we ultimately exist, so that it would appear to undermine itself. But we have no reason to believe that they would interpret their reply in this way.

§ 3.10 Vasubandhu's claim to present the middle way

Heretical views concerning the existence of persons, Vasubandhu concludes, have arisen amongst the disciples of the Buddha. Although the theory of persons held by the Tīrthikas is the eternal transcendence view about which the Buddha explicitly warns his followers, Vasubandhu seems to conclude here that the theory of the Pudgalavādins is just a subtle version of that eternal transcendence theory. What the two theories share is the denial that we ultimately exist without being the same in existence as collections of aggregates, and hence, according to Vasubandhu, they share the consequence that they are committed to the view that we are other than collections of aggregates.

Another theory that has arisen among the Buddha's followers, Vasubandhu adds, is that nothing exists. This is surely the view of Nāgārjuna, who taught not only that persons do not ultimately exist, but that even the collection of aggregates in dependence upon which they are conceived does not ultimately exist. Vasubandhu believes that this teaching deprives us of a metaphysical foundation upon which reference to persons can be made. (The Pudgalavādins would agree.) That nothing ultimately exists, of course, means here that nothing exists apart from being conceived. The no ultimate existence theory of phenomena is nihilistic, Vasubandhu believes, precisely in the sense that the Buddha means when he tells his followers to avoid nihilism. Nihilism is the view that when we talk and think about persons there is nothing about which we are talking or thinking that exists apart from our talking and thinking about them.

We have already seen how Vasubandhu in Section 1.2 used the no-self argument to avoid the eternal transcendence view and used the ultimate existence argument to avoid the nihilism view. The extreme views against which he was arguing in his middle way argument are that we can be identified independently and that we do not exist at all. At least one nihilism view against which he was arguing, we can assume, is Nāgārjuna's denial of the ultimate existence of all phenomena, including both persons and the aggregates. In the "Refutation" he offers no explanation of his omission of any consideration of Nāgārjuna's arguments for his view. The most likely explanation of Vasubandhu's omission seems to be that he did not think that it is as dangerous a heresy as that of the Pudgalavādins, which, if accepted, would undermine his efforts to get us to abandon the mistaken view of a self. It does not seem to occur to Vasubandhu that the no ultimate existence theory of persons may be given the subtle form it is given by Candrakīrti, who lived centuries after Vasubandhu, and that ultimately it might pose the greatest challenge to his own interpretation of the Buddha's theory of persons.

6

COMMENTARY ON SECTION 4

Vasubandhu's replies to the objections of the Tīrthikas

§ 4.0 Why Tīrthika views must be considered

In Section 4 Vasubandhu prefaces his exchange with the Tīrthikas by saying that those who accept their theory are prevented from achieving liberation from suffering. Since the basic differences between their accounts of why we suffer and Vasubandhu's account I have already explained in the Commentary on Section 1, I will not repeat them here. I have already explained, as well, why I believe that in Section 4 Vasubandhu considers only the views and arguments of the Nyāya-Vaiśeṣikas, which is that their objections to the sort of theory held by Vasubandhu are likely to have encouraged the Pudgalavādins to reject that theory and adopt a theory similar to theirs. Although in Section 4 many of the objections raised against Vasubandhu's theory may be similar to objections that were likely to have been raised by the Pudgalavādins themselves, Vasubandhu's replies are directed to the objections in the form in which the Nyāya-Vaiśeṣikas would raise them.

§ 4.1 The Tīrthikas' objection, that if there is no self and minds are momentary, an account of a memory or recognition of an object is not possible, and Vasubandhu's reply

The Vaiśeṣikas' account of memory is presented in the *Padārthadharmasaṃgraha* of Praśastapāda. He says that it arises from a particular kind of contact between a self (*ātman*) and an internal organ (*manas*) and depends on the awareness of a memory-impression that stimulates its occurrence. What is remembered is an object previously experienced in some way, and the memory of the object itself may give rise to recognition, inference, desire, aversion, or another memory. A self, which is an owner or possessor of such mental states, is the agent that uses a memory-impression to perform the action of remembering the object. If a self is to remember an object, Vātsyāyana claims in his *Nyāyasūtrabhāṣya*, it cannot remember what has not been apprehended or what has been apprehended by a different self; it can remember only what it itself has apprehended previously. Hence, it follows, he thinks, that the self that previously apprehended the object is the same as the self that remembers it, and, as owner or possessor of the previous cognition and subsequent memory, is other than it.

In Section 4.1, Vasubandhu's Nyāya-Vaiśeṣika opponents object that his denial of the existence of a self and acceptance of the doctrine that minds are momentary phenomena make it impossible for him to account for our ability to remember objects we have previously perceived. Since Vasubandhu denies that there is a self, which is an independently identifiable owner or possessor of minds, and claims that minds are momentary in existence, how can he explain the fact that we remember or recognize an object we perceived in the past? The person who remembers an object, the opponents assume, must be the same person as the person who previously perceived it, which is possible only if there is just one person who both owns or possesses these different minds and uses a memory-impression of the object to grasp the object. In Section 4.1.1 their assumption, that what remembers an object is the same as what perceived it, surfaces in an objection they make to Vasubandhu's explanation of the occurrence of a memory, while in the next two sections, their assumptions, that what remembers an object and perceives it is an owner or possessor of both the memory and the perception and that their owner or possessor is an agent that uses a memory-impression to grasp the object, are made the basis of two more objections to Vasubandhu's theory of persons.

The Nyāya-Vaiśeṣika objection made in Section 4.1 is an argument for the existence of a self that has been reformulated as an objection to Vasubandhu's theory of persons. The objection, which is not fully stated, begins with the argument that if (I) an object remembered is previously perceived, and (II) what remembers an object is the same in existence as what previously perceived the object if the object remembered is previously perceived, then (III) what remembers an object is the same in existence as what previously perceived the object. However, the Nyāya-Vaiśeṣikas believe, (IV) if we are the same in existence as collections of momentary aggregates, then what remembers an object is a mind, what previously perceived the object is a mind, and the mind that remembers the object is not the same in existence as the mind that previously perceived the object. In addition, (V) if what remembers an object is a mind, what previously perceived the object is a mind, and the mind that remembers the object is not the same in existence as the mind that previously perceived the object, then what remembers an object is not the same in existence as what previously perceived the object. Therefore, from (III), (IV), and (V) we may infer that (VI) we are not the same in existence as collections of momentary aggregates. Since (VI) is true, the Nyāya-Vaiśeṣikas reason, Vasubandhu's thesis, that we are the same in existence as collections of momentary aggregates, is false. To formulate their argument for the existence of a self we simply add that (VII) if what remembers an object is the same in existence as what previously perceived the object, there is a self. Therefore, from (III) and (VII) we may infer that (VIII) there is a self.

The Nyāya-Vaiśeṣikas' objection, as stated in Section 4.1, is that Vasubandhu cannot explain how a memory of an object arises, since he denies the existence of a self and asserts that minds are momentary phenomena. So in his reply to the objection, as stated, he need only explain, without reference to a self, but with reference to momentary minds, how a memory of an object arises. His explanation, which may be called his no-self account of memory, is that a memory of an object arises from a mind that (1) is causally connected to a prior discrimination of a character of the object, (2) is attracted to the object, (3) possesses, among other things, a discrimination of a character of an object associated with or similar to the object that was previously discriminated, and (4) is not inhibited in its action of producing the memory of the object. Since only momentary minds are mentioned in this explanation, Vasubandhu believes, he has explained, without reference to a self, how a memory of an object arises. The implication is that what makes it possible to speak of what both perceived and remembers an object is that the perception and the memory are properly causally related. The same account, Vasubandhu says, can be given of the recognition of an object, since a recognition of an object arises from a memory of an object. His no-self account of memory, although sketchy, seems to serve the purpose for which it is intended, which is to answer the objection as stated.

What is not intended when he gives his no-self account of memory is that it should provide a paraphrase of what we mean, or what is meant, when we say that we remember an object. Vasubandhu has no obligation to show that he can translate, without loss of meaning or information, sentences about persons remembering things into sentences about the occurrence of certain causal connections in the continuum of aggregates in the collections in dependence upon which the persons are conceived. In fact, Vasubandhu would say that the sentences used to assert that we remember things, when understood according to their ordinary meanings, cannot be translated, without loss of meaning, into the sentences he uses to explain the occurrence of memories of things. For the former sentences are about persons according to their conventional reality, while the latter are about collections of aggregates, and collections of aggregates, although the same in existence as persons, are not persons. Finally, we should recall that Vasubandhu, like other Indian Buddhists, believes that what is discovered about persons, from the point of view of their ultimate reality, should not lead us to abandon what we say about persons as conventional realities.

Nor are the Nyāya-Vaiśeṣikas objecting that we cannot translate, without loss of meaning or information, sentences we use to say that we remember objects we previously experienced into sentences in which no reference to us is included. Their point is that a self is needed, as an additional cause, of the arising of a memory of an object, since a memory of an object cannot arise simply from a prior perception of the object. It cannot do so, they believe, since a necessary condition for the arising of a memory of an object is that the memory of the object arises in a self that has previously perceived the object. Both the Nyāya-Vaiśeṣikas and Vasubandhu are aware that their theories of persons are not accounts of what sentences about ourselves mean or what we mean when we use them, but accounts of the production of phenomena in which, respectively, a self does and does not have a causal role to play, and if it does, what its role is, and if it does not, why it does not. In the present case, the disagreement concerns whether or not a self plays a causal role in the production of a memory of an object, and if it does not, how a memory of an object can arise. The Nyāya-Vaiśeṣikas imply that its production is not possible unless we are permanent phenomena, while Vasubandhu implies that an explanation does not require that we be permanent phenomena.

§ 4.1.1 *The Tīrthikas' objection, that Vasubandhu's no-self account of how a memory of an object occurs implies that one mind can remember what another perceived, and Vasubandhu's replies*

The Nyāya-Vaiśeṣikas are made to object in Section 4.1.1 that Vasubandhu's no-self account of how a memory of an object occurs is incorrect, since it implies that one mind perceives an object and another mind remembers it, when in fact one mind cannot remember an object another mind perceived. That one mind cannot remember an object another mind perceived is supported by the example that a mind of Yajñadatta cannot remember an object that a mind of Devadatta perceived. The objection is based on the assumption that what remembers an object must be the same in existence as what previously perceived the object.

Vasubandhu first replies that his no-self account of how a memory of an object occurs does not imply that what a mind of Devadatta perceived a mind of Yajñadatta can remember, since these minds are not causally connected in the way the minds in the continuum of just one of them are. What is implied, at best, is that one of Devadatta's minds perceived what another of his minds remembers. But he does not say, he adds, that one mind remembers what another perceived. He does not explain why he denies saying this, but it would seem to be because it implies that a mind that remembers an object need not be caused by a mind that perceived it. Because a mind that remembers an object and a mind that perceived it can arise in a single causal continuum of minds, but not in different causal continua of minds, he does not simply say that one mind remembers what another perceived.

Vasubandhu assumes that the existence of a causal relation between the mind that perceived an object and the mind that remembers the object explains why we say that the same person both perceived and remembers the object. He does not reply to the Nyāya-Vaiśeṣika's objection by arguing that when we say that a person who remembers an object is the same as the person who previously perceived it we mean that in a collection of aggregates that exist in a causal continuum, the aggregate, a memory of an object, caused to arise by another aggregate, a perception of the object. He does not think that a collection of aggregates in a causal continuum is what a person is or that "a person" means "a collection of aggregates in a causal continuum." His view is that the convention, according to which we assume that it is the same person who both perceived an object and now remembers it, is based on the fact that the aggregate in the collection in dependence upon which we say that the person remembers an object is caused to arise, in the same causal continuum, by the aggregate in dependence upon which we say that he perceived the object. There is no implication, either, that what we say about ourselves remembering an object can be translated, without loss of meaning or information, into statements about a memory of an object being caused by a previous perception of the object in the same causal continuum.

Vasubandhu also assumes that the absence of a certain causal relation between the minds of Devadatta and Yajñadatta explains why we do not say that what a mind of Devadatta perceived a mind of Yajñadatta can remember. He implies that even though minds in the same causal continuum are other than one another, one can be said to remember what the other perceived if they are appropriately causally related. Minds in different causal continua of aggregates, he assumes, cannot be appropriately causally related, but he does not explain what constitutes aggregates being appropriately causally related or what constitutes aggregates belonging to different causal continua of aggregates. He cannot distinguish the causal continua of the aggregates in dependence upon which different persons are conceived as the Nyāya-Vaiśeṣikas do, by saying that they are present in different selves. The closest he seems to come to an account of how they are distinguished is in his *Commentary*, where he argues, in his discussion of verse 36 of Chapter 2 of the *Treasury*, that only causal relations between phenomena are needed to bind them together. In this passage he is rejecting the orthodox Vaibhāṣika theory that a separate substance is required in order to bind phenomena together into a single causal continuum. His view is that when we look for what ties together the phenomena in such a continuum only their causal connections can be found. Unfortunately, this view does not explain how different causal continua of aggregates are to be distinguished from one another. It seems to be to this very passage that he refers when, in support of his claim that his account of how a memory of an object occurs does not omit the causal connection between the mind that perceived an object and the mind that remembers the object, he mentions an earlier discussion on developments (*pariṇāma*-s) within a continuum.

Vasubandhu's reference to his account of what connects phenomena into a single causal continuum is meant to suggest that the only thing found to connect a perception of an object to a memory of an object is their causal connection. But what exactly does it mean for such a causal connection to be found? Vasubandhu believes that a causal connection between phenomena is a connection that exists between phenomena that are other than one another. But since, in his view, a cause ceases to exist before its effect arises, a perception of a causal connection would seem to be impossible. So if the causal connection is found, it is found by correct inference. What form this correct inference would take is not explained. Presumably, he would infer the existence of a causal connection between phenomena on the basis of their perceived regularities and on the basis of the Buddha's claim that they are causally connected. So the difference between Vasubandhu's no-self account of a memory of an object and the Nyāya-Vaiśeṣikas' account would seem to consist, at least in part, in different causal inferences. Since the Nyāya-Vaiśeṣikas' objection is that an account of a memory of an object is not possible without a causal inference to the existence of a self, Vasubandhu simply provides such an account.

At the end of his reply to the Nyāya-Vaiśeṣikas' elucidation of their first objection, Vasubandhu states that the account he has given of how a memory of an object occurs can be used to explain how a recognition of an object occurs, since a recognition of an object occurs in dependence upon a memory of the object. In this statement Vasubandhu gives his answer to the second part of the initial objection set out in Section 4.1, where it was objected that there can be no memory or recognition of an object experienced in the past if there is no self and minds are momentary phenomena.

There are further questions this interchange raises. For instance, Vasubandhu's opponents may complain that he at best explains memories *of objects*. Memories of oneself perceiving objects cannot be explained in the same way. Vātsyāyana argues, in his *Nyāyasūtrabhāṣya*, for instance, that the occurrence of a memory or recognition of an object shows that a self exists, since what is remembered or recognized is not simply the object perceived, but also oneself having perceived the object. What does the work of his argument is that part of what is remembered or recognized is oneself having perceived the object. So in the content of the memory or recognition itself the possessor of the memory or recognition of the object is identified with the perceiver of the object.

Could Vasubandhu explain a memory or recognition of this sort? No, but he would surely try to explain it away. Presumably, he would claim that the content of a memory or recognition cannot contain an identification of oneself as what perceived an object, and that, to the extent that it seems to contain it, it arises in dependence upon our false appearance as selves, and so need not be addressed, since it is mistaken. The Nyāya-Vaiśeṣikas, of course, deny that it is mistaken, since they believe that they have other arguments that establish the existence of a self. So it seems that this exchange about how a memory and a recognition of an object arise does not by itself settle the dispute.

What would Vasubandhu say about claims made about our conventional idea of our identity over time on the basis of thought experiments in which it would seem that one person would remember an object another experienced, since they are made to be causally related in an appropriate way? For instance, it has been suggested that there is a possibility, if we should transplant portions of the brain of one person into the brain of another, that the second person would remember an object the first experienced. It might seem that Vasubandhu could agree that under such circumstances one person can be said to remember what the other person experienced, since the memory and the original experience are causally connected, while the Nyāya-Vaiśeṣikas could not, since in their view the same person would not possess the memory and the original experience. However, neither could agree that such a transplant could have this result. For even if such a transplant were to occur, both would say, it could not be said that one person remembers what another person experienced, since the law of actions and their results would be violated, which is not possible. It seems that most of the many thought-experiments used by contemporary philosophers to deconstruct the conventional idea of ourselves and/or our personal identity over time are deemed impossibilities by Vasubandhu, since they involve a violation of the law of actions and their results.

§ 4.2 The Tīrthikas' objection, that Vasubandhu's denial of the existence of a self implies that there is no agent of remembering, and Vasubandhu's reply

In Section 4.2 the Nyāya-Vaiśeṣikas are made to argue that since to remember an object is to do something, and hence, to perform an action, a self is needed as an agent that performs this action. When they ask who remembers, the Nyāya-Vaiśeṣikas are asking who performs the action of remembering. Remembering, apparently, is defined as the action of grasping an object by the use of a memory as an instrument. In this objection a memory is conceived to be a memory-impression, and remembering is conceived to be the action of a self grasping an object with the help of the memory-impression of the object created by a previous experience of the object. Since Vasubandhu's theory of persons implies that there is no self that grasps an object previously perceived by using a memory-impression as an instrument of this action, this argument for the existence of a self is used as an objection to Vasubandhu's theory.

The Nyāya-Vaiśeṣikas' objection begins with the assumptions that (I) to remember an object is for an agent to perform the action of grasping the object by using a memory of the object as an instrument, and that (II) if to remember an object is for an agent to perform the action of grasping the object by using a memory of the object as an instrument, there is a self that is an agent that uses a memory of an object as an instrument to perform the action of grasping the object. Therefore, from (I) and (II) we may infer that (III) there is a self that is an agent that uses a memory of an object as an instrument to perform the action of grasping the object. However, they imply, (IV) if there is a self that is an agent that uses a memory of an object as an instrument to perform the action of grasping the object, we are not the same in existence as collections of aggregates. Therefore, from (III) and (IV) we may infer that (V) we are not the same in existence as collections of aggregates.

Vasubandhu's reply to the objection is to argue that the Nyāya-Vaiśeṣikas' own explication of the action of this self shows that there need be no self responsible for the remembering of an object. His reply begins with a statement of their definition of remembering. Vasubandhu himself, of course, rejects this definition of remembering. It will be instructive to explore briefly what reason he would have for rejecting it. The Nyāya-Vaiśeṣikas accept the definition, it seems, because they have adopted many Sanskrit grammatical categories of discourse as the basis for the construction of their metaphysical categories. In particular, since in Sanskrit grammar there exist different cases of nouns and pronouns for agents of action, instruments of action, and objects of action, as well as various verb inflections for action, and these categories provide the grammatical structure of Indian discourse about the world, Nyāya-Vaiśeṣikas assume that these categories of discourse mirror categories of entities in the world represented through them. But from Vasubandhu's viewpoint, these categories are valid only as conventions. In addition to being an owner or possessor of aggregates, for instance, a self is thought by the Nyāya-Vaiśeṣikas to be an agent of actions that uses instruments to perform actions.

Vasubandhu surely assumes, therefore, that the Nyāya-Vaiśeṣikas' definition of remembering an object merely reflects a picture of reality embedded in Sanskrit discourse, and that this picture is known to be a mere convention on the basis of an analysis that reveals the ultimate reality of the objects of discourse. In such a picture, Vasubandhu believes, it will be true that if there is a self that acts as an agent that uses a memory of an object as an instrument to perform the action of grasping the object, the action of an agent grasping the object is not the same in existence as the memory of the object. Vasubandhu next denies the truth of the consequent of this conditional, claiming that to grasp an object by using a memory of the object as an instrument is the same in existence as the memory of the object. He believes that this claim is true, presumably, because when he looks within his own experience for something corresponding to the action of remembering an object, what he finds is simply a memory of the object. Vasubandhu then assumes that if to grasp an object by using a memory of the object as an instrument is the same in existence as the memory of the object, then the action of an agent grasping an object is the same in existence as the memory of the object. Therefore, he would have us infer that the so-called action of an agent grasping the object to be remembered is the same in existence as the memory of the object. Therefore, he believes, we are to infer that there is no self that acts as an agent that uses this memory as an instrument. Should the Nyāya-Vaiśeṣikas object that if the action of grasping an object with the help of a memory of an object were the same in existence as the occurrence of a memory of the object, there would be nothing that produces the memory, Vasubandhu answers by reminding them that he has already explained in Section 4.1 how, without a self, a memory of an object is produced.

But why do we say that Caitra remembers an object if Caitra is not a self that performs the action of grasping an object with the help of a memory? In response to this question Vasubandhu answers that we say this because we perceive a memory that occurs in the continuum of the collection of aggregates called Caitra. When he says that Caitra is said to remember because we perceive a memory that occurs in Caitra's continuum of aggregates, he can hardly be taken to mean that we somehow literally perceive a mind in someone else's continuum of minds. He must be using "perceive" here in a nontechnical sense to signify a belief that depends upon perception. It is important to notice once again that Vasubandhu does not claim that what we mean, or what is meant, when we say that Caitra remembers is that a memory is perceived within the continuum of aggregates called Caitra. He is simply pointing out that we say that Caitra is said to remember because a memory is perceived in the continuum of his aggregates.

In his translation of this argument La Vallée Poussin represents Vasubandhu as asking the Pudgalavādins whether the grasping that they identify with remembering is something other than the occurrence of a memory, and the Pudgalavādins as replying that it is other, since a memory is the agent of the action of grasping. He then has Vasubandhu respond by claiming that the agent of the action of grasping is the special sort of mind that produces a memory. La Vallée Poussin seems to have been misled by Paramārtha's interpretation. I have adopted the more straightforward interpretation that Vasubandhu is asking a rhetorical question, and is suggesting that since remembering an object is grasping it, and grasping the object, in this case, is a memory of the object, remembering the object is simply a memory of the object. The conclusion is that remembering does not need a self as an agent. Then the objector protests that, even so, this memory needs to be produced by a self, and Vasubandhu replies that he has already explained what produces the memory.

To Vasubandhu's claim, that the grasping of an object with the help of a memory of the object to be remembered is the same in existence as the occurrence of a memory of the object, the Nyāya-Vaiśeṣikas may object that Vasubandhu has illegitimately identified the remembering of an object with the memory-impression used to facilitate it. A memory of an object, as conceived in their objection, is an impression stored in the self and is created by a prior perception of the object. Even Vasubandhu, they can object, believes that such an impression is needed in order to explain how we can remember an object. Their account of how we can remember an object, therefore, cannot be identified with the simple mental occurrence of remembering an object, since it includes reference to the memory-impression that Vasubandhu himself believes to be needed if a remembering of an object is to occur. Hence, in Vasubandhu's argument, they may claim, there is an equivocation in the use of the term "a memory," since the memory of an object used by a self to grasp the object is an impression and the memory of the object that constitutes remembering the object is not. Vasubandhu's reply, therefore, they may conclude, does not disarm the objection.

Although Vasubandhu does not explicitly consider the objection that he has equivocated on "a memory," he would seem to have a reply ready at hand. He can deny that he has identified the memory-impression used by a self to grasp an object with the remembering of the object, since the point of his claim, that to grasp an object by using a memory of an object as an instrument is the same in existence as the memory of the object, is that the Nyāya-Vaiśeṣikas' definition of the remembering of an object includes a reference to a memory-impression that is not found when we use introspection to look for it among the phenomena in dependence upon which we conceive the remembering of an object. Although by convention we might say, when we remember an object, that we are using a memory-impression of the object, this manner of speaking is misleading.

§ 4.3 The Tīrthikas' objection, that Vasubandhu's denial of the existence of a self implies that a memory and a consciousness are without an owner or possessor, and Vasubandhu's reply

In Section 4.3 the Nyāya-Vaiśeṣikas are made to object that there must be a self that owns or possesses the memory of an object even if a self is not needed to produce the memory. Once again we are given a Nyāya-Vaiśeṣika argument for the existence of a self under the guise of an objection to Vasubandhu's theory of persons. The argument is that there must be a self, since a memory is an instrument of the action of remembering, an instrument requires a possessor in order to be used, and the possessor must be a self. If there were no self to possess a memory, the memory could not be directed to the object to be remembered so that it can be remembered. Once again, a memory of an object is conceived as an impression that arises in dependence upon a previous perception of the object. What we might describe as the calling up of a memory-impression the Nyāya-Vaiśeṣikas call directing a memory to the object to be remembered.

In this objection Vasubandhu assumes that the Nyāya-Vaiśeṣikas believe that the self uses a memory of an object to remember the object by directing the memory somewhere, and asks them to what the memory is directed. They reply that it is directed to the object for the sake of the self remembering it. Their objection is basically that (I) just as a cow can be milked for the sake of obtaining milk because the cow has a possessor, so a memory can be directed to an object for the sake of remembering the object because the memory has a possessor. (It need not be implied in (I) that we possess a cow in the very same sense that we possess a memory, only that what is used by us must, in a general sense, be in our possession.) The objection continues with the assumptions that (II) if a memory can be directed to an object for the sake of remembering the object because the memory has an owner or possessor, the memory has an owner or possessor, and that (III) if the memory has an owner or possessor, there is a self. Therefore, from (I), (II), and (III) we may infer that (IV) there is a self. However, (V) if there is a self, we are not the same in existence as collections of aggregates. Therefore, from (IV) and (V) we may infer that (VI) we are not the same in existence as collections of aggregates. Hence, Vasubandhu's theory of persons is false.

Vasubandhu's reply begins with the assumption that (I) remembering an object is the same in existence as the occurrence of a memory of the object. His reason for making his assumption, of course, is the same as his reason for assuming that to grasp an object by using a memory of an object as an instrument is the same in existence as the occurrence of the memory of the object: when he looks for this phenomenon in his own experience, what he finds is simply a memory of the object occurring. He now assumes, I believe, that (II) if remembering an object is the same in existence as the occurrence of a memory of the object, then if a memory is directed to an object for the sake of remembering the object because the memory has an owner or possessor, a memory owned or possessed is directed to an object for the sake of the occurrence of the memory in its owner or possessor. Therefore, from (I) and (II) we may infer that (III) if a memory is directed to an object for the sake of remembering the object, then a memory owned or possessed is directed to an object for the sake of the occurrence of the memory in its owner or possessor. At this point, Vasubandhu assumes that the consequent of (III) is absurd. He does not say why it is absurd. He merely says, "For this itself must be directed for sake of this." I am assuming, with Stcherbatsky, that the first "this" refers to the memory owned or possessed and the second "this" refers to the memory for the sake of the possession of which the other memory is directed to the object. Vasubandhu apparently thinks that it is absurd for a memory already possessed to be directed to an object for the sake of possessing a memory. Hence, he assumes that (IV) a memory owned or possessed is not directed to an object for the sake of the occurrence of the memory in its possessor. From (III) and (IV) Vasubandhu would have us infer that (V) a memory is not directed to an object for the sake of remembering the object because the memory has an owner or possessor. In this portion of Vasubandhu's reply to the objection from the agent of remembering, he has attempted to show that their definition of remembering is incoherent, since it implies the absurdity that a memory owned or possessed is directed to an object for the sake of the occurrence of the memory in its owner or possessor.

But is this implication of the definition an absurdity? For the memory directed to the object, according to the Nyāya-Vaiśeṣikas, is surely a memory-impression, while the memory for the sake of whose possession it is directed to the object to be remembered is the occurrence of a memory of the object. So this implication, as they interpret its meaning, is not absurd. Vasubandhu thinks that the implication is absurd because he has identified the memory-impression with the memory-experience. So it is clear that (IV), if interpreted as the Nyāya-Vaiśeṣikas would, is just false. Hence, Vasubandhu's argument is unsound.

Vasubandhu's reply to the Nyāya-Vaiśeṣikas' objection continues by probing the means by which they believe a memory of an object is directed to the object. In what follows I will disambiguate Vasubandhu's use of "a memory" so that it does not cause confusion. He says that (VI) the owner or possessor of a memory-impression directs it to the object to be remembered either by producing the memory-experience or by sending it to the object. What exactly are these two ways of directing a memory-impression to the object to be remembered? If the alternative of sending the memory-impression to the object were to be acceptable to the Nyāya-Vaiśeṣikas, the meaning would not be that the memory-impression is somehow literally moved to the object, since this is obviously impossible, which Vasubandhu points out. If this alternative is to make sense within their view, it is that a self sends the internal organ to the memory-impression of the object, and when the organ makes contact with the memory-impression, the object is apprehended with the help of the memory-impression. But Vasubandhu does not entertain this interpretation, and proceeds to reject the alternative. He argues that if it is true that (VII) if the owner or possessor of a memory-impression sends it to the object to be remembered, a memory-impression can be moved, and that (VIII) a memory-impression cannot be moved, it follows that (IX) the owner or possessor of a memory-impression does not send it to the object. Therefore, from (VI) and (IX) we may infer that (X) the owner or possessor of a memory-impression directs it to the object to be remembered by producing the memory-experience. Vasubandhu now claims that (XI) if the owner or possessor of a memory-impression directs it to the object to be remembered by producing the memory-experience, the possessor of a memory-impression is the cause of the memory-experience. Therefore, from (X) and (XI) we may infer that (XII) the possessor of a memory-impression is the cause of the memory-experience. But he has already argued in Section 4.1 that (XIII) the cause of a memory-experience is a mind that occurs earlier in the continuum of aggregates of which the memory-experience is a part. Therefore, from (XII) and (XIII) he would have us infer that (XIV) the owner or possessor of a memory-impression is a mind that occurs earlier in the continuum of aggregates of which the memory-experience is a part. He then generalizes this result, claiming that in this case the existence of the relation between an owner or possessor and what is owned or possessed is nothing but the existence of the relation between a cause and its effect.

The obvious weakness of this portion of Vasubandhu's argument is that in (VI) he allows the Nyāya-Vaiśeṣikas only two ways of directing a memory-impression to the object to be remembered, when in fact there are numerous accounts they may give of this phenomenon, one of which I have already suggested. Hence, the Nyāya-Vaiśeṣikas would most likely object to (VI).

Vasubandhu concludes this reply by saying that what apprehends an object and what possesses a consciousness of an object are to be explained in the same way he has explained what remembers an object and what possesses a memory of an object. If the explanations are parallel, what apprehends an object is to be explained by reference to the fact that the activity of apprehending an object is the same in existence as the occurrence of a consciousness of an object, and what possesses a consciousness of an object is explained by reference to the fact that the possession of a consciousness of an object is the same in existence as the cause of the consciousness of an object. But the cause of the memory of an object is the special kind of mind described in Section 4.1, while the cause of a consciousness of an object is the conjunction of an organ of perception, an object of perception, and attentiveness. Attentiveness is added as a cause of a consciousness of an object because if a consciousness does not pay attention to the object to which it has access by means of an organ of perception, it does not perceive the object.

Vasubandhu is claiming that if we look for the possessor of a consciousness of an object among the phenomena in dependence upon which its possessor is conceived as its possessor, what we will find is an organ of perception, the object of perception and attentiveness to the object. At first sight, this claim is odd, since there is no way in which these three phenomena can be said to possess a consciousness of an object. But the oddness disappears when we recall that Vasubandhu is not attempting to explain what it means to say that a consciousness of an object has a possessor, but what the phenomena are that are the basis of conceiving a consciousness to have a possessor. The convention that we possess a consciousness of an object succeeds because it is grounded in the fact that in the continuum of the aggregates in the collection in dependence upon which we are conceived a consciousness of an object arises not only in dependence upon the object of the consciousness, but also in dependence upon the presence in this same continuum of an organ of perception and the mental factor of attentiveness.

Vasubandhu also argues that the Nyāya-Vaiśeṣikas' example of Caitra being said to be the owner or possessor of a cow can also be explained in terms of the causal connections we assume to exist between the continuum of aggregates in the collection in dependence upon which Caitra is conceived and the continuum of aggregates in the collection in dependence upon which the cow is conceived. Because of these assumed causal connections, which he says result in changes of place and changes of quality in the continuum of the aggregates of which Caitra is composed, we say Caitra possesses the cow. These connections, he thinks, are the metaphysical bases of our conceptions of Caitra as owner or possessor and the cow as the thing owned or possessed.

When Vasubandhu says that there is no relation between a possessor and what is possessed other than that between a cause and its effect, he means that when we use a causal basis analysis to look for a relation between what we by convention call the possessor and what it possesses, we find only the relation between a cause and its effect. He does not mean that the meaning of "possessor" and "possessed" is "cause" and "effect." He means that, when he searches for a relation between a possessor and what it possesses among the phenomena in dependence upon which the idea of that relation is formed, he finds only a relation between a cause and its effect.

But how does Vasubandhu think a relation between a cause and its effect is to be found between these phenomena? Since, according to Vasubandhu, a cause must cease to exist before its effect is produced, it is clear that no causal relation between these phenomena can be directly perceived. Hence, he must think that a causal relation can be correctly inferred to exist. But how can this be inferred? Is the basis of the inference direct perceptions of constant conjunctions of earlier and later similar kinds of phenomena? He does not seem to think that such conjunctions are directly perceived. Perhaps he believes that when the phenomena in these conjunctions are perceived, their specific causal powers are discriminated. In any case, he owes his opponents both an account of how specific causal relations are known to exist and replies to the objections they may raise to the account.

§ 4.4 The Tīrthikas' objection, that a self is needed to explain the occurrence of a consciousness of an object

In this section the Nyāya-Vaiśeṣikas present another objection to Vasubandhu's denial of the existence of a self. In this objection, a self (*ātman*) is identified as "an agent [signified by a noun to which an active verb is attached]" (*bhāvitṛ*), and apprehending an object (*vijānāti*) is identified as "an activity [signified by an active verb]" (*bhāva*). The claim is made that since an activity signified by an active verb exists in dependence upon an agent signified by a noun to which the active verb is attached, and apprehending an object is an activity signified by an active verb, there must be an agent responsible for the activity of apprehending an object. This agent is the self. It is assumed, of course, that the activity of apprehending an object is what Vasubandhu has just called a consciousness of an object.

Since Vasubandhu ended Section 4.3 by claiming that he can explain how a consciousness of an object arises by reference to the presence of an organ of perception, an object, and attentiveness, this objection can also be interpreted as an objection to his explanation of how a consciousness of an object arises. The objection is that this explanation is incomplete, since an agent signified by a noun to which "apprehends" (*vijānāti*) is attached must exist if a consciousness of an object exists; for a consciousness apprehending an object is an activity signified by "apprehends," which is attached to a noun that signifies an agent. Specifically, it is argued that just as walking, which is an activity signified by "walks," as in "Devadatta walks," exists in dependence upon Devadatta, the walker, so the activity signified by "apprehends" exists in dependence upon an agent signified by a noun to which this verb is attached.

The example of Devadatta and his walking is an analog of the self and its apprehending an object. The idea is that, just as in everyday discourse we attribute the activity of walking to an empirical self that we believe to be an agent of walking when we say that Devadatta walks, so we attribute the activity of apprehending an object to the real self that is an agent of this activity when we say that we apprehend an object. The grammatical analogy of the two cases, it seems, is supposed to warrant our inferring that what apprehends an object is an agent, just as an empirical self is. The agent signified by a noun to which "apprehends" is attached, the opponents simply assume, can only be a self. The general principle that every activity signified by an active verb exists in dependence upon an agent signified by a noun to which the active verb is attached is used to warrant the move from the example of Devadatta walking to a self apprehending an object.

Although Yaśomitra seems to attribute this objection to the Vaiyākaraṇas, I have been unable to find it in the extant works of the Vaiyākaraṇas, either as an argument for the existence of a self or as an objection to a Buddhist account of how a consciousness of an object arises. This raises the possibility that Yaśomitra's comment may mean no more than that the objection is based on an analogy to a point of grammar set out by the Vaiyākaraṇas. But neither have I found an objection of this form presented in the extant works of either the Nyāya-Vaiśeṣikas or the Sāṃkhyas, the other two Tīrthikas that Yaśomitra identifies for us. It is, nonetheless, more closely related to arguments used by the Nyāya-Vaiśeṣikas to prove the existence of a self, since the Sāṃkhyas reject the view that a self is an agent of any sort, while the Nyāya-Vaiśeṣikas argue that a self exists because there must be an agent that produces purposive bodily motion. But the Nyāya-Vaiśeṣikas' argument does not, as the objection in Section 4.4 does, rest on a grammatical analogy or on the use of an active verb to signify consciousness of an object as an activity. It pertains specifically to an agent that is a cause of purposive bodily motion. So whose objection is it that is presented in this section?

Any answer to this question, it seems, will be guesswork. My own inclination is to think that it is in fact an objection put forward by the Nyāya-Vaiśeṣikas. For there is another argument of the Nyāya-Vaiśeṣikas that is closely related to the objection in Section 4.4. This is the argument that a self exists because there must be an underlying support in which a consciousness of an object inheres and a consciousness of an object cannot inhere in any underlying support other than a self. A consciousness of an object, although classified by the Nyāya-Vaiśeṣikas as an attribute of the self, is considered by them to be an activity of the self. This does not mean that they think of consciousness of an object as an action (*karma*) in the sense in which "action" is defined within their system of categories. An action, according to that system, is or involves a bodily motion. From a grammatical point of view, I believe, a consciousness of an object is understood by them to be an activity of the self, even if it is included in the category of attributes.

The grammatical analog to the Nyāya-Vaiśeṣikas' argument, that a self must exist because consciousness of an object cannot reside in anything else, is the argument that there must be an agent signified by a noun to which "apprehends" is attached. This argument from grammar also bears a resemblance to the Nyāya-Vaiśeṣikas' argument for the existence of a self from the need for an agent to cause purposive bodily motions, since in both cases the need for an agent to explain the functioning of what the Buddhists call aggregates is stressed. In effect, this argument uses a grammatical point to extend the idea that an agent is needed to explain physical motions such as walking to the idea that an agent is needed to explain mental activity. If this is correct, the objection in Section 4.4 is primarily based on a grammatical consideration rather than on the metaphysical doctrines upon which these other two arguments are based. The Nyāya-Vaiśeṣikas may then be taken to be relying on the belief that we make a consciousness of an object an activity signified by an active verb attached to a noun that signifies a self.

The objection, which I will assume is put forward by the Nyāya-Vaiśeṣikas, begins with the claim that (I) an activity signified by an active verb exists in dependence upon an agent signified by a noun or pronoun to which the active verb is attached. For instance, (II) the activity of walking, which is signified by the active verb, "walks," in "Devadatta walks," exists in dependence upon Devadatta, who is an agent signified by "Devadatta." In the same way, (III) the activity of apprehending an object, which is signified by the active verb, "apprehends," in "X apprehends an object," exists in dependence upon a self, which is an agent signified by a noun to which the active verb is attached. But (IV) if the activity of apprehending an object, which is signified by the active verb, "apprehends," in "X apprehends an object," exists in dependence upon a self, which is an agent signified by a noun to which the active verb is attached, then a self exists. Therefore, from (III) and (IV) we may infer that (V) a self exists. We are to infer not only that a self exists, but that since apprehending an object requires the existence of a self, a consciousness apprehending an object is not to be explained simply by reference to an organ of perception, an object of perception, and attentiveness.

§ 4.4.1 *Vasubandhu's reply to the objection*

In Section 4.4.1 Vasubandhu responds to this objection by arguing that the Nyāya-Vaiśeṣikas cannot use (II) to support (III). In other words, he claims that the grammatical analogy between "Devadatta walks" and "X apprehends [an object]" does not warrant the supposition that X is a self. For if they assume that the Devadatta who is said to walk is a self, they are assuming the existence of a self, which is what they are trying to prove. But if Devadatta being said to walk simply implies that Devadatta is a man, which Vasubandhu himself understands to be the same in existence as a collection of aggregates, Devadatta walking is not analogous to a self apprehending an object. Hence, since the Nyāya-Vaiśeṣikas cannot assume that Devadatta is either a self or the same in existence as a collection of aggregates, it cannot be said that X being said to apprehend an object implies that X is a self on the ground that "walks" and "apprehends" signify activities that exist in dependence upon agents signified by nouns or pronouns to which these verbs are attached.

Vasubandhu's claim that (II) cannot be used to support (III) seems to be correct. The implication is that (I) is true simply as a point of grammar, and cannot warrant the claim that the agent signified by a noun or pronoun attached to an active verb is a self or a person that is the same in existence as a collection of aggregates. In other words, the mere use of an active verb does not, without further argumentation, determine the ultimate mode of existence of what is signified by a noun or pronoun attached to the verb. Although it may true, he can say, that we assume, when we attach active verbs to nouns or pronouns, that there are activities signified by the verbs and that they cannot exist apart from agents signified by nouns or pronouns to which these verbs are attached, it does not follow that there are such activities or agents. In general, he can argue, we need not accept the Nyāya-Vaiśeṣikas' metaphysical explanation of why we ascribe activities to ourselves if there is available an alternative metaphysical explanation. In particular, he believes, an inquiry into the truth conditions of sentences in which we attach active verbs to nouns or pronouns in order to ascribe activities to ourselves can uncover the false assumption that we are selves or substantially real agents.

§ 4.5 The Tīrthikas' objection, that if we are not selves, we cannot walk, and Vasubandhu's reply

The Nyāya-Vaiśeṣikas are now on the verge of asserting the view I believe to have inspired the grammatical argument presented in 4.4. For in Section 4.5 they ask, in response to his claim in Section 4.4.1, that Devadatta walks even though he is not a self, how Devadatta can walk. The question is asked because they believe that a person's purposive bodily motions are caused by a self. They believe, of course, that Vasubandhu's thesis, that we are the same in existence as collections of momentary aggregates, will prevent him from being able to explain how it is possible for Devadatta to walk, since the aggregates of Devadatta are momentary phenomena, and walking, as a bodily motion, is not possible for a causal continuum of momentary aggregates. Their question, therefore, amounts to the objection that Vasubandhu cannot explain how it is possible for Devadatta to walk, since he believes that Devadatta is the same in existence as a collection of momentary aggregates. Vasubandhu's reply to the implicit objection is to explain why it is said that Devadatta walks in spite of his aggregates not being said to walk. He first notes that we conceive a collection of aggregates that exist in a causal continuum as a single being possessed of a body, conceive Devadatta in dependence upon this collection, and say that Devadatta walks. We say that he walks because we say that we walk. We say that we walk, he explains, because we believe that we cause the continuum of our own bodily aggregates to arise in different places at different times, and use "walking" to refer to the arising of the continuum of these bodily aggregates in different places at different times. Then, having implicitly inferred that Devadatta too causes the continuum of his own bodily aggregates to arise in different places at different times, we say that he walks.

In Vasubandhu's explanation of why we say that Devadatta walks he makes it clear that the Devadatta who walks is being conceived as the same person at different moments as he walks by saying that Devadatta's walking is conceived in dependence upon change of place being attributed to the causal continuum of his bodily aggregates. In general, we may assume, when reference to a person is made in the context of a person being conceived to be engaging in an activity that occurs over a period of time, Vasubandhu thinks that the person is being conceived in dependence upon the causal continuum of the aggregates in the collection of aggregates in dependence upon which he is being conceived. The aggregates themselves, of course, are not thought to be capable of change, but the causal continuum of the aggregates in the collection in dependence upon which the person is conceived can change. A person walking, as a conventionally real phenomena, exists in dependence upon the mind (1) conceiving a person in dependence upon a collection of aggregates that exist in a causal continuum, (2) conceiving the causal continuum of the bodily aggregates in this collection as occupying different places at different times, and (3) conceiving the causal continuum of these bodily aggregates that occupies different places at different times as "walking."

He adds that we attribute change of place to ourselves for the same reasons we attribute change of place to fire and sound. We need to keep in mind, when he says this, that the analogies to fire and sound are intended only to support this explanation of how change of place can be attributed to Devadatta. For instance, Vasubandhu does not think that the elements in the collection of elements in dependence upon which we speak of the same fire or the same sound over time exist in a beginningless causal continuum. The fact that our own aggregates exist in a beginningless causal continuum is irrelevant to his use of the analogies. He also adds that the same sort of analysis can be used to explain why we speak of Devadatta apprehending an object.

Vasubandhu's explanation of why it is said that Devadatta apprehends an object, if analogous to his explanation of why it is said that he walks, consists of two claims. These are the claims that we assume (1) that Devadatta, like ourselves, is one thing, even though he is the same in existence as the collection of his momentary aggregates existing in a causal continuum, (2) that the different consciousnesses of objects in Devadatta's continuum are caused to arise by this one thing, Devadatta, just as we ourselves cause our different consciousnesses of objects to arise, even though in fact they arise in dependence upon different objects and different organs of perception, and (3) that Devadatta apprehends objects when different consciousnesses of objects arise in his continuum of consciousnesses, just as we apprehend objects when different consciousnesses of objects arise in our continua.

Since the Nyāya-Vaiśeṣikas' implicit objection is that Vasubandhu cannot explain, from an ultimate point of view, why we say that Devadatta walks without including mention of a self that causes his walking, his reply need only provide such an explanation. This objection, like the objection in Section 4.1, does not include an argument used to support it, and so Vasubandhu makes no attempt to discredit the argument that lies behind the objection. In this case, the argument is that a self is needed as an agent to explain how Devadatta can walk, and so Vasubandhu does not address this argument.

§ 4.6 The Tīrthikas' objection, that Vasubandhu makes a consciousness into a self by making it an agent of the activity of apprehending an object, and Vasubandhu's reply

In Section 4.6 the opponents argue that Vasubandhu cannot escape the metaphysical assumption that we are selves when we use "apprehends" because the Buddha himself said that a consciousness apprehends an object. The force of the objection, it seems, is that since the Buddha himself made this assumption in using this active verb, Vasubandhu is committed to the existence of a self, except that in this case the self is called "a consciousness." Since the Nyāya-Vaiśeṣikas employ a version of this argument against those who would have the internal organ (*manas*) perform the functions of a self, we may presume that the objection Vasubandhu is here considering is one of theirs. They mean to be objecting, therefore, that since Vasubandhu's own scriptures show that a consciousness is an agent signified by a noun and an agent signified by a noun is a self, he is still committed to the view that there is a self.

Vasubandhu's reply is to say that a consciousness apprehending an object is an effect that conforms to its cause, which is its object, and that an effect that conforms to its cause receives a form like that of its cause and is not an agent that engages in an activity. So since a consciousness apprehending an object just is its reception of a form like that of its cause, which is its object, it is not an agent that engages in an activity. As an aside, Vasubandhu explains why, even though a consciousness of an object also has an organ of perception as a cause, it is not said to be conscious of the organ. The reason, he says, is that when a perception occurs the consciousness does not conform to the organ, but to the object, which possesses the character (*ākāra*) the consciousness receives.

He then admits that there may be a sense in which a consciousness is an agent. For if that which causes a consciousness may be called an agent or producer (*kartṛ* may also be translated as "a producer"), then since in a causal continuum of consciousnesses one consciousness produces another in the next moment, a consciousness is an agent. But in this case, of course, the consciousness is not called an agent or producer because it is signified by a noun to which the active verb, "apprehends," is attached, but because it produces another consciousness. Vasubandhu likens this case to that in which it is said that a ring of a bell is an agent or producer. It is an agent or producer in the sense that in a causal continuum of rings of a bell a ring at one moment produces a ring in the next moment. He is not saying, of course, that the ring at one moment, by itself, produces the next ring, since the causal conditions for the continued ringing must also be present.

Vasubandhu also presents an account of why we say that a consciousness apprehends an object even though it is not an agent or producer signified by a noun to which "apprehends" is attached. He explains it by analogy to his explanation of why we say that the flame of a butterlamp moves even though it is not an agent signified by a noun to which "moves" is attached. The account is similar to that given in Section 4.5 for why we say that Devadatta walks even though he is not an agent signified by "Devadatta" in "Devadatta walks." Here he says that since the momentary flames within the continuum of such flames arise in different places at different times and common people mistakenly grasp this continuum as one thing, they say that the flame moves, even though it does not move. He uses a second analogy to show that the use of "apprehends" need not imply that the consciousness is an agent signified by "a consciousness" to which "apprehends" is attached. The analogy is that, just as we can say that a bodily form arises and endures for a moment without implying that the bodily form is an agent signified by "a bodily form," to which "arises and endures" is attached, so a consciousness can be said to apprehend an object without implying that there is an agent signified by "a consciousness," to which "apprehends" is attached.

Vasubandhu's reply contains no significant new information about his views, and seems to be an appropriate reply to the objection.

§ 4.7 The Tīrthikas' objection, that if minds arise from other minds the same kinds of minds always arise or they arise in a fixed order, and Vasubandhu's reply

In Section 4.7 Vasubandhu has the opponents, whom Yaśomitra identifies as the Vaiśeṣikas and Stcherbatsky identifies as the Sāṃkhyas, pose a problem for his view that there is no self and that a mind arises from an immediately preceding mind in the same causal continuum of minds. If Stcherbatsky's identification is correct, the opponents' objection is grounded in the belief that objects of consciousness, including what Vasubandhu calls minds, are ultimately produced by a fundamental nature (*prakṛti*) so that the self (*purūṣa*), which they believe to be pure consciousness, may enjoy them. The Sāṃkhyas agree that what the Buddhists call minds are impermanent phenomena that are causally conditioned by other minds, but disagree with their account of what their nature is and how they arise. They claim that minds are caused to arise by the fundamental nature for the sake of the enjoyment of selves. So if there were no selves, minds would not arise at all. If it is this belief that gives rise to the objection in Section 4.7, the opponents are assuming that if there were no self, then even if minds were produced by the fundamental nature, these minds would always be the same, since it would produce variation only for the enjoyment of the self, or if it did produce different minds, it would produce them in the same order, as things with reproductive cycles are produced, since without a self to enjoy different minds, different minds would at best arise only as a part of such cycles. The point would be that there is no way to explain the sorts of variations that occur in the causal continua of minds, since there are no selves for the sake of whose enjoyment different minds or different orderings of different minds would be produced.

Although it is possible that the Sāṃkhyas would have presented such an objection, it seems highly unlikely, since I have found no comparable argument in the Sāṃkhya texts known to me. There certainly is no such argument in the *Sāṃkhya Kārikas* of Īśvarakṛṣṇa (second century CE), which is the only surviving text of the school that predates Vasubandhu's "Refutation." The original text of the school, composed by Kāpila (seventh century BCE) has been lost, but it could not have contained any arguments directed against the teachings of the Buddha (sixth century BCE). The remaining possibility is that the argument is recorded in the *Mahāvibhāṣā*, the compendium of Vaibhāṣika school theses upon which Vasubandhu draws in composing the *Treasury*. There are Chinese translations of the *Mahāvibhāṣā*, but there is in English no complete translation of the Chinese translation. There is in English a summary of its contents made by Shohei Ichimura with Kosho Kawamura, Robert Buswell Jr, and Collett Cox in vol. VII of Karl Potter's *Encyclopedia of Indian Philosophies* (Motilal Banarsidass: Delhi, 1996, pp. 511–68). But neither the portions of the Chinese translation translated into English nor its summary make reference to a Sāṃkhya argument of the sort found in Section 4.7 of the "Refutation." Hence, I have been unable to find support for Stcherbatsky's attribution of the objection to the Sāṃkhyas.

If Yaśomitra's identification of the opponents with the Vaiśeṣikas is correct, the argument is that if a self did not exist as an agent that produces different kinds of minds there would be no explanation of the fact that different kinds of minds do arise in the continuum of minds of a person, or, if different kinds of minds do arise, that they do not arise in a fixed order in the way in which things without a self arise, for instance, in the order of sprout–stem–leaf. In Vātsyāyana's *Nyāyasūtrabhāṣya*, a commentary on Gotama's *Nyāya Sūtras*, it is argued in his discussion of verse 3 of Chapter 1 of Book III of the *Nyāya Sūtras*, that an agent is needed in order to explain the different orders in which perceptions of the different qualities of the same object occur. This argument, it would appear, closely resembles the argument on the basis of which the objection Vasubandhu considers in Section 4.7 is formulated. Vātsyāyana argues that the presence of an agent of perception is required in order to explain the fact that these perceptions can occur in different orders. The implication is that if there were no agent, the order would be fixed, as it is in the case of things like sprout–stem–leaf, in which there is no agent that can change the order. The presence of this argument in a Nyāya text strongly suggests that Vasubandhu's opponent is, as Yaśomitra contends, the Vaiśeṣikas. We may assume that his reference includes both the Nyāya and Vaiśeṣika schools.

The Nyāya-Vaiśeṣikas are made to argue, first of all, that from the assumptions that if (I) there is no self (an agent that changes the order in which minds arise) and minds arise from minds that immediately precede them in the same mind-continuum, either the same kinds of minds will always arise or minds of different kinds will arise in a fixed way for the sake of their reproduction, and (II) the same kinds of minds do not always arise and minds of different kinds do not arise in a fixed way for the sake of their reproduction, we may infer that (III) either there is a self (an agent that changes the order in which minds arise) or minds do not arise from minds that immediately precede them in the same mind-continuum. Vasubandhu, of course, believes that (IV) minds arise from minds that immediately precede them in the same mind-continuum. Therefore, the Nyāya-Vaiśeṣikas would have us infer from (III) and (IV) that (V) there is a self (an agent that changes the order in which minds arise).

Vasubandhu's reply to this objection is to argue that (I) is false, since minds are by nature different in kind and arise from different kinds of impressions. First, he argues that if it is true that (I)′ minds in the same mind-continuum are causally conditioned phenomena, and that (II)′ causally conditioned phenomena are by nature different in kind from moment to moment, then (III)′ minds in the same mind-continuum are by nature different in kind from moment to moment. In support of (III)′ Vasubandhu also argues that a meditator could not release himself from concentration on an object by letting go of his effort of holding the minds in his mind-continuum on the same object unless minds are by nature different in kind from moment to moment. He continues by saying that (IV)′ if minds in the same mind-continuum are by nature different in kind from moment to moment, the same kinds of minds do not always arise in the same mind-continuum. Therefore, from (III)′ and (IV)′ we may infer that (V)′ the same kinds of minds do not always arise in the same mind-continuum. Hence, he has shown that (VI)′ the same kinds of minds always arising need not be a consequence of there being no self and minds arising from minds that immediately precede them in the same mind-continuum.

But the Nyāya-Vaiśeṣikas may still claim that if there is no self (an agent that changes the order in which minds arise) and minds arise from minds that immediately precede them in the same mind-continuum, minds of different kinds will always arise in a fixed way for the sake of their reproduction. That this claim is also false Vasubandhu begins to argue by stating that (VII)′ minds of different kinds arise from the same kinds of minds in different mind-continua because different kinds of impressions are present in each continuum. For instance, he points out, in the mind-continuum of a bhikṣu who has, for the sake of safeguarding his vow of chastity, meditated on the repulsiveness of the female body, the idea of a woman gives rise to a feeling of repulsion, yet in the mind-continuum of a layperson who has met the woman's husband and son, the idea of the woman gives rise to the thought of her husband and son.

Vasubandhu also explains that different kinds of minds are produced in a single mind-continuum in dependence upon the relative strengths of the different kinds of impressions present in it and can give rise to these different kinds of phenomena, unless there is a special bodily condition or external condition that inhibits the production of the kinds of minds to which it would give rise. One kind of impression is stronger than another, he adds, if it is created by a more common, intense, or recent association of minds than the association that creates the other. Nonetheless, the kind of impression that is stronger does not always produce its result because the causally conditioned minds that must be present in order for them to exert their causal efficacy differ in kind from moment to moment and this difference enables a different kind of result to be produced from a different kind of impression.

Since Vasubandhu's account makes it clear that these different kinds of minds do not arise in a fixed order for the sake of reproduction, we may add to his argument the premise that (VIII)′ if different kinds of minds arise from the same kinds of minds in different mind-continua because different kinds of impressions are present in each, then different kinds of minds will not always arise in a fixed way for the sake of their reproduction. It follows from (VII)′ and (VIII)′ that (IX)′ different kinds of minds will not always arise in a fixed way for the sake of their reproduction. Consequently, since Vasubandhu has argued that (VI)′ and (IX)′ are true, they may be conjoined and used, along with the Nyāya-Vaiśeṣikas' initial claim, (I), to conclude that (X)′ either there is no self (an agent that changes the order in which minds arise) or minds do not arise from minds that immediately precede them in the same mind-continuum. And since Vasubandhu himself, of course, claims that (XI)′ minds do arise from minds that immediately precede them in the same mind-continuum, he believes that we may infer, from (X)′ and (XI)′, that (XII)′ there is no self (an agent that changes the order in which minds arise). He himself, of course, does not explicitly draw all of these consequences in his discussion, but merely draws the conclusion that it is false that if there is no self and minds arise from minds that immediately precede them in the same mind-continuum, either the same kinds of minds will always arise or different kinds of minds will always arise in a fixed way for the sake of their reproduction.

Vasubandhu's reply would seem to be satisfactory insofar as it explains, on Buddhist principles, why minds of the same kind are not always produced and why minds of different kinds are produced in the different orders in which they are produced. What is missing is an account and criticism of the Nyāya-Vaiśeṣikas' own explanation of how minds of different kinds are produced because of a self. He saves this account for Section 4.7.1, where he uses the same basic objection to criticize the Nyāya-Vaiśeṣikas' own theory of how minds are produced by a self with the help of the internal organ.

§ 4.7.1 *Vasubandhu's critique of a Tīrthika theory of how minds are produced in a self*

A Tīrthika theory that minds arise from a self

The long and complicated argument in Section 4.7.1 has as its aim a demonstration that the false consequence the Nyāya-Vaiśeṣikas believe is entailed by Vasubandhu's account of how minds are produced is in fact a consequence entailed by their own theory that minds arise from a self.

The Nyāya-Vaiśeṣikas' "theory of the production of minds" (TPM), in which I will include theses concerning the self, minds, and the internal organ, may be summarized for our purposes as a set of twelve theses. For each I will assign a descriptive name. The first is

TPM(I) The agency thesis: minds arise from a self when the self is conjoined with an internal organ.

It is basically the consistency of the agency thesis with the remaining theses of the theory that Vasubandhu is challenging. Included in minds are what the Nyāya-Vaiśeṣikas call cognitions, desires, aversions, and feelings of pleasure and pain, The most important of the remaining theses for our purposes are as follows:

TPM(II) The permanent self thesis: a self is a permanent phenomenon.
TPM(III) The permanent organ thesis: an internal organ is a permanent phenomenon.
TPM(IV) The different minds thesis: the same kinds of minds do not always arise and different kinds of minds do not always arise in the same order.
TPM(V) The pervasion thesis: a self pervades the body.
TPM(VI) The organ-presence thesis: an internal organ is present in the body.
TPM(VII) The organ-mobility thesis: an internal organ moves from one place to another.
TPM(VIII) The immobility thesis: a self is immovable.
TPM(IX) The indestructibility thesis: a self is indestructible.
TPM(X) The partlessness thesis: a self is partless.
TPM(XI) The underlying support thesis: a self is the underlying support for minds.
TPM(XII) The otherness thesis: a self is other than minds.

The Nyāya-Vaiśeṣikas claim that minds arise from a self (that is permanent, pervades the body, is immovable, partless, and indestructible, and is other than the minds for which it provides an underlying support) when the self is conjoined with an internal organ (that is permanent, present in the body, and moves from one place in the body to another). The self that is conscious of a sense-object, for instance, is said to have sent the internal organ to a sense-organ of the body that the self pervades. When the internal organ makes contact with the sense-organ, which is itself in contact with its object, a mind, which is a consciousness of the sense-object, arises in a self. So a mind arises from a self when the self is conjoined with an internal organ.

The root objection to the theory

Vasubandhu's root objection to the Nyāya-Vaiśeṣikas' theory of the production of minds is that TPM(I), TPM(II), TPM(III), and TPM(IV) are inconsistent. In order for Vasubandhu to show that TPM(I), TPM(II), TPM(III), and TPM(IV) are inconsistent, he needs to assume, I believe, that if a self is a permanent phenomenon, an internal organ is a permanent phenomenon, and a self is conjoined with an internal organ, then a self is always conjoined with an internal organ. Vasubandhu thinks that this assumption is true because he believes that if a self and an internal organ were to cease to be conjoined, they would change from being conjoined to not being conjoined and a permanent phenomenon cannot change. He also assumes that if a self is always conjoined with an internal organ and minds arise from a self when the self is conjoined with an internal organ, then either the same kinds of minds always arise or different kinds of minds always arise in the same order. His reason for making this assumption would seem to be that a permanent conjunction, if it could produce many minds as its effect, could only produce many minds not different in kind, or, if it could produce many minds different in kind, it could produce them only in one kind of order. In fact, Vasubandhu, like other Buddhists, does not even believe that a permanent conjunction of a self with an internal organ could produce many effects of the same kind, since all believe that each effect would require its own separate cause. Vasubandhu seems to grant the possibility of multiple effects of a single cause in order to employ, against the Nyāya-Vaiśeṣikas' own account of the production of minds, their own objection to his theory that minds arise, without being possessed by a self, from other minds.

From TPM(I), TPM(II), TPM(III), and the above two assumptions, Vasubandhu would have us draw the conclusion that either the same kinds of minds always arise or different kinds of minds always arise in the same order. This conclusion contradicts TPM(IV), which is that the same kinds of minds do not always arise and different kinds of minds do not always arise in the same order. Hence, he believes, TPM(I), TPM(II), TPM(III), and TPM(IV) are inconsistent.

The Nyāya-Vaiśeṣikas do not believe, as Vasubandhu will report, that if a self is a permanent phenomenon, an internal organ is a permanent phenomenon, and a self is conjoined with an internal organ, then a self is always conjoined with an internal organ. For they think that the permanence of phenomena is compatible with their successive conjunctions and disjunctions as relational attributes they possess. Since they believe that the attributes of substances like a self and an internal organ are not the same in existence as the substances in which they inhere, they believe that the substances do not change when their attributes do. Why does Vasubandhu think that if a self is a permanent phenomenon, an internal organ is a permanent phenomenon, and a self is conjoined with an internal organ, then a self is always conjoined with an internal organ? He believes that the attributes of a substance are the same in existence as the substance itself, and that for this reason, if a self and an internal organ have the attribute of being conjoined they cannot lose this attribute if they are permanent entities. But this reply does not occur until another is first attempted.

The first reply to the root objection: the reply from different conjunctions

The Nyāya-Vaiśeṣikas' first reply to Vasubandhu's root objection is to give an account of how different kinds of minds arise from a self in accord with their theory that conjunctions, as relational attributes of substances, can change without change in the substances themselves. Hence, they claim, the cause of the arising of different kinds of minds in a self is a different conjunction. The reply is that (I) different kinds of minds arise from a self when the self and an internal organ enter into different con-junctions. The Nyāya-Vaiśeṣikas believe that (II) if different kinds of minds arise from a self when the self and an internal organ enter into different conjunctions, the same kinds of minds do not always arise. Hence, they conclude, (III) the same kinds of minds do not always arise. So they believe that, even though different kinds of minds arise from a self when the self is conjoined with an internal organ and both a self and an internal organ are permanent phenomena, it is not true that the same kinds of minds always arise, since a self having different conjunctions with an internal organ is the cause of the arising of different kinds of minds.

Three objections to the reply from different conjunctions: the objection from the otherness of conjunction, the objection from the definition of conjunction, and the objection from organ motion

Vasubandhu presents three objections to the reply from different conjunctions. The first of these objections relies on TPM(III), TPM(IV), and the reply from different conjunctions. It begins, I believe, with the assumption that (I) if different kinds of minds arise from a self when the self and an internal organ enter into different conjunctions, then the conjunction of a self with an internal organ is not the same in existence as either the self or the internal organ. The Nyāya-Vaiśeṣikas, of course, accept the truth of (I). But for Vasubandhu, it must also be true that (II) if the conjunction of a self with an internal organ is not the same in existence as either the self or the internal organ, the conjunction of a self with an internal organ is other than both the self and the internal organ. Although (II) might seem innocuous, and so, acceptable to the Nyāya-Vaiśeṣikas, its meaning, according to Vasubandhu, is that if the conjunction is not the same in existence as what it conjoins, it must be other in the sense of being a separate substance. But if this is the meaning of (II), the Nyāya-Vaiśeṣikas do not believe that it is true. In their view, conjunction is an attribute (*guṇa*) that inheres in two or more substances, and although an attribute is not the same in existence as the substances in which it happens to inhere, it is not itself a separate substance, since attributes exist in dependence upon the substances in which they inhere.

In the text Vasubandhu next claims that the Nyāya-Vaiśeṣikas have not proved that the conjunction of a self with an internal organ is other than the self and internal organ in which it inheres. His reason for making this claim, it appears, is that he knows that they cannot prove this. He is assuming that the otherness in question is a difference in substance. So let us take him to be asserting that (III) the conjunction of a self with an internal organ is not other than both the self and the internal organ. Therefore, from (I), (II), and (III), Vasubandhu would have us infer that (IV) different kinds of minds do not arise from a self when the self and an internal organ enter into different conjunctions. But if (IV) is true, TPM(IV), which is the different minds thesis, is false. Hence, Vasubandhu would have us believe that the Nyāya-Vaiśeṣikas' reply from different conjunctions fails to overturn his root objection to their theory.

But his reply is flawed to the extent that the Nyāya-Vaiśeṣikas can argue that either "is other than" is used in the same sense in (II) and (III), in which case one or the other is false, or "is other than" is used in different senses in (II) and (III), in which case the argument is invalid. So if Vasubandhu's objection is to work, it seems that he would have to argue that the Nyāya-Vaiśeṣikas cannot prove that attributes can be not the same in existence as substances without being other in substance than them. He would need to show, on the basis of the views of the Nyāya-Vaiśeṣikas themselves, that the notion of attributes not being the same in existence as the substances without being different substances is incoherent.

Vasubandhu's second objection to the reply from different conjunctions begins with a statement of the definition of conjunction given by Praśastapāda, which is that (I) conjunction is contact between things not in contact before being conjoined. But Vasubandhu believes that it is also true that (II) if conjunction is contact between things not in contact before being conjoined, then if different kinds of minds arise from a self when the self and an internal organ enter into different conjunctions, a self and an internal organ are not in contact before they are conjoined. Therefore, from (I) and (II) he would have us infer that (III) if different kinds of minds arise from a self when the self and an internal organ enter into different conjunctions, a self and an internal organ are not in contact before they are conjoined. But Vasubandhu claims that (IV) if a self and an internal organ are not in contact before they are conjoined, a self and an internal organ are in separate places. Therefore, from (III) and (IV) we may infer that (V) if different kinds of minds arise from a self when the self and an internal organ enter into different conjunctions, a self and an internal organ are in separate places. Vasubandhu now calls attention to the consequence of the definition of conjunction on the possibility of different conjunctions of a self with an internal organ. For this purpose, he focuses on the pervasion thesis and the organ-presence thesis, which are TPM(V) and TPM(VI) of the Nyāya-Vaiśeṣikas' theory of the production of minds. In conjunction, they are the statement that (VI) a self pervades the body and an internal organ is present in the body. But now a problem arises. For (VII) if a self pervades the body and an internal organ is present in the body, a self and an internal organ are not in separate places. Therefore, from (VI) and (VII) we may infer that (VIII) a self and an internal organ are not in separate places. Therefore, from (V) and (VIII) we may infer that (IX) different kinds of minds do not arise from a self when the self and an internal organ enter into different conjunctions. Vasubandhu concludes that the reply from different conjunctions does not enable the Nyāya-Vaiśeṣikas to avoid the root objection to their theory of how different kinds of minds arise from a self.

How could the Nyāya-Vaiśeṣikas reply to this objection? One possible reply, I believe, is that the definition of conjunction employed in the objection is meant to be applied only to the conjunction of physical substances, not to the conjunction of a self with an internal organ. But this reply will not adequately answer the objection unless a definition of conjunction that does apply to the conjunction of a self with an internal organ is supplied. (Such a definition can be found in the *Vaiśeṣika Sūtras*, Book VII, Chapter 2, verse 9.) Another possible reply to Vasubandhu's objection would be to define "not in contact" in such a way that a self not being in contact with an internal organ does not imply that they are in separate places. In fact, when the Nyāya-Vaiśeṣikas do reply to Vasubandhu's objections to their reply from different conjunctions by claiming that different parts of the self conjoin with the internal organ, they are in effect redefining "not in contact" in an attempt to escape the objection from the definition of conjunction.

Vasubandhu's third objection to the Nyāya-Vaiśeṣikas' reply from different conjunctions is a continuation of the second insofar as it relies on a conclusion they draw from its premises. It begins with the Nyāya-Vaiśeṣikas' acceptance of TPM(VII), which is the organ-mobility thesis. This is the thesis that (I) an internal organ moves from one place to another. But according to TPM(IV), which is the different minds thesis, (II) different kinds of minds arise from a self when the self and an internal organ enter into different conjunctions. As he did in the objection from the definition of conjunction, Vasubandhu calls upon the claim that (III) if different kinds of minds arise from a self when the self and an internal organ enter into different conjunctions, then a self and an internal organ are in separate places. Therefore, from (II) and (III) he would have us conclude that (IV) a self and an internal organ are in separate places. But Vasubandhu claims that (V) if a self and an internal organ are in separate places and an internal organ moves from one place to another, then if an internal organ moves to a place occupied by a self, the self either moves out of the way or is destroyed. Therefore, from (IV), (V), and (I) we may infer that (VI) if an internal organ moves to a place occupied by a self, a self either moves out of the way or is destroyed. But the Nyāya-Vaiśeṣikas accept the truth of TPM(V), which is the pervasion thesis, TPM(VI), which is the organ-presence thesis, and TPM(VII), which is the organ-mobility thesis. In conjunction these are the theses that (VII) a self pervades the body, an internal organ is present in the body, and an internal organ moves from one place to another. But Vasubandhu claims that (VIII) if a self pervades the body, an internal organ is present in the body, and an internal organ moves from one place to another, then an internal organ moves to a place occupied by a self. Therefore, from (VII) and (VIII) we may infer that (IX) an internal organ moves to a place occupied by a self. Therefore, from (VI) and (IX) we may infer that (X) a self either moves out of the way or is destroyed. Vasubandhu believes that the Nyāya-Vaiśeṣikas must agree that (XI) if a self either moves out of the way or is destroyed, either a self is movable or a self is destructible. Therefore, from (X) and (XI) we may infer that (XII) either a self is movable or a self is destructible. But the Nyāya-Vaiśeṣikas accept the truth of TPM(VIII), which is the immobility thesis, and TPM(IX), which is the indestructibility thesis, which in conjunction are the thesis that (XIII) a self is immovable and a self is indestructible. Hence, since (XII) and (XIII) are contradictory, and a contradiction has been derived from this set of premises, if the other theses of the Nyāya-Vaiśeṣikas' theory of how a self produces minds are true, the different minds thesis is false.

The second reply to the root objection: the reply from partial conjunctions

The Nyāya-Vaiśeṣikas now present, in reply to Vasubandhu's root objection, a second account of how a self can produce different kinds of minds. The simplest form of the reply is that since (I) different kinds of minds arise from a self when an internal organ is conjoined with different parts of a self, and (II) the same kinds of minds do not always arise if different kinds of minds arise from a self when an internal organ is conjoined with different parts of a self, it follows that (II) the same kinds of minds do not always arise. If an internal organ is conjoined with different parts of a self, as opposed to the whole, the self and the internal organ are not in different places and yet the self need not move or be destroyed when differently conjoined with an internal organ.

Vasubandhu's objection to the reply from partial conjunctions: the objection from partlessness and nondifference

Vasubandhu's objection to the reply from partial conjunctions begins with a statement of TPM(X), which is the partlessness thesis. This is the thesis that (I) a self is partless. Vasubandhu claims that (II) if a self is partless, then different kinds of minds do not arise from a self when the internal organ is conjoined with different parts of a self. Vasubandhu does not explain why he thinks that (II) is true, but the reasoning is easy to supply. If a self is partless, the internal organ cannot be conjoined with different parts of a self, and so, a self cannot produce different kinds of minds when the internal organ is conjoined with different parts of a self. Therefore, from (I) and (II) he would have us infer that (III) different kinds of minds do not arise from a self when the internal organ is conjoined with different parts of a self. Since (III) is the contradictory of their claim that different kinds of minds arise from a self when the internal organ is conjoined with different parts of the self, Vasubandhu believes, the reply from partial conjunctions fails to overturn the root objection.

But even if the Nyāya-Vaiśeṣikas abandon their view that a self is partless, according to Vasubandhu, a problem arises, since they must agree that (IV) if a self has parts, its parts are not different from one another. Why Vasubandhu thinks that they must agree to (IV) is not clear, since they deny that a self has parts. Perhaps the reasoning is that since the self pervades the body and the body has parts, the self may be said to have parts in dependence upon the parts of the body it pervades. But if a self has parts in this extended sense, its parts will not really be different from one another. Vasubandhu also assumes that the Nyāya-Vaiśeṣikas believe that (V) the internal organ is not different. The meaning of (V) seems to be that the internal organ does not change even if it were to conjoin with different parts of a self. Vasubandhu believes that (VI) if the parts of a self are not different from one another and the internal organ is not different, then the conjunction of an internal organ with different parts of a self cannot be different. The idea seems to be that if an internal organ were to conjoin with different parts of a self, the conjunction in each case would be different, which is impossible if the parts of the self are not different and the internal organ is not different. Therefore, from (IV), (V), and (VI)

Vasubandhu would have us infer that (VII) if a self has parts, then the conjunction of an internal organ with different parts of a self cannot be different. According to the Nyāya-Vaiśeṣikas themselves, (VIII) if the conjunction of an internal organ with different parts of a self cannot be different, then different kinds of minds do not arise from a self when an internal organ is conjoined with different parts of a self. Therefore, from (VII) and (VIII) we may infer that (IX) if a self has parts, different kinds of minds do not arise from a self when an internal organ is conjoined with different parts of a self. Hence, regardless whether a self is or is not partless, the reply from partial conjunctions cannot overturn the root objection.

The weakest part of this objection, if it has one, might be (VIII), since it presupposes that the only way in which different kinds of minds arise from a self when an internal organ is conjoined with different parts of a self is if in each case the conjunction is different. That the Nyāya-Vaiśeṣikas would accept this presupposition is implied by their earlier claim that different kinds of minds are produced by a self when the self is differently conjoined with the internal organ.

The rejection of the protest that different cognitions in fact arise

The Nyāya-Vaiśeṣikas, I believe, are now made to protest that since the cognitions that arise from the conjunction of a self with an internal organ are different in kind, the conjunctions themselves must be different. Stcherbatsky and La Vallée Poussin try to make what the Nyāya-Vaiśeṣikas say here into an attempt to ground their view in the doctrine that a cognition (*buddhi*) is an attribute of the self. But how they can make sense of this interpretation escapes me, since a cognition is simply an example of what Vasubandhu has been calling a mind. Not every statement Vasubandhu puts into the mouths of his opponents needs to be a point of doctrine. The more obvious interpretation of the statement made here is that the Nyāya-Vaiśeṣikas are protesting that their account of how different cognitions arise must be true, since different kinds of cognitions do in fact arise. Vasubandhu's response is simply to point out that this protest does not address his root objection to their view, which is that different kinds of minds cannot arise from a conjunction between a self and a mental organ that are permanent phenomena.

The third reply to the root objection: the reply from the influence of different impressions on conjunctions

Although the next move in the argument of the Nyāya-Vaiśeṣikas takes the form of answering the question, "How will these cognitions be different?," the answer in fact constitutes their third reply to the root objection, since a cognition is simply an example of a mind. So the Nyāya-Vaiśeṣikas' third reply to the root objection is that different kinds of minds arise from the conjunction of a self and an internal organ because the conjunctions are influenced by different kinds of impressions. The reply is that since it is true that (I) different kinds of cognitions arise when the conjunction of a self with an internal organ arises under the influence of different kinds of impressions, and that (II) if different kinds of cognitions arise when the conjunction of a self with an internal organ arises under the influence of different kinds of impressions, then the same kinds of cognitions do not always arise, it follows that (III) the same kinds of cognitions do not always arise. This is the third attempt of the Nyāya-Vaiśeṣikas to explain why, even though minds arise from a self when the self and an internal organ are conjoined, the same kinds of minds do not always arise.

Vasubandhu's objection to the reply: the objection from the causal irrelevance of conjunction

The point of Vasubandhu's objection to the Nyāya-Vaiśeṣikas' third reply to the root objection is that if different kinds of impressions influencing the conjunction of a self with an internal organ cause the conjunction to produce different kinds of cognitions, the addition of the conjunction of a self and an internal organ to the causal process explains nothing. So there is no reason to suppose that the conjunction of a self with an internal organ has anything to do with the production of the different kinds of cognitions, since what makes the difference in the resulting cognitions is the influence on minds of the different kinds of impressions. Minds alone produce different kinds of cognitions under the influence of different kinds of impressions, Vasubandhu adds, because there is no perception of a power of a self to produce different kinds of cognitions. For there to be no such perception, presumably, means that there is no perception of a self in which such a power is discriminated and no correct inference to the existence of a self possessed of such a power. Vasubandhu likens the power of a self to produce different kinds of cognitions to the power of a magic formula to cure a disease. What produces the cure is in fact something other than what has been said to do so. Just as a medicine in fact produces the cure, so minds alone, under the influence of different kinds of impressions, produce different kinds of cognitions.

The Tīrthikas' reply to Vasubandhu's objection from the causal irrelevance of conjunction: the reply from the need for an underlying support of cognitions and impressions

At this point in the argument Vasubandhu introduces a reply the Nyāya-Vaiśeṣikas would make to his claim that minds alone may be said to produce different kinds of cognitions under the influence of different kinds of impressions. They argue that minds alone cannot be said to do this, since minds and impressions do not exist unless a self is their underlying support. The reply begins with the claim that a self is the underlying support for minds and impressions. They claim that if the underlying support for minds and impressions does not exist, minds and impressions do not exist, and if minds and impressions do not exist, minds alone may not be said to produce different kinds of cognitions under the influence of different kinds of impressions. But according to Vasubandhu, a self does not exist. Therefore, we may infer, they believe, that the underlying support for minds and impressions does not exist. It follows that since minds and impressions do not exist, minds cannot be said to produce different kinds of cognitions under the influence of different kinds of impressions. Hence, the Nyāya-Vaiśeṣikas imply, their own account of how different kinds of cognitions are produced is to be preferred.

Vasubandhu's objection to the reply from the need for an underlying support for cognitions and impressions: the objection from the lack of physical resistance and a separate place

Vasubandhu's objection to this reply is to assume that if a self is an underlying support for minds and impressions it is an underlying support in the way a wall is an underlying support for a picture or a bowl is an underlying support for fruit. On this basis, he argues that a self is not an underlying support of this sort, since a self does not offer physical resistance to minds or impressions and does not have a place of its own. In this argument, he also assumes that a wall and a bowl underlie and support a picture and fruit, respectively, by offering physical resistance to them and having separate places of their own.

This objection would seem to be based on a conception of an underlying support that was explained by the Nyāya-Vaiśeṣikas by reference to examples of a relation between two different physical entities. The Nyāya-Vaiśeṣikas may have explained these conceptions in this way, but they need not have intended the meaning of the conceptions to be defined by the specific natures of the examples used. That they did not have this intention is shown by the different example they are about to give of the relation between an underlying support and what it underlies and supports.

The Tīrthikas' reply to the objection from the lack of physical resistance and a separate place: the reply from earth as the underlying support of its sensible qualities

Vasubandhu next considers the Nyāya-Vaiśeṣikas' view that a self is the underlying support for minds and impressions in the way earth is the underlying support for its odors and other sensible qualities. The implication is that because a self is the underlying support for minds and impressions in the way earth is the underlying support for its odors and other sensible qualities, and its odors and these other sensible qualities cannot exist without the earth in which they inhere, so minds and impressions cannot exist without a self in which they inhere. The general doctrine, that certain kinds of attributes must inhere in certain kinds of substances, is not specifically mentioned. The Nyāya-Vaiśeṣikas argue that since earth is the underlying support for its odors and other sensible qualities, the odors and other sensible qualities of earth do not exist if earth does not exist. They believe that since a self is the underlying support for minds and impressions in the way earth is the underlying support for its odors and other sensible qualities and the odors and other sensible qualities of earth do not exist if earth does not exist, then minds and impressions do not exist if a self does not exist. But minds and impressions do exist; so a self must exist. The implication of the account of how a self is an underlying support for minds and impressions is that Vasubandhu's objection misses the mark, since a self is not an underlying support for them in the way a wall is an underlying support for a picture, but in the way earth is an underlying support for its odors and other sensible qualities.

Vasubandhu's objection to the reply from earth as the underlying support of its sensible qualities: the objection from the nonotherness of earth and its sensible qualities

Vasubandhu's objection to the Nyāya-Vaiśeṣikas' account of how a self is an underlying support for minds and impressions is based on the idea that the example of earth as an underlying support for its odors and other sensible qualities may be interpreted as he himself interprets it rather than in the way in which they do. His objection is that, as he interprets the example, it is false that a self is the underlying support for minds and impressions in the way earth is the underlying support for its odors and other sensible qualities. The objection begins with a statement of the Nyāya-Vaiśeṣikas' view that (I) a self is other than minds and impressions. Then he adds that (II) if a self is the underlying support for minds and impressions in the way earth is the underlying support for its odors and other sensible qualities, then earth is other than its odors and other sensible qualities. He then claims that (III) if earth is other than its odors and other sensible qualities, then earth is perceived without its odors and other sensible qualities being perceived, and that (IV) earth is not perceived without its odors and other sensible qualities being perceived. Therefore, from (III) and (IV) we may infer that (V) earth is not other than its odors and other sensible qualities. Therefore, from (I), (II), and (V) we may infer that (VI) a self is not the underlying support for minds and impressions in the way earth is the underlying support for its odors and other sensible qualities. Hence, since the Nyāya-Vaiśeṣikas believe that a self is other than minds and impressions, they cannot employ the analogy to earth and its odors and other sensible qualities to avoid Vasubandhu's reply to their self as an underlying support objection to his view that minds alone, under the influence of different impressions, produce different cognitions.

The Tīrthikas' reply to the objection from the nonotherness of earth and its sensible qualities: the objection from earth's possession of sensible qualities

Why, if earth is not other than its odors and other sensible qualities, the Nyāya-Vaiśeṣikas ask, do we distinguish earth from its odors and other sensible qualities by saying that they are possessed by earth? Is not the possessor of these sensible qualities other than them? According to Vasubandhu himself, moreover, earth is the underlying support for its odors and other sensible qualities. Therefore, earth is the underlying support for its odors and other sensible qualities and it is other than its odors and other sensible qualities. But if earth is the underlying support for its odors and other sensible qualities and it is other than its odors and other sensible qualities, then if a self is the underlying support for minds and impressions in the way that earth is the underlying support for its odors and other sensible qualities, then a self is the underlying support for minds and impressions and it is other than them. Hence, Vasubandhu cannot claim to have shown that a self is not the underlying support for minds and impressions in the way earth is the underlying support for its odors and other sensible qualities.

Vasubandhu's objection to the reply from earth's possession of sensible qualities: the objection from the need to distinguish different collections of sensible qualities

Vasubandhu's objection is that even though we say that odors and other sensible qualities are possessed by earth, we do so in order to distinguish its odors and other sensible qualities from the sensible qualities possessed by fire and other such things, not because earth is other than its odors and other sensible qualities, which are the collection of elements in dependence upon which it is conceived. He believes that since earth, as a conventional reality, is conceived in dependence upon its odors and other sensible qualities, earth is the same in existence as its odors and other sensible qualities. His supporting example implies that he believes that just as we say that a body is possessed by a wooden statue in order to distinguish it from the body possessed by a clay statue, we say that odors and other sensible qualities are possessed by earth in order to distinguish its odors and other sensible qualities from the sensible qualities possessed by fire.

Vasubandhu's objection succeeds to the extent that it shows that our practice of saying that odors and other such "qualities" are possessed by earth does not imply that earth is other than these "qualities." But it does not establish the truth of his own account of this practice. It merely shows us how Vasubandhu himself explains it.

The fourth reply to the root objection: the reply from the influence of different impressions on the self

Vasubandhu now takes up one final reply the Nyāya-Vaiśeṣikas might give to the root objection, which was that if minds arise from a self because the permanent self and permanent internal organ are conjoined, the same kinds of minds will always arise. The reply to this objection is that different kinds of cognitions or minds arise from a self when the self is conjoined with an internal organ because of the influence of different kinds of impressions on the self. The Nyāya-Vaiśeṣikas' third reply to the root objection was that the influence of different kinds of impressions on the conjunction of the self and the internal organ explains why the cognitions that arise from the conjunction are different in kind. This fourth reply is that the influence of different kinds of impressions on the self conjoined with an internal organ explains why the cognitions that arise from the conjunction are different in kind.

Vasubandhu's objection to the reply from the influence of different impressions on the self: the objection from the simultaneous production of different cognitions

Vasubandhu objects that the fourth reply to the root objection has the consequence that the different kinds of cognitions would arise simultaneously, since a self is a permanent phenomenon and the different kinds of impressions under whose influence cognitions arise from the self are always present in the self. The different kinds of impressions would always be present in the self, Vasubandhu believes, since they are the seeds planted in the self by prior minds of different kinds and these seeds are reproduced from moment to moment until the conditions are present for them to produce their own kinds of results. The Nyāya-Vaiśeṣikas' fourth reply to the root objection was that (I) when the self is conjoined with an internal organ different kinds of cognitions arise from a self because the self is under the influence of different kinds of impressions present in the self. Vasubandhu contends that the Nyāya-Vaiśeṣikas themselves believe that (II) all of the different kinds of impressions are always present in the self. But in that case, Vasubandhu believes, (III) if when the self is conjoined with an internal organ different kinds of cognitions arise from a self because the self is under the influence of different kinds of impressions present in the self, and all of the different kinds of impressions are always present in the self, then all of the different kinds of cognitions arise simultaneously. But the Nyāya-Vaiśeṣikas agree that (IV) all of the different kinds of cognitions do not arise simultaneously. Therefore, from (I), (II), (III), and (IV) we may infer that (V) different kinds of cognitions do not arise from a self because a self is under the influence of different kinds of impressions present in the self. Hence, the reply from the influence of different impressions on a self may be rejected.

The Tīrthikas' reply to the objection from the simultaneous production of different cognitions: the reply from the influence of a stronger impression

But is the objection from the simultaneous production of different cognitions conclusive? Vasubandhu takes up a possible Nyāya-Vaiśeṣika reply. It consists of an account of why, although different kinds of impressions are always present in the self, all of the different kinds of cognitions are not produced simultaneously. The reply begins with the same two premises with which Vasubandhu's objection began, which are that (I) when the self is conjoined with an internal organ different kinds of cognitions arise from a self because the self is under the influence of different kinds of impressions present in the self, and that (II) different kinds of impressions are always present in the self. But now they add the consideration that (III) a stronger impression present in the self blocks the influence of the others. The Nyāya-Vaiśeṣikas claim that (IV) if different kinds of impressions are always present in the self and a stronger impression present in the self blocks the influence of the others, then different kinds of cognitions do not simultaneously arise from a self. Therefore, from (II), (III), and (IV) we may infer that (V) different kinds of cognitions do not simultaneously arise from a self. Hence, Vasubandhu's objection is not valid.

Vasubandhu's objection to the reply from the influence of a stronger impression: the objection from the continuous production of the same cognition

Vasubandhu's objection to their reply is to argue that if a stronger impression blocks the influence of the others, then since the stronger impression and the other impressions are always present in the self, the same kinds of cognitions will always arise from the self; for a stronger impression will always give rise to its own kind of cognition. According to the Nyāya-Vaiśeṣikas, (I) a stronger impression present in the self blocks the influence of the others. But (II) both a stronger impression and the other impressions are always present in the self, and surely it is true that (III) if a stronger impression present in the self blocks the influence of the others and both the stronger impression and the other impressions are always present in the self, then the same kinds of cognitions always arise from the self. Therefore, from (I), (II), and (III) we may infer that (IV) the same kinds of cognition always arise from the self. But (V) if the same kinds of cognitions always arise from the self, then when the self is conjoined with an internal organ different kinds of cognitions do not arise from a self because the self is under the influence of different kinds of impressions present in the self. Therefore, from (IV) and (V) we may infer that (V) when the self is conjoined with an internal organ different kinds of cognitions do not arise from a self under the influence of different kinds of impressions present in the self.

The Tīrthikas' nature of impressions reply to the objection from continuous production of the same cognitions, and Vasubandhu's objection to the reply: the objection from the subsequent causal irrelevance of the self

Vasubandhu next considers the reply that a stronger impression does not always produce the same kind of cognition because it is the nature of impressions to differ from moment to moment. He first points out that if it is the nature of impressions to produce different kinds of cognitions from moment to moment, then when a self is conjoined with an internal organ different kinds of cognitions do not arise from a self because the self is under the influence of different kinds of impressions present in the self. Moreover, he says, if it is the nature of impressions to produce different kinds of cognitions from moment to moment, then when a self is conjoined with an internal organ different kinds of cognitions do not arise from a self because the self is under the influence of different kinds of impressions present in the self. Therefore, he concludes, when a self is conjoined with an internal organ, different kinds of cognitions do not arise from a self because the self is under the influence of different kinds of impressions present in the self. Hence, Vasubandhu believes that the Nyāya-Vaiśeṣikas cannot use the view that it is the nature of impressions to differ from moment to moment to avoid his objection from the continuous production of the same cognition.

Appraisal of the exchange between Vasubandhu and the Nyāya-Vaiśeṣikas

A review of this long and complicated exchange raises two important questions. First, since Vasubandhu's root objection to the Nyāya-Vaiśeṣikas' account of how a self produces minds depends on his rejection of their view that the conjunction of a self with an internal organ can come to be and pass away without affecting their permanence, it fails to show that the consequence of the same kinds of minds always arising from a self follows from views they themselves accept. Hence, it is revealing that Vasubandhu's first objection to their first reply, which is that minds different in kind arise because the conjunctions of a self with an internal organ are different, is to reject their view that conjunctions, as relational attributes, are not the same in existence as the things conjoined, simply by saying that they have not proved that conjunctions are other than the things conjoined. He has not argued, as he needs to do if he is to reject their view on proper grounds, that such conjunctions are the same in existence as the things conjoined. So his rejection of their reply is based on a view that the Nyāya-Vaiśeṣikas themselves do not accept. If they were to speak for themselves, we can be sure, they would have demanded that Vasubandhu prove that such conjunctions are the same in existence as the things conjoined. How he could do this on the basis of views they themselves accept is not clear.

The second question raised by the exchange is why the Nyāya-Vaiśeṣikas offer, or at least are made to offer, a series of replies to the root objection, when in fact their initial reply is very likely the actual reply they would give and would not relinquish. So what is the point of the lengthy exchange? My guess is that its point is to parade in review possible replies the Nyāya-Vaiśeṣikas might make to the root objection so that Vasubandhu's own disciples may come to understand the various theses of the Nyāya-Vaiśeṣikas' own theories of persons and cognition with which these replies are inconsistent and with which the theses of Vasubandhu's own philosophy are inconsistent. In this way, he may have thought that his disciples could come to know how and why their theses are different from those of the Nyāya-Vaiśeṣikas. Vasubandhu's treatment of the theses of the Nyāya-Vaiśeṣikas in this exchange, from this point of view, would seem to be comparable to his treatment of the Pudgalavādins' theses in the exchanges in Sections 2 and 3 of the "Refutation."

§ 4.8 The Tīrthikas' objection, that a self is needed as an underlying support for minds, and Vasubandhu's reply

In Section 4.8, Vasubandhu introduces one of the Nyāya-Vaiśeṣikas' most commonly used arguments for the existence of a self under the guise of an objection to his theory of persons. This is the argument that minds are attributes (*gūṇa*-s) that require for their own existence a substance (*dravya*) in which to inhere and that they are not in any substance other than selves.

The Nyāya-Vaiśeṣikas' argument relies heavily upon the acceptance of their views that there are a certain number of permanent substances of different sorts in which attributes inhere and that minds cannot inhere in any of the other known kinds of substances. For this reason, it seems, Vasubandhu simply objects that the Nyāya-Vaiśeṣikas have not independently established the existence of attributes, that his own theory is that all phenomena are substances, and that the existence of an underlying support for attributes has already been rejected. When Vasubandhu says that they have not established the existence of attributes, he means the existence of attributes that are not the same in existence as the things to which they belong. He also believes that they cannot establish the existence of such attributes. But he need not attempt to demonstrate that such attributes cannot exist, since he assumes that the burden of proof falls on those who champion their existence. His use of the quotation from the sūtras, moreover, cannot be meant to refute the view that attributes exist, since the Nyāya-Vaiśeṣikas do not accept the authority of the sūtras. Nor, for the same reason, is his use of the quotation meant to prove to them that all phenomena are substances. His use of the quotation, apparently, is simply to explain why he himself believes that all phenomena are substances.

The quotation Vasubandhu uses to explain why, as a Buddhist, he holds the view that all phenomena are substances requires some explanation. He cannot mean to imply that there are no phenomena that are substantially established realities. The quotation, therefore, seems in fact to be used to explain why Vasubandhu accepts the thesis that the world is ultimately composed of causally conditioned phenomena, which are substances or collections of substances, and causally unconditioned phenomena, which are substances. Although in the passage only the five uncontaminated aggregates and nirvāṇa are mentioned, they are the only substances mentioned because the fruits of spiritual practice are being enumerated. But the clear implication is that the five contaminated aggregates and causally unconditioned phenomena other than nirvāṇa itself are also substances. It would seem, therefore, that in this passage Vasubandhu agrees with the Vaibhāṣikas' view that all of these phenomena are substances. In the *Commentary*, where Vasubandhu comments on verse 55 of Book II of the *Treasury*, he represents a dispute between the Vaibhāṣikas and the Sautrāntikas concerning whether or not causally unconditioned phenomena exist in the sense of performing a function. Vasubandhu appears there to side with the Sautrāntikas' view that they do not exist in this way, but here in the "Refutation" he is clearly siding with the Vaibhāṣikas, since if nirvāṇa is to be counted as a substance, it surely performs a function. The function it performs, we may conjecture, is that of providing a metaphysical basis for the statement of the ultimate goal of Buddhist practice. The five uncontaminated aggregates would seem to be the fruits of spiritual practice during the life in which a nirvāṇa with remainder is reached, and nirvāṇa without remainder would seem to be what is here simply called nirvāṇa.

When Vasubandhu says that he has already subjected the notion of an underlying support to analysis, he seems to be referring to his rejection of the existence of an underlying support for attributes in Section 4.7.1, when he was rejecting the Nyāya-Vaiśeṣika views that minds and impressions need an underlying support in which to inhere and that the underlying support for them is the self. Vasubandhu objected that minds and impressions do not need a self as an underlying support in which to inhere either in the sense that a bowl is an underlying support for fruit, since the self offers no physical resistance to them and does not exist in a different place, or in the sense that earth is an underlying support for its odors, since earth is not other than its odors.

§ 4.9 The Tīrthikas' objection, that without a self there is nothing for whose sake action is undertaken, and Vasubandhu's reply

In Section 4.9, the Nyāya-Vaiśeṣikas argue that the denial of the existence of a self implies that there is nothing for whose sake an action is undertaken. It is being assumed, as the examples make clear, that the reason we undertake an action is self-interest and that without a self there can be no self-interest. No account is provided of why the self in whose interest an action is undertaken is a person that is other than a collection of aggregates. The account, presumably, is that only if we are other than a collection of aggregates, which is momentary in existence, can what we do at one time have an effect on us at another time, and when we act in our own interest we intend to do what will have an effect on us at a later time. The Nyāya-Vaiśeṣikas believe that we must be permanent entities if we are to benefit from or be harmed by our actions. The usual Buddhist objection to this account is that if we are permanent entities we cannot benefit from or be harmed by our actions, since permanent entities cannot change.

Are the Nyāya-Vaiśeṣikas assuming that we act only out of self-interest? Surely not. Since, according to the law of actions and their results, an action performed in the interest of another is also in one's own interest, and the Nyāya-Vaiśeṣikas accept this law, they surely believe that some actions are undertaken in the interest of others. Why then do they assume that without self-interest there is no reason to undertake an action? Perhaps they believe that if there can be no reason to undertake an action in one's own interest, there can be no reason to undertake an action in the interest of another, since action undertaken in the interest of another is not possible unless action can be undertaken in the interest of oneself. If this is their view, Vasubandhu, at least from a conventional point of view, would agree. Moreover, Vasubandhu and the Nyāya-Vaiśeṣikas seem to agree that what acts for the sake of being happy and avoiding suffering, is the object of the mind that conceives an "I." That about which they do not agree is whether this object is the same in existence as a self or is the same in existence as a collection of aggregates.

Since the Nyāya-Vaiśeṣikas are not made to explain why, if there is no self, there is nothing for whose sake an action is undertaken, the question of whether or not a person is a permanent entity is not raised. Instead,

Vasubandhu supposes that the objection is that the object of the mind that conceives an "I" must be a self, since there is nothing else in whose interest an action is undertaken. So Vasubandhu's reply to this argument is simply to state that that for whose sake an action is undertaken is known to be the same in existence as a collection of aggregates, since it is to the aggregates in this collection that we are attached when we act out of self-interest, and it cannot be attachment to a self, since attributes of the body are ascribed to us and such attributes cannot be ascribed to a self, which is other than the body.

Vasubandhu assumes that (I) that in whose interest an action is undertaken is that to which there is attachment. Since in this case, Vasubandhu claims, attachment is attachment to a collection of aggregates, (II) that to which there is attachment is the same in existence as a collection of aggregates. Therefore, from (I) and (II) we may infer that (III) that in whose interest action is undertaken is the same in existence as a collection of aggregates. But if it is the same in existence as a collection of aggregates, it is not a self. Moreover, Vasubandhu adds, (VI) if we are selves, the attributes of a body are not ascribed to us. Since (VII) the attributes of a body are ascribed to us, it follows that (VIII) we are not selves.

In Section 4.9.1 the Nyāya-Vaiśeṣikas raise an objection to Vasubandhu's reply. I shall discuss that objection in my commentary on that section. But Vasubandhu's use of the claim, that that to which there is attachment is the same in existence as a collection of aggregates, raises a question we need to discuss before we deal with their own. The question arises because Vasubandhu himself believes that one of the causes of suffering is attachment to a self. Hence, it appears that he must acknowledge that there is attachment both to a collection of aggregates, which is the same in existence as the object of the mind that conceives an "I," and to a self, which is not, and that it is for the sake of both a collection of aggregates and a self that we act. But how is attachment to a collection of aggregates related to attachment to a self?

Vasubandhu's view, surely, is that there is no attachment to a collection of aggregates if it is not believed that they belong to a self. In fact, Vasubandhu would not want to say that there is attachment to a collection of aggregates independently of attachment to a self, since a separate attachment to a collection of aggregates would perpetuate our rebirth in saṃsāra. Moreover, were there to be attachment to a collection of aggregates without attachment to a self, we would not have any reason to seek nirvāṇa, which involves the cessation of the continuum of aggregates. What then is implied by Vasubandhu's claim that that for whose sake we act is a collection of aggregates because it is to a collection of aggregates rather than to a self that we are attached?

The claim cannot imply that we are attached to a collection of aggregates rather than to a self and act for its sake rather than for the sake of a self. What Vasubandhu must mean is that since a collection of aggregates exists and a self does not, the attachment, in the end, is to the collection of aggregates. What he does not say, but should have said to make his point clear, is that, from a conventional point of view, we act out of self-interest, and that, since there is no self, and we are the same in existence as a collection of aggregates, which does exist, that in whose interest we act is the same in existence as a collection of aggregates rather than a self. This is a reply to the Nyāya-Vaiśeṣikas' charge that there is nothing in whose self-interest action is undertaken if there is no self. What he does not make clear is that self-interested action is action undertaken for the sake of the conventionally real person, and that we need not assume the existence of a self in order to explain such action.

Another version of the Nyāya-Vaiśeṣikas' argument is that the denial of the existence of a self implies that there is nothing for whose sake an action is undertaken because we cannot act out of self-interest unless we remain the same over time and we cannot remain the same over time unless there is a self. Perhaps he ignores this way of understanding the argument because he thinks that, so understood, the issue it raises has already been discussed in Section 4.1.1, which concerned the objection that one person could remember an object perceived by another if memories are produced by minds and there is no self. If the Nyāya-Vaiśeṣika argument were given this second interpretation, his reply, as in Section 4.1.1, would simply be to explain the convention that persons seek their own good in the future because they conceive themselves to be the same over time in dependence upon the fact that the aggregates in the collection in dependence upon which they are conceived exists in an unbroken causal continuum.

Vasubandhu's account of why we assume and say we are the same over time does not imply that we should or even can abandon the convention that we are rational to act in our own self-interest. For he believes that, even though the aggregates in dependence upon which we conceive ourselves in the present and the aggregates in dependence upon which we conceive ourselves in the future are other than one another, he would reject a theory of rational action or a theory of moral reasons formulated on this basis. For he believes that our conventional conception of ourselves, albeit deceptive concerning our mode of identity over time, is what enables us to achieve nirvāṇa by providing conventionally valid reasons for seeking this goal. Practical rationality and morality, he believes, are conventional realities. The theory of practical rationality he accepts is simply a conventionalist form of the theory that actions performed for the sake of others are in our own interest, and therefore it is rational to act for the sake of others. So-called impersonal theories of rational action and moral reasons, from Vasubandhu's perspective, would not only be irrelevant to our attempts to achieve freedom from suffering, but would also undermine the initial motivation we would have for making the attempt. For until we have become Arhats, our actual motivation is in fact at least in part egoistic, and our practice of morality, conventionally understood as the practice of action that does not harm others, is ultimately pursued for the sake of the elimination of our own suffering. What would be our motivation for action once we become Arhats? According to Vasubandhu, I believe, it would be to free others from their suffering out of compassion developed on the path.

§ 4.9.1 *The Tīrthikas' objection, from the figurative application of "I" to the body, and Vasubandhu's reply*

In Section 4.9.1 the Nyāya-Vaiśeṣikas are made to object that the fact, that the attributes of the body are ascribed to the object of the mind that conceives an "I," cannot be used to support Vasubandhu's denial that the object of this mind is a self. The reason it cannot be so used, they object, is that in "I am fair-skinned," etc. a name for a self is applied in a figurative way to the body because the body acts on behalf of a self in much the same way that in "My servant is I myself" the master of the servant figuratively applies "I" to the servant because he acts on behalf of the master. A figurative application of a name, apparently, is the application of the name of one thing to a second because of some special relation it has to the first. It is a secondary application of a name, as opposed to a primary application. Presumably, the Nyāya-Vaiśeṣikas believe that in "I possess a body" the "I" has a primary application, since it is used to refer to a self. This account of why we ascribe physical attributes to ourselves is employed in all the Hindu philosophical schools in which the separate substance theory of persons is held.

Vasubandhu replies that even if a name for a self is figuratively applied to a body that acts on its behalf, a name for a self is not applied to the object of the mind that conceives an "I." In this reply, he is simply challenging the assumption upon which the objection is predicated. It cannot be proved that "I" in "I am fair-skinned," etc. is being figuratively applied to a body that acts on behalf of a self unless it is first proved that "I" is a name for a self, and this proof has not been presented. Hence, the Nyāya-Vaiśeṣikas' objection, he believes, fails.

Buddhists do not find it necessary to distinguish primary and secondary uses of "I" in order to explain how it is possible to ascribe both the attributes of our bodies and the possession of bodies to ourselves. For they believe that the object of the mind that conceives an "I" is the conventionally real person and that this object is neither other than nor the same in existence as its body and mind, individually considered. In Section 2.5.1, for instance, Vasubandhu assumes not only that we are not other than collections of aggregates, but also that we are not the same in existence as each of the aggregates in the collection. But then, since we are not other than our bodies and minds, Buddhists can say, we can ascribe their attributes to ourselves, and since we are not the same in existence as either of them, individually considered, we can ascribe the possession of bodies and minds to ourselves. Hence, they can say that there is no ambiguity in the application of "I" in these different cases, since we are neither other than our bodies and minds nor the same as each of them. In this way, the Buddhists manage, by means of their theories of persons, to avoid the view that "I" has primary and secondary uses. The Nyāya-Vaiśeṣikas must resort to the fiction of primary and secondary uses of the first-person singular pronoun.

§ 4.9.2 *The Tīrthikas' objection, that Vasubandhu's reply does not enable him to explain why "I" is not applied to the bodies of others, and his explanation of why it is not applied to the bodies of others*

In Section 4.9.2 Vasubandhu has the Nyāya-Vaiśeṣikas object to Vasubandhu's reply to their objection in Section 4.9.1. They object that if, when a person says, "I am fair-skinned," the objective support for the mind that conceives an "I" is simply a body, there is no way to explain why "I" is applied to the body of the person that uttered the statement rather than to the body of someone else. (This claim is made, in fact, in the *Nyāya Sūtras*, Book III, Part II, verse 4.) But they have the explanation that "I" is applied figuratively only to the body used by the particular self that utters the statement. Vasubandhu then supplies an explanation and thereby implies that their objection fails. His explanation is that the body to which "I" is applied differs from a body to which it is not applied because the first body is included in the same causal continuum of aggregates in which the mind that conceives the "I" is included, while the second body is not. The success of this objection, of course, depends on whether or not Vasubandhu can distinguish a causal continuum of aggregates that includes the mind that conceives the "I" from one that does not without making reference to a self. He makes no attempt to do this.

Although Vasubandhu says that the mind that conceives an "I" is a habit that exists in beginningless saṃsāra, I take this to mean that it arises as a result of a mental habit, in the beginningless continuum of a collection of contaminated aggregates to conceive an "I," and by means of conceiving an "I," to create the appearance of a self. Vasubandhu's explanation of why the bodies of others are not objective causes of the minds that conceive an "I" would seem to be a genuine alternative to the explanation offered by the Nyāya-Vaiśeṣikas.

§ 4.10 The Tīrthikas' objection, that without a self to possess it there can be no mind that conceives an "I," and Vasubandhu's reply

In Section 4.10 the Nyāya-Vaiśeṣikas are made to object that, even if Vasubandhu can explain why the bodies of others are not causes of the minds that conceive an "I," nonetheless, the mind that conceives an "I" cannot exist unless it is possessed by a self. Vasubandhu replies by alluding to his earlier argument that there need be no self to which a memory of an object belongs, since a memory is caused to arise by something other than a self. The reference is to Section 4.1, in which the cause of a memory is said to be a special kind of mind produced by a prior discrimination of the object. The cause of the mind that conceives an "I," he says, is a contaminated mind that has as its object its own continuum and arises in dependence upon a previous mind that conceives an "I." What exactly this statement means is not clear. What is this contaminated mind? By what is it contaminated? Why is this contaminated mind said to have its own causal continuum for its object? And how and why does this contaminated mind arise from previous minds that conceive an "I"?

If we were to answer the first, second, and fourth of these questions on the basis of an extrapolation from the paraphrase-like translations of Stcherbatsky and de La Vallée Poussin, we might say that the contaminated mind is itself just a previous mind that conceives an "I," that its contamination is that it conceives an "I," that the contaminated mind itself arises from previous minds that conceive an "I" because each mind in the continuum of minds arises from the immediately preceding mind, and that all of these minds are contaminated because they conceive an "I." This is a possible interpretation, but I very much doubt that it is correct. For it is not clear to me that when Vasubandhu refers to the contamination of the mind he is referring to the conceiving of an "I." The mind that conceives an "I," in fact, would seem to be the mind that creates the conventionally real person in dependence upon a collection of aggregates, and its contamination to be the mistaken view of a self, which consists in assenting to the false appearance created by the conceiving of an "I." So we can agree that Vasubandhu means that the mind from which the mind that conceives an "I" arises is a mind that conceives an "I," but we should probably not agree that he means that its contamination consists in conceiving an "I," but in being contaminated by the mistaken view of a self.

Vasubandhu, the Pudgalavādins, and Candrakīrti, I believe, think that the mistaken view of a self is the assent the mind gives to the false appearance of the "I" it creates when it conceives an "I" in dependence upon a collection of aggregates. The false appearance of an "I" this mind creates, according to Vasubandhu and the Pudgalavādins, is that of possessing an identity independently of the collection of aggregates, and according to

Candrakīrti, is that of possessing independent reality. The mind's assent to the false appearance of the "I" is its beginningless contamination, and only when the mind is freed from its assent to this false appearance will the suffering caused by the assent be eliminated. Vasubandhu believes, as other Buddhists do, that it is possible, without eliminating the mind that conceives the "I," to purge the mind's assent to the false appearance of the "I" it creates when it conceives the "I." So three of my initial questions have in effect been answered. The mind that is contaminated is the mind that conceives an "I," its contamination is the mistaken view of a self, and each of these contaminated minds has arisen in dependence upon its immediate predecessor.

The third question I asked was: why does Vasubandhu say that the object of the contaminated mind is the continuum of aggregates in which this mind is present? First of all, it seems clear that a continuum of aggregates is not what the object of this mind is; nor is a collection of aggregates that exists in a causal continuum what the object of this mind is. The object of the mind that conceives an "I" is the conventionally real person. When Vasubandhu's view is more carefully stated, it is that the object of the contaminated mind is the same in existence as the collection of aggregates that exist in a causal continuum. This collection of aggregates is the causal basis of the conception of a person, not the person itself. Consequently, Vasubandhu, I believe, is speaking loosely when he says that the continuum of aggregates is the object of the contaminated mind.

Vasubandhu's objection to the Nyāya-Vaiśeṣikas' argument does seem to show that there need be no self that possesses a mind that conceives an "I" insofar as it provides an alternative explanation of how this mind arises. What he might have added, but does not, is that the appearance of this mind being possessed by a self is created by the mind itself when it conceives an "I." That there is no owner or possessor of this mind that can be identified independently of aggregates, Vasubandhu is convinced, is shown by the fact that when in meditation we search for a self among the phenomena in dependence upon which we conceive ourselves, it cannot be found.

§ 4.11 The Tīrthikas' objection, that feelings cannot exist unless there is a self as an underlying support in which they arise, and Vasubandhu's reply

The Nyāya-Vaiśeṣikas object that since pleasure and pain require an underlying support in which they come to be and only a self can be such a support, there must be a self. This argument is similar to the argument presented in Section 4.8, where it was said that a memory and other forms of cognition require the existence of a self as an underlying support. In Section 4.11 the question raised concerns where such minds could come to be, as opposed to where they could exist, and the only minds mentioned are pleasure and pain. Instead of repeating his argument in Section 4.8, that the Nyāya-Vaiśeṣikas have not established that the existence of minds requires the existence of a self as an underlying support in which they exist, here in Section 4.11 he offers an alternative account of the underlying support in which pleasure and pain come to be. His view is simply that they come to be in the six internal bases of cognition in the sense in which flowers come to be in a tree and fruit comes to be in a garden. The six internal bases of perception are the six organs of perception, the last of which, the mental organ, is consciousness itself. As opposed to the Nyāya-Vaiśeṣika view, according to which the underlying support in which feelings come to be is a substance, he proposes that they come to be in the collection of aggregates with which they arise in the same causal continuum. The point is basically the same as that made in Section 4.7.1, where Vasubandhu says that odors are in earth, which, as an underlying support for odors, is not other than its odors. Earth is the same in existence as a collection of odors and other sensible qualities, just as we are the same in existence as collections of aggregates, including pleasure and pain, which come to be in us, but not as in a substance.

§ 4.12 The Tīrthikas' objection, that without a self there is no agent of actions or subject that experiences their results

In Section 4.12 the Nyāya-Vaiśeṣikas say that the existence of a self cannot be denied because if it does not exist, there is no agent of actions or subject that experiences the results of actions. They assume that this is an unacceptable consequence of the denial, since they believe that the law of actions and their results, which Vasubandhu accepts as true, requires the existence of an agent of actions that experiences the results of its actions. From a conventional point of view, Vasubandhu thinks, there is an agent of actions and a subject that experiences the results of actions, since to deny this, from that point of view, undermines the view that there is a law of actions and their results. From an ultimate point of view, he believes, there is no agent of actions or subject that experiences their results. The Nyāya-Vaiśeṣikas would seem to be arguing that unless a self exists, there would not be, even from a conventional point of view, an agent of actions or subject that experiences their results.

In his reply to this objection, of course, Vasubandhu needs to show that the non-existence of a self does not imply that there is, even from a conventional point of view, no agent of actions or subject that experiences the results of actions. He begins by asking for definitions of an agent of actions and a subject that experiences their results. After rejecting their attempt to define them by the use of mere synonyms, he represents the Nyāya-Vaiśeṣikas as adopting a definition of an agent given by Pāṇini, the grammarian, and adopted by the Lakṣaṇikas. The definition, as stated, is that an agent is independent. The word translated as "independent" is *svātantra*, which literally means "self-powered." No explanation is provided of what it means to say that an agent is defined as independent or of how this definition is supposed to lend support to the argument for the existence of a self. Hence, we need to reconstruct what exactly the definition means and what it contributes to their objection to the denial of the existence of a self.

If the definition is to be used to support the objection, that there is, even from a conventional point of view, no agent of actions unless there is a self, it means, I believe, that an agent of actions is independent *of causes and conditions*. I express this idea in the Translation as the view that an agent of actions is causally independent. The view that an agent of actions is causally independent is not by itself *a definition* of an agent of actions, but at best a statement of what differentiates an agent of actions from other things in the same genus. To obtain a complete definition we need to add to this statement of the differentia of an agent of actions a reference to the genus to which an agent of actions belongs. This genus, we may be sure, is that of being a cause of actions. Hence, a full statement of the definition of an agent of actions used by the Nyāya-Vaiśeṣikas is that it is a causally independent cause of actions. The point of the definition in this way becomes clear: it is to distinguish an agent of actions from other kinds of causes of actions by saying that it is a causally independent cause. The other causes of actions, the Nyāya-Vaiśeṣikas believe, are themselves caused, as for instance the cognitions, desires, aversions, and volitions in dependence upon which an agent of actions causes bodily motions.

What then of the Nyāya-Vaiśeṣikas' example of the causal independence of Devadatta being recognized by the world? What does this contribute to their argument? It would appear that it is used to show that the definition of an agent of actions as a causally independent cause of actions is the one accepted by the world. In other words, it is used to show that, even from a conventional point of view, an agent is a causally independent cause of actions. Devadatta is recognized by the world to be a causally independent cause of actions, they say, because it is said in the world that Devadatta prays, eats, walks, etc. It is assumed that Devadatta is in fact the sort of thing the world recognizes to be an agent of the actions of praying, eating, walking, etc.

But how does the Nyāya-Vaiśeṣikas' use of this definition show that a self must exist? The argument for the conclusion that a self exists requires that we add to the premises, that an agent of actions exists by convention and that an agent of actions, by convention, is a causally independent cause of actions, the premise that a causally independent cause of actions is a self. Hence, we may suppose that the Nyāya-Vaiśeṣikas are making this assumption. So their argument begins with the assumption that (I) an agent of actions exists. Vasubandhu himself, they assume, must accept the truth of (I) from the conventional point of view. Then the Nyāya-Vaiśeṣikas explicitly call upon Pāṇini's definition of an agent of actions, which we may elaborate as the thesis that (II) to be an agent of actions is to be a causally independent cause of actions. In support of the view that (II) is a definition of an agent of actions accepted from the conventional point of view, they claim that (III) the world recognizes the causal independence of Devadatta in relation to his being a cause of praying, eating, walking, and so on. If the Nyāya-Vaiśeṣikas are to argue, on this basis, that a self exists, they must be assuming that (IV) if the world recognizes the causal independence of Devadatta in relation to his being a cause of praying, eating, walking, and so on, a causally independent cause of actions exists. Therefore, from (I), (II), (III), and (IV) it may be inferred that (V) a causally independent cause of actions exists. At this point, it is assumed that (VI) a causally independent cause of actions is a self. In other words, it is assumed that a causally independent cause of actions is a substance that exists apart from a collection of aggregates. Therefore, from (V) and (VI) we may infer that (VII) a self exists. Hence, they believe, if there is an agent of actions, there must be a self.

§ 4.12.1 *Vasubandhu's reply to the objection that the existence of a self cannot be denied because a self is needed as an agent of actions*

Vasubandhu's first reply to the objection, that there can be no agent of actions if there is no self, is an attempt to show that what the world recognizes about Devadatta cannot be used in the argument to prove that a self exists. He argues that it cannot be assumed, without begging the question, that Devadatta is the same in existence as a self, since the assumption occurs in an argument used to establish the existence of a self. On the other hand, if this Devadatta is assumed to be the same in existence as a collection of aggregates, then a collection of aggregates rather than a self is what is conceived as an agent of actions, in which case it is not true that a causally independent cause of actions exists because the world recognizes the causal independence of Devadatta in relation to his being a cause of praying, eating, walking, and so on. It is not true because there is no causal independence of Devadatta in relation to his being a cause of praying, eating, walking, etc.

This first reply seems to ignore the point that in the Nyāya-Vaiśeṣikas' argument "Devadatta" is not being used to refer either to a self or to a collection of aggregates, but to what by convention the world calls an agent, whatever an agent might be from an ultimate point of view. Vasubandhu's error here is like the error he committed when he claimed in Section 3.4.2 that the Pudgalavādins could not use the example of a grammarian coming to be to explain what they meant by "coming to be," since the grammarian is either an independently existent inexplicable person or a collection of aggregates, and it cannot be an independently existent inexplicable person, which would beg the question of the independent existence of an inexplicable person, and cannot be a collection of aggregates, in which case the example cannot be used to argue that a person comes to be by acquiring new aggregates. The error in both cases is that of interpreting an appeal to what is conventionally believed as an appeal to what ultimately exists.

What Vasubandhu needs to argue here, and perhaps meant to argue, is that it cannot be inferred, from the world's recognition of Devadatta as a causally independent cause of actions, that Devadatta is in fact a causally independent cause of actions. Even if a causally independent cause of actions is recognized by the world, why should we believe that what the world recognizes is what ultimately exists? The point is that the Nyāya-Vaiśeṣikas cannot establish the ultimate existence of an agent simply on the ground that the world believes that it exists.

Vasubandhu next simply states that there is no causally independent cause of actions. Actions of body and speech, he says, arise from actions of the mind, which arise from other phenomena that arise from other phenomena, and so on. He then states the thesis that underlies his denial of the existence of a causally independent cause of actions: all things, which include causes, arise in dependence upon causal conditions. He claims that (I) every action is an action of either body, speech, or mind, that (II) an action of body arises in dependence upon an action of mind, that (III) an action of speech arises in dependence upon an action of mind, and that (IV) an action of mind arises in dependence upon a mind that arises in dependence upon another mind, and so on. Therefore, from (I), (II), (III), and (IV) we may infer that (V) every action arises in dependence upon a mind that arises in dependence upon another mind, and so on. He next points out that (VI) if every action arises in dependence upon a mind that arises in dependence upon another mind, and so on, then a causally independent cause of actions does not exist. Therefore, from (V) and (VI) we may infer that (VII) a causally independent cause of actions does not exist. Vasubandhu then notes that (VII) also follows from the general principle that all things, which include causes, exist in dependence upon causal conditions.

Vasubandhu's denial of causally independent causes raises a question every thoughtful Buddhist sooner or later ponders. If all causes of actions are themselves caused and there is no self that, as a causally independent cause of actions, intervenes in the chain of causes of our actions, how is it possible for us to use our knowledge of the law of actions and their results to our advantage? Is not what we do determined already by our past actions, and those by actions even earlier in the causal continuum of the collection of aggregates in dependence upon which we are conceived, etc.? Although this is not an issue raised by the Nyāya-Vaiśeṣikas, it is an issue for Buddhists who read this text. The Buddhists, it seems, did not discuss the problem. Two questions naturally arise: why is the problem not discussed by Vasubandhu (or by the Indian Buddhists in general) and what would be the Indian Buddhist solution, if any, to the problem?

Vasubandhu next argues that the Nyāya-Vaiśeṣikas have simply assumed, without proof, that a causally independent self can cause actions. But if it is to be established that a self exists, it needs to be proved that a self, as a causally independent entity, can cause actions. "Its causality cannot be assumed," he says. But the Nyāya-Vaiśeṣikas do not in their argument simply assume that a causally independent entity can cause actions, since they argue that it can on the basis of what the world recognizes. What cannot be assumed is that what the world recognizes to be the case is in fact the case.

Vasubandhu's final reply to the objection is to argue that, if there is, from an ultimate point of view, an agent that causes actions, that agent is not a self, but one or more of the causally conditioned causes of actions, since a self that causes actions is not found by perception to exist among their causes. He implies that the causally conditioned causes of actions can be perceived, and so, if they are called agents, the existence of agents of actions is established from an ultimate point of view. He also assumes in this account that causally independent phenomena cannot be perceived. To illustrate how actions arise from their causally conditioned causes he gives an account of how a bodily action arises from its causes. He says that (I) if a causally independent self is a cause of actions, a causally independent self is perceived among the causes of actions, but (II) a causally independent self is not perceived among the causes of actions. Therefore, (III) a causally independent self is not a cause of actions. Moreover, he argues, if (III) is true, and (IV) if a causally independent self is not a cause of actions, and a causally independent self is not an agent of actions, it follows that (V) a causally independent self is not an agent of actions. He then supposes that we assume that (VI) a causally dependent cause of actions is an agent of actions. It is true that (VII) if a causally dependent cause of actions is an agent of actions, a causally dependent cause of actions is perceived among the causes of actions. Therefore, from (VI) and (VII) we may infer that (VIII) a causally dependent cause of action is perceived among the causes of actions. But (IX) if a causally dependent cause of actions can be perceived among the causes of actions, a causally dependent cause of actions exists. Hence, from (VIII) and (IX) we may infer that (X) a causally dependent cause of actions exists. Therefore, from (VII) and (X) we may infer that (XI) an agent of actions exists. So Vasubandhu contends that, even though a self is not an agent of actions, it can be said that an agent of actions exists in ultimate reality.

Vasubandhu presents an account of how an action of body or speech arises in which a self does not play the role of a cause. The cause of an action of body or speech is a prior mind, not a self, as we observe in ourselves: a memory of an object causes a desire for it, this desire being the principal cause of the action by virtue of causing a consideration of how to obtain the object, which in turn causes an effort of the mind to move the body for the sake of satisfying the desire, which effort causes a movement in the wind channels, which in turn causes the bodily action.

§ 4.12.2 *Vasubandhu's reply to the objection that the existence of a self cannot be denied because a self is needed as a subject that experiences the results of actions*

The remainder of Vasubandhu's reply to the Nyāya-Vaiśeṣikas' objection is concerned with the claim that if a self does not exist, there is, from a conventional point of view, no subject that experiences the results of actions. His objection to this claim is abbreviated, and lacks the sophistication of his objection to their claim that if a self does not exist there is, from a conventional point of view, no agent that experiences the results of actions. But the strategy of the objection is the same. The Nyāya-Vaiśeṣikas think that the conventional reality of the experience of suffering as a result of the performance of contaminated actions is not possible unless there exists, in ultimate reality, a self. Vasubandhu asks them in what, from the ultimate point of view, the experience of the results of actions consists, so that he can show that their account does not explain why, from the conventional point of view, there is a subject that experiences the results of actions. Since the result of contaminated actions is suffering, let us take the case of experiencing physical pain as a result of the past performance of contaminated actions. In answer to Vasubandhu's question, the Nyāya-Vaiśeṣikas say, in accord with their view that a self does not really suffer, that it consists in the perception by a self of physical pain in the body. Vasubandhu now need only point out that he has already argued, in effect, that a self cannot be a perceiver, since to be a perceiver it must own or possess a consciousness by means of which it perceives the result of actions and there is no more reason to believe that a self can own or possess a consciousness by means of which it can perceive physical pain in the body than there is reason to believe that a self owns or possesses a memory by means of which it remembers an object. Since this reply is essentially the same as the earlier argument against the existence of an owner or possessor of a memory of an object, we need not discuss it further.

§ 4.13 The Tīrthikas' objection, that the existence of a self is required to explain why beings not in saṃsāra do not accumulate merit and demerit in the way that beings in saṃsāra do, and Vasubandhu's reply

In Section 4.13 the Nyāya-Vaiśeṣikas are made to object to Vasubandhu's denial that a self need exist if there is, by convention, an agent of actions and a subject that experiences the results of actions. If there is no self, they claim, it cannot be explained why a being not in saṃsāra (i.e. a being that is neither an agent of actions nor a subject that experiences the results of its actions) does not accumulate merit and demerit in the way in which a being in saṃsāra does. They do not state their reason for believing that such an explanation cannot be given. Their reason would seem to be their beliefs that beings not in saṃsāra lack a self and only beings in saṃsāra can accumulate merit and demerit. Because they do not state this reason, Vasubandhu need only supply an account of why beings not in saṃsāra do not accumulate merit and demerit without making reference to a self in order to show that their argument fails. His account is that beings not in saṃsāra do not accumulate merit and demerit because they lack the underlying support for the feelings that result from the accumulation of merit and demerit. To forestall the objection that the underlying support for feelings is a self, he adds that this support has already been established in Section 4.11 to be the six internal bases of perception.

The Nyāya-Vaiśeṣikas' argument may be construed as yet another argument for the existence of a self. The argument begins with the statement that (I) if there is no self, no beings are in saṃsāra. The belief that at least some beings can accumulate merit and demerit, which is accepted by both Vasubandhu and the Nyāya-Vaiśeṣikas, may be expressed by saying that (II) some beings can accumulate merit and demerit. But (III) if no beings are in saṃsāra and some beings can accumulate merit and demerit, then beings not in saṃsāra can accumulate merit and demerit. Therefore, from (I), (II), and (III) we may infer that (IV) if there is no self, beings not in saṃsāra can accumulate merit and demerit. However, (V) beings not in saṃsāra cannot accumulate merit and demerit. Therefore, from (IV) and (V) we may infer that (VI) there is a self. This reconstruction of their argument shows why the Nyāya-Vaiśeṣikas believe both that if there is no self, it cannot be explained why beings not in saṃsāra do not accumulate merit and demerit, and that this fact shows that a self exists.

Vasubandhu's reply is simply to provide an explanation of why beings not in saṃsāra do not accumulate merit and demerit. The explanation is in effect an explanation of why it is false that if there is no self, no beings are in saṃsāra. He claims that since beings not in saṃsāra lack an underlying support for the feelings that result from the accumulation of merit and demerit because they do not possess the six internal bases of perception, beings not in saṃsāra do not accumulate merit and demerit. Since Vasubandhu has provided an account why beings not in saṃsāra do not accumulate merit and demerit, and has excluded a self from that account, he believes that he has shown that we need not accept the Nyāya-Vaiśeṣikas' view that no beings are in saṃsāra if there is no self.

§ 4.14 The Tīrthikas' objection, that a past action cannot produce a future result if there is no self, and Vasubandhu's reply

The Nyāya-Vaiśeṣikas object that Vasubandhu's denial of the existence of a self does not enable him to explain how an action that has ceased to exist can produce its result. Let us call an action that has ceased to exist before its result is produced a past action and its result a future result. Since it is implied in their statement of this objection that they can explain how the existence of a self makes it possible for a past action to produce a future result, Vasubandhu asks for their explanation. He first criticizes their own explanation and then presents his own.

Their explanation is that unless a self exists as an underlying support in which the merit or demerit of the past action inheres, the past action cannot produce its future result, since the merit or demerit of the past action is the cause of the result and cannot exist without a self as an underlying support in which to inhere. Vasubandhu's criticism of their explanation is that since he has already established in Section 4.8 that a self is not an underlying support in which attributes inhere, and the Nyāya-Vaiśeṣikas believe that a past action does produce its future result, they must admit that a future result of a past action is produced without a self as an underlying support in which the merit or demerit of the past action inheres. His claim, that they are committed to the view that a future result of a past action is produced without a self, of course, is a rhetorical way of stating that they have not established the existence of a self as an underlying support for merit and demerit. His reply to the Nyāya-Vaiśeṣikas' original objection is to deny that he claims that a past action produces a future result, and then to explain, without reference to a self, why it is said that an action produces its result.

Vasubandhu's denial that he claims that a past action produces a future result would seem to mean that he does not claim that a past action by itself produces a future result. For Vasubandhu explains that his actual view is that an action produces a result by means of initiating a causal continuum of phenomena in which a special development occurs that directly produces the result. A result produced in this way, he believes, is produced in the way a seed produces a fruit. He says that just as a fruit arises from a seed by way of arising from a special development in the continuum produced by the seed, so the result of an action arises from an action by way of arising from a special development in the continuum produced by the action. In both cases, he says, the power to produce the effect is transmitted by means of this causal continuum to this special development. In the case of an action, the power to produce its result is transmitted through a sequence of minds that constitutes a causal continuum of minds produced by the action. Vasubandhu uses the analogy simply to explain why it is said that an action produces a result. He is careful in his explanation to define for us what he means by the continuum of an action, a development in the continuum it produces, and a special development in this continuum. Vasubandhu's reply may be set out as a series of analogies. He believes that just as a fruit does not arise immediately from a seed, so a result does not arise immediately from an action. He also believes that just as a seed produces a continuum of phenomena in which a flower produces a fruit, so an action produces a continuum of minds in which a special development produces a result. Finally, he believes, just as we say that a seed produces a fruit because the power to produce the fruit is causally transmitted to the flower, so we say that an action produces its result because the power to produce the result is causally transmitted to the special development that produces its result.

Vasubandhu believes that he has explained how an action produces a result without recourse to a self as an underlying support in which merit and demerit produced by the action inhere and remain until the result is produced. But he probably does not believe that the merit or demerit produced by the action can exist without an underlying support. In his view, the merit or demerit of an action is simply its power to produce the kind of result it can produce according to the law of actions and their results. And this power, therefore, would be transferred from one mind to the next in the continuum of minds that makes up a person's mind. So, just as he has previously explained that there is a sense in which earth is an underlying support for what are called its sensible qualities and a sense in which the internal bases of cognition are called the underlying support for minds, he most likely believes that the minds in a continuum that possess the power to produce the result of an action may be called the underlying support for the merit or demerit of an action.

Vasubandhu's claim, that a seed and an action possess the powers to produce a fruit and a future result, respectively, is not clear. First of all, strictly speaking, if a seed possesses a power in relation to a fruit, should it not be the power to produce a causal continuum of phenomena the last of which possesses the power to produce a fruit? If the seed really possessed the power to produce a fruit, it should itself be able to produce the fruit. So when Vasubandhu says that a seed possesses the power to produce a fruit, he must be speaking from the point of view of the convention according to which a seed, a conventional reality, is the cause of a fruit, not speaking from the perspective of the ultimate reality of the seed. Even if he believes that, should the ultimate reality of the seed – the collection of substances of which it is composed – be perceived or correctly inferred to exist, one or more causal powers would be discriminated, it is difficult to believe that the power to produce a fruit would be one of the powers so discriminated. Second, Vasubandhu omits from his account the role played by the causal conditions that must obtain if the causal continuum produced by a cause is to give rise to an effect. In the case of the seed, at least some of these causal conditions are well-known, especially the presence of the seed in soil that is moist and warm and contains the necessary nutrients, and so on. By not specifying what the causal conditions are for the production of a result in the causal continuum produced by an action Vasubandhu fails to close the door to the claim that one such causal condition is the presence of the causal continuum produced by the action in a self. Third, and most importantly, it may be objected, as Nāgārjuna would, that the appeal to a power of a cause to produce an effect cannot be used to explain the coming to be of an effect, since, when the cause exists, no power to produce an effect can be discriminated, since the effect does not yet exist and may not in fact ever exist unless the causal conditions for its arising are present. Since the cause and its effect, according to Vasubandhu, are other than one another, how can they be said, from their own side, to stand in a causal relation? This objection is not available to the Nyāya-Vaiśeṣikas, who believe, as Vasubandhu does, that an effect and its cause independently exist.

Vasubandhu presents, as an example of an action that produces a result, an action that produces a rebirth. According to the standard Buddhist view, an action whose result does not arise in the same life can have any one of three different kinds of results: the kind of rebirth a person may have, the kind of suffering a person may have in a rebirth, or the kind of circumstance in which a person is found in a rebirth. Here Vasubandhu discusses only the first of these three. The causal continuum produced by an action that produces a rebirth has as a special development a mind that occurs at the time of death. It may be called a rebirth-producing mind. Vasubandhu tells us what kinds of actions have the most power to produce rebirth-producing minds and what their relative strengths are to produce them.

The three kinds of actions that he believes have the most power to produce a rebirth-producing mind at the time of death, mentioned in the order of greater strength, are the weighty, the recent, and the habitual. According to the standard Buddhist account, a weighty action, which has the most power, is weighted according to the nature of the action, the force of the motivation of the action, the amount of suffering inflicted by the action, the value of the object of the action, the frequency of the action, and the use of counter-measures. An example of a very weighty action is the violent killing of one's own parents out of anger and without remorse. An action performed close to the time of death has greater power to give rise to a rebirth-producing mind than an action performed earlier if both are equally weighty. Other things being equal, an action habitually performed has more power to give rise to a rebirth-producing mind at the time of death than an action not habitually performed. These actions, Vasubandhu adds, lose their power to produce these rebirths after they produce them.

Having provided the example of an action that produces a rebirth and stating that it loses its power to produce another rebirth after it has produced a rebirth, Vasubandhu explains how rebirth comes to an end. In the second chapters of the *Treasury* and its *Commentary* Vasubandhu distinguishes effects that are not like their causes from effects that are. He says that effects that are not like their causes, such as the results of actions, require maturation, while those that are like their causes, such as minds produced by prior minds in the same mind-continuum, arise immediately from their causes. In a causal continuum of phenomena in which effects are like their causes each effect is in turn a cause of the next effect. If a mind in a continuum of minds is afflicted with ignorance, it produces a mind that is like itself afflicted, and if the mind is unafflicted with ignorance, it produces a mind that is like itself unafflicted. Afflicted minds in a continuum lose their power to produce afflicted minds, he says, when the antidotes to the afflictions are applied. Unafflicted minds lose their power to produce effects like themselves (other unafflicted minds) when nirvāṇa is attained. The import of this account is that rebirth comes to an end when the afflictions are destroyed and the lifetime in which they have been destroyed comes to an end.

§ 4.14.1 *Vasubandhu's explanation of why effects that require maturation do not produce further effects that require maturation*

The analogy Vasubandhu made in Section 4.14 to a fruit arising from a seed might seem to imply that another result could arise from the result of an action, just as another fruit could arise from the fruit that has arisen from a seed. Vasubandhu seems to be anticipating an objection the Nyāya-Vaiśeṣikas might make to his use of the analogy. They might object that his use of this analogy seems to commit him to a view inconsistent with one implication of the law of actions and their results. The implication of the law with which it seems to be inconsistent is that a result of an action, once it occurs, will not reproduce itself. When Vasubandhu said that the power of an action to produce a rebirth is lost once it has produced a rebirth, it would seem to be implied that the rebirth that occurs as a result of the prior action cannot itself produce another rebirth. But the analogy he used seems to imply that more than one result could arise from an action, since a fruit produced by a seed can in turn be a seed from which another fruit arises, and so on. Such an objection is not explicitly stated in the text, but that Vasubandhu had it in mind explains why he bothers to go on to explain in such detail why it is that another result does not arise from the result of an action in the way another fruit arises from a fruit.

The objection in question, if the Nyāya-Vaiśeṣikas did in fact offer this objection, would most likely be based on the idea that Vasubandhu's comparison of an action producing a result to a seed producing a fruit fails to explain why the delayed result of an action does not produce another result, just as a fruit produced by a seed produces another fruit. So if an action produces a result in the way that a seed produces a fruit, it may be objected, there is no reason why the result may not, as a fruit does, produce another effect like itself. That Vasubandhu himself thinks that this idea underlies the objection is suggested by his first response, which is that not every effect that requires maturation is like the fruit, which is said to produce another fruit. The meaning of the response, in this case, is that the analogy was not meant to be extended in this way, since it was used only to explain how, without reference to a self, an effect that requires maturation can arise from a cause. In general, he might have added, an analogy is not meant to be applicable in every respect to that to which it is applied.

Vasubandhu introduces the apparent objection simply by asking why another effect that requires maturation does not arise from an effect that requires maturation in the way a fruit arises from another fruit as from a seed. His initial answer, as I have just mentioned, is meant to suggest that the opponent has grasped on to a feature of the analogy that is not relevant to the use to which it was put, which was to help explain how, without reference to a self, a result can arise from an action. Then Vasubandhu argues that it is not true that another fruit arises from a fruit as from a seed. He claims that the fruit from which another fruit arises is not itself a seed from which it arises. The actual seed that produces a sprout from which eventually a fruit arises is a causally conditioned special development in the continuum of the fruit that is merely called a seed because it gives rise to this development or is like it.

In the same way, he states, a result of an action does not produce another result in the same causal continuum. What produces another result is a causally produced special development in the continuum of the prior result. Vasubandhu uses the example of positive and negative changes that occur in one's contaminated mental continuum because of prior actions. These changes are not the cause of more changes, but when a special development occurs in the continuum of minds in which they occur, for instance, the hearing of correct or incorrect teachings on virtue, more changes are caused. Just as a special development in the continuum of a fruit is what causes another fruit to arise, so a special development in the continuum of a prior change in the mind is what causes another change to occur.

The second example he gives concerns a red keśara fruit, which does not produce another red keśara fruit, since it arises only from a special development in its continuum, which in this case is the staining of the mātuluṅga flower that occurs in its continuum by the red juice of a lākṣā plant. The point once again is that from an effect that requires maturation, in this case, a red keśara fruit, another effect that requires maturation, i.e. another red keśara fruit, does not arise. A red keśara fruit arises only from the special development in the continuum of the earlier red keśara fruit.

So Vasubandhu has explained in Sections 4.14 and 4.14.1 how actions can yield results without the need of a self as an underlying support for their merit or demerit. He has told us that the collection of aggregates in a causal continuum is perpetuated both from moment to moment and from lifetime to lifetime by afflicted actions. This process, he has argued, can come to an end, since when the result of an action is attained the power of the action to produce the result is lost. Once all afflicted minds have been destroyed by the application of the antidotes to the afflictions, nirvāṇa is obtained, and actions no longer produce rebirth as one of their results.

He finishes this explanation of the workings of the law of actions and their results by confessing that it is coarse and lacks the refinements the Buddha could add. He quotes a passage in which it is stated that only the Buddha fully understands the teachings on our actions, the developments in the continuum of our actions, the benefits we gain from these developments, and the results of our actions.

BIBLIOGRAPHY

PT: Peking edition of the Tibetan Tripiṭaka; Ṅu, Ñu, and Thu: numbers given to different boxes in the PT (the following numbers being folio numbers, and the "a" or "b" attached to the folio numbers being the front and back sides of the folios numbered); TT: Taisho edition of Chinese Tripiṭaka (the numbers that follow the volume numbers are the page numbers in the volume, and the letters signify columns on the page).

Primary texts, translations, and summaries

Editions of the "Refutation" of Vasubandhu, textual studies, and index

Pradhan, Prahlad (1967) *Abhidharmakośabhāṣyam of Vasubandhu*, Tibetan Sanskrit Works Series vol. VII. Patna: K. P. Jayaswal Research Institute, pp. 461–79.

Hirakawa, Akira *et al.* (1973) *Index to the Abhidharmakośabhāṣya (P. Pradhan Edition), Part One, Sanskrit–Tibetan–Chinese*. Tokyo: Daizo Shuppan.

Haldar, Aruna (1975) *Abhidharmakośabhāṣyam of Vasubandhu*, revised second edition of Pradhan's edition, with introduction and indices, Tibetan Sanskrit Works Series, vol. VIII. Patna: K. P. Jayaswal Research Institute, pp. 461–79.

Ejima, Yasunori (1987) "Textcritical Remarks on the Ninth Chapter of the *Abhidharmakośa-bhāṣya*." *Bukkyo Bunka*, 20: 1–40.

Shastri, Swami Dwarikadas (1998) *The Abhidharmakośa and Bhāṣya of Acarya Vasubandhu with Sphuṭārthā Commentary of Acarya Yaśomitra*, Bauddha Bharati Series, vols 7–8 in one volume. Varanasi: Bauddha Bharati, pp. 923–57.

Translations and summaries of the "Refutation"

Jinamitra and dPal brtsegs, *Chos mṅon paḥi mdsod kyi bśad pa*, PT 5591 (Ṅu 93b7–109a7).

Paramārtha (561 CE) *Ē-pí-dá-mó-jù-shè-shì-lùn*, TT 1559 (vol. 29, 304a17–310c17).

Xúanzàng (651 CE) *Ē-pí-dá-mó-jù-shè-lùn*, TT 1558 (vol. 29, 152b23–159b15).

Stcherbatsky (Ščerbatskoj), Th. (1919) "The Soul Theory of the Buddhists." *Bulletin de l'Académie des Sciences de Russie*, VI Série, vol. XIII: 823–54 and 937–58.

La Vallée Poussin, Louis de (1925). "*L'Abhidharmakośa de Vasubandhu, septième et huitième chapitres, neuvième chapitre ou Réfutation de la Doctrine du Pudgala.*" Paris: Paul Geuthner; reprint Bruxelles: Institut Belge des Hautes Études Chinoises, 1971, pp. 227–302.

Duerlinger, James (1988) "Vasubandhu's Refutation of the Theory of Selfhood." *Journal of Indian Philosophy*, 17: 129–87.

Oetke, Klaus (1988) *"Ich" und Das Ich*. Stuttgart: Franz Steiner Verlag Wiesbaden GmbH.

Pruden, Leo. M. (1990) *Abhidharmakośabhāṣyam by Louis de La Vallée Poussin*, vol. 4. Berkeley: Asian Humanities Press, pp. 1313–80.

Anacher, Stefan (1999) "Abhidharmakośa, Chapter Nine: Refutation of the Self," in *Encyclopaedia of Indian Philosophies, vol. VIII, Buddhist Philosophy from* AD *100 to 350*, Potter, Karl, ed. Delhi: Motilal Banarsidass, pp. 510–16.

Commentaries on the "Refutation" and its Chinese translations

Pû-guâng (664 CE) *Jù-shè-lùn-jì*, TT 1821 (vol. 41, 438c15–452b4).

Yuán-huî (654 CE) *Jù-shè-lùn-sòng-shū*, TT 1823 (vol. 41, 978a9–981c14).

Fâ-bâu (703 CE) *Jù-shè-lùn-shū*, TT 1822 (vol. 41, 803b14–812c1).

Pūṇarvardhana (700 or 800 CE) *Chos mṅon paḥi mdsod kyi ḥgrel bśad mtshan ñid kyi rjes su ḥbraṅ ba shes bya ba* (*Abhidharmakośa-tīkā Lakṣanāṇusāriṇī-nāma*), PT 5594 (Ñu 365a3–390b6).

Wogihara, Unrai (1937) *Yaśomitra's Sphuṭārthā Abhidharmakośavyakhyā*. Tokyo: Publishing Association of the *Abhidharmakośavyakhyā*, pp. 697–723.

English translations and summaries of the Pudgalavādins' treatises

Venkataramanan, K. (1953) "*Sāṃmitīyanikāya Śāstra.*" *Visva-Bharati Annals*, 5: 153–242.

Skilling, Peter (1977) "History and Tenets of the Sāṃmitīya School." *Linh-Son publication d'études bouddhologiques*, 19, pp. 38–52.

Buswell, Robert, Jr (1996) "Summary of the *Sāṃmitīyanikāya Śāstra*" in *Encyclopaedia of Indian Philosophies, Buddhist Philosophy from* AD *100 to 350*, vol. VIII, Potter, Karl, ed. Delhi: Motilal Banarsidass, pp. 353–65.

Châu, Thích Thiên (1999) *The Literature of the Personalists of Early Buddhism* (an English translation by Sara Boin-Webb of his 1977 doctoral dissertation, *Les Sectes personnalistes* (*Pudgalavadin*) *du bouddhisme ancien*). Delhi: Motilal Banarsidass, pp. 43–83 (contains a summary of the *Tridharmaka Śāstra*).

Priestley, Leonard C. D. C. (1999) *Pudgalavāda Buddhism, The Reality of the Indeterminate Self*, South Asian Studies Papers, no. 12, Monograph no. I. Toronto: University of Toronto Centre for South Asian Studies.

Modern translations of Buddhist critiques of the Pudgalavādins' theory of persons

Aung, Shwe Zan and C. A. F. Rhys-Davids (1915) *Points of Controversy*. London: Pali Text Society (translation of Chapter 1 of the *Kathāvatthu*).

La Vallée Pousin, Louis de (1925) "La Controverse du Temps et du Pudgala dans le *Vijñānakāya*" in *Études asiatiques oubliées à l'occasion du 25e anniversair de l'École-française de l'Extrême Orient*, vol. 1, pp. 343–76 (French translation of Chapter 2 of the *Vijñānakāya-Śāstra*).

Jha, Ganganatha (1926) *Tattvasaṃgraha of Śāntarakṣita with the Commentary of Kamalaśīla*, vol. 1. Delhi: Motilal Banarsidass, pp. 217–24 (translation of Pudgalavāda section of Chapter VII of the *Tattvasaṃgraha*).

Shastri, N. Aiyaswami (1975) *Satyasiddhiśāstra of Harivarman*, vol. 2. Baroda: Gaekwad's Oriental Series 165, pp. 67–74 (translation of Sections 34–5 of the *Satyasiddhiśāstra*).

Iida, Shotaro (1980) *Reason and Emptiness*. Tokyo: Hokuseido, pp. 173–6 (translation of Bhāvaviveka's treatment of the Pudgalavādin theory of persons).

Watanabe, Fumimaro (1983) *Philosophy and its Development in the Nikayas and Abhidhamma*. Patna: Motilal Banarsidass, pp. 177–208.

Huntington, C. W., Jr with Geshé Namgyal Wangchen (1989) *The Emptiness of Emptiness: An Introduction to Early Indian Mādhyamika*. Honolulu: University of Hawaii Press, 175 (translation of verses 146–9 of Chapter 6 of the *Madhyamakāvatāra*).

Translations and summaries of relevant treatises of the Nyāyas and Vaiśeṣikas

Gough, Archibald E., trans. (1875) *The Vaiśeṣika Aphorisms of Kanāda: with the Upaskāra of Śaṅkara Miśra and the Vṛṭṭi of Jaya Narāyana Tarkapachanana*. Benaras: E. J. Lazarus; reprint (1915), New Delhi: Oriental Books.

Basu, B. D., ed. (1911) *The Sacred Books of the Hindus, The Vaiśeṣika Sūtra. The Vaiśeṣika Darśaṇa with the commentaries of Śaṅkārā Miśra and Jayanarayana Tarka Pañchanana*, Jayanarayana Tarka Pañchanana, ed. Allahabad: Panini Office; reprint (1974), New York: AMS Press.

Jha, Ganganatha (1912–19) *The Nyāya Sūtra of Gautama (with the commentaries of Vātsyāyana and Uddyotakara)*, 4 vols; reprint (1986), Delhi: Motilal Banarsidass.

Jha, Ganganatha (1916) *Padārthadharmasaṃgraha of Praśāśtapāda, with Nyayakandalī of Śrīdhara*. Allahabad: E. J. Luzac; reprint (1982), Varanasi: Chaukhambha Orientalia.

Potter, Karl, ed. (1977) *Encyclopaedia of Indian Philosophies, Indian Metaphysics and Epistemology: The Tradition of Nyāya-Vaiśeṣika up to Gaṅgeśa*. Princeton: Princeton University Press (contains summaries of the *Vaiśeṣika Sūtra*, *Nyāya Sūtra*, *Nyāya Bhāṣya*, and the *Padārthadharmasaṃgraha*).

Gangopadhyay, Mrinalkanti, trans. (1982) *Nyāya Sūtra with Vātsyāyana's Commentary*. Calcutta: Indian Studies.

Modern discussions and summaries of primary sources

Samskrtyayana, Rahula (1937) "Second Search of Sanskrit Palm-Leaf MSS in Tibet." *Journal of the Bihar and Orissa Research Society*, 23: 1–57.

Conze, Edward (1962) *Buddhist Thought in India*. London: Allen and Unwin.

Dutt, Nalinaksha (1970) *Buddhist Sects in India*. Calcutta: Firma K. L. Mukhopadhyay.

Stcherbatsky, Th. (1970) *Central Conception of Buddhism and the Meaning of the Word "Dharma."* Delhi: Motilal Banarsidass.

Dube, S. N. (1980) *Cross Currents in Early Buddhism*. Delhi: Manohar Publications.

Williams, Paul (1981) "On the Abhidharma Ontology." *Journal of Indian Philosophy*, 9: 227–57.

Chakrabarti, Arindam (1982) "The Nyāya Proofs for the Existence of the Soul." *Journal of Indian Philosophy*, 10: 211–39.

Watanabe, Fumimaro (1983) *Philosophy and its Development in the Nikāyas and Abhidhamma*. Patna: Motilal Banarsidass.

Châu, Thích Thiên (1984) "The Literature of the Pudgalavādins." *Journal of the International Association of Buddhist Studies*, 7: 7–160.

—— (1987) "Les Réponses des Pudgalavadin aux Critiques des Écoles Bouddhiques." *Journal of the International Association of Buddhist Studies*, 10(1): 33–53.

Skilling, Peter (1987) "The *Saṃskṛtāsaṃskṛta-Viniścāya* of Daśabalaśrimitra." *Buddhist Studies Review*, 4: 3–23.

Oetke, Klaus (1988) *"Ich" und Das Ich*. Stuttgart: Franz Steiner Verlag Wiesbaden GmbH.

Potter, Karl, ed. (1993) *Encyclopaedia of Indian Philosophies, vol. VI. Indian Philosophical Analysis, Nyāya-Vaiśeṣika from Gaṅgeśa to Raghunātha Śiromaṇi*. Princeton: Princeton University Press.

Cousins, L. S. (1994) "Person and Self" in *Proceedings: "Buddhism into the Year 2000."* Khlong Sam, Khlong Luang, Patumthani, Thailand: Dhammakaya Foundation, pp. 15–31.

Potter, Karl, ed. (1996) *Encyclopaedia of Indian Philosophies, vol. VII, Abhidharma Buddhism to AD 150*. Delhi: Motilal Banarsidass.

Chakrabarti, Kisor Kumar (1999) *Classical Indian Philosophy of Mind: the Nyaya Dualist Tradition*. Albany: State University of New York Press.

Potter, Karl (1999) *Encyclopaedia of Indian Philosophies, vol. VIII, Buddhist Philosophy from AD 100 to 350*. Delhi: Motilal Banarsidass.

Priestley, Leonard C. D. C. (1999) *Pudgalavāda Buddhism, The Reality of the Indeterminate Self*, South Asian Studies Papers, no. 12, Monograph no. I. Toronto: Centre for South Asian Studies.

INDEX